ECHEVERIA

Eric Walther in Strybing Arboretum, Golden Gate Park
Photography by Owen Pearce

ECHEVERIA

Eric Walther

CALIFORNIA ACADEMY OF SCIENCES
San Francisco 1972

Library of Congress Catalog Card Number 76-174452

Copyright © 1972 by the California Academy of Sciences:
All rights reserved.

Distributed by the California Academy of Sciences,
Golden Gate Park, San Francisco, California 94118

Printed in the United States of America by
George Waters Photolithography, San Francisco

Designed by Adrian Wilson

Composition by Brekas of Berkeley, California
Binding by Vince Mullins Cardoza-James

Contents

About Eric Walther and This Book

Eric Walther was a horticulturist, the first Director of Strybing Arboretum, and a specialist in the Crassulaceae. He was an employee of the Park Department of San Francisco for thirty-nine years, during which time he developed the Arboretum, introduced many kinds of ornamental plants into California cultivation, and made important contributions to the gardening world.

Mr. Walther was born in Dresden, Germany, August 14, 1892, and emigrated to California in 1909. He was without formal training in horticulture or botany, but was always interested in gardening and plants. He worked on the Mortimer Fleishhacker estate in Woodside from 1914 to 1916, then for a nursery and landscape firm in San Francisco. On February 16, 1918, John McLaren hired him, starting his career in Golden Gate Park which lasted until his death in 1959. He had retired in 1957.

Three friends encouraged young Walther's botanical interests in his early years: Alice Eastwood of the California Academy of Sciences, who gave him access to the Academy herbarium and library, which he used regularly throughout his life; Charles Abraham, nurseryman and succulent plant collector; and John McLaren, the Superintendent of Parks who employed him, then gave him his confidence, and later the responsibility for developing Strybing Arboretum.

Eric Walther's desire to learn all about the plants with which he worked became the dominant force in his life. The Academy's herbarium and botanical library were research resources which enabled him to fulfill that desire. He became an authority on cultivated plants. He had a photographic memory which enabled him to recall illustrations and descriptions of species—he could often instantly identify a plant he had not seen before. At meetings of the California Horticultural Society Walther was a never-ending source of information about plants which were brought for identification or discussion and study.

The insect pests of cultivated plants and the control of those pests held Eric Walther's attention for several years. He worked with the biological control of insects as early as 1928, and had charge of an insectary where parasites were reared for release in the Park.

The building of Strybing Arboretum and Botanical Garden in Golden Gate Park was Eric Walther's greatest achievement. Made possible by a bequest from Helene Strybing, the Arboretum occupied the last twenty years of his life, and it remains a monument to the donor's generosity and to Mr. Walther's vision and industry.

Eric Walther probably became interested in succulent plants through Charles Abraham's collection. His first publications about succulents were in 1929, and that year he spent three months identifying the succulent plants of the Huntington Botanical Gardens in San Marino. By 1930 his interest focused on the genus *Echeveria;* in 1933 he visited the major herbaria of the United States in his studies of echeverias and their distribution; and in 1934 and 1935 he traveled in Mexico to observe the plants in the wild and collect living specimens for introduction into cultivation and subsequent study.

It was Mr. Walther's intention to write a monograph of *Echeveria,* but the work begun in the early and mid 1930's was interrupted by the demands of the new Arboretum. It was only after his retirement in 1957 that he returned to the monograph, and resumed publishing papers about *Echeveria.* In 1958 and 1959 he again made field trips to Mexico, and he rewrote much of the manuscript of this book. Unfortunately he died before it was completed.

Eric Walther was unassuming, sincere, and kind. He tended to conceal his shyness and modesty with artificial gruffness, but he was always ready to communicate his knowledge and to learn from others. He published about two hundred notes, articles, and scientific papers. He received several honors and awards in recognition of his contributions to horticulture and to Strybing Arboretum. He was a Life Member, Research Associate, and Fellow of the California Academy of Sciences.

Before his death on July 1, 1959, Eric Walther arranged that the Academy should use his modest estate to publish the *Echeveria* monograph on which he had worked for so many years. The manuscript, however, was not yet completed or in final draft when he died. Mr. John Thomas Howell undertook the long and difficult task of editing and preparing it for publication, and our sincere appreciation is extended for his efforts for his friend. Dr. Elizabeth McClintock wrote a biography of Walther and assembled a bibliography which are sources for these remarks. Some editorial suggestions also came from Dr. Reid Moran, Curator of Botany at the San Diego Natural History Museum, a student of the Crassulaceae with a special interest in *Echeveria.* It should be stressed, however, that his suggestions were merely editorial and did not lead to the addition of any new material or to any changes in interpretation.

Unfortunately, Mr. Walther did not reach the point of preparing the illustrations for his monograph. We are depicting as many as possible of the species with illustrations that he cited, including many from the original publications of the species. Among those cited are some from the United States National Herbarium which, through the kindness of Richard S. Cowan, Director of the United States Museum of Natural History, are published here for the first time; these include eight watercolors by Frederick A. Walpole and 25 photographs, all of plants in the study collection of Dr. J. N. Rose shortly after 1900.

Fortunately, we are able to reproduce many of Mr. Walther's own published photographs and drawings, mostly from the original photoengraved plates. Mr. Charles Glass, Editor of the Cactus and Succulent Journal, lent us numerous plates; Mrs. Glenn B. Eastburn, Executive Director of the American Horticultural Society, lent those from an article in the National Horticultural Magazine; and Dr. Jorge Meyrán, Editor of Cactáceas y Suculentas Mexicanas, sent some of Walther's original photographs and drawings. To all three we are most grateful.

To fill in some gaps, Dr. Moran has kindly provided 58 photographs. So far as possible, these are of cited plants or of plants from cited localities, including type localities. Plants not thus indirectly authenticated by Mr. Walther are shown only when the species are so distinct and his concepts so clearly evident that there seems no possibility of misinterpretation. Even so, data are given for each plant so that students can make their own evaluations.

We are also indebted to Mr. Paul C. Hutchison for two drawings by Mrs. May Blos and to Miss Ethel Z. Bailey of the Bailey Hortorium for the use of a plate for a cited illustration from Gentes Herbarum.

In the twelve years since Eric Walther's death, much new information about *Echeveria* has come to light, and several new species have been published. Although most of this information would have affected Walther's interpretations, we have followed his express wishes in not tampering with the manuscript to inject the opinions of others. Rather, we have left it his monograph of *Echeveria,* up to date to the time of his death.

In any case Eric Walther's monograph of the genus *Echeveria* is presented herewith. We feel it is a fitting tribute to a fine horticulturist.

George E. Lindsay

GEORGE E. LINDSAY
Chairman, Publications Committee
California Academy of Sciences

Preface

A complete revision of the genus *Echeveria* has been long overdue since determination of unknown material, on the basis of the available literature, has been both difficult and unsatisfactory. One reason for this has been the intractable nature of this succulent genus, notoriously difficult to convert into acceptable herbarium specimens owing to the tendency to fragment or in some other way become scarcely recognizable.

Moreover, garden hybrids are numerous and often difficult to distinguish from valid species. Only by a careful comparison with field-collected topotypes and a comprehensive study of all accessible herbarium material, including all recorded literature, has it been possible to clarify many of the specific components of *Echeveria*.

While I was fortunate in being able to undertake four field trips to Mexico (as well as one trip to Europe) it is certain that, with the rapid multiplication of good roads and other travel facilities, further field collecting will become easier and hence more frequent. I hope that my present survey may facilitate such future work and study.

My initial interest in *Echeveria* was prompted by its popularity as a garden ornament and this interest provided the incentive for my study of the genus. The undeniable appeal held by *Echeveria* to many plant lovers arises, no doubt, largely from the charming symmetry of its leaf rosettes, in many of its species of the most striking perfection. This sense of orderliness inherent in these regular spirals of leaves is so pronounced that one may well doubt their accidental origin. Rather than having been the product of mere fortuituous evolution, they appear to be the result of creative imagination, striving to express the basic unity of the true and beautiful with the practical utility that follows from complete utilization of all available space and sunlight. One may well wonder why such a promising model has not been used more widely by modern designers, or speculate what inspiration the artists of ancient Hellas might not have found in *Echeveria,* had this been native to ancient Greece.

In the photographs an attempt has been made to capture some of this perfection of form, nobility of line, and delicacy of texture found in *Echeveria,* but quite incapable of representation in monochrome are the fine nuances of opalescent bloom that covers leaves, bracts, and flowers, the translucent texture of such species as *E. elegans,* or the delicate pastel shades of, say, *E. potosina.* As one example of the decorative motifs provided by *Echeveria,* I offer a picture of the gracefully nodding buds of *E. agavoides.* The enlarged representation of the diminutive corolla of *E. potosina* serves as a perfect illustration of the term "urceolate," for it is an almost perfect replica of a Grecian urn, while the magnified carpels of *E. setosa* have been compared, not inappropriately, with a set of modernistic perfume containers. Whether contemplating the stout candelabras in species of the series Gibbiflorae, admiring the scorpioid racemes in the series Secundae gracefully uncoiling toward the life-giving sun, or contemplating the velvety pile coating all exposed portions of plants in the series Echeveria, we can find on every hand novel beauty of line and form, texture, and color.

But not only does *Echeveria* appeal strongly to the esthetic sense, it also presents a host of novel interests to intellectual curiosity. Tracing its numerous special features from apparently ingenious modifications of a simple fundamental model is a task well worthy of our efforts. In the field of taxonomic botany, dry as this may often seem to the layman, *Echeveria* offers many unsolved, difficult, yet fascinating problems to the student, and equally fascinating is its history, both botanical and horticultural. Unsolved cultural questions still challenge the skilled grower of *Echeveria.* Thorough testing of all available species and forms as to their adaptability and utility is as yet far from completed. So too, further intelligent hybridization would appear to promise much.

Acknowledgments

In the course of my studies I have been privileged to receive generous help from numerous friends, associates, and correspondents—many of whom are listed herewith:

Charles Abraham
H. Baker
Helia Bravo
N. L. Britton
J. R. Brown
N. E. Brown
A. D. Cotton
R. Craig
Leon Croizat
L. Cutak
R. Flores
H. A. Gleason
D. B. Gold
J. M. Greenman
A. Guillaumin
Christian Halbinger
William Hertrich
J. T. Howell
E. Hummel
P. C. Hutchison
D. A. Johansen
E. P. Killip
J. F. Macbride
Thomas MacDougall
E. Matuda
William Maxon

E. P. Meinicke
H. Sánchez Mejorada
J. Meyrán
Reid Moran
M. W. Morgan
B. Y. Morrison
C. V. Morton
E. Oestlund
E. O. Orpet
F. W. Pennell
K. von Poellnitz
M. Polido
V. Reiter, Jr.
B. L. Robinson
J. N. Rose
M. Sanches
A. C. Seward
V. J. Sexton
D. B. and M. Skinner
T. A. Sprague
P. C. Standley
C. H. Uhl
E. Werdermann
J. West
J. Whitehead

And to Miss Alice Eastwood I must record my particular thanks for that help, encouragement, and inspiration without which the preparation of this monograph would have been quite impossible. I dedicate it to her and to my mother.

ECHEVERIA

Introduction

BOTANICAL HISTORY

"Cotyledon" was the name first applied to some unidentified plant by Hippocrates, father of Medicine. Its earliest recognizable use was by Dioscorides, Cilician-Greek physician of Nero's Court, at about 50 A.D. The best extant example of his much copied work is the *Codex Vindobonensis,* originally prepared for the Emperor Justinian in approximately 527 A.D., later brought to Vienna by the Austrian Ambassador Busbecq, and recently, in 1906, reproduced in facsimile at Leyden. This illustrates what we know today as *Umbilicus erectus,* under the name *Cotyledon,* from the Greek root "Kotyle," meaning "socket," presumably a reference to the peltate, concave leaves typical of *Umbilicus.* In Bauhin's *Pinax* of 1623, one of the better of the early printed herbals, six species of *Cotyledon* are listed, all of them Old World plants. Tournefort, in his *Elemens de Botanique,* dedicated to Louis XIV, defines the genus *Cotyledon* as consisting of four species, all belonging to the modern *Umbilicus.*

When modern botany began with publication of Linnaeus' *Species Plantarum* in 1753 seven species were enumerated under *Cotyledon* as follows:

1. *Cotyledon orbiculata,* the type of our modern *Cotyledon*
2. *C. hemispherica,* now *Adromischus hemisphericus* (Linnaeus) Berger
3. *C. serrata,* now *Rosularia serrata* (Linnaeus) Berger
4. *C. spinosa,* now *Orostachys spinosus* (Linnaeus) Berger
5. *C. Umbilicus repens,* now *Umbilicus erectus* DeCandolle
6. *C. Umbilicus tuberosus,* now *Umbilicus pendulinus* DeCandolle
7. *C. laciniata,* now *Kalanchoe laciniata* (Linnaeus) Person.

All of these are plants of the Old World, and, except for *Rosularia,* all have a terminal inflorescence. It was only in the 1790's that the first New World cotyledon reached Europe, when *C. coccinea* was cultivated at the Madrid Botanic Garden and in 1793 described and illustrated by Cavanilles in his *Icones,* plate 170. Not until 1828 was *Echeveria* named and described as a genus by A. P. DeCandolle in his *Prodromus.*

DeCandolle included in his new genus four species: two plants then cultivated at Geneva, one being the aforesaid *E. coccinea,* and the other from California, *Dudleya caespitosa;* and two others, known to him only from two drawings made in Mexico by Señor Atanasio Echeverria. DeCandolle referred to him as a distinguished Mexican botanical painter and showed his appreciation by naming this new genus in his honor. An Echeverria had been employed by Moçiño and Sessé in making drawings of numerous Mexican plants, to be used for illustrating a projected *Flora Mexicana*. For more detailed recital of the fascinating story of these pictures, the reader is referred to Standley's *Trees and Shrubs of Mexico*, pages 13 to 18; also A. P. DeCandolle's *Mémoires et Souvenirs*, page 288.

The two Echeverria drawings were published in DeCandolle's *Mémoire sur la Famille des Crassulacées* in the year 1828 which also saw the publication, by A. Haworth, of the description of *E. grandifolia*.

I have not been able to uncover further information about Sr. Echeverria. The two species of the genus based on his own drawings and named in his honor were *Echeveria gibbiflora*, quite clearly recognizable, and *E. teretifolia*. The latter is still unidentified, since the drawing in question consists merely of one-half of the bifid inflorescence, without any basal leaves. The nearest I have been able to come in my attempt to match this is with *E. bifurcata*.

In the same *Prodromus*, DeCandolle also listed two species of *Sedum*, both collected by Humboldt and Bonpland in South America, *Sedum bicolor* and *S. quitensis*, with the indication by DeCandolle that they might be referable to *Echeveria*.

The earliest monographic treatment of *Echeveria* is that by Schlechtendal of 1839, in *Hortus Halensis*, wherein 22 species are admitted, of which five, however, belong to *Dudleya*. Schlechtendal grouped his species in five main groups, as follows:
1. Inflorescence equilateral.
    a. Caulescent (*E. coccinea, E. pubescens, E. rosea*).
    b. Stemless (*E. racemosa, E. lurida, E. mucronata, E. peruviana*).
2. Inflorescence secund, simple (*E. secunda*).
3. Inflorescence with two or three branches (*E. bifida, E. scheerii, E. retusa, E. bracteolata*).
4. Inflorescence paniculate (*E. gibbiflora, E. grandifolia, E. acutifolia, E. campanulata*).
5. Flowers erect (*Dudleya caespitosa*).

Except for the inclusion of *Dudleya*, the arrangement is quite sound and foreshadows our modern classification. Schlechtendal was first to recognize the true nature of the so-called pedicels in the equilaterally flowered species as reduced branches characterized by their persistent bracteoles.

In 1848 D. Dietrich, in his *Synopsis Plantarum*, reduced *Echeveria* to a section of *Cotyledon*, in which unfortunate treatment he was followed by Bentham and Hooker in their *Genera Plantarum*. The otherwise high quality of the last mentioned work and the high reputation of its authors were responsible for the unduly long persistence of this misconception.

Charles Lemaire gave a summary of all known species of *Echeveria* in 1862 in *L'Illustration Horticole*, where the first mention is made of *E. agavoides, E. linguaefolia*, etc. The first really adequate monograph is that of J. G. Baker in Saunders' *Refugium Botanicum* in 1869, wherein a total of 29 species, many well illustrated, are treated and keyed. *Dudleya* is still included, with five species, as is *Pachyphytum* with two species. All are treated as *Cotyledon*. In

1874 Ed. Morren gave a list of cultivated echeverias, in *La Belgique Horticole,* where we find the first record of such hybrids as *E.* 'Scaphophylla,' *E.* 'Glauco-Metallica,' and *E.* 'Pachyphytoides.' From then until 1903, only a few scattered items appeared in print, such as those mentioning *E. schaffneri, E. chiclensis, E. pringlei, E. chilonensis,* and *E. subrigida.*

In 1903 a new chapter opened in the history of *Echeveria,* with the publication by Britton and Rose, in the *Bulletin of the New York Botanical Garden,* of 11 new species, as well as the establishment of the distinct genus *Dudleya.* This was followed in 1905, by the same authors, in the *North American Flora,* by 14 other new species. Between 1909 and 1911 another 11 species were named by J. N. Rose, some of them in collaboration with J. A. Purpus and N. L. Britton; and a few more by J. A. Purpus and J. N. Rose came out before 1930. That year saw the appearance, in Engler's *Natürlichen Pflanzenfamilien* of A. Berger's monographic treatment of the Crassulaceae, wherein he treats *Dudleya* as a subgenus of *Echeveria,* and creates the new combinations of *E. tobarensis* and *E. purpusorum,* the latter change due to the reduction of *Urbinia* to *Echeveria. Oliveranthus* is also reduced, but its specific name is retained, leading to the needless *E. perelegans* Berger.

The years 1935 and 1936 saw the publication, by von Poellnitz in Fedde's *Repertorium,* of five new species, and in the latter year, of a complete monographic treatment of *Echeveria.* Owing to the fact that this was based largely on dried material, its usefulness was far short of expectations. A total of 88 species were treated, of which I estimate 13 to be untenable, some belonging to other genera, as *E. tepeacensis* to *Thompsonella* and *E. minutifoliata* to *Graptopetalum.*

In 1935 my own publications in *Echeveria* began, with eight new species, in *Cactus and Succulent Journal of America,* followed by another three species in 1938. In 1941 E. J. Alexander of the New York Botanical Garden published descriptions of four species. My species *E. craigiana* was described in 1952, and *E. semivestita* Moran in 1954. After my retirement in 1957, I proposed a number of new species, all of them based on living plants studied either in cultivation or in the field. And bringing it up to 1959, E. Matuda in 1958 published the description of the interesting *E. tolimanensis.*

HERBARIUM COLLECTIONS AND FIELD WORK

Since validation of any taxon is based on the type concept, preservation of type specimens, etc., in herbaria is essential. Unfortunately, study of such dried material is often disappointing, and critical characters are often not discernible because of the nature of succulent specimens. Recognition of the importance of living material for effective studies by Dr. Rose led him in 1905 to cultivate over 1000 living plants in the Washington greenhouses. Since 1933 I have had opportunities to examine practically all the herbarium material, both in the United States and Europe, of *Echeveria* specimens from various sources, amounting in all to a little over 1000 sheets (see Table 1 for symbols designating institutions where specimens are deposited). The largest and most important collections are those where Drs. Britton and Rose were active, at the United States National Herbarium at Washington, D.C., and at the New York Botanical Garden. Of special value I found the many photographs Dr. Rose had made from the living plants, particularly the types of his new species. Even more useful were the fine, carefully prepared watercolors of Frederick A. Walpole, which were most useful in clarifying several of Rose's types (*E. cuspidata,* etc.).

TABLE 1.   *Symbols used to designate institutions where* Echeveria *specimens are found.*

AHFH	Herbarium of the Allan Hancock Foundation, University of Southern California, Los Angeles, California.
B	Botanisches Museum, Berlin-Dahlem, Germany.
BH	Bailey Hortorium, Cornell University, Ithaca, New York.
BR	Jardin Botanique de l'Etat, Bruxelles, Belgium.
CAS	California Academy of Sciences, San Francisco, California.
CGE	Botany School, University of Cambridge, Cambridge, England.
CU	Wiegand Herbarium, Cornell University, Ithaca, New York.
DS	Dudley Herbarium, Stanford University, Palo Alto, California.
F	Field Museum of Natural History, Chicago, Illinois.
G	Conservatoire et Jardin Botaniques, Genève, Switzerland.
GH	Gray Herbarium, Harvard University, Cambridge, Massachusetts.
HAL	Institut für Systematische Botanik und Pflanzengeographie der Martin-Luther Universität, Halle, Germany.
K	The Herbarium, Royal Botanic Gardens, Kew, England.
MA	Jardin Botanico, Madrid, Spain.
MEXU	Herbario Nacional del Instituto de Biologia, Universidad Nacional de México, México.
MO	Missouri Botanical Garden, St. Louis, Missouri.
NY	New York Botanical Garden, New York, New York.
P	Muséum National d'Histoire Naturelle, Paris, France.
PH	Academy of Natural Sciences, Philadelphia, Pennsylvania.
SD	San Diego Museum of Natural History, San Diego, California.
UC	Herbarium, University of California, Berkeley, California.
UCBG	University of California Botanical Garden, Berkeley, California, used in citing growing plants.
US	United States National Museum, Washington, D.C.
W	Naturhistorisches Museum, Wien, Austria.

Other collections of importance consulted were those at the Field Museum at Chicago, the Missouri Botanical Garden at St. Louis, the Philadelphia Academy of Natural Sciences, the Bailey Hortorium at Ithaca, the Gray Herbarium at Cambridge, Massachusetts, the University of California at Berkeley, the California Academy of Sciences at San Francisco, the Biological Institute at Mexico City, and in Europe the herbaria at Kew, Brussels, Geneva, Vienna, and Berlin (although very little was left at the last-mentioned herbarium).

Of the numerous field collectors we can only mention the most active ones. I found nothing collected either by Moçiño and Sessé or by Cervantes, the oldest material seen being Humboldt and Bonpland's of *E. bicolor* and *E. quitensis.* Next comes Schiede's Jalapa material of *E. racemosa* followed by Meyen's *E. peruviana.* C. Ehrenberg furnished Schlechtendal with specimens of *E. bifida, E. pubescens,* and *E. mucronata;* and he must have been one of the first botanists to visit the Barranca de Venados, where grows the well-known *Cephalocereus senilis.*

In the following years, *Echeveria* material was incidentally gathered by a number of collectors: Wright, Wislizenus, Hartweg, Galeotti, Bourgeau, C. S. Smith, Ball, O. Kuntze, R. Spruce, Botteri, Wawra. The last-mentioned accompanied Emperor Maximilian on a journey through Mexico, and a specimen of his collecting of *E. nuda* from the vicinity of Mt. Orizaba is preserved at Vienna.

The most active field collecting done in the recent past was that of C. G. Pringle, who made numerous trips to Mexico and who knew how to make good specimens of succulent material. He collected numerous duplicates which were named and widely distributed by Asa Gray. Later much of Pringle's collecting was done for Rose, many of whose new species were based on Pringle's material. Edward Palmer also collected for Rose in Mexico, and like Pringle, he furnished Rose with living plants. Rose himself made several field trips to Mexico, usually in company with one or more assistants. About this time, too, were active such collectors as Goldman, White, Holway, and Arsene. C. A. Purpus was an important collector of *Echeveria,* both of living plants and specimens. He must be credited with the discovery of *E. purpusorum, E. setosa, E. pilosa, E. microcalyx, E. gigantea, E. subalpina, E. rubromarginata, E. derenbergii, E. parrasensis, E. turgida,* etc. Most of these were sent, as living plants, from Mexico to Washington, D.C., La Mortola, Darmstadt, etc.

Of recent years a large number of collectors have been active, both in Mexico and South America, of which I may note the following: Pittier, Goldman, Holway, White, Runyon, Steyermark, Camp, E. K. Balls, Craig and Lindsay, J. West, Backeberg, Rogers and Meyer, Hinton, Moore, Dressler, Gentry, R. Flores, C. Halbinger, R. Moran, H. Johnson, P. C. Hutchison. Most useful, of course, are collections of living plants, since these are easily multiplied and furnish ample specimens identical with the type. Lately some intensive collecting has been done in Oaxaca and Chiapas by Mr. Thomas MacDougall, many of whose discoveries I have been privileged to name. My own modest contribution in the field amounts to about six new species; most of my efforts have been directed to the collection of topotypes, *i.e.,* specimens from the locations from which new species have been named.

MORPHOLOGY

A full understanding of *Echeveria,* as of any other group of plants, requires at least some knowledge of its vegetative and floral structures. In the following pages a brief discussion is given of the more obvious forms and structures in the various species. These observations by no means exhaust the subject, and since they are intended for the lay student and amateur grower rather than the trained plant morphologist, abstruse technicalities have been avoided and the use of a microscope will only rarely be necessary.

ROOTS

The roots of *Echeveria* are usually poorly developed, often quite superficial, and of relatively limited extent. This is rather surprising, in view of the rocky substratum generally inhabited by *Echeveria,* almost devoid of soil except a small amount of leaf mold, collected in small crevices. Only in the series Mucronatae are the lateral roots developed into fleshy fusiform storage roots, also found to a very limited extent in the series Angulatae. Root innovations arise freely both from detached portions of the stems and the aerial portions of plants growing in shady locations. Most of such adventive roots spring from the leaf scars, but in detached cuttings they may develop almost anywhere. Separated leaves and bracts, too, give off new roots from their lower ends, usually from the vascular bundles. Such adventive roots are often negatively phototropic. True taproots are practically unknown, but an old clump of *Echeveria pumila* var. *glauca,* collected at about 12,000 feet altitude on Ixtaccihuatl in 1957, while obviously a single plant, still preserved a long, strong, main root, attached to the oldest central rosette. We have seen no trace of either mycorrhiza or bacterial nodules. Red root-tips, as mentioned by Molisch, were observed in *E. gibbiflora* var. *metallica* and several others (K. Reiche).

Figure 1. *Echeveria* 'Mutabilis'. From an article by Eric Walther. (Cactus and Succulent Journal, volume 8, page 191.)

STEMS

Postulating the descent of *Echeveria* from an ancestor similar to species of *Sedum* in Berger's sections *Pachysedum* and *Dendrosedum,* we may assume that a primitive "Proto-Echeveria" had a subshrubby habit and an evident branching stem with subrosulate or scattered leaves. Such stems are typical of our series Nudae and Spicatae, and are also to be found in the series Echeveria. From this primitive stem type evolution produced two lines, one elongated, the other reduced. On the one hand it produced the greatly enlarged stem of the series Gibbiflorae which may attain a height of several feet and a thickness of nearly two inches. K. Reiche states that this highly developed stem of *E. gibbiflora* has as its most conspicuous feature the scattered distribution of the conducting elements, whether these be sieve tubes of the phloem or vessels of the xylem. Although this is foreign to the general concept of dicotyledonous stem structure, such scattering of vessels is not unknown in several other groups, as in the Piperaceae, for instance, which share with the Crassulaceae a more or less succulent nature. The thick, fleshly, moisture-turgid body of these plants apparently calls for a correlated wide distribution of conducting elements. As a further consequence of this, as well as of the crowded leaf arrangement, the woody skeleton is often strongly reminiscent of that found in various cacti, as *Opuntia.* Reiche concludes by terming the Crassulaceae "terrestrial aquatics," a comparison especially apt in view of the possible derivation of the Crassulaceae, so decidedly xerophytic, from some such hygrophilous ancestor as *Tillaea.*

In the other direction, the stem of *Echeveria* has been reduced, first to the simple, unbranched, often short caudex found in the series Elatae, in *E. montana,* etc., and some species of the series Gibbiflorae and Retusae, as for instance in *E. subrigida* and *E. palmeri.* A further reduction of stem is evident in the series Secundae, Urceolatae, Angulatae, and Pruinosae, in which it may be either simple or more or less branching. The greatest degree of branching is found in the cespitose species of the series Secundae, where as many as 20 rosettes may be connected to the original central one. Such lateral stems are comparable to stolons and may reach considerable lengths, 20 cm. being reported for *E.* 'Perbella.' The unique side branches produced by *E. pallida* may be even longer. Greatest reduction of stem is found in the series Mucronatae, where the caudex is merely a crown-like plate atop the diverging, fleshy fusiform roots, which apparently have taken over some of the storage functions normally performed by the fleshy stem.

The bark of the stems presents some unusual features in *E. multicaulis,* where the epidermis bears irregular outgrowths, somewhat granular in nature, that surround the leaf scars and form irregular hexagons. In the series Echeveria the trichomes may extend to the stem surface. The prominent leaf scars of the series Gibbiflorae, etc., exhibit the phyllotaxy typical of the genus, and often clearly demonstate the crowded arrangement of the bundle traces typical of the genus.

The stem structure of *E. quitensis* has been described by G. von Lagerheim as follows: "The corky layer of the stem arises from a subepidermal layer of cells. Cells slightly thickened through collenchyma constitute the outer barklayer. Numerous bundles of bast-fibers occur in the bark, but hard fibers are scarce, as in other Crassulaceae. In stems 2 cm. thick, the walls of the woody cylinder will be about 2 mm. thick; it is continuous and without medullary rays. Most of the xylem consists of woody fibers with small, slitlike, oblique pores. The vessels are arranged in small groups and consist of spiral and annular tracheal tubes and transitions between these."

The often popular crests or fasciations are aberrations following from the conversion of the growing point to a line; they are usually perpetuated by vegetative propagation, but in some instances, as in *E. pumila* var. *glauca,* have appeared spontaneously among seedlings raised from Mexican seed.

LEAVES

Much of the popularity of *Echeveria* is due to the attractive colors, form, and arrangement of its leaves. Even without flowers, many species and hybrids present a unique charm in the spirals of their dense rosettes, unequalled in any other plant. This leaf arrangement or "phyllotaxy" is most readily discerned in such plants as *E. pumila* var. *glauca, E. alpina,* and *E.* 'Imbricata,' where the alternate leaves, while crowded, permit tracing the fundamental arrangement in an orderly spiral, which, after eight full turns and 21 leaves, returns to a point opposite the first leaf. The angle between successive leaves closely approximates 137° 8′ 34″, known to mathematicians as the Fibonacci angle, named after Leonardo of Pisa, who in the Thirteenth Century first demonstrated its peculiar properties. The Fibonacci angle constitutes $\frac{8}{21}$ of a full circle, which leads to the designation of this leaf arrangement as 8/21 phyllotaxy. Such an angle is commonly found in organs like pine cones with their crowded scales. To what an extent this applies to the leaves, bracts, and flower arrangement of other species is yet to be determined.

Most striking is the variation in size of *Echeveria* leaves. There is quite a step from such tiny leaves as are found in *E. amoena,* where they do not exceed a length of 20 mm. and a width of 8 mm., or *E. bella,* where they may be only 12 mm. long and 2 mm. broad, to the largest known, in the series Gibbiflorae, where I have measured leaves 45 cm. long and 30 cm. broad, and weighing, when fresh, an even 15 ounces. Most of this bulk is of course moisture, for in the last instance the leaf in question weighed, after complete drying for herbarium preservation, less than half an ounce.

The manner in which *Echeveria* leaves are attached to the stem is distinctive and of importance in defining the genus. It may be most readily studied in species with an evident stem and scattered leaves, as for instance in *E. fimbriata.* While the petiole sits on the stem with a broad and thick base, this is actually attached to the stem solely by a quite constricted central bundle of vascular strands. The leaf is maintained in its appropriate position by the turgid base of the petiole which bulges strongly above, below, and on each side of the slight central attachment. In the case of the floral bracts, technically transformed leaves, this basal bulge is sometimes changed into a distinct, 1- to 3-toothed spur, also serving to hold the bract in its proper pose.

If we assume the average *Echeveria* leaf to have a shape described as obovate-cuneate and mucronate, and to be fleshy and of moderate thickness, a few of the more conspicuous departures from this norm may be mentioned. In the series Paniculatae the leaves and bracts are decidedly thick, subterete to clavate; in the series Urceolatae too, they are thicker than usual, as they are in most species of the series Angulatae and Pruinosae, as well as in *E. nodulosa, E. pulvinata, E. setosa, E. macdougallii, E. johnsonii, E. sedoides,* and *E.*

longissima. On the other hand, they are thinner than usual in the series Spicatae, *E. nuda, E. quitensis,* and in the series Secundae, *E. megacalyx,* etc. Markedly narrower are the leaves of *E. subalpina, E. sprucei, E. bella, E. tolimanensis, E. tenuifolia, E. chilonensis,* etc.

While in most cases the leaves are broadly sessile, with only a slight contraction toward the base, in the series Gibbiflorae and series Retusae a distinct, well developed petiole is present. This last is usually markedly thickened, and often winged and keeled toward the base. In many cases the lower side of the blade presents a distinct keel, most strongly developed in several species with subtriquetrous leaves, such as *E. nodulosa, E. purpusorum.*

Most leaves are shallowly concave on the upper side, with a few exceptions where they may be convex above, as in *E. tolimanensis,* or in several cases where the upper surface is more or less deeply concave or channeled, as in *E. canaliculata, E. bifurcata, E. lutea,* and *E. walpoleana,* the last three belonging to the series Angulatae.

Longitudinally the leaves may at times be strongly upcurved toward the apex, as in *E. lutea* and *E. sprucei.*

Generally the venation is scarcely visible, except in the series Gibbiflorae, where the central vascular bundle constituting the midrib is accompanied on each side by three or more parallel veins, always more or less convergent toward the base. Similar venation exists in the closely related series Retusae.

Most commonly the apex is mucronate, occasionally acuminate, sometimes becoming apiculate or aristate; and in *E. chiclensis* the apiculus is cartilaginous. The margins are often prominently red edged, as in *E. subrigida* and *E. lozani,* and in the series Urceolatae they are generally more or less hyaline-translucent, in keeping with the crystalline-hyaline epidermis of this series. In a few species the margins may be lacerate, denticulate, or undulate. Selected forms or hybrids are frequently cultivated in which the last character is especially pronounced.

Palisade cells are very rare in *Echeveria,* and to my knowledge confined to *E. longissima.*

The leaf coloration is usually modified by the frequently present wax coating of the various species. In other cases a decided reddish tinge is developed, particularly on plants in sunny locations. This may be due to concentration of acid anthocyan. In *E. purpusorum* this red cell sap is confined to individual cells, or idioblasts, often deep within the parenchyma of the leaves. The greatest development of such coloration is found in *E. gibbiflora* var. *metallica, E. lurida, E. lutea* var. *fuscata, E. acutifolia, E. atropurpurea,* and *E. affinis,* the latter becoming almost dark enough to justify its name 'Black Echeveria.'

Epidermis

Always of special interest are the various means by which succulents store and conserve moisture, and the nature of the epidermis frequently is an important part of this essential protection against loss of cell moisture. *Echeveria* does not possess such strongly thickened cuticle and epidermal cell walls as are present in the Cactaceae. The epidermal cells are rather smaller than those of the parenchyma, quite thin, and present the common, irregular, interlocking margins; or they may be roughly arranged into longitudinal series. Sometimes the epidermal cells are more or less strongly convex or lenticular, as in *E. carnicolor* in which they are responsible for the iridescence characteristic of this species. True papillae are present in *E. nodulosa* in which every cell bulges into a bulbous projection; the papillae of *E. backebergii,* too, are of this type. In *E. spectabilis* the leaf surface bears scattered rather distant projections and may be termed "muriculate."

Many *Echeveria* species have leaves distinctly bifacial, and stomata ought to be unequally distributed between the two surfaces, but data are lacking. The stomata are fairly numerous, not at all specialized as in many other xerophytes. They are accompanied by the usual guard cells, forming a ring of two to three accessory cells, sometimes reinforced by a second ring of three cells, all rather smaller than the other epidermal cells. While the latter are colorless, the guard cells as usual contain green chloroplasts. Especially crowded, under a particularly thick cuticle, are the epidermal cells in *E. purpusorum.* The striking crystalline appearance of the leaves of *E. agavoides* and its allies may be due to the presence of large intercellular air spaces. Most epidermal cells appear to have their longest dimension parallel to the leaf axis.

TRICHOMES

True hairs are present in one group of obviously related species, the series Echeveria. From these must be excepted *E. semivestita*, in which anomalous species the hairs are limited to the leaf surface and lower portion of the peduncle. In *E. fimbriata* the very young leaves are distinctly hairy, but these hairs appear to arise from its cuticle, are quite solid and colorless, and rapidly disappear as growth continues. In the series Echeveria two distinct types of trichomes are found and seem to indicate two separate lines of descent. In *E. pringlei, E. carminea, E. amphoralis,* and *E. harmsii* the hairs are simple, ap-

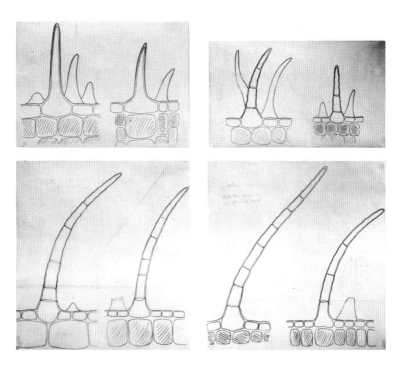

Figure 2.   Hairs of *Echeveria.*

parently single celled and ordinarily do not exceed a length of 200 microns. In *E. setosa, E. ciliata, E. pilosa, E. coccinea, E. pubescens, E. pulvinata,* and *E. leucotricha,* the trichomes vary in length from 280 to 3000 microns (see table 2). In such obviously closely related pairs of species as *E. coccinea* and *E. pubescens, E. pulvinata* and *E. leucotricha,* the hairs too are very similar. In

TABLE 2.   Echeveria *trichomes: (dimensions in microns)* .

Species	Length	Basal diameter	Central diameter	Diameter of apical cell	No. of cells
E. setosa	3000	100	60	40	8
E. pilosa	960	80	60	35	3–4
E. pulvinata	1100	120	60	35	4–6
E. leucotricha	800	100	65	40	3
E. pubescens	520	90	60	20	4
E. coccinea	280– 400	50	35	20	3
E. pringlei	100– 200	50	30	25	1
E. harmsii	200	40	30	15	1
E. nodulosa	25	25	5–7	8–10	1
E. fimbriata	900	70	60	65	0

Thickness of outer, cuticular wall of trichome cells appears to average around 4 microns.

these uniseriate trichomes, the number of cells varies from three to eight, but is fairly constant within each species. The hairs are outgrowths of certain specialized epidermal cells, distributed rather regularly among the normal epidermal cells. That these cellular hairs are alive is demonstrated by their assumption of red color (in *E. pulvinata*) under the influence of intense sunlight. Speculation as to their function differs widely, but they may be protective. In *E. ciliata* the hairs are confined to the margins and keel; if protective, this function would seem to be effective only at the tips of the very youngest leaves. Trichomes usually extend to the caudex, peduncle, bracts, pedicels, sepals, and the outside of the corolla, except for *E. semivestita,* where the corolla is glabrous. I have seen no glandular leaves in the genus as stated by Wagner.

The trichomes usually taper from base to apex, are often deflexed toward the base of the leaf, especially in the case of the longer ones. Interspersed with the normal type are often to be found numbers of smaller, less fully developed trichomes. *Echeveria macrantha* was described as having follicles "sparsely pubescent ventrally with brownish hairs," but I have been unable to substantiate this statement through examination of the type specimen.

INFLORESCENCE

Like other members of the subfamily Echeverioideae, *Echeveria* is readily distinguished from other Crassulaceae by union of its petals at their base and by the lateral axillary inflorescence. In other words, its vegetative axis is indeterminate and continues to grow and elongate indefinitely and the main branches end in a leaf cluster, while the flowering shoots arise from lower portions of the branches or rosettes, attain full maturity in one season, and die after flowering and producing seeds. While basically the floral scape is analogous to a sterile shoot, it differs in the greater elongation of its internodes, the gradual reduction in size of its leaves or bracts, and the production of flowers in its upper portion.

The basal portion of this scape, here termed peduncle, may be stout or slender, tall or short, erect or spreading or decumbent. In size it varies from the short, slender flower stalk of *E. amoena* where it may be less than 2 mm.

thick, to the stout peduncles of the series Gibbiflorae, which may reach a height of about 2 m. and a thickness of nearly 20 mm. In view of their short life expectancy, the peduncles do not possess extensive storage facilities for either moisture or reserve food, as do the vegetative stems. In the larger stalks particularly, the interior of the thin vascular cylinder is filled with medullary pith, and only the rather thick fleshy periderm may function as a storage organ.

The leaves of the flowering stem, here termed bracts, are strictly homologous with the leaves of the sterile shoots in structure, usually in shape, and essentially in function if not in duration. In many cases they also share the

Figure 3. Inside of flower of *Echeveria setosa,* much enlarged. From an article by Eric Walther (American Horticultural Magazine, volume 39, page 89).

Figure 4. *Echeveria fimbriata* illustrating
the growth pattern of the floral racemes and
the persistence of both basal bractlets.

8/21 phyllotaxy of the rosette leaves. Sometimes the bracts are readily detached and may serve to spread the species, as in *E. amoena* and its allies, also
in *E. lurida, E. westii, E. carnicolor,* etc. Here each bract bears at its base a
dormant bud, which readily produces roots and new leaves. The swollen base,
discussed above in the section on leaves, is often especially developed into
distinct basal spurs, with one or two teeth, presumably serving to hold the
bracts in an erect position. These bracts are particularly numerous in the
series Angulatae (*E. heterosepala,* etc.), also in the series Gibbiflorae. In the
latter group they attain the largest dimensions. They are much reduced in
other cases, in both numbers and size, as in the series Urceolatae.

FLORAL BRANCHING

The number of floral shoots borne by each branch or rosette varies, from
only a single one in such series as the Mucronatae, to quite numerous ones (in
E. derenbergii for example), often a consequence of environmental factors.
The number of branches in an individual inflorescence, however, is rather constant in each species and even in each series. The arrangement of these floral

branches falls, in the great mass of *Echeveria* species, into two main types. From a primitive ancestral form with several secund branches, *Echeveria* has evolved these two main types here designated as "secund" and "equilateral." More than half of all species known are referable to the first category, with floral branches consisting of one or more secund racemes. Technically, the term "cincinnus" would be more accurate, which differs from a true secund raceme ("drepanium" of Rickett) in that its flowers do not all lie in a single plane on one side of the axis, but rather in two distinct rows. Schlechtendal recognized that each single flower of such a cincinnus was terminal at the end of its branch, further growth of which could take place only from the axil of one or two basal bractlets. The resultant zigzag growth of the floral racemes is well shown in my photograph of *E. fimbriata* (fig. 4). This also shows the occasional persistence of both basal bractlets, ordinarily reduced to a single one, but I found it also to be present occasionally in *E. gibbiflora, E. agavoides,* etc. Although the number of secund racemes composing the inflorescence varies in the various secund-flowered series, it is constantly solitary in the series Secundae and in numerous species of other affinities.

The drastically different type of inflorescence here termed equilateral may be understood most readily if we assume its derivation from a tall paniculate one with several relatively short lateral branches. An approach to such an inflorescence may be seen in *E. subrigida,* etc., where the several branches have been reduced to as few as two to four flowers each, while the rachis retained its full length.

The individual flowers, spreading radially around the central axis, appear to be borne singly on the lateral pedicels, but closer examination of these "pedicels" reveals that each bears two small bractlets, aside from the large, subtending, basal bract borne on the rachis. These bracteoles indicate that formerly further flowers were borne here, making these pseudopedicels in fact reduced branches, otherwise quite similar to the secund racemes of the secund-flowered series. Frequently the lowest "pedicels" will bear several flowers, while the uppermost are single flowered. Sometimes the same plant will have all flowers solitary, and later at another season will have a truly paniculate inflorescence, with most branches bearing numerous flowers, as in *E. maculata.* Schlechtendal first called attention to the true nature of these "pseudopedicels."

The pedicels, whether true or not, vary in length, but for diagnostic purposes this character needs to be employed with caution. At times they are very short as in the series Angulatae, or they may reach a length of 15 mm. or more. In the series Urceolatae they are often turbinately thickened below the calyx. Although nodding before anthesis, the pedicels usually spread horizontally at flowering time, later to become erect, at least in the secund-flowered series. The pseudopedicels of the equilateral flowered series mostly spread horizontally, especially when short, but may become ascending to erect where their length permits. In all of these equilaterally flowered groups the actual pedicels, while present, are usually quite short, and not to be confused with the shortened lateral branches here termed "pseudopedicels."

The so-called "upper bracts" subtend the pedicels of the individual flowers and do not ordinarily differ from the lower bracts except in their smaller size. However, in the series Spicatae they are often reduced to very narrow, linear organs, colored bright rose, and no doubt serve as an attraction. In *E. rosea,* for instance, the uppermost bracts are sterile and do not subtend any flower.

Numbers of flowers borne on one inflorescence vary greatly, sometimes reaching 100 or more in *E. gibbiflora* and its allies, while in *E. harmsii* the number is reduced to one or two.

Before anthesis the tips of the floral branches in all secund-flowered species are strongly nodding, whether from negative geotropism or mere weakness is uncertain. The erect rachis of the equilaterally flowered species does not show any such pre-floral nutation except in two species, *E. eurychlamys* and *E. megacalyx*, of the series Racemosae.

Simple as this division of the genus on the basis of inflorescence type ap-

Figure 5. *Echeveria* 'Haageana'. From the Cactus and Succulent Journal, Volume 9, page 20. [Note: The photograph was mislabelled; see correction in the Cactus and Succulent Journal, volume 9, page 82.]

pears, it becomes complicated in the remaining groups. In the series Echeveria, for instance, we find both equilaterally spicate and racemose inflorescences, as well as one species with a paniculate, another with a secund-racemose one, while finally in *E. harmsii* the inflorescence is reduced to two large flowers. On the basis of trichome characters all of these species are closely related, and they intercross freely. In the series Paniculatae the branching of the inflorescence seems to be rather indefinite, so that this cannot be placed clearly in either of the main groups. The same is true also of the series Longistylae, for the flower cluster of its sole species, *E. longissima,* is difficult to classify.

SEPALS OR CALYX-LOBES

In some species of *Echeveria* the parts of the outer floral envelope are somewhat united at base and should perhaps be called "calyx-lobes," while in other cases the sepals are quite free to the very base. Every transition exists, so that it is simpler to use the term "sepal." In related genera, as *Dudleya, Pachyphytum, Graptopetalum,* the sepals are closely appressed to the base of the corolla, as they are also in most species of *Sedum* (and in the bud stage in *Echeveria*). If we assume this to be the original primitive condition, it by no means follows that all species of *Echeveria* with appressed sepals are primitive. This would certainly not apply to the series Spicatae, nor to *E. whitei, E. megacalyx, E. moranii, E. proxima, E. pulvinata, E. leucotricha,* etc., even if probably true of the members of the series Paniculatae and Urceolatae. Their original function may have been protective, but with the development of a highly colored corolla it would appear valueless to hide this with appressed sepals. Reflexed sepals are present in *E. sprucei, E. canaliculata,* etc.

In the bud stage, the available space is unequal for uniform development of all sepals, with the consequence that the innermost sepals are often much shortened, with the two outermost the longest. Normally the length of the sepals is correlated with the length of the corolla, but they are much shortened in some species of the Paniculatae and the Urceolatae, as in *E. purpusorum.* The sepals are greatly lengthened in *E. rosea,* where they are colored bright red, and with the similarly colored upper bracts they attract pollinating agents indifferent to the pale corolla.

Normally the sepals agree in texture, color, and approximate shape with the bracts, but they may be more intensely tinged with red, owing to light intensity. Particularly brilliant red are the sepals in *E. strictiflora.* In a few cases one or more of the sepals may be articulated and spurred at the base, as in *E. lutea.* In other instances a distinct suture can be seen separating individual sepals, as in *E. pulvinata* and others. In *E. platyphylla* the sepals appear to become accrescent after anthesis, *i.e.,* they continue to grow and surround the developing follicles.

COROLLA

The erect petals of its corolla are foremost among the special features that make the *Echeveria* flower an advanced type, clearly distinct from the more primitive type of flower of the Sedoideae. Actually the corolla tube itself is rather short, the erect petals owing most of their pose to their thickness, prominent dorsal keel, and basal rigidity arising from strongly united petal bases. Where the base of the petals is prominently hollowed within, the resultant pseudospherical shape adds further to the rigidity of the corolla tube. Whether the cochleate-imbricate aestivation of the petals also contributes rigidity is uncertain. Least rigid is the corolla tube in the series Spicatae and in *E. linguae-folia*, where the petals also are usually quite pale in color.

The *Echeveria* corolla, often described as pentagonal, actually is a regular 10-sided prism, with five exterior and five interior angles. This does not apply to members of the series Paniculatae, Urceolatae, etc., where the corolla has an almost circular cross section. In the two mentioned series the petals are rather thinner than in the ideal norm, they are faintly or not carinate, and they are scarcely hollowed at the base within, with nectaries correspondingly small.

Size of the corolla is fairly constant in most species, averaging for the genus around 10 mm. in length and somewhat less in diameter. The smallest flowers are those of *E. amoena* and *E. microcalyx; E. maxonii* too has a rather small corolla. The series Gibbiflorae includes several species with a corolla over 20 mm. in length, as does also the series Echeveria, in which last the flowers of

Figure 6. *Echeveria* 'Mutabilis'. Inflorescence, approximately × 1.5. From an article by Eric Walther (Cactus and Succulent Journal, volume 8, page 192, figure 2).

E. harmsii and *E. amphoralis* usually are over 30 mm. long. Longest is the slender corolla of *E. longissima,* often to 32 mm. long.

The often quite brilliant color of *Echeveria* flowers is usually some shade of red or scarlet, less often yellow, and very rarely white, with the inside of the petals and their overlapping edges rather paler, usually yellowish. My own rather superficial observations indicate that the yellow color is due to colored cell sap, rather than to plastids as is the case in many other yellow flowers. Such yellow pigmentation should perhaps be classed with the anthoxanthins, glucosides having a xanthone or flavone nucleus. These yellow anthoxanthins are readily converted into red pigments by action of an enzyme, resulting in the so-called anthocyan pigments. Because of the known acidity of the cell contents, the result is nearly always some shade of red, with the intensity correlated to that of light. The delicate pastel shades of many *Echeveria* flowers are modifications of the basic red color by a superficial waxy coating, adding the effect of diffraction and refraction to the absorption and transmission effects of the cell anthocyan. Clear yellow is the corolla in *E. lutea* and *E. maculata,* without any trace of red. White are the petals in *E. linguaefolia* and *E. chilonensis;* and in some members of the series Spicatae they are very pale. In the series Urceolatae it is not uncommon for the petal tips to be greenish. The so-called 'Blue Echeveria,' *E. semivestita,* owes its misleading appellation to the purplish tinge of the sepals. Where the external portions of the plant bear trichomes, these extend to the outer surface of the corolla, with the sole exception of *E. semivestita* in which the corolla is quite glabrous even though the leaves, bracts, and lower part of the peduncle are puberulent.

The closely related genus *Pachyphytum* differs from *Echeveria* in, among other things, bearing on the inside of each petal, at each side of the base of the epipetalous filament, an appendage which consists of a thin layer of cells, perhaps helping to exclude unwanted pollinators. Similar appendages may occur in *Echeveria,* as in *E. heterosepala* and *E. longissima,* but there they represent abnormalities of rare occurrence. Different is the case in *E. dactylifera* closely allied to *E. palmeri* and *E. subrigida,* but distinct from those species in the quite normal possession of two finger-like processes attached to the upper rim of the basal petal cavity and definitely restricting the size of the passage leading to the nectar store.

STAMENS

As do most members of the Crassulaceae, with the exception of the subfamily Crassuloideae and a few aberrant items, *Echeveria* has 10 stamens. Five of these are attached to the petals, near the upper edge of the basal cavity, into the center of which the base of the filament may be decurrent. The episepalous stamens are attached to the base of the petals where these are joined to the rather short corolla tube, but the filament usually remains free to the base. The reputed union of the stamens into a tube, as claimed for *Courantia rosea (Echeveria rosea)* has escaped me completely. The episepalous stamens are slightly longer than the epipetalous ones, but all are included in the corolla, with the sole exception of *E. linguaefolia,* where the tips of the anthers equal the petal tips. In some cases the episepalous filament may be somewhat flattened radially toward the base, as in *E. bifida.* In about 55 percent of all species examined, the stamens equal in length the carpels with their styles, and in only about 10 percent are the stamens slightly longer than the carpels. The anthers are terminal, introrse, and attached to the filaments by the rear or outer part of the connective. They are usually oblong, always much longer than thick, display the longitudinal furrows suggestive of the locules, and are distinctly cordate at base and shortly apiculate at the apex. Before dehiscence their color is usually pale yellowish, and they are always decidedly proterandrous, shedding their pollen long before the stigmas become receptive.

POLLEN

Pollen in *Echeveria* is usually abundant and commonly remains adherent to the anthers because of its agglutinate nature. While apparently yellowish, the individual pollen grains are colorless. The pollen is odorless, not at all foetid as is that of *Graptopetalum*.

With the exception of Link, Klotzsch, and Otto, no one seems to have mentioned *Echeveria* pollen, those authors having included pollen grains in their illustration of *E. bracteolata (E. bicolor)*. In shape, the pollen grains of *Echeveria* are of a type commonly found in the higher dicotyledons, and are called "ellipsoid-tricolpate" by R. P. Wodehouse. Their shape may be described as an elongated ellipsoid of revolution with three longitudinal furrows. Each of these furrows contains one germ-pore. In polar view the grains, especially when turgid, appear almost circular in outline except for the three furrows, separated from each other by 120 degrees. The exact shape of each grain varies with the amount of contained moisture; with increasing dessication the hard exine or outer skin permits shrinkage by folding inward along the three aforementioned furrows. From my very limited observations I offer the following dimensions:

Species	Microns in length	Microns in diameter
E. gibbiflora	49	23
E. coccinea	38	23
E. maxonii	36	23
E. multicaulis	45	27

CARPELS

The gynoecium of *Echeveria* is apocarpous, consisting as it does of five separate carpels or megasporophylls which are free practically to the base. Only rarely do the carpels cohere near their base for as much as one-third of their length, but the character is of slight use diagnostically. The carpels are best described as bottle-shaped (Chianti bottle); the separate ones taper above rather gradually into the more or less elongated styles. Below, the carpels are decidedly flattened on their outer face, to make room for the enlarged nectaries. On the inner side, the individual carpels display a distinct suture, the overlapping margins of which form the elongated placentae within each locule, these bearing the numerous, crowded ovules.

Usually the styles equal the ovaries proper in length, but taper (bulge in *E. carminea, E. alata,* etc.) into these very gradually, making comparisons difficult. Often there is a decided difference in color, the styles being often darker greenish, yellowish, or reddish than the paler ovaries. In the exceptional *E. longissima* the styles may be as much as four times as long as the ovaries, reaching a total length of over 20 mm. Their length is of course correlated to that of the corolla. Deep scarlet are the styles in *E. subrigida,* as are its nectaries. In the series Gibbiflorae most species have rather long and slender styles, at first erect, but at full maturity strongly outcurved at their apex and probably permitting self-pollination.

The stigmas of *Echeveria* are usually obliquely truncate and scarcely thicker than the styles. Stigmatic exudate may create an appearance of capitate stigmas which I have observed in *E. setosa* and a hybrid between *E. agavoides* and *E. derenbergii.* In the series Gibbiflorae and Retusae, the stigmas are quite uniformly dark red to maroon.

NECTARIES

In nearly all genera of the Crassulaceae, well developed nectaries are present at the base of the carpels, which are variously termed scales, hypogynous glands, or nectaries. Considerable diversity exists in both size and form of these nectaries, which reach their greatest development in *Monanthes,* where they have become petaloid and as large as the petals. Similarly enlarged are the nectaries of *Sedum longipes* from Mexico, far removed from *Monanthes,* both geographically and in relationship.

In size, bright color, tubular shape, and carriage of corolla at anthesis, *Echeveria* represents adaptations for attracting definite pollinating agents such as hummingbirds. A corollary development is the increase in size of the nectaries of many *Echeveria* species, which usually are larger than those found in

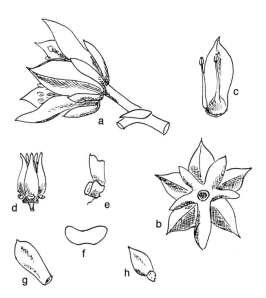

Figure 7. *Sedeveria* 'Hummeli' E. Walther, a hybrid between *Echeveria derenbergii* and *Sedum pachyphyllum.* Explanation: (a) flower, × 2; (b) flower from below, × 2; (c) inside of petal, × 2; (d) carpels, × 2; (e) nectary, side view, × 8; (f) nectary, front view, × 8; (g) leaf, × 0.4; (h) bract, × 0.4. From the original publication (Cactus and Succulent Journal, volume 25, page 21, figure 14).

Dudleya, Stylophyllum, and most Mexican species of *Sedum.* Within the genus *Echeveria,* some relation is evident between the shape and size of the nectaries and other characters utilized for delimitation of the series. The nectaries are smaller and usually thinner in the series Paniculatae, and most of the species in the series Urceolatae; they are larger and thicker in the series Gibbiflorae and in most species of the series Echeveria. The statement by Lemaire, repeated by Rose and Berger, that in *E. rosea* the nectaries are very small or lacking is not borne out by my observations.

In shape the nectaries of *Echeveria* vary from narrowly lunate to rhomboid reniform, with the face grading from quite sharp to broadly, often obliquely, truncate. At their base they are contracted into a distinct, if short, stout stipe. The smallest nectaries are those found in species of the series Paniculatae, some of the members of the series Urceolatae, also in *E. coccinea, E. pringlei, E. derenbergii, E. maxonii,* etc., while the largest, found in *E. subrigida, E. palmeri, E. crenulata,* and *E. amphoralis,* may reach a width of over 4 mm. In color most nectaries of *Echeveria* agree with the respective carpels, but often tend to be rather more yellowish. A striking exception to this rule are the bright scarlet-red nectaries of *E. subrigida* and *E. palmeri,* clearly visible when the corolla is viewed end-on, just as they would be to any visiting hummingbird.

Supplementing the nectaries are the usually highly developed petal-cavities that store the secreted nectar. In species with thick keeled petals, the base of the latter is usually deeply hollowed within, with the upper edge of the cavity often forming a prominent thick ridge on each side of the epipetalous filament. Here may be found the origin of the so-called petal appendages characteristic of the genus *Pachyphytum.*

It may be noted that nectaries of related species are often quite similar in form and size. Numerous exceptions, which possibly prove a rule, prevent utilization of nectary-shape as more than a minor character for specific delimitation, even if it were possible to describe them in simple terms.

FOLLICLES AND SEEDS

While before and at anthesis, the flowers and their contents are usually poised in a horizontal position, later the pedicels often turn so as to hold the mature follicles upright. Exceptions may be found in species with very short pedicels, particularly where the inflorescence is equilateral. This upright position permits the gradual discharge of the ripe seeds by wind gusts, to which arrangement the term "censer-mechanism" has been applied.

Before maturity all carpels are borne in an erect position, but later, in nearly all species with the possible exception of members of the series Mucronatae, the ripe follicles diverge widely. This is brought about by the drying of the carpel walls, and differential shrinking relatively of the dorsal and ventral sides. The rigid margins of the ventral suture shrink less than the softer dorsal face, so that the sutures gape open widely.

Scattering of the seeds over a longer period of time is obviously an advantage. The follicles contain a large amount of chaff consisting of unfertilized ovules, from which the viable seeds may readily be distinguished by their plumpness. Normal seeds usually approximate a shape that may be described as oblong-pyriform to obovoid, with the apex obtusely rounded to acute. The base is usually more or less tapered to the point of attachment. The outer integument or testa is often more or less roughened or tuberculate, and is commonly light to dark brown in color. No extensive measurements can be cited, but in *E. coccinea* the length of ripe seeds averages 480 microns, by a width of about 230 microns. In *E. strictiflora* these dimensions are, respectively, 660 to 400 microns.

EMBRYOLOGY

From the work of Johan Mauritzon (Studien über die Embryologie der Familien Crassulaceae und Saxifragaceae, Lund, 1933), I cite the following most interesting conclusions, based on the study of *E. agavoides, E. amoena, E. derenbergii, E. elegans, E. fulgens, E. gibbiflora (?), E. harmsii, E. palmeri, E. pilosa, E. pittieri, E. pulvinata, E. purpusorum, E. setosa, E.* 'Parva,' *E.* 'Weingartii.'

The subfamily Echeverioideae possesses a distinctive type of chalazal endosperm haustorium, and except in the Sedoideae, each subfamily has its own distinctive type. The subfamilies Crassuloideae and Kalanchoideae particularly are quite distinct in this regard. Within the Sedoideae are to be found both the *Sempervivum*-type and the *Echeveria*-type. The Echeverioideae also have a distinctive type of embryo not found elsewhere. In *E.* 'Weingartii,' *E.* 'Parva,' *E.* 'Set-oliver,' and *E.* 'Pulv-oliver' normal completion of the embryo sac occurs in very few ovules, owing perhaps to the cytological complications arising from the incompatible chromosome number of the parents (that is, *E. setosa* $n = 25$, and *E. purpusorum* $n = 40$).

In *E. agavoides, E. elegans, E. alata, E. sessiliflora, E. carminea, E. spectabilis,* and *Graptopetalum (Pachyphytum) amethystinum,* the placentae are lobulate, which is not the case in the other species studied.

Crassula and *Tillaea* are considered to be derived, not primitive. This is in contrast to the opinion expressed by Froederstroem that *Tillaea,* because of its primitive characters and hygrophilous adaptation, is the oldest representative of the family Crassulaceae and probably the origin of the historically known crassulaceous flora. As previously stated by Wettstein (Handbuch der syst. Botanik, 1924), there is some evidence of relationship with the families Podostemonaceae and Hydrocharitaceae, both of which are wholly aquatic.

Berger and Harms (in Engler's Nat. Pflanzenf., ed. 2, vol. 18a, p. 377) mention that in the Crassulaceae the endosperm is reduced, consisting of oil and aleurone grains. This conclusion is supported by Mauritzon's findings.

TERATOLOGY

The readiness with which particular forms of *Echeveria* may be preserved through vegetative propagation has led to the gradual accumulation in gardens of a large number of forms departing from normal in one or more ways. It by no means follows that *Echeveria* is more liable to such abnormalities than are other genera. Most popular among gardeners and collectors of the unusual are the so-called crests or "cristates," in which the normal growing point of the vegetative shoot has been transformed into a transverse line, resulting in a fasciated stem. Such fasciation often arises quite spontaneously, as in *E. pumila* var. *glauca,* to my own knowledge; and probably is attributable to some genetic change in the cells of the growing meristem at its apex. As a consequence, these multiplying cells increase more rapidly along the two opposite radii than those in the rest of the circumference of the growing tip. From the widened apex arise a greatly increased number of leaves, usually much smaller than the normal ones. Such crests are on record for *E. pumila* var. *glauca, E. crenulata, E. lozani, E. elegans, E. coccinea,* etc. Fasciation of the flowering stem has been noted in *E. grandifolia,* and *E.* 'Metallica-Glauca.'

Sometimes the normally lateral inflorescence will arise from the center of the foliage rosette, as I have seen in *E.* 'Imbricata'; but even more frequent is the production of leaf rosettes on the flowering shoot, as in *E. grandifolia, E. peacockii, E. elegans, E. derenbergii,* etc. Similar in character would seem to be the occasional production of floral bracts larger or more numerous than is usual, as in *E. agavoides,* Rose's *E. obscura* having been founded on such an abnormal specimen.

Appearance of six-merous flowers in a genus normally five-merous, is not unusual, and occasionally occurs in *Echeveria* too. An extra sepal may occur, and then usually is articulated and free at its spurred base, best perhaps interpreted as a misplaced bract. Sometimes one or more of the sepals may be free and spurred at the base, as in *E. lutea.*

Strongly undulate margins may arise in species with leaves normally flat, as in *E. crenulata* and *E. gibbiflora,* a character to some extent transmissible through the seed. A supernumerary mucro may be found, as in *E. reglensis.* Variegation in *Echeveria* is fairly rare, occurring in *E.* 'Hoveyi,' *E.* 'Raymondii,' and *Pachyveria* 'Scheideckeri .' Nematode infestation was responsible for a remarkable malformation of roots, stem, and inflorescence of *E. bifurcata,* the abnormality including virescence of the petals and swelling of the carpels. In *E. pubescens* var. *tortuosa,* the leaves are strongly decurved and twisted, as well as slightly discolored, and have all the appearance of suffering from a virus infection.

Vegetative organs

Of the several physiological peculiarities of *Echeveria,* the most interesting are of course those concerned with moisture conservation. The singular phenomenon of succulency is as much one of biochemistry and metabolism as it is of a distinct type of anatomic structure. As succinctly stated by H. Evans (Quart. Review Biol., vol. 7, p. 3, 1932): "Succulency must mean something definite and characteristic in type of metabolism, which, unlike many other features, is not defined by family relationships, but which must nevertheless be capable of hereditary transmission. It remains for further research to discover what this is. . . . Of the various attempts to explain the peculiar nature of succulent plants, neither the morphological nor anatomical ones appear valid. Thicker cuticle does not necessarily prevent transpiration from being generally greater in succulents than in other xerophytes. Of explanations involving the essentially metabolic nature of the problem, the pentosan or mucilage theory is merely an attempt without definite proof. One important aspect in which succulents differ from other plants is that their gas exchange is such that transpiration, especially at night, results in absorption of oxygen in excess of the carbon dioxide given off, an unquestioned advantage to plants in dry habitats. The cause of this may be linked with the peculiar acid metabolism of succulents, since malic acid in some form has long been known to be abundant in the tissues of succulents, and of the Crassulaceae in particular, but its presence does not explain the whole problem. As far as examined, the hydrogen-ion concentration in the cell sap of succulent plants seems to range between pH-3.9 and 5.7, the malic acid salts in effect constituting a buffer solution. The solving of this problem regarding the true nature of succulents, may lie in this direction, but probably no single factor can explain the singular problem of succulency."

It would seem that succulents, such as *Echeveria,* may practice anaerobic or intramolecular respiration, by which they can obtain energy from food stored within their tissues, without losing any moisture in the process, as would be inevitable with the ordinary aerobic respiration of other plants. Pertinent here are the observations of Askenasy (Bot. Zeit., vol. 33, p. 441, 1875) and Ursprung (Bibl. Bot., vol. 60, p. 1, 1903) that, in succulents like *Sempervivum,* the leaf temperature may rise as much as 18°C. to 25°C. above that of the surrounding air, where in normal non-succulent leaves this difference only rarely exceeds a fraction of 1 degree (Miller and Saunders, Jour. Agr. Res., vol. 26, p. 15, 1923).

Generalizations based on study of such thorough xerophytes as cacti should be applied to *Echeveria* only with great caution, for, in Mexico at least, *Echeveria* is of relatively rare occurrence in the true cactus regions with their high temperatures and scarcity of moisture. The need of *Echeveria* to conserve moisture is obvious when, even without considering the rainless winter months, we find them inhabiting so uniformly in their native habitat exceedingly steep declivities where the frequent summer rains cannot alter the fundamentally arid nature of the substratum.

The root system of *Echeveria* is in general rather scanty, consisting mainly of undifferentiated fibrous roots, usually without any trace of a distinct taproot except in the youngest seedlings. However, a cluster of about 15 rosettes of *E. pumila* var. *glauca,* found at 12,000 feet on Ixtaccihuatl in 1957 and clearly a single plant, displayed a long taproot attached to the oldest central rosette. Only in the series Mucronatae are the main lateral roots developed into fleshy storage organs. I have seen nothing of the mycorrhiza, said to inhabit the fusiform lateral rootlets in *E. gibbiflora* and *E. mucronata* (Berger and Harms. *In* Engler, Nat. Pflanzf., ed. 2, vol. 18a, p. 354, 1930).

In *Echeveria,* as in other Crassulaceae, adventitious roots are produced freely, both from the ends of cut stems and at bases of detached leaves or bracts, arising readily even in rather dry air, or even on herbarium specimens pressed without having been killed properly. On stems these roots usually arise from the bundle traces of the leaf scars, or even from any phloem tissue on cut stems. Roots emitted from aerial stem portions may function as holdfasts, especially in epiphytic species. These aerial roots are strongly, negatively phototropic.

Technically, *Echeveria* species may be called nanophanerophytes and chamaephytes, terms which mean that their lateral buds are borne at or slightly above ground level. This condition hardly applies to the shrubby species and the large species of the series Gibbiflorae. *Echeveria* has no true rhizomes, for the structures so-called are never truly subterranean. The stem apex appears to be strongly and positively phototropic, with the growing tip pointing toward the strongest light source, but this does not apply to the apex of the flowering stems, which are mostly strongly nodding. In *E. purpusorum* the upper end of the inflorescence is strongly recurved (see fig. 61), evidently because of its negatively phototropic nature. Even in members of series having an erect equilateral inflorescence, several exceptional instances have been observed where this apex of the floral stem becomes strongly recurved, perhaps the result of negatively phototropic character in *E. megacalyx* and *E. eurychlamys* (fig. 198).

Dormant buds of the lower leaf axils may be forced into growth by decapitating the stem. The thick stems, whether long or short, undoubtedly serve as storage organs for both reserve food and moisture, a fact demonstrated by the tenacity with which such stems persist in trying to grow.

In species with laxly arranged leaves, as those of the series Gibbiflorae, the aspect or port of these leaves depends on the turgor of the thick petiole base. Species with densely crowded leaves probably gain an advantage from the mutual protection involved, where the young, innermost, tender leaves are sheltered by the old, outer leaves, even after the latter are quite dry. For instance, *E. subalpina,* a high alpine species habituated to a moist environment among the clouds at 13,500 feet near San Antonio Atzitzintla, during the dry winter season becomes an apparently dead, dried-up ball of dessicated leaves which closely invests the few remaining green living central leaves of the rosettes. In cultivation, with a more constant supply of moisture, this phenomenon is not observable.

The trichomes of the hairy species in the series Echeveria would appear to have protective functions, as would also the papillae of *E. nodulosa.* K. M. Weigand (Bot. Gaz., vol. 49, p. 430, 1910) found hairs effective in reducing transpiration. He states that they are most effective in dry, moving air, being much less so in a still, humid atmosphere. How far this finding applies to trichomes whose cells contain living protoplasm is an open question. A thick cuticle and waxy pulverulence may be equally efficient in preventing undue loss of moisture in both still and moving, dry or moist air.

The generally protective palisade-parenchyma is almost totally lacking in the genus *Echeveria,* with the sole known exception being *E. longissima.* The crystalline-hyaline leaf surface found in most members of the series Urceolatae may have some protective function, such as light reflection, in keeping with the rather decidedly xeric habitat of the species in question. A protective function is often attributed to leaf color, but its occurrence on the underside of the leaves and in deep seated idioblasts casts doubt on such a hypothesis. Anthocyan red, the most common *Echeveria* pigment, depends on the acidity of the cell sap for its intensity, which is greatest in such plant parts as are exposed to the most intense insolation, so that its development is an effect rather than a cause.

REPRODUCTIVE ORGANS

From the presence of chlorophyll in all green floral organs we may assume that these participate in photosynthesis. The more immediate function of upper bracts, sepals, and fleshy petals is undoubtedly protective, sheltering the essential reproductive organs, the nectar, pollen, and ovules. What advantage, if any, *Echeveria* derives from having a lateral inflorescence, rather than a terminal one, must remain conjectural. The nodding racemes found in many species of *Echeveria* are a beautiful example of the complex interaction of phototropism and geotropism, both positive and negative. The subject, as it pertains to the prefloral nutations in *E. agavoides, E. purpusorum,* etc., is discussed in detail by K. Troll (Flora, vol. 115, p. 325, 1922).

Flowers borne in a nodding attitude may represent an adaptation to heavy rainfall, unless their aspect is especially suited to a particular pollinating agent, in the case of *Echeveria*, hummingbirds. The tubular, often elongated bright red corolla, the well-developed nectaries and corresponding nectar cavities in the petals, all are designed for the convenience and attraction of specialized visitors, undoubtedly one or more species of hummingbirds. Cross pollination is favored by the decided proterandry of *Echeveria* flowers, but self fertilization is not unusual, for with maturity the styles become strongly outcurved and finally contact the anthers and any pollen these may still retain. The exceptionally long styles of *E. harmsii* and *E. longissima* are apparently too long for effective penetration by pollen tubes of smaller flowered species and may constitute an effective barrier.

As stated by M. C. Rayner (New Phytologist, vol. 15, p. 136, 1916), the pollen of *E. fulgens* germinates readily in hanging drop solutions of 15 percent cane sugar, forming tubes with unusual rapidity. At 24°C. the average rate of tube growth is 0.54 mm. per hour. Rapid germination and preference for solutions of high osmotic pressure may be biologic features of plants occurring in xeric locations. Although the pollen grains of *Echeveria* belong to a class termed by R. P. Wodehouse "ellipsoid-tricolpate," they are by no means entomophilous, as is further contraindicated by their agglutinate nature.

After pollination the petals shrivel, but sometimes remain more or less connivent around the immature follicles, as for instance in the series Mucronatae. The pedicels, usually spreading or drooping at anthesis, generally become erect before dehiscence, preventing premature scattering of the ripe seeds. With maturity the follicles too, become erect and usually widely spreading. As they dry, the edges of their ventral sutures finally bulge apart, apparently because of the differential drying of the thinner walls and thicker edges, and so permitting the gradual release of the ripe seeds. These may be scattered gradually, by stronger gusts of wind, and represent an example of the well-known "censor-mechanism." The rather small seeds appear to be short-lived and are presumably distributed by wind, and perhaps rain runoff. In view of the steep habitat of many species, gravity also must play a role in this. The inconspicuous reticulations of the seed tests appear inadequate for attachment to insects or other animals.

Echeveria IN NATURE

Detailed information on the occurrence of the individual species of *Echeveria* is given under each, but a brief summary may be in order here. The genus has a range of well over 4,000 miles, extending from southwestern Texas to northwestern Argentina. It follows the American Cordillera throughout, few or no species being found below 3,000 feet, others reaching an altitude of over 14,000 feet. The greatest concentration of species is found in Mexico, whence over 117 are now known, and undoubtedly here is the present center of speciation.

With very few exceptions, *Echeveria* is of quite localized occurrence, and even the individual species are only rarely abundant in any one locale. The reason for this is the definite preference of *Echeveria* for rocks, cliffs, steep slopes, and recent lava flows, possibly because of lessened competition in such spots where its own succulent nature enables it to survive periods of more or less prolonged drought. The nature of the subsoil appears to be of slight importance, the several series occurring quite indifferently on lava basalt, rhyolite, re-cemented breccia, and limestone.

Climatically, *Echeveria,* with few exceptions, belongs in the warm temperate and subtropical regions. Several groups of species show some adaptation to special habitats.

Members of the series Spicatae are commonly found as epiphytes in tropical cloud forest or rain forest, while various members of the series Urceolatae and Mucronatae exhibit definite xerophytic characters. Members of the series Secundae are often true alpines, ascending to the snowline; while species of the series Gibbiflorae are rather tender and prefer lower elevations.

To assign *Echeveria* to any particular plant association is difficult, but a brief mention may be made of several species of *Echeveria* known to occur in definite vegetation zones as discussed by A. S. Leopold (Vegetation Zones of Mexico, Ecology, vol. 30, p. 507, 1950).

TEMPERATE ZONE

1. Boreal Forest. (Canadian and Hudsonian zones of Merriam's Life Zones.)
    a. Open pine forest and bunch-grass, 10,000 to 14,000 feet, with *Pinus montezumae, Juniperus* species.
        E. alpina
        E. byrnesii
        E. subalpina
        (*E. chiclensis* of Peru)
    b. Pine-alder-fir forest, 7000 to 8500 feet, with *Pinus montezumae, Alnus* species.
        E. elatior
        E. pumila var. *glauca*
        E. crassicaulis

2. Pine-oak Forest. (This is the largest, most important vegetational type in Mexico. Most Mexican pines and oaks occur in this zone, and more species of *Echeveria,* too, are to be found here. The zone extends from the border of the United States to Guatemala and beyond.)
    a. Pine forest, mostly *Pinus montezumae*
        E. pinetorum
        E. sessiliflora
        E. obtusifolia
    b. Pine-oak woodland
        E. cornuta
        E. palmeri
        E. shaviana
        E. semivestita
        E. fulgens
        E. grandifolia
        E. elegans
    c. Pinyon-juniper woodland, *Pinus cembroides*
        E. cuspidata

3. Mesquite-grassland and Desert. (Here these are treated together. Trees and shrubs belong to Cactaceae, *Cordia, Yucca, Agave, Prosopis, Acacia,* etc.)
        E. agavoides
        E. nodulosa
        E. bifida
        E. humilis
        E. subsessilis
        E. heterosepala
        E. amoena
        E. meyraniana
        E. strictiflora

TROPICAL ZONE

1. Cloud Forest

        E. rosea
        E. chiapensis
        E. nuda

2. Tropical Evergreen Forest

        E. racemosa
        E. carnicolor
        E. chiapensis
        E. crenulata
        E. grisea

Mexican topography is notoriously broken, either through extreme erosion that has created such chasms as the Barranca de Metztitlan in Hidalgo and the Barranca de Cobre in the Sierra Madre Occidental, or else through extreme vulcanism which has built up such peaks as Popocatepetl, Ixtaccihuatl, Oriza-ba, and the Nevado de Toluca. A consequence of this is the existence of a series of microclimates that appear to violate the broad outlines of the vegetation zones which frequently become intricately interwoven.

The broad division into Temperate and Tropical zones is based on minimum winter temperatures and is borne out in that *Echeveria* species from the former zone are usually quite hardy out-of-doors in California, while those from the Tropical Zone require greenhouse protection. Moisture-supply is more important than nature of the substratum. Most species of *Echeveria* are habituated to summer rains and a dry, almost completely rainless winter. The heaviest rainfall experienced by any species is probably that in Costa Rica, where *E. australis* enjoys as much as 12 inches of precipitation in the month of September. Not more than 10 inches annual precipitation is recorded for the habitat of *E. agavoides, E. strictiflora,* and *E. paniculata. Echeveria,* far from being truly xerophytic, nearly always seeks the shelter of low bushes and the shadier north slope of a hill with denser tree cover and more humus deposits.

Varying light intensity, too, is of importance, and some of the special morphological modifications (as hairiness, glaucous covering, papillose or lenticular epidermis, thickened cuticle) may be responses to this. Most striking is the apparent division of *Echeveria* species into winter-flowering types and late spring-flowering forms. This difference, being maintained in cultivation, must be a response to length of day, rather than to temperature or rainfall.

The effect of these biotic factors on the occurrence of *Echeveria* no doubt is important, but almost totally unknown. The presence of man, with his agricultural activity involving the destruction of original plant- and tree-cover, (by fires, etc.) and with his introduction of grazing animals (such as goats) no doubt plays an increasing role in the limitation of *Echeveria,* both in numbers and locations. Notorious is the fact that botanists collecting *Echeveria* must be better cliff-climbers than the ubiquitous goats. An interesting light is thrown on this aspect by the results of two visits to the vicinity of Esperanza in southeastern Puebla. Here in 1934 I had found *E. rubromarginata* and *E. nuda* in abundance, while *E. subalpina* and *E. nodulosa* had been relatively scarce. By 1957 conditions were reversed, so that *E. rubromarginata* seemed to have become quite extinct and of *E. nuda* only a single plant was found, while on the other hand *E. nodulosa* had become exceedingly abundant and *E. subalpina* also appeared to be more plentiful. Whatever factor was active was clearly selective in its effects. Possibly an explanation might be found in the fluctuations of such natural enemies of *Echeveria* as injurious insects and diseases. The most common injurious insect we have noticed was *Mitoura spinetorum,* a lycaenid butterfly, whose range extends to southern California. Its larvae mine into the tender tips of the young, growing shoots, but the leaves may also be attacked.

With few exceptions, *Echeveria* species in nature are relatively short-lived, and since they must depend upon abundant reproduction for continuance of the species, factors affecting seedling survival are important. Even the very earliest leaves are decidedly succulent and turgid with moisture. Seedling vigor is another such factor and depends largely on effective cross pollination. To assure this, *Echeveria* depends on its large, colorful flowers, typical humming-bird flowers. Lagerheim (Gartenflora, p. 68, 1893) reports frequent visits of an unidentified hummingbird to the blossoms of *E. quitensis* near Quito. Else-where in Colombia, this species is known locally as "Chupa-hueva" or egg-sucker, no doubt in reference to such a visitor. Interesting is the fact that the range of the genus *Echeveria* coincides very nearly with that of one particular group of hummingbirds. Another, perhaps pertinent observation is that the flowers of *Cuphea micropetala,* also Mexican, are typical hummingbird flowers, and in their internal structure, including nectaries, nectar-cavities, and flatten-ing of carpels, they strikingly simulate the structure of *Echeveria* flowers, even though the plant belongs in an unrelated family.

There remains the need to explain how the various species of *Echeveria* have managed to attain the range they now exhibit. It appears unlikely that in the recent past climatic conditions have been such as to permit *Echeveria* spe-cies to have a more continuous uninterrupted range, since the competitive ele-ment would remain unchanged. We must grant that the mechanism for seed dispersal, however inefficient it may appear, is adequate for the purpose.

ASSOCIATED PLANTS

During the several field trips to Mexico, mainly to re-collect the various species at their type localities, I found it interesting to note the various other plants sharing the peculiar habitat of *Echeveria.* Details are recorded under each species in question, but a brief summary of the more striking features may be in order.

Most commonly associated with *Echeveria* was a fern *Notholaena aurea,* which curiously enough has almost the same natural range as the genus *Eche-veria.* Almost as striking was the occurrence, with *Echeveria,* of other members of the family Crassulaceae. We may cite *Sedum palmeri* and *S. confusum* growing with *E. simulans, Sedum stahlii* with *E. nuda* and *E. nodulosa,* the remarkable *Sedum longipes* with *E. fimbriata, Sedum dendroideum* and *Thomp-sonella platyphylla* quite near *E. grisea, Sedum lucidum* with *E. nuda, Grapto-petalum occidentale* with *E. craigiana, Sedum dendroideum* and *S. oxypeta-lum* with *E. pumila* var. *glauca* and *E. gibbiflora,* and *Sedum moranense* and *S. confusum* with *E. elatior.*

More remarkable still is the occurrence of two quite distinct species of *Echeveria* in the same locality, and in the closest proximity. My observations show records for *E. rubromarginata* growing with *E. subalpina* near Esperanza, *E. chiapensis* with *E. racemosa* near Banderilla, *E. subrigida* and *E. byrnesii* at Tultenenago, *E. palmeri* and *E. cornuta* near Encarnacion, *E. amoena* and

E. meyraniana at Laguna El Chicico, *E. coccinea* and *E. pumila* var. *glauca* on Peñas Cosas, D. F., and *E. grandifolia* and *E. tolucensis* near Toluca. It is notable that no evidence of intercrossing could be found, not too surprising since most of the species paired belong to different series and have quite distinct flowering times. Exceptions to this last rule are *E. amoena* with *E. meyraniana* and *E. chiapensis* with *E. racemosa*. What prevents intercrossing in nature of species most readily hybridizing in cultivation is uncertain. Either there is a genetic barrier or the distinct flowers of the different species cater to different pollinating agents.

Geographical Occurrence

Below is given a summary of the occurrence of the various species of *Echeveria* by countries and, for Mexico, by states. Since more detailed information is recorded under each species, this list should be sufficient here.

Countries of North and South America

Argentina:	*E. peruviana.*
Bolivia:	*E. chilonensis, E. whitei.*
Colombia:	*E. ballsii, E. bicolor, E. quitensis.*
Costa Rica:	*E. australis.*
Ecuador:	*E. cuencaensis, E. quitensis, E. sprucei.*
Guatemala:	*E. fulgens, E. guatemalensis, E. macrantha, E. maxonii, E. montana, E. pinetorum, E. pittieri.*
Honduras:	*E. australis.*
Mexico:	See below for distribution detailed by states.
Nicaragua:	*E. guatemalensis.*
Panama:	*E. australis.*
Peru:	*E. chiclensis, E. eurychlamys, E. excelsa, E. peruviana, E. westii.*
United States (Texas):	*E. strictiflora.*
Venezuela:	*E. bicolor, E. quitensis (?), E. venezuelensis.*

States of Mexico

Chiapas:	*E. bella, E. canaliculata, E. chiapensis, E. goldmani, E. pallida, E. pinetorum, E. sessiliflora.*
Chihuahua:	*E. chihuahuensis, E. craigiana, E. paniculata, E. strictiflora.*
Coahuila:	*E. cuspidata, E. floresiana, E. mucronata, E. parrasensis, E. peacockii, E. shaviana, E. strictiflora, E. turgida, E. walpoleana.*
Distrito Federal:	*E. coccinea, E. crassicaulis, E. glauca, E. grandifolia, E. platyphylla.*
Durango:	*E. dactylifera, E. fulgens, E. mucronata, E. paniculata, E. tobarensis.*
Guanajuato:	*E. hyalina, E. walpoleana.*
Guerrero:	*E. grisea, E. longiflora, E. multicaulis.*
Hidalgo:	*E. agavoides, E. alpina, E. bifida, E. bifurcata, E. coccinea, E. cornuta, E. elatior, E. elegans, E. hernandonis, E. halbingeri, E. humilis, E. longipes, E. lutea, E. maculata, E. mucronata, E. palmeri, E. pubescens, E. pulidonis, E. sanchez-mejoradae, E. secunda, E. semivestita, E. tenuifolia, E. tolimanensis, E. trianthina.*
Jalisco:	*E. dactylifera, E. fulgens, E. lozani, E. pringlei.*
Mexico:	*E. alpina, E. byrnesii, E. coccinea, E. crassicaulis, E. fulgens, E. grandifolia, E. harmsii* (cultivated), *E. platyphylla, E. pumila* var. *glauca, E. subrigida, E. tolucensis.*
Michoacan:	*E. colorata, E. fulgens, E. grisea, E. pinetorum.*
Morelos:	*E. crenulata, E. fimbriata, E. gibbiflora, E. grandifolia, E. obtusifolia.*
Nuevo Leon:	*E. mucronata, E. shaviana, E. strictiflora, E. walpoleana.*
Oaxaca:	*E. acutifolia, E. alata, E. amphoralis, E. carminea, E. chiapensis, E. ciliata, E. fulgens, E. gigantea, E. globuliflora, E. juarezensis, E. macdougallii, E. megacalyx, E. montana, E. morani, E. nodulosa, E. penduliflora, E. pinetorum, E. proxima, E. pulvinata, E. scheerii, E. sedoides, E. skinneri, E. spectabilis, E. viridissima.*
Puebla:	*E. alpina, E. amoena, E. chiapensis, E. coccinea, E. crassicaulis, E. derenbergii, E. gigantea, E. gracilis, E. heterosepala, E. leucotricha, E. longissima, E. meyraniana, E. microcalyx, E. nodulosa, E. nuda,*

	E. pilosa, E pubescens (?), *E. purpusorum, E. rubromarginata, E. schaffneri, E. setosa, E. subalpina, E. subsessilis.*
Queretaro:	*E. maculata, E. trianthina.*
San Luis Potosí:	*E. agavoides, E. humilis, E. lutea, E. palmeri, E. rosea, E. schaffneri, E. walpoleana.*
Sinaloa:	*E. affinis, E. dactylifera.*
Tamaulipas:	*E. shaviana, E. walpoleana.*
Tlaxcala:	*E. alpina, E. pubescens.*
Veracruz:	*E. microcalyx* (?), *E. carnicolor, E. chiapensis, E. lurida, E. nuda, E. racemosa, E. rubromarginata, E. subalpina.*
Zacatecas:	*E. paniculata, E. tenuis.*

As is evident from the list, the greatest concentration of species is found in the Mexican states of Hidalgo, Oaxaca, and Puebla. Among them, these three states account for over 60 species, three times the number known from all the rest of North and South America outside of Mexico. Unquestionably this part of Mexico is the central headquarters of *Echeveria*, where the greatest amount of speciation has occurred and is still taking place. Here are to be found the most highly specialized forms, the most peculiar chromosome numbers; and no doubt here or nearby is where the genus had its beginning. The further removed from this region a species occurs, the fewer neighbors does it have, and the more ancient should be its type.

On this hypothesis the original *Echeveria* was a subshrubby species with scattered rather small leaves and an equilaterally spicate or racemose inflorescence, as for instance in *E. quitensis*. To the north are to be found fewer equilaterally flowered species, and possibly the most ancient form found there is one like *E. strictiflora* with a simple secund inflorescence and a haploid number of chromosomes of $n = 12$. Of the various series, the series Nudae would appear to have the greatest range and age. The series Secundae would appear to be a high-montane group of species of relatively recent origin subsequent to the volcanic uplift of central Mexico. The series Urceolatae and the series Angulatae and Pruinosae as well appear to be northern xerophytic adaptations. In view of its simple structure, the indefinite branching of its inflorescence, and its thin petals and small nectaries, the series Paniculatae may be the most primitive and ancient now to be found in Mexico, unless it should be a recent side-shoot. Hairy species, constituting the series Echeveria, are a specialty that arose in central and southern Mexico and today reach their southern limit in Guatemala with *E. macrantha*. *Echeveria* finds the climax of its evolution in such highly specialized forms as in numbers of the series Gibbiflorae and in *E. harmsii* with its very large corolla. The last is duplicated in *E. longissima,* the species which in many ways appears to be the very apex of evolution in *Echeveria*. Another peculiar specialization is the series Spicatae, in which the epiphytic habit seems to be general. The fleshy-fusiform roots of the series Mucronatae, too, are unique.

ORIGIN OF *Echeveria* AND ITS DIFFERENTIATION

Actual knowledge of the origin of *Echeveria,* like that of most other genera, is of course non-existent. In the absence of any eye-witnesses because of lack of any fossil material, our observations must in their very nature be mainly speculative rather than that objective presentation of factual data which supposedly is the essence of scientific record. However, if the course of evolution of a genus, whether speculative or not, is duly considered, one's ability to judge properly the importance, taxonomic or otherwise, of its various morphological characters becomes more comprehensive.

As a genus, *Echeveria* shared of course the history of the family Crassulaceae, including the latter's origin and subsequent migrations. If we assume with L. Croizat (Manual of Phytogeography, 1953) that the family had its origin somewhere to the south of South Africa and Madagascar, its further development included the segregation of the subfamilies Crassuloideae, with stamens as many as the petals, the Kalanchoideae, with four united petals, and the Cotyledonoideae, with five united petals, often opposite leaves, and terminal inflorescence. Farther to the north in the Mediterranean Area, the Sempervivoideae with a greater multiplication of floral parts, originated from the primitive stock which must have resembled greatly what is now grouped in the subfamily Sedoideae.

This subfamily is now of wide distribution largely in the Northern Hemisphere, and has become greatly varied. When it reached Central America, presumably by a route where today are located the Canary Islands and the Caribbean Sea, it finally gave rise to the subfamily Echeverioideae. As the immediate ancestor of this subfamily, I should like to postulate a shrubby species of *Sedum* with alternate leaves and a lateral inflorescence, the latter probably cymose with secund branches. Within the subfamily Sedoideae, a number of genera, otherwise wholly sedoid in character, have developed a more or less tubular corolla with erect connate petals but still have a terminal inflorescence, as in *Gormania* and *Altamiranoa* (or else even a lateral inflorescence may exist with otherwise sedoid characters, as in *Rosularia*).

The tendency towards development of a more or less tubular corolla seems to be inherent in the nature of the family Crassulaceae, for it appears in quite remote groups, as in the subfamily Kalanchoideae, the subfamily Cotyledonoideae, and even in the Crassuloideae (as in *Rochea*). Its undoubted advantage in reserving nectar for the benefit of special pollinating agents probably was responsible, as it must have been in the case of the subfamily Echeverioideae. Once this general tendency is recognized, we escape the temptation to consider all tubular-flowered Crassulaceae as closely related and descended from one common ancestor; and *Dudleya* can logically be traced to a separate origin from some sedoid form such as *Gormania*.

The true progenitor of *Echeveria* should, in theory at least, have possessed one or more of the following characters and peculiarities:

1. A lateral, axillary inflorescence.
2. Petals more or less united and erect.
3. A shrubby habit.
4. A cymose inflorescence with secund-racemose branches.
5. Bractless pedicels.
6. Slender styles.
7. Erect stamens.
8. Pollen agglutinate, not foetid.
9. Large nectaries.
10. Carpels spreading when mature.
11. Spreading sepals.
12. Ability to intercross with related forms.
13. Similar chromosome numbers, *i.e.*, 12 or more, but not 17.
14. Similar geographical range.
15. Similar climatic, soil, and moisture requirements.
16. Similar habitat preferences.

Most of the points enumerated point towards *Bergerosedum,* but do *not* apply to *Dudleya,* which is not closely related. Aside from *Bergerosedum, Echeveria* finds its nearest allies in the genera *Pachyphytum, Graptopetalum,* and *Thompsonella.* Of these *Graptopetalum* closely approximates the hypothetical ancestor of *Echeveria,* including forms with relatively tall, shrubby stems, others with dense, acaulescent rosettes, all intercrossing freely with *Echeveria,* but differing in having spreading red-lined petals, stamens reflexed at maturity, and foetid pollen.

If I were to nominate one series as the most primitive of the genus *Echeveria,* this would have to be the series Paniculatae. Within this series the most primitive, *Sedum*-like species appears to be *E. linguaefolia,* for which unfortunately no definite Mexican locality is known. In foliage, habit, and type of inflorescence this is very similar to *Sedum cremnophila (Cremnophila nutans),* differing mainly in its erect, white petals. Its chromosome number is reported by Dr. Johansen of Stanford to be $n = 48$, which fits well with the otherwise lowest-recorded $n = 12$ of *E. strictiflora.*

Aside from this primitive group with its rather indeterminate manner of floral branching, the remaining series fall, with just a few exceptions, into two main groups. These differ primarily in having either an equilateral inflorescence, or one consisting of one or more secund branches. In the former the flower-stalks represent formerly many-flowered branches; their true nature is revealed by the continued presence, on the pseudopedicels, of usually two, rarely three, bractlets. Occasionally one or more of the lowermost pseudopedicels may bear two or three flowers, as in *E. australis, E. maxonii, E. viridissima, E. paniculata,* and *E. maculata.*

In the series Longistylae, the branching of the inflorescence seems rather indeterminate, too, but the well developed corolla and long styles argue for a high state of development here, as they do in *E. harmsii.* In the secund-flowered species, development appears to have led to the appearance of one series with small sepals, an urceolate corolla, and small nectaries, with correspondingly thin, scarcely angled or hollowed petals. The series Urceolatae is further peculiar in the quite thick leaves and dense rosettes of its species. Another branch leads to the species with very sharply angled corollas, here divided between the series Angulatae and Pruinosae, of which only the latter is pruinose. The remainder of the secund-flowered species are closely related, differing mainly in the degree of branching of the inflorescence, the latter's size, and the number and size of the leaves. The zenith of development is attained in the series Gibbiflorae, where the inflorescence may exceed a height of six feet, as in *E. gigantea.* The large petiolate leaves of this series too are distinctive, sometimes reaching a weight of over one pound each.

The individual flowers in the several series having a more or less equilateral inflorescence are borne on what are actually short branches rather than bractless pedicels. This applies also to the species in the series Echeveria, with the exception of *E. setosa* and *E. ciliata.* In this series, two distinct lines may be traced, species with multicellular trichomes and those with simple hairs. The latter group terminates in the large flowered species *E. carminea, E. amphoralis,* and *E. harmsii,* the last with an inflorescence reduced to two large flowers. In the rest of the group we can trace a line of descent from *E. pulvinata,* with appressed sepals, to *E. coccinea* with these widely spreading. *Eche-*

veria pilosa, with its paniculate inflorescence, agrees with the secund-racemose-flowered *E. setosa* in type of trichome, and comes close in chromosome number.

The remainder of the equilaterally flowered species fall into two main groups, those with an evident shrubby stem and rather small leaves, and those practically stemless. Of the former, the series Spicatae is distinct by reason of its densely thyrsoid-spicate inflorescence and its predominantly epiphytic habit, and in having chromosome numbers based on the number 17, otherwise very rare in *Echeveria.* In our series Elatae, the stem is evident, if short, but usually simple, the leaves are rather large, and the inflorescence is a notably tall spike or raceme. The remaining species are stemless and fall into two branches, of which the series Mucronatae has fleshy-fusiform roots and often semideciduous leaves.

Generally, there does not appear to be any barrier to intercrossing within the genus, so that almost any combination of characters mentioned above may be found in garden plants. Whether hybridization occurs in nature is uncertain, one obstacle there being the present isolation of most species. Only very rarely do more than one species occur in any one locality, and even when this is the case, these species rarely flower simultaneously to permit cross-pollination. The only exceptions known to what might be a natural law are found in the instances where *E. chiapensis* grew with *E. racemosa* and *E. amoena* grew with *E. meyraniana.* No hybrids between these quite distinct species could be found.

It is uncertain whether there is a genetic barrier to intercrossing between *E. chiapensis* and *E. racemosa,* but *E. chiapensis* is recorded to have $n = 51$ chromosomes, a multiple of 17, otherwise almost unknown in *Echeveria.* The possibility of dependence on a quite distinct pollinating agent must also be kept in mind, for one species is epiphytic while the other is terrestrial, one has a dense spike of pale yellow flowers, while the other has typically coral-red corollas. In view of the presently very localized occurrence of *Echeveria* in its native habitat, hybridization can have played only a minor role, if any, in recent speciation in *Echeveria.* It needs to be mentioned though that several species, such as *E. scheerii, E. multicaulis, E. microcalyx,* while of undoubted Mexican origin, display chromosomal irregularities ordinarily associated with intercrossing.

In preparing my keys, I have usually been able to group together obviously related species, even if the need of making these keys workable had to take precedence.

THE CONCEPT OF SERIES AND SPECIES IN *Echeveria*

CONCEPT OF SERIES

Past attempts of subdividing the genus *Echeveria* have not been very successful, and the segregation of *Courantia, Oliveranthus,* and *Urbinia* could not be maintained in view of increased knowledge and the many new species which have been discovered and which form connecting links. Even as subgenera, sections, or series, these groups are untenable, not only for the reason stated, but further because of nomenclatural complications, such as the requirements of conserving the oldest names for serial designations. This would lend an undue emphasis to these groups, and perhaps include within their limits a large number of species entirely foreign to the original concept, whether justifiably or not.

Offhand, *Echeveria* might be divided into two groups of species, those with a secund inflorescence having bractless pedicels, and the other species with an equilateral inflorescence and two or more bractlets on the pseudopedicels. A number of species are difficult to fit into this grouping: those which Berger placed in his series Paniculatae, the several hairy species which are obviously related to each other more closely than to the other groups, and the aberrant *E. longissima*. For our present purpose we have found the simple series concept much more useful, practical, and quite logical from the phylogenetic aspect. Chromosome numbers in *Echeveria*, while highly variable, lend considerable support to our arrangement.

Member species of the 14 series here proposed show evident similarities to each other, and in some cases have formerly been combined into one broad species. As novel species have been discovered, they have usually fitted without question into one of the series here adopted.

Under the recommendations of the International Rules, designations of series should be descriptive adjectives with due regard for priority, and with these rules we have tried to comply as fully as possible.

CONCEPT OF SPECIES

At present, in the genus *Echeveria* no absolute decision is possible as to what is a valid species and what should be treated as a subordinate form. In a measure this sort of judgment is subjective and personal, but even wide experience and sound views, with an unbiased and critical approach, make any final decision difficult at this time. In the history of any genus several stages are passed through, of which the initial one, following the recognition of the genus, requires discrimination only between a limited number of species. These are generally quite easily distinguished, but as the number of known species grows, the entities are obviously not all equally distinct. At this stage it would be premature to be concerned unduly about the degrees of differences, whether the new forms at hand are species, subspecies, varieties, or forms. Expediency requires that these novelties be placed on record as species, until such time as more nearly complete knowledge of the genus will permit preparation of a more definitive treatment. The present understanding of *Echeveria* has by no means reached such a stage; the present study is a recapitulation of the current sum of knowledge.

SYSTEMATIC POSITION OF THE GENUS *Echeveria*

Family CRASSULACEAE

Annual, biennial, or perennial herbs or subshrubs, usually more or less succulent; leaves opposite, alternate, or whorled, often densely rosulate, exstipulate, mostly persistent, rarely deciduous; flowers actinomorphic, with as many petals as carpels; stamens as many, or twice as many, as petals and carpels; the carpels free except at base; hypogynous nectaries usually evident, very rarely lacking.

KEY TO SUBFAMILIES

A. Stamens as many as petals and carpels. . . . . CRASSULOIDEAE
A. Stamens twice as many as petals and carpels.
  B. Flowers 4-parted; corolla more or less tubular; leaves mostly opposite.
                                                         KALANCHOIDEAE
  B. Flowers with 5 or many parts.
    C. Flowers 6- to 32-parted; leaves mostly rosulate, often ciliate. SEMPERVIVOIDEAE
    C. Flowers usually with 5 petals, sepals, and carpels, but with 10 stamens.
      D. Inflorescence mostly terminal, rarely lateral; petals usually free to base, less
        often connate and then the inflorescence terminal.
        E. Petals connate into a long corolla-tube; plants of the Old World.
                                              COTYLEDONOIDEAE
        E. Petals free or only slightly connate at base, usually spreading above; plants
          of both the Old and New Worlds. . . . . SEDOIDEAE
      D. Inflorescence normally, without exceptions, lateral and axillary; petals con-
        nate at base, above erect or spreading; plants of the New World.
                                              ECHEVERIOIDEAE

SUBFAMILY ECHEVERIOIDEAE

Perennial herbs or subshrubs, with indeterminate vegetative axis and axillary, lateral inflorescences; leaves always alternate, scattered, or densely rosulate, usually persistent; flowers five-parted; petals either clearly united below, or connivent above into pseudotube or both; stamens 10; carpels five, free to base or nearly so, at first erect but often widely divergent at maturity; plants of the New World, southwestern Texas to northwestern Argentina.

Typical genus: *Echeveria* DeCandolle

KEY TO GENERA

A. Corolla-segments more or less rotately spreading from the middle.
  B. Inflorescence a narrow, equilateral panicle or thyrse with many short, few-flowered
    branches; petals evenly and closely lined red on inner surface; stamens remaining
    erect; pollen not foetid; Mexico. . . . . THOMPSONELLA Rose
  B. Inflorescence otherwise, usually with elongated secund branches, or else with bracte-
    olate pedicels.
    C. Inner face of petals with conspicuous red dots often forming transverse bands;
      stamens reflexed at maturity; pollen foetid or musty-scented; Arizona to Mexico.
                                         GRAPTOPETALUM Rose
    C. Petals mostly whitish, yellowish or uniformly tinged purplish; stamens erect;
      pollen not foetid.
      D. Leaves and flowers arising from a subterranean corm, leaves thin, deciduous;
        California. . . . . HASSEANTHUS Rose
      D. Caudex not cormous; leaves evergreen, thick; petals white or tinged purplish;
        southern California and northern Baja California
                             DUDLEYA Britton and Rose, subgenus
                         STYLOPHYLLUM (Britton and Rose) R. Moran
A. Corolla-segments erect or nearly so, at most slightly spreading at tips, more or less
  tubular-connate below.
  B. Petals with pair of scale-like appendages within at base of epipetalous stamens;
    Mexico. . . . . PACHYPHYTUM Link, Klotzsch and Otto
  B. Petals normally without any appendages (except in abnormal plants of *Echeveria*
    heterosepala and *E. longissima* and in normal *E. dactylifera*).
    C. Leaves and bracts broadly sessile with base more or less stem-clasping, not readi-
      ly detached, veins parallel to base or slightly converging, departing from leaf by
      as many separate bundles; inflorescence mostly cymose-racemose with secund
      branches; flowers small to medium-sized, often pale or dull colored, less often
      bright red or yellow; petals thinnish, scarcely keeled on back, not deeply hol-
      lowed within at base, usually spirally convolute in bud; sepals mostly equal and
      appressed; anthers short, broad; pollen dry-powdery in most species; carpels slen-
      der, straight; nectaries small, thinnish; chromosome number $n = 17$ or some mul-
      tiple thereof; plants of California, Arizona, and Baja California, not present in
      the rest of Mexico. . . . . DUDLEYA Britton and Rose, subgenus
                             DUDLEYA

C. Leaves with bases scarcely stem-clasping, with veins convergent to base and with a single bundle-trace, the leaf-like bracts similar; inflorescences various, either secund or with secund branches, or else equilateral with bracteolate pedicels; flowers often large and showy, bright red and yellow, less often pale; petals mostly thick, distinctly keeled on back and deeply hollowed within at base, in bud cochleate-imbricate, not convolute, aestivation some variant of quincuncial arrangement; sepals often unequal, mostly spreading at anthesis; anthers oblong; pollen agglutinate; carpels often short and stout, less often slender and elongated; nectaries mostly large, thick, truncate, rarely small and thin; chromosome numbers various, at present only three species known with $n = 17$ or multiple thereof; plants of Mexico, Central and South America, with one species reaching southwestern Texas, not known from California, Baja California, or Arizona. Includes *Courantia, Oliveranthus,* and *Urbinia.* . . . ECHEVERIA DeCandolle

Echeveria DeCandolle

Echeveria DeCandolle, Prodromus, vol. 3, p. 401, 1828.
Courantia Lemaire, Jard. Fleur., vol. 1, misc. p. 92, 1851.
Oliverella Rose, Bull. New York Bot. Gard., vol. 3, p. 2, 1903; not Van Tieghem.
Urbinia Rose, Bull. New York Bot. Gard., vol. 3, p. 11, 1903.
Oliveranthus Rose, *in* Britton and Rose, N. Amer. Fl., vol. 22, p. 27, 1905.

Succulent perennials or subshrubs, with indeterminate vegetative axis; roots fibrous or sometimes fusiform-thickened; stems simple or branched, very short to elongated; leaves usually evergreen, rarely semideciduous, spirally alternate in 8/21 phyllotaxy, densely rosulate or scattered, fleshy, thin or more often turgid, mostly entire, rarely with lacerate or fimbriate margins, usually sessile, less often narrowed below into a distinct stout petiole, base articulate, not amplexicaul, at apex usually mucronate, apiculate to aristate, often glaucous or pruinose, sometimes papillose or muriculate, or pubescent with trichomes simple and single-celled or with several uniseriate cells; palisade-parenchyma lacking in all species studied with the exception of *S. longissima;* venation usually obscure, but in series Retusae and Gibbiflorae three to five or more parallel longitudinal veins arise from base; inflorescences normally always lateral and axillary, simple or variously compound, secund or with secund branches (cincinni), through reduction of these secund branches often becoming an equilateral raceme, spike or thyrsoid panicle, the inflorescence rarely reduced to one or two flowers only; peduncle stout or slender, in its lower portion bearing leaf-like bracts, the bracts large or much reduced, smaller above, never cordate or amplexicaul at base, often readily detached, upper bracts one or two at base of each pedicel; pedicels elongated or sometimes much shortened, bractless, the bracteolate pseudopedicels of the series Nudae, Spicatae, Elatae, Mucronatae, and Racemosae, really representing reduced branches, upper bracts much reduced, bracteoles when present still smaller; flowers perfect, five-merous, proterandrous; sepals five, free or more or less united at base, unequal or subequal, more or less spreading or ascending, less often appressed, rarely reflexed, usually large, rarely reduced; corolla mostly strongly pentagonal, rarely subrotund, cylindrical to urceolate, often somewhat campanulate at apex, color mostly reddish to orange, less often pale, yellowish to pinkish; petals five, imbricate in bud, quincuncial, shortly connate at base, connivent above into a pseudotube, mostly thick and keeled on back, with prominent nectar-cavity at base within, less often thinnish and then neither keeled nor much hollowed at base, generally without any appendages at base of epipetalous filaments; stamens 10, quite free from each other, unequal, the epipetalous ones attached at top of nectar-cavity, the episepalous ones at top of corolla-tube, usually somewhat shorter than petals, rarely equalling these; filaments flattened-subulate; anthers basi-fixed, oblong, to 6 mm. long, pollen agglutinate, tricolpate to tetrahedroid-spherical; carpels five, united at base, erect at anthesis, at base bearing promi-nent nectar-glands, these usually thick, truncate, reniform or lunate, stipitate, less often small thin and sharp-edged, secreting an abundance of nectar; styles mostly slender; stigmas small, rarely decidedly clavate or capitate, often dark colored; follicles usually widely divergent at maturity, with many small ovoid-pyriform seeds, their testa smooth or reticulate.

TYPE. *E. coccinea* (Cavanilles) DeCandolle.

KEY TO THE SERIES

A. Plants hairy on all exterior portions, inclusive of corolla. .   .   .   Series 13 Echeveria
A. Plants glabrous, rarely papillose or muriculate (leaves puberulous, but corolla glabrous in *E. semivestita*).
  B. Corolla to 33 mm. long, 2 to 3 times as long as thick; styles greatly elongated, to 4 times as long as ovaries; leaves possessing palisade-cells. .   Series 14 Longistylae
  B. Corolla shorter or broader; styles mostly shorter, less than 20 mm. long inclusive of ovaries, rarely more than twice as long as ovaries.
    C. Leaves thick, turgid, clavate-subterete, often obtuse; stem often evident even if short; peduncle mostly slender, usually with readily detachable bracts; inflores-cence cymose to paniculate; petals thin, scarcely keeled; nectaries small, thin; sepals small and obtuse, or else appressed. .   .   .   .   .   Series 1 Paniculatae
    C. Plants largely otherwise in most characters
      D. Inflorescence or its branches secund; pedicels bractless.
        E. Corolla urceolate, subrotundate, scarcely pentagonal; petals mostly thin, rarely with deep basal cavity; pedicels slender, sometimes turbinately thick-ened below calyx; leaves mostly thick, turgid, often with epidermis crystal-line and margins hyaline; lower bracts often few, small, appressed; sepals mostly small, sometimes connate, rarely spreading or reflexed; nectaries mostly small, thin. .   .   .   .   Series 2 Urceolatae
        E. Corolla conoid-cylindroid, bluntly or sharply pentagonal; petals thickish, with well-defined basal cavity; sepals larger, spreading, ascending or ap-pressed; nectaries large, thick, truncate; leaves thick or thinnish, large or small, neither crystalline nor hyaline.
          F. Corolla sharply pentagonal, with petals prominently keeled; pedicels usually short or none; basal nectar-cavity usually well defined; leaves mostly rather thick; bracts numerous or few, often subterete; sepals large, ascending to erect; nectaries large, thick, truncate.
            G. Leaves, bracts, and sepals strikingly pruinose-glaucous; bracts flat and broad. .   .   .   .   Series 7 Pruinosae
            G. Leaves, bracts, and sepals scarcely or not pruinose-glaucous; bracts mostly subterete. .   .   .   .   Series 6 Angulatae
          F. Corolla bluntly pentagonal, never sharply angled; pedicels mostly slen-der, elongated, rarely short; sepals spreading to ascending or reflexed; bracts mostly flat.
            G. Plants small to medium sized; rosettes dense, usually cespitose, with stem short or none; leaves small to medium sized; inflorescences small to medium sized, usually a simple secund raceme; lower bracts often few, small; styles pale, greenish. .   .   .   Series 3 Secundae
            G. Plants medium sized to large; stem evident, often stout, mostly sim-ple; leaves relatively few, medium sized to large, often petioled; in-florescence medium sized to large, with 2, 3, or many branches; lower bracts often numerous, flat; corolla sometimes large; styles mostly dark, red to black.
              H. Plants medium sized; leaves rather small, sometimes retuse; stem short; inflorescence small, with at most 2 tor 3 branches.
Series 4 Retusae
              H. Plants large to very large; caudex large, stout; leaves large, often distinctly long-petioled; inflorescence a tall many-branched panicle.
Series 5 Gibbiflorae

D. Inflorescence equilateral; pedicels bracteolate.
   E. Plants with evident, often branching stem.
      F. Leaves relatively small, rosulate, subrosulate, or alternate.
         G. Inflorescence densely subspicate; pedicels short; sepals slightly spread-
           ing to appressed; petals often yellowish. . . . Series 9 Spicatae
         G. Inflorescence laxly spicate, racemose or subpaniculate.
                               Series 8 Nudae
      F. Leaves larger, longer, rosulate or scattered; inflorescences mostly tall
        racemes . . . . Series 10 Elatae
   E. Plants stemless or nearly so, the stem if present mostly simple; leaves small,
     less often medium sized.
      F. Roots fleshy-fusiform; leaves sometimes deciduous; pedicels, at least of
        uppermost flowers, short; sepals often ascending; corolla mostly rather
        broad . . . . Series 12 Mucronatae
      F. Roots all fibrous; pedicels often elongated; corolla often narrow, to
        20 mm. long; sepals usually widely spreading. . Series 11 Racemosae

Figure 8. *Echeveria 'Victor'.* From an article by Eric Walther (American Horticultural Magazine, volume 39, page 86).

HORTICULTURAL, UNCERTAIN, AND EXCLUDED NAMES OF *Echeveria*

Echeveria Abramsii (Rose) Berger . . .	*Dudleya Abramsii* Rose
Echeveria abyssinica Otto	*Hypagophytum abyssinicum* (Hochstetter) Berger
Echeveria acuminata (Rose) Berger . . .	*Dudleya acuminata* Rose
Echeveria adunca Otto	*Pachyphytum Hookeri* (Salm) Berger
Echeveria albida (Rose) Berger	*Stylophyllum albidum* Rose
Echeveria albiflora (Rose) Berger . . .	*Dudleya albiflora* Rose
Echeveria aloides (Rose) Berger	*Dudleya aloides* Rose
Echeveria amadorana Berger	*Dudleya gigantea* Rose

Echeveria amethystina, hortorum*   .   .   .   *Graptopetalum amethystinum*
(Rose) E. Walther

* Hortorum = of the garden, referring to plants of garden or unknown origin.

Echeveria amethystina, hortorum . . .	*Echeveria violescens* E. Walther
Echeveria angulosa, hortorum	*Echeveria pulchella* Berger
Echeveria angustiflora (Rose) Berger . .	*Dudleya angustiflora* Rose
Echeveria Anthonyi (Rose) Berger . . .	*Dudleya Anthonyi* Rose
Echeveria argentea Lemaire	*Dudleya pulverulenta*
	(Nuttall) Britton & Rose
Echeveria arizonica	
(Rose) Kearney & Peebles	*Dudleya arizonica* Rose
Echeveria arizonica, hortorum	*Graptopetalum paraguayense*
	(N. E. Brown) E. Walther (?)
Echeveria attenuata (S. Watson) Berger .	*Stylophyllum attenuatum* Britton & Rose
Echeveria Baileyi, hortorum	(?)
Echeveria Bartramii	
(Rose) Kearney & Peebles	*Graptopetalum Bartramii* Rose
Echeveria Bergeriana, hortorum	*Pachyveria* 'Sodalis'
Echeveria bernardina (Britton) Berger . .	*Dudleya bernardina* Britton
Echeveria bracteosa	
(Link, Klotzsch & Otto) Lindley . . .	*Pachyphytum bracteosum*
	Link, Klotzsch & Otto
Echeveria Brandegei (Rose) Berger . .	*Dudleya Brandegei* Rose
Echeveria Brauntonii (Rose) Berger . .	*Dudleya Brauntonii* Rose
Echeveria brevipes (Rose) Berger . . .	*Dudleya brevipes* Rose
Echeveria Brittonii Nelson & Macbride . .	*Gormania Hallii* Britton
Echeveria Bryceae (Britton) Berger . . .	*Dudleya Bryceae* Britton
Echeveria caespitosa	
(Haworth) DeCandolle	*Dudleya caespitosa* (Haworth) Britton & Rose
Echeveria californica Baker	*Dudleya Cotyledon* (Jacquin) Britton & Rose
Echeveria calophana, hortorum	*Echeveria acutifolia* Lindley
Echeveria campanulata, hortorum . . .	*Echeveria violescens* E. Walther
Echeveria Candelabrum (Rose) Berger . .	*Dudleya Candelabrum* Rose
Echeveria candicans, hortorum	(?)
Echeveria candida (Britton) Berger . . .	*Dudleya candida* Britton
Echeveria Collomae	
(Rose ex Morton) Kearney & Peebles .	*Dudleya Collomae* Rose ex Morton
Echeveria compacta (Rose) Berger . . .	*Dudleya compacta* Rose
Echeveria congesta (Britton) Berger . . .	*Dudleya congesta* Britton
Echeveria Cooperi Otto	*Adromischus Cooperi* (Baker) Berger
Echeveria Cotyledon	
(Jacquin) Nelson & Macbride	*Dudleya Cotyledon* Britton & Rose
Echeveria crispa, hortorum	*Echeveria crenulata* var. (?)
Echeveria cultrata (Rose) Berger . . .	*Dudleya cultrata* Rose
Echeveria cymosa Lemaire	*Dudleya cymosa* (Lemaire) Britton & Rose
Echeveria debilis	
(Watson) Nelson & Macbride	*Gormania debilis* (Watson) Britton
Echeveria decipiens (Baker) Ed. Morren,	
Belg. Hortic., vol. 24, p. 159, 1874 . .	*Villadia decipiens* (Baker) Jacobsen
Echeveria delicata (Rose) Berger . . .	*Dudleya delicata* Rose
Echeveria densiflora (Rose) Berger . . .	*Stylophyllum densiflorum* Rose
Echeveria diaboli Berger	*Dudleya humilis* Rose
Echeveria Eastwoodiae (Rose) Berger . .	*Dudleya Eastwoodiae* Rose
Echeveria edulis (Nuttall) Berger . . .	*Stylophyllum edule* (Nuttall) Britton & Rose
Echeveria elongata (Rose) Berger . . .	*Dudleya elongata* Rose
Echeveria eximia, hortorum	(?)
Echeveria farinosa Lindley	*Dudleya farinosa* (Lindley) Britton & Rose
Echeveria fulgida, hortorum	*Echeveria fulgens* Lemaire
Echeveria gerbella, hortorum	*Echeveria* 'Perbella'
Echeveria gibba Burchard	(?)
Echeveria gibbosa var. *viridis*, hortorum .	*Echeveria grandifolia*
	cv. 'Green-leaf' E. Walther
Echeveria globosa, hortorum	*Echeveria pumila* var. *glauca*
	(Baker) E. Walther

Figure 9. *Echeveria* 'Imbricata'. From an article by Eric Walther (American Horticultural Magazine, volume 39, page 80).

Echeveria Goldmani
   (Rose) Berger (not Rose) . . . . . *Dudleya Goldmani* Rose
Echeveria Gormanii Nelson & Macbride . *Gormania laxa* Britton
Echeveria grandiflora (Rose) Berger . . . *Dudleya grandiflora* Rose
Echeveria grandis Ed. Morren . . . . . *Echeveria gibbiflora* DeCandolle
Echeveria Greenei (Rose) Berger . . . . *Dudleya Greenei* Rose
Echeveria Greenii de Smet . . . . . . *Cotyledon* species (?)
Echeveria Hallii
   (Rose) Nelson & Macbride . . . . . *Dudleya Hallii* Rose
Echeveria Hassei (Rose) Berger . . . . *Stylophyllum Hassei* Rose
Echeveria Helleri (Rose) Berger . . . . *Dudleya Helleri* Rose
Echeveria Hookeri Lemaire . . . . . *Pachyphytum Hookeri* (Salm) Berger
Echeveria ingens (Rose) Berger . . . . *Dudleya ingens* Rose
Echeveria insularis (Rose) Berger . . . *Stylophyllum insulare* Rose
Echeveria Jepsonii Nelson & Macbride . . *Dudleya paniculata* Britton & Rose
Echeveria lagunensis Munz . . . . . *Dudleya lagunensis* (Munz) E. Walther
Echeveria lanceolata Nuttall . . . . . *Dudleya lanceolata* (Nuttall) Britton & Rose
Echeveria laurifolia, hortorum . . . . (?)
Echeveria laxa Lindley . . . . . . *Dudleya laxa* (Lindley) Britton & Rose
Echeveria linearis (Greene) Berger . . . *Dudleya linearis* (Greene) Britton & Rose
Echeveria Lingettolii, hortorum . . . . (?)
Echeveria linguaformis, hortorum . . . *Dudleya caespitosa* (Haworth) Britton & Rose
Echeveria lingula
   (S. Watson) Nelson & Macbride . . . *Dudleya lingula* (S. Watson) Britton & Rose
Echeveria lucida Steudel . . . . . *Echeveria lurida* Haworth (acc. Index Kew.)
Echeveria macrantha, hortorum . . . . *Cotyledon macrantha* Berger (?)
Echeveria macrophylla, hortorum . . . *Echeveria grandifolia* Haworth (?)
Echeveria McCabei, hortorum . . . . *Echeveria Runyonii* var. *Macabeana*
                            E. Walther
Echeveria mexicana, hortorum . . . . *Echeveria coccinea* (Cavanilles) DeCandolle
Echeveria minor (Rose) Berger . . . . *Dudleya minor* Rose
Echeveria minutiflora Rose . . . . . *Thompsonella minutiflora*
                            (Rose) Britton & Rose
Echeveria minutifoliata Poellnitz . . . . *Graptopetalum pachyphyllum* Rose
Echeveria Monicae Berger . . . . . . *Dudleya lurida* Rose
Echeveria Muelleriana, hortorum . . . (?)
Echeveria nevadensis
   (S. Watson) Nelson & Macbride . . . *Dudleya nevadensis*
                            (S. Watson) Britton & Rose
Echeveria nubigena (Brandegee) Berger . *Dudleya nubigena*
                            (Brandegee) Britton & Rose
Echeveria obtusata
   (A. Gray) Nelson & Macbride . . . . *Gormania obtusata* (A. Gray) Britton
Echeveria Orcuttii (Rose) Berger . . . . *Stylophyllum Orcuttii* Rose
Echeveria oregana
   (Nuttall) Nelson & Macbride . . . . *Gormania oregana* (Nuttall) Britton
Echeveria ovaliformis, hortorum . . . . (?)
Echeveria ovatifolia (Britton) Berger . . *Dudleya ovatifolia* Britton
Echeveria ovifera Fournier . . . . . . (?)
Echeveria oviformis, hortorum . . . . (?)
Echeveria Pachyphytum Ed. Morren . . *Pachyphytum bracteosum*
                            Link, Klotzsch & Otto
Echeveria palensis Berger . . . . . . *Stylophyllum Parishii* Britton
Echeveria Palmeri
   (S. Watson) Nelson & Macbride . . . *Dudleya Palmeri* Britton & Rose
Echeveria paniculata Moçiño & Sessé . . *Fouquieria spinosa* Humboldt, Bonpland &
                            Kunth (acc. Index Kew.)
Echeveria Parishii (Rose) Berger . . . . *Dudleya Parishii* Rose
Echeveria parva Berger . . . . *Dudleya pumila* Rose
Echeveria pauciflora (Rose) Berger . . . *Dudleya pauciflora* Rose
Echeveria planifolia Berger . . . . . *Thompsonella platyphylla* Britton & Rose
Echeveria Plattiana
   (Jepson) Nelson & Macbride . . . . *Dudleya Plattiana* (Jepson) Britton & Rose
Echeveria pulverulenta Nuttall . . . . *Dudleya pulverulenta*
                            (Nuttall) Britton & Rose

Figure 10. *Echeveria* 'Set-oliver'. From an article by Eric Walther (American Horticultural Magazine, volume 39, page 78).

Echeveria Purpusii K. Schumann	*Dudleya Purpusii* (Schumann) Britton & Rose
Echeveria reflexa (Britton) Berger . . .	*Dudleya reflexa* Britton
Echeveria rhombifolia Otto	*Adromischus rhombifolius* (Haworth) Lemaire
Echeveria rigida (Rose) Berger	*Dudleya rigida* Rose
Echeveria rigidiflora (Rose) Berger . . .	*Dudleya rigidiflora* Rose
Echeveria robusta (Britton) Berger . . .	*Dudleya robusta* Britton
Echeveria rosaeformis de Smet	(?)
Echeveria rubens (Brandegee) Berger . .	*Dudleya rubens* (Brandegee) Britton & Rose
Echeveria Rusbyi (Greene) Nelson & Macbride	*Graptopetalum Rusbyi* (Greene) Rose
Echeveria saxosa (M. E. Jones) Berger . .	*Dudleya saxosa* (M. E. Jones) Britton & Rose
Echeveria Scheideckeri de Smet	*Pachyveria* 'Scheideckeri' E. Walther
Echeveria Schmidtii, hortorum	(?)
Echeveria semiteres (Rose) Berger . . .	*Stylophyllum semiteres* Rose
Echeveria septentrionalis (Rose) Berger .	*Dudleya septentrionalis* Rose
Echeveria Setchellii (Jepson) Nelson & Macbride	*Dudleya Setchellii* (Jepson) Britton & Rose
Echeveria Sheldonii (Rose) Berger . . .	*Dudleya Sheldonii* Rose
Echeveria sobrina Berger	*Pachyveria* 'Sobrina'
Echeveria sodalis Berger	*Pachyveria* 'Sodalis'
Echeveria spathulata Bull	*Kalanchoe spathulata* DeCandolle
Echeveria spathulifolia de Smet	*Sedum spathulifolium* Hooker
Echeveria spicata Moçiño & Sessé . . .	*Fouquieria formosa* Humboldt, Bonpland & Kunth (acc. Index Kew.)
Echeveria tenuis (Rose) Berger (not Rose)	*Dudleya tenuis* Rose
Echeveria tepeacensis Poellnitz	*Thompsonella minutiflora* (Rose) Britton & Rose
Echeveria tortuosa Ed. Morren	(?)
Echeveria Traskae (Rose) Berger . . .	*Stylophyllum Traskae* Rose
Echeveria uniflora, hortorum	*Pachyphytum uniflorum* Rose (?)
Echeveria velutina, hortorum	(?)
Echeveria villosa de Smet	(?)
Echeveria virens (Rose) Berger	*Stylophyllum virens* Rose
Echeveria viscida (S. Watson) Berger . .	*Stylophyllum viscidum* (S. Watson) Britton & Rose
Echeveria Watsonii (Britton) Nelson & Macbride	*Gormania Watsonii* Britton
Echeveria Weinbergii T. B. Shepherd . .	*Graptopetalum paraguayense* (N. E. Brown) E. Walther
Echeveria Xanti (Rose) Berger	*Dudleya Xanti* Rose

Echeveria Hybrids

It has never been easy to have any competent botanist express definite opinions on the exact identity of the various kinds of *Echeveria* grown in our local gardens. This caution is due to the inevitable confusion that has followed from the lack of any adequate monograph on the genus, the scarcity of correctly determined herbarium material, and the presence in gardens of numerous hybrids, many of them nameless and often confusingly simulating true species. *Echeveria* is constant enough when propagated vegetatively, but seedlings grown from garden-collected seeds, are most variable, owing to the readiness with which almost any species or hybrid will cross with any other that happens to be close by. In nature, hybrids are almost unknown, for most species are quite isolated, and where two species do occur together, they usually have distinct flowering seasons, with very few known exceptions. However, cytological studies by Dr. Uhl show chromosomal irregularities in *E. scheerii, E. expatriata, E. gilva,* and *E. pulchella,* which suggest that at least some of these owe their origin to hybridization.

Figure 11. *Echeveria* 'Set-Oliver'. From an article by Eric Walther (Cactus and Succulent Journal, volume 8, page 172).

No genetic studies as to the limits of possible intercrossing appear to have been made in *Echeveria*, but from my observations it seems that members of all the various series will hybridize with each other quite freely. This applies even to distinct genera, as *Graptopetalum, Pachyphytum,* and even *Sedum.* For the reception of these hybrids the categories Graptoveria, Pachyveria, and Sedeveria have been devised, which deserve separate consideration.

Some wide crosses within *Echeveria,* as with *E. harmsii,* appear to be sterile, never producing any seed. Similar information is on record for *E.* 'Weingartii' and *E.* 'Parva'; no doubt other hybrids too are sterile. Scarcity of hybrids in nature may be due to sterility of the F_2 generation.

Many hybrids, of known parentage, are strictly intermediate between their parents, of which fact crosses between hairy and smooth species provide numerous examples. Numerous hybrids have been made, for instance, with *E. setosa* for one parent. In the resultant offspring, the long, dense hairs of *E. setosa* are represented by smaller scattered trichomes often confined to the edges and keels of the leaves, bracts, and sepals, as for example in *E.* 'Weingartii' and *E.* 'Derosa.' In *E.* 'Mutabilis' the leaf-surface is minutely papillose, a character readily accounted for if *E. carnicolor* was one of its parents, as I believe is the case.

Seeds from garden-grown echeverias may yield hybrids of some slight interest, but rarely are of sufficiently high quality to deserve distinctive names. This last does not apply to crosses made deliberately by skilled growers, whose aim is the creation of new plants of superior beauty. Historically such hybridization was carried on most intensively by Deleuil of Rue Paradis, Marscilles, who listed numerous named hybrids in his catalogs for 1873 and 1874 as reprinted in *La Belgique Horticole* of those years. Several of his hybrids are still extant in local gardens, and one at least appears to be the most commonly cultivated *Echeveria* in California. This is *E*. 'Imbricata,' a cross of *E. glauca* and *E. metallica,* and commonly misnamed *E. secunda-glauca.* Other breeders of that time were de Smet, Rendatler of Nancy, and Wm. Bull of Kings Road, Chelsea, London. The latter's *E*. 'Glauco-Metallica' was listed by Veitch in their 1873 catalog and is still grown today.

More recently numerous fine hybrids have been raised in Germany, as for instance *E*. 'Derosa' by von Roeder, also *E*. 'Weingartii' and *E*. 'Haageana.' With the growing popularity of *Echeveria* in California, local growers too, whether commercial or amateur, have undertaken hybridization, with some notable results. Mr. Hummel of Inglewood and Carlsbad has managed to cross *Echeveria (E. derenbergii)* not only with *Graptopetalum* and *Pachyphytum,* but even with *Sedum (S. pachyphyllum, S. nussbaumerianum, S. compressum,* and *S. treleasii),* a most interesting bigeneric hybrid named 'Sedeveria' by me.

Mr. Victor Reiter, Jr., of San Francisco has made many crosses, with the deliberate purpose of combining the known, superior qualities of certain parent-species and so producing fine garden plants. Among his most successful hybrids are *E*. 'Set-Oliver,' *E*. 'Victor,' and *E*. 'Pulv-Oliver'; which owe their superiority, including extra large flowers, to the influence of *E. harmsii,* formerly known as *Oliveranthus elegans.*

Figure 12. *Echeveria 'Pulv-Oliver'.* From an article by Eric Walther (Cactus and Succulent Journal, volume 9, page 92).

Several echeverias in cultivation, said to be of Mexican origin, have not been found again in nature and may be suspected to be of hybrid origin. Among such possible hybrids masquerading as species are *E. expatriata* and *E. pulchella,* perhaps descended from *E. amoena;* and *E. gilva,* whose amber-colored leaves point to *E. agavoides* as a putative parent. More illuminating is the case of *E. stolonifera,* stated by Baker to have come from Mexico but never yet found there. No plants of this were ever planted in the grounds of the Strybing Arboretum, yet several were found there, apparently being spontaneous seedlings. The conclusion is inescapable that these seedlings are the result of accidental intercrossing of some of the other species planted nearby. Of these *E. glauca* and *E. grandiflora* are the most likely parents, for the characters of *E. stolonifera* are exactly those to be expected in other hybrids of similar origin.

As garden ornaments, hybrids are not necessarily better or more beautiful than species are, and being often nameless, fail to satisfy the owner's deeper interest. On the other hand, named hybrids, deliberately raised for combining the good qualities of the parents, are in a different class, and often prove su-

Figure 13. *Echeveria elegans,* one of the finest species, shown in an informal manner in the rock garden of Victor Reiter, Jr., San Francisco. From an article by Eric Walther (American Horticultural Magazine, volume 39, page 73).

perior to any species, especially in vigor. For the guidance of local growers I
suggest the following superior, locally available hybrid echeverias:

E. 'Imbricata'	*E.* 'Ex-Palmeri'	*E.* 'Pulv-Oliver'
E. 'Derosa'	*E.* 'Flammea'	*E.* 'Glauco-Metallica'
E. 'Weingartii'	*E.* 'Atrosanguinea'	*E.* 'Blue-Boy'
E. 'Mutabilis'	*E.* 'Set-Oliver'	*E.* 'Doris Taylor'
E. 'Haageana'	*E.* 'Victor'	*E.* 'Orpet's Chocolate'

Echeveria IN CULTIVATION

HISTORY OF CULTIVATION

In its native habitat, *Echeveria* leaves may sometimes be used as a poultice,
as an antiscorbutic, or for other purposes, but its introduction into gardens is
of course motivated by its ornamental esthetic qualities. Even in Mexico today,
Echeveria is frequently planted in both private and public gardens and parks,
usually as a border, often in a fanciful design simulating a turtle. Such use may
antedate the Conquest; it may even have some now obscure religious significance, as has today the utilization of *Echeveria* flowers for decorating altars
and wayside crosses at Christmas time. As stated by Robert Redfield in *Tepoxtlan, a Mexican Village,* page 131, "the flowers (of *E. gibbiflora*) are sold in
the market only (?) on the day before Christmas"; they apparently are cultivated in Tepoxtlan homesteads for the purpose, or may be collected in the
native habitat of the species in the Sierra de Tepoxtlan. In Guatemala *E. montana* is said to be used similarly (*Flora of Guatemala,* Standley and Steyermark, page 409).

The several vernacular names applied to various species of *Echeveria* indicate local familiarity; the Nahuatl name for *Echeveria,* presumably *E. grandifolia,* was "Tetzmixochitl," meaning "flower of the plant with thick leaves,"
but "Siempreviva" is quite as commonly applied to other Crassulaceae as to
species of *Echeveria.* This may be merely a transfer of the Old World name
for *Sempervivum tectorum,* probably brought from Spain along with *Aloe vera,*
the latter now a widespread escape in Mexico, including Baja California. "Flor
de pietra," or "flower of the rocks," is also applied to *Echeveria* and its allies.
In Venezuela *E. bicolor* goes under the name "Repollo," or cabbage. "Chupa-
hueva" or "egg-sucker" is a local name for *E. quitensis* in parts of Colombia,
which might be freely translated "honeysuckle," and derived from the habit of
hummingbirds visiting the flowers. Endlich reports that the Tarahumare Indians of Western Chihuahua apply the term "Mec" to an *Echeveria,* possibly to
E. chihuahuaensis. "Orejo de burro" is the name of *E. paniculata, E. walpoleana,* and *E. grandifolia,* whose leaves do resemble the ear of a donkey, while
such species as *E. elegans* and its allies are known as "concha" or shells. "Galli-
nata" (little rooster) is the name applied to *E. montana,* in Guatemala.

Illustrating the widespread cultivation of *Echeveria* in modern Mexico is
the following list of species which I have found planted:

E. alpina	Federal District; Hostel on Popocatepetl.
E. byrnesii	Park in Toluca.
E. coccinea	Pachuca.
E. elegans	Omitlan, Pachuca, Actopan.
E. fulgens	Churchyard at Tenancingo.

E. glauca	Coatapec; Federal District. Salvador (?).
E. gibbiflora	Tepoxtlan; El Parque.
E. grandifolia	Federal District, Huitzilac.
E. harmsii	Amecameca; Mihuatlan.
E. obtusifolia	Huitzilac.
E. racemosa	Jalapa (?).
E. rubromarginata	Plaza at Puebla.
E. setosa	Plaza at Tehuacan.
E. palmeri	Encarnacion.
E. runyonii	Matamoros.
E. tolucensis	Railroad station at Toluca.

Perhaps the significance of this extensive planting of *Echeveria* is their being emblematic of remembrance, as are our forget-me-nots.

European cultivation of *Echeveria* is complicated by the fact that there they are not hardy, requiring winter protection from frost. Aside from scientific collections of botanic gardens, naturally housed in heated greenhouses, some species, such as *E. glauca,* have been used extensively in design bedding and for formal borders, a type of gardening once very popular. The plants could be carried over the winter in cold frames or a frost-free cellar, a practice still followed to some extent.

The first species to be grown in Europe was *E. coccinea,* at the Botanic Garden in Madrid before 1793, and was presumably sent there by Dr. Cervantes from Mexico City, where the species is wild within the city limits even today. By 1828 *E. grandifolia* was grown in England, when Haworth named and illustrated it; by 1837 *E. racemosa* appears to have been in cultivation at

Figure 14. *Echeveria elegans* as grown in a farm yard in Omitlán, Hidalgo, Mexico. From an article by Eric Walther (American Horticultural Magazine, volume 39, page 77).

Berlin, and soon after at Glasgow and Claremont. In that year *E. secunda* was sent to England from Real del Monte by John Rule, mine superintendent, and flowered for the first time in 1838 at Carclow, near Penryn, Cornwall. *Echeveria rosea* first flowered in England in 1841, a plant having been presented to the London Horticultural Society by the Nursery firm of Lee & Co., Vineyard, Hammersmith. This may have been collected by Karl Theodore Hartweg, then in Mexico, commissioned by said Society to collect seeds and plants; he also sent home *E. acutifolia* from Oaxaca, pictured in the Botanical Register for 1842, and also *E. fulgens (E. retusa)*, illustrated in the same publication the same year.

By 1863, 34 "species" were enumerated by Charles Lemaire, in *L'Illustration Horticole,* indicating that *Echeveria* had attained great popularity, which reached its zenith in 1869 with the publication by Baker, in Saunders' *Refugium Botanicum,* of the first comprehensive, well illustrated monograph, based almost wholly on living plants then in cultivation. Most of these were grown by Mr. W. Wilson Saunders at Reigate, who seems to have acquired Haworth's collection. Active at this time was also Mr. Justus Corderoy of Blewbury, Didcot, still remembered today by *E. corderoyi.* Other growers of the time were W. Bull, J. G. Henderson, Cooper, Shirley Hibbard, Carnell, Croucher, Wilson, and Peacock.

Aside from the aforementioned Charles Lemaire, Van Houtte, and Verschaffelt, who were prominent growers on the continent, L. de Smet was an early active hybridizer and the first grower of *E. peacockii.* Deleuil of Marseilles at this time turned out numerous hybrids, including our most common one, *E.* 'Imbricata.' By 1874 Ed. Morren listed nearly 100 names under *Echeveria,* in *La Belgique Horticole,* supposedly grown in Belgium at that time. In Germany the most extensive grower of the time seems to have been Otto of Hamburg, who also assigned Baker's species to their proper genus.

More recently the most active growers in Europe appear to have been such firms as Haage & Schmidt and F. A. Haage, Jr., of Erfurt, R. Graessner of Perleberg, Blossfeld of Potsdam, Schenkel of Hamburg, Winter of Frankfurt, all German firms offering numerous species and hybrids. Mention should be also made of DeLaet of Contich near Antwerp, Engelmann, Neal, Theobald, S. Smith & Sons, L. Lawrence, and Sir O. Leese of Worfield Gardens in England.

All of the aforementioned were commercial growers, but even more important is the extensive cultivation of *Echeveria* in the various botanic gardens in Europe, starting with *E. coccinea* at Madrid before 1793. When the Darmstadt Botanic Garden had for its director J. A. Purpus, brother of C. A. Purpus, the Mexican collector, its collection was the first European home of numerous new species, including *E. leucotricha, E. derenbergii, E. pilosa, E. gigantea, E. setosa, E. microcalyx, E. purpusorum, E. turgida, E. subalpina, E. rubromarginata,* and *E. carnicolor.* My new *E. parrasensis* was grown here too, and published as *E. cuspidata.* At the Royal Botanic Garden at Kew, England, quite a number of interesting items were cultivated at this time, including *E. devensis (E. acutifolia), E. pulvinata, E. harmsii* (as *Oliveranthus elegans*), *E. setosa,* and *E. subrigida.* The Kew Handlist enumerated 13 valid species in 1931. An important collection was that at the Hanbury Gardens of La Mortola in Italy, where Alwin Berger was active and grew *E. pusilla (E. amoena), E. pulchella, E. parrasensis,* and listed a total of 27 species in the *Hortus Mortolensis* in 1912.

At present the largest collection would appear to be that at the Kiel Botanic Garden, where Dr. Jacobsen compiled his *Succulent Plants,* of which the 1933 edition lists 27 kinds of *Echeveria.* Other botanic gardens in Europe growing substantial numbers of *Echeveria* are those at Zurich, where the Municipal Cactus and Succulent Collection is a leader in this field, as are also the gardens at Berlin-Dahlem, Frankfurt (Palmengarten), and Cologne (Flora). At Paris the Jardin des Plantes devotes a large greenhouse to succulents, including *Echeveria,* but the most extensive French collection is that of Marnier-Lapostolle at Les Cedres, Cap Ferrat, near Nice. The well known Jardin Exotique at Monte Carlo includes *Echeveria* among its show-plants, and nowhere have I seen *E. pilosa* in better form. Small collections are to be found at the Botanic Gardens at Edinburgh, Glasgow, and Dublin, of which the first mentioned is perhaps the most comprehensive. All such displays aim largely to illustrate the diversity of plant life, of which cacti and succulents represent a unique departure. Specialized research seems to be rare; to mind comes only that of Mauritzon, of Lund, Sweden.

Figure 15. A California rock garden featuring all sorts of *Echeveria* species and hybrids. From an article by Eric Walther (American Horticultural Magazine, volume 39, page 91).

CULTIVATION IN THE UNITED STATES OF AMERICA

Early cultivation of *Echeveria* in the United States reflected European practice, both as to kinds grown and purposes for which they were utilized. Paucity
of accurate records prevents giving of exact dates for the first arrival in the
United States of any definite items, and few of them left any permanent im-
pression on our gardens. However, *Echeveria metallica* was mentioned by
Blanc in his *Hints on Cacti* of 1891; and it was pictured in the Cactus Journal
of Baltimore in 1898. Of other growers of the period we mention Mr. Hovey
of Boston, still remembered through *E. hoveyi* which he originated; his portrait
still graces the offices of the Massachusetts Horticultural Society. Mention
should be made here of Manda's Universal Horticultural Establishment of
South Orange, New Jersey, where succulents, including *Echeveria,* were grown
and a number of still extant hybrids raised.

Eastern botanic gardens featured *Echeveria,* if to a limited extent. More
intensively was the genus grown at the New York Botanical Garden, during the
directorship of the late Dr. N. L. Britton, who then was collaborating with Dr. J.
N. Rose of the U.S. National Herbarium on both the Cactaceae and the Crassulaceae. In 1905, Dr. Rose's collection at Washington, D.C., included over
1000 pot-grown plants of *Echeveria, Sedum,* etc., many of them types of newly
discovered species. All of these were grown under the direction of Mr. E. M.
Byrnes, Superintendent of Gardens and Grounds, U.S. Dept. of Agriculture,
Washington, D.C., termed by Dr. Rose "a most skillful grower of *Echeveria,*"
and commemorated in Dr. Rose's genus *Byrnesia,* and *Echeveria byrnesii.* Mr.
Byrnes may have been responsible for rearing such hybrids as *E.* 'Clevelandii,'
long grown locally as *E. nobilis,* and probably referable to *Pachyveria.*

Dr. Rose's interest was primarily systematic botany, but the more desirable
of his new introductions soon found their way into more general cultivation.

More recently several novelties from Oaxaca have been named by Dr. Alexander of the New York Botanical Garden, and grown at the garden, *i.e., E.
bella, E. spectabilis, E. carminea,* and *E. alata.*

CULTIVATION IN CALIFORNIA

California's mild climate permits most species of *Echeveria* to be grown
out-of-doors the year round, a fact which accounts for their past and present
popularity here. As long ago as 1875, one San Francisco nurseryman listed 40
different kinds of *Echeveria* for sale, most of which had come from Europe
where the genus was popular at the time. Despite California's close proximity
to Mexico, few species of *Echeveria* were introduced directly until quite lately.
Much of the material grown here is traceable to Dr. Rose's introductions, as for
instance, *E. nuda, E. nodulosa, E. carnicolor, E. elegans, E. multicaulis, E.
turgida, E. lozani, E. gigantea, E. acutifolia,* and *E. crenulata.* Numerous novelties were first grown at the Western Nursery by the late Charles Abraham,
San Francisco, as for instance *E. grandifolia, E. peacockii, E. setosa, E. elegans, E. amoena, E. lozani, E. gilva, E.* 'Multicaulis,' *E.* 'Imbricata,' *E.* 'Glauco-Metallica,' *E.* 'Flammea,' and *E.* 'Atrosanguinea.'

A more recent and important grower of rarities was the late E. O. Orpet of
Santa Barbara, in whose collections I first saw *E. goldmani, E. violescens, E.
runyoni, E. stolonifera, E. bifurcata, E. gracilis,* and *E. pinetorum.* Of late
years the number of growers featuring *Echeveria* has grown too great for enu-

meration here, but of the larger commercial growers that ship large quantities of *Echeveria* we must mention Mr. Hummel of Inglewood and Carlsbad, and Harry Johnson of Paramount. For further information the interested reader is referred to the pages of the *Cactus and Succulent Journal.* Aside from the commercial growers, many private amateurs have taken up *Echeveria*, and not always merely because of its esthetic appeal. They are responsible for the organization of numerous local clubs, as well as the Cactus and Succulent Society of America and the publication of its journal, and the recent creation of the International Succulent Institute, Inc., Mr. J. W. Dodson of Millbrae, secretary.

Scientific collections in California are to be found at the Huntington Botanical Gardens, San Marino; at the Strybing Arboretum, Golden Gate Park, San Francisco; and at the University of California Botanical Garden at Berkeley. The last collection owed its inception to the efforts of the late James West, who, under the directorship of Dr. T. H. Goodspeed, first built it up to respectable proportions. Of late its management has been assumed by Dr. Herbert Baker, with Paul C. Hutchison, Senior Botanist, and Myron Kimnach as grower.

I have no private facilities for growing the material, and must depend upon my friends for help, among whom Mr. Victor Reiter of 1195 Stanyan Street, San Francisco, has been foremost. The latter is also responsible for the raising of some superior hybrids, as *E.* 'Set-Oliver,' *E.* 'Victor,' *E.* 'Pulv-Oliver,' and many others. Here were grown many of my own novelties introduced from Mexico, either personally or through friendly collaborators, such as C. Halbinger and members of the newly organized Sociedad Mexicana de Cactologia. Further data on the introduction and cultivation of the various species are given under each item.

CULTURAL NOTES

Aside from any scientific interest presented by *Echeveria,* its prime appeal must always be the esthetic one. This is not the place to discuss the proper manner to grow, plant, and arrange *Echeveria,* but I shall make a few observations drawn from my experience. In modern gardens few opportunities exist for creation of the stiff formal effects for which *Echeveria* was utilized formerly, even if there are exceptions to this rule. Informal arrangements, as in a sunny rock garden, furnish ample opportunities to display echeverias to advantage. Where a home gardener is looking for a subject to grow as a hobby, *Echeveria* and other succulents may be recommended. Not only do these present a large amount of interesting and varied plant material, they have the additional advantage of being able to survive with little care during the owner's absence, whether on a business trip or a two-weeks' vacation.

Permanently successful plantings require recognition of the cultural requirements of *Echeveria*, which include well-drained but moist soil, not absolutely devoid of plant food. Sprenger, German nurseryman of Naples, goes on record on the need of *Echeveria* seedlings for frequent and abundant applications of fertilizer through the growing season. Too many plantings I have seen were disappointing because the plants were diseased or pest-infested. Some effective means of excluding and controlling pests and diseases are essential and not too difficult with available modern insecticides, means of soil sterilization, etc. Stringent precautions in obtaining only absolutely healthy plants are essential.

The most serious enemies of *Echeveria* in cultivation, aside from frost, would seem to be nematodes and *Brachyrhinus*, the latter a snout-beetle commonly known as the strawberry crown-weevil. Its larvae feed on the stem at ground level, but several effective insecticides are available and should be used freely. Oil sprays are injurious to *Echeveria* and are best avoided. Occasional replanting during which the roots, etc., are discarded and only the rerooted tops of the plants used, helps to reduce losses from this pest. Soil sterilization and planting of wholly clean material, without roots, if these are not known to be wholly clean, should keep down losses from nematodes. Aphids, thrips, and mealy-bugs, may cause injury, in greenhouses especially, but are easily controlled by continuous vigilance. Frequent overhead syringing tends to keep down the incidence of such superficial insects. From my insistence on using clean plants follows the raising of new plants from seeds, for these are sure to be clean to start with. To be true to name, seed must be of species, for hybrids do not come true to name, and in cultivation plants grown together intercross so readily that care must be taken to prevent accidental hybridization. Most accidental hybrids are quite worthless and a mere nuisance to the student and botanist.

Propagation of *Echeveria* is no problem, and does not differ from that of similar plants. Division of cespitose kinds is only too easy; leaves and bracts, carefully detached from the stem so that an axillary bud is taken, provide a ready means of increasing the stock. Decapitation of tall stalks, as in the series Gibbiflorae, will not only permit rerooting the tip for creation of a smaller, more manageable plant, but the numerous sprouts arising from the stump will serve for further propagation. Removal of all buds from the flower stem may also induce the latter to form leaf buds suitable for rooting. Ordinarily, grafting succulents is unnecessary, but the finest specimen of *E. harmsii (Oliveranthus elegans)* I have ever seen had been grafted on *Sedum praealtum,* with eminent success. Much soil used for growing *Echeveria* in pots is devoid of all plant food, a serious mistake if well-grown specimens are wanted. Good drainage is desirable, but need not result in complete starvation. While in California partial shade is harmless, elsewhere plants need full light, for in too deep shade they do not develop their normal habit and color.

Relative frost hardiness may be inferred from the natural habitat of the species. *Echeveria alpina, E. subalpina, E. byrnesii, E. glauca, E. elatior,* and *E. crassicaulis,* occurring naturally at elevations of 8,000 to 14,000 feet, are of course the hardiest. On the other hand, most of the series Gibbiflorae, as *E. gibbiflora, E. gigantea, E. acutifolia, E. pallida, E. subrigida, E. palmeri, E. fimbriata, E. grisea,* and *E. violescens,* only rarely grow at elevations of more than 7,600 feet, and hence need winter protection even in some parts of California. Each garden is of course a separate problem, and often some warm sheltered corner, with perhaps a wall or tall tree to the north, will prove a happy home for even rather tender species. The old practice of carrying echeverias through the winter in a cold-frame or cellar, and planting them out after danger from frost is past, is still recommended. At home *Echeveria* is quite dry during the rainless winters characteristic of Mexico's climate, which hints that sharp drainage for plants left in the open should help them through the winter. Regularly exposed to frost, and even snow, in Mexico, are *E. alpina, E. byrnesii,* and *E. elatior,* from my own personal observations.

Systematics

Series 1. PANICULATAE Berger

Echeveria, ser. Paniculatae BERGER, *in* Engler Nat. Pflanzenf., ed. 2, vol. 18a, p. 472,
   1930, *pro parte;* E. WALTHER, Leafl. West. Bot., vol. 9, pp. 1, 4, 1959.
Echeveria, ser. Amoenae E. WALTHER, Cactus and Succ. Jour. Amer., vol. 30, p. 105,
   1958.

Plants glabrous; stem evident, but often short, simple or branching below;
leaves thick, often clavate, obtuse and mucronate, rarely aristate-mucronate;
inflorescence cymose to elongate-paniculate; peduncle erect or ascending to
decumbent, its bracts usually readily detached, mostly subterete; pedicels usually slender, occasionally bracteolate; sepals short, thick, turgid, or else elongated to more than half length of corolla, always more or less appressed; corolla
cylindroid to campanulate, rarely over 11 mm. long; petals mostly thin, with
dorsal keel blunt or none and basal hollow poorly developed, rarely sharply
keeled; stamens at times as long as petals; nectaries mostly small and thin.

TYPICAL SPECIES. *Echeveria amoena* L. de Smet.

REMARKS. Berger's series Paniculatae appears to constitute a quite natural
group after eliminating *E. setosa* with its strictly secund-flowered racemes and
sharply angular corolla. *Echeveria craigiana* and *E. affinis* may seem to be
out of place here, but they fit this series better than any other. *Echeveria pulchella* and *E. expatriata* are most likely hybrids that originated in some Italian
or French garden or nursery; I treat them here provisionally only. *Echeveria
linguaefolia* is known only from cultivated material; it has not been found wild
in Mexico. In habit, foliage, and inflorescence it greatly resembles *Sedum
cremnophila* (*Cremnophila nutans* Rose). Series Paniculatae may be considered as probably the most primitive one of the genus by reason of the small
nectaries, poorly developed petal-cavity and keel, and the rather indeterminate
type of inflorescence.

KEY TO THE SPECIES

A. Sepals at least half the length of the corolla, longest to 7 mm. long or more, deltoid-oblong or ovate-deltoid, acute.

  B. Leaves dark green, neither glaucous nor brownish, to over 2 cm. broad, often more or less remote or scattered; inflorescence an elongated, trailing panicle with many short few-flowered branches; sepals nearly as long as corolla; petals whitish. Source uncertain. . . . . 1. *E. linguaefolia*

  B. Leaves more or less brownish green, rosulate, inflorescence erect; corolla light or bright red.

    C. Leaves broadly oblanceolate, 5 cm. long or less, 2 cm. broad, acuminate; inflorescence rarely over 15 cm. tall, with about 3 short, horizontally spreading branches, cymose rather than paniculate; pedicels 6 to 8 mm. long; corolla often rather shorter. Sinaloa. . . . . 6. *E. affinis*

    C. Leaves narrow-oblong, to 8 cm. long or more, at apex acute and aristate; inflorescence erect, to over 50 cm. tall, with an elongated axis and 5 or more short branches; pedicels 10 mm. long or more; longest sepals to 9 mm. long; corolla to 11 mm. long. Southwest Chihuahua. . . . . 7. *E. craigiana*

A. Sepals less than half the length of the corolla; petals pinkish to red, scarcely keeled, with basal hollow only faintly developed.

  B. Leaves green tinged red, not at all glaucous; bracts appressed, obovate; pedicels stout, to 5 mm. long; sepals ovate-deltoid; corolla short, broad. Probably a garden hybrid. . . . . 4. *E. pulchella*

  B. Leaves more or less glaucous-green; bracts spreading; pedicels slender, to 10 mm. long; corolla pinkish or rose-colored.

    C. Leaves 25 mm. long or less, more or less pruinose; stem short or none; scape low, usually not over 8 cm. tall; corolla bright rose-doree. Puebla and Veracruz. 3. *E. amoena*

    C. Leaves to 45 mm. long, glaucous-pruinose; stem evident; scape longer, to 20 cm. tall; corolla pale, pinkish to light salmon-orange.

      D. Sepals orbicular; inflorescence erect, few-branched; petals erect, light salmon-orange. Puebla and Veracruz. . . . . 2. *E. microcalyx*

      D. Sepals ovate; inflorescence spreading to decumbent, many branched; petals more or less spreading, pinkish. Probably a garden hybrid. 5. *E. expatriata*

1. **Echeveria linguaefolia** Lemaire.

   (Figures 16–18.)

   Echeveria linguaefolia LEMAIRE, Ill. Hort., vol. 10, misc. p. 81, no. 20, 1863; BRITTON AND ROSE, N. Amer. Fl., vol. 22, p. 15, 1905; POELLNITZ, *in* Fedde Repert., vol. 39, p. 234, 1936.

   Talinum linguaeforme Hort. *ex* LEMAIRE, *loc. cit.* in synonymy.

   Anacampseros linguaefolia Hort. *ex* LEMAIRE, *loc. cit.* in synonymy.

   Cotyledon linguaefolia Hort. *ex* LEMAIRE, *loc. cit.* in synonymy.

   Cotyledon linguaefolia (Lemaire) BAKER, *in* Saunders Refug. Bot., vol. 1, pl. 58, no. 8, 1869; LEMAIRE, *loc. cit.*, in synonymy acc. Index Kew.

   Pachyphytum lingua Hort., as synonym *in* BAKER, *loc. cit.*, and *in* ED. MORREN, La Belg. Hort., vol. 24, p. 162, 1874.

   ILLUSTRATIONS. Saunders Refug. Bot., vol. 1, pl. 58, 1869; Cactus and Succ. Jour. Amer., vol. 8, p. 87, 1936.

Stem evident, branching to 20 cm. long or more, decumbent from weight of foliage; leaves scattered or subrosulate, obovate-cuneate, to 8 cm. long and to 4 cm. broad, narrowed to 15 mm. at base, to 12 mm. thick, above flat, rounded beneath, upcurved, obtusish or faintly mucronate; inflorescence a spreading or decumbent panicle with many short branches; peduncle to 10 mm. thick at base; lower bracts few, elliptic-obovate, to 35 mm. long, semiterete, acutish, spreading; panicle with 10 or more branches, rachis to 15 cm. long, to 6 mm. thick, with conspicuous swellings at base of branches, the latter to 4 cm. long, recurved, each with two to five flowers, the uppermost often single-flowered, all branches rigid and bearing linear-deltoid, obtuse bractlets; ultimate pedicels stout, 2 mm. long; sepals as long as or somewhat shorter than corolla, sub-

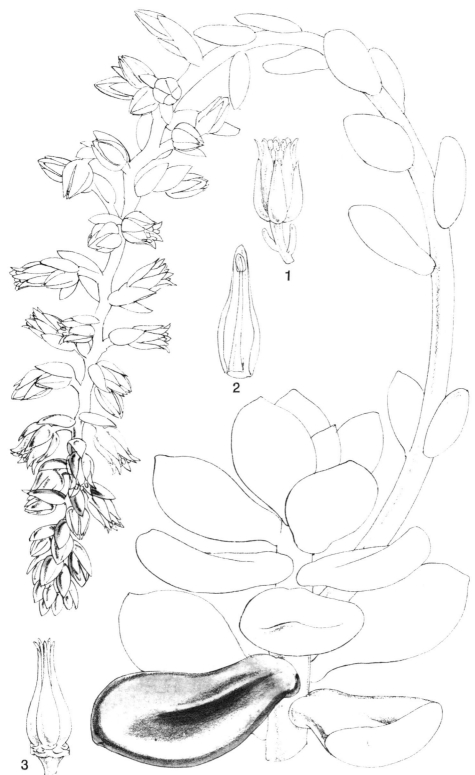

Figure 16. 1. *Echeveria linguaefolia* Lemaire. Flowering plant evidently natural size; flower and parts enlarged. Plant grown by W. W. Saunders in Reigate, England; received "from one of the Belgium nurseries." From Baker's monograph (Saunders Refugium Botanicum, volume 1, plate 58). This plate is designated neotype for the species.

equal, longest to 9 mm. long, deltoid-oblong, appressed, obtusish or acute; corolla to 9 mm. long; petals free nearly to base, thin, only faintly keeled, scarcely hollowed, erect or slightly spreading, minutely apiculate; stamens to 9 mm. long, equaling corolla, filaments with a few longitudinal brown lines; nectaries narrowly lunate, to 1.5 mm. wide. Flowers January to March. Description based on plants grown locally.

Color. Leaves spinach-green, not at all glaucous; peduncle cosse-green tinged acajou-red; sepals corydalis-green, glaucous in bud; petals deep seafoam-green to white; carpels as petals; styles chrysolite-green; nectaries nearly white.

Type. None designated. Neotype: Saunders Refugium Botanicum, volume 1, plate 58, 1869.

Figure 17. 1. *Echeveria linguaefolia* Lemaire. Inflorescence, × 1.5. Plant flowering in San Diego 19 December 1969; collected at Malinalco, State of Mexico (Moran 14778).

Figure 18. 1. *Echeveria linguaefolia* Lemaire. Plant about to flower, × 0.5. Plant of unknown origin (Moran 10998), photographed in San Diego 10 January 1965.

OCCURRENCE. Stated to have come from Mexico, but no definite locality is known at present.

COLLECTIONS. *Cultivated:* New York Bot. Gard. in 1909, the plant from Kew (CAS); New York Bot. Gard., 10/63337 (NY,US); Washington Bot. Gard., *Rose,* 02/6382 (US); garden of V. Reiter, San Francisco, *Walther* in 1932 (CAS).

REMARKS. Dr. D. A. Johansen (when at Stanford) informed me that the haploid chromosome number of this species is 48. Recent field collections in Mexico have failed to reveal a definite locale for this species, so that its exact status must remain in doubt, and any speculations on its phylogenetic position are futile. Its primitive nature is suggested by the scattered leaves, evident caudex, subpaniculate inflorescence, long, appressed sepals, thin, pale petals, long stamens, and minute nectaries. In some of the points enumerated, *E. linguaefolia* shows a strong resemblance to *E. amoena* and *E. microcalyx*, which may well be related. Even closer is the resemblance to *E. expatriata*, but here this is apparently due to hybridization; the decumbent panicle and long stamens are suggestive. Even more striking is the similarity between *E. linguaefolia* and *Sedum cremnophila* (*Cremnophila nutans* Rose), the latter of which has very similar foliage, a decumbent, subpaniculate inflorescence, but free, spreading petals.

2.   **Echeveria microcalyx** Britton and Rose.

> *Echeveria purpusii* BRITTON, *in* Britton and Rose, N. Amer. Fl., vol. 22, p. 26, 1905; *not* Schumann, Gartenflora, vol. 45, p. 608, 1896.
> *Echeveria microcalyx* BRITTON AND ROSE, Contrib. U.S. Nat. Herb., vol. 13, p. 295, 1911; POELLNITZ, *in* Fedde Repert., vol. 39, p. 253, 1936.

Stem evident, to 5 cm. tall, branching below; leaves many, crowded, obovate-spathulate, to 45 mm. long and 18 mm. broad, thick, convex beneath, nearly flat above, faintly mucronate, narrowed to 6 mm. at base, more or less glaucous-pruinose; inflorescences two or three, to over 15 cm. tall, laxly cymose-paniculate with two or three branches; peduncle erect, slender; bracts many, readily detached, ascending-spreading, subterete, obovate-oblong, obtusish, to 2 cm. long; pedicels slender, drooping, sometimes bracteolate; sepals ovate-orbicular, obtusish unequal, longest to 3 mm. long, thick, connate at base but with evident sutures; corolla cylindric, 8 to 9 mm. long, to 5 mm. in basal diameter, scarcely angled; petals obtusish, scarcely hollowed at base; longest stamens 6 mm. long, shorter than petals; nectaries very thin, sharp-edged, to 1.5 mm. wide. Flowers from March on. Description based on locally grown plants traceable to Dr. Rose.

Color. Leaves deep greenish glaucous, but kildare-green without bloom; peduncle onionskin-pink; bracts as leaves but tinged vinaceous-russet; sepals opaline-green, pruinose; corolla light salmon-orange; petals inside buff-yellow; carpels naphthalene-yellow below to amber-yellow above; anthers empire-yellow; nectaries amber-yellow.

TYPE. *Purpus,* 1903/R-939, between Esperanza and Orizaba, Mexico (NY).

OCCURRENCE. Mexico. Puebla-Veracruz border, Boca del Monte; Perote, pass in limestone hills just west of Perote.

COLLECTIONS. Mexico. Puebla: between Esperanza and Orizaba, *Purpus,* 03/R-939 (NY,type); near Esperanza, *Purpus,* 04/R-944 (NY,UC); below Boca del Monte, *Purpus,* 07/R-393 (GH,US); *Purpus,* 12/5823 (MO,UC); Tehuacan, rocky slopes, *Purpus,* 04/944 (GH,US). *Cultivated:* Brooklyn Bot. Gard., *Baldwin,* 23/542 (BH).

REMARKS. *Echeveria amoena* is very closely related but differs as stated under that species. Only further field studies can determine to what extent these two species may intergrade. Britton, *loc. cit.,* states that the sepals of *E. microcalyx* differ in not being appressed to the base of the corolla, which I was unable to verify. The specific name *"purpusii"* belongs to *Dudleya purpusii,* named by Schumann in 1896 as *Echeveria.*

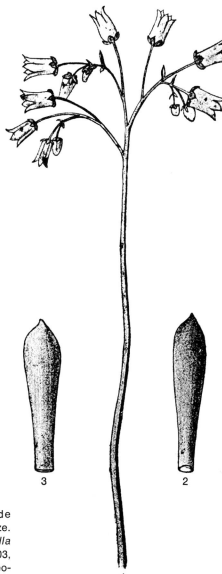

3

2

1

Figure 19. 3. *Echeveria amoena* L. de Smet. Leaves and floral stem, natural size. From the original publication of *E. pusilla* Berger (Gartenflora, volume 53, page 203, figure 30). This figure is designated neotype of *E. amoena*, of which *E. pusilla* is a synonym.

Abb. 80. E. pusilla. A. B.

3.   **Echeveria amoena** L. de Smet.
   (Figure 19.)

> *Echeveria amoena* L. DE SMET, Catalogue of 1875; ED. MORREN, La Belg. Hort., vol. 25, p. 216, 1875; BRITTON AND ROSE, N. Amer. Fl., vol. 22, p. 26, 1905; POELLNITZ, *in* Fedde Repert., vol. 39, p. 251, 1936.
> *Echeveria pusilla* BERGER, Gartenflora, vol. 53, p. 206, 1904.
> ILLUSTRATION. Gartenflora, vol. 53, p. 203, fig. 30, 1904.

Stem short, branching from base and forming dense mats; rosettes dense; leaves thick, clavate, semiterete or slightly flattened, oblanceolate-spathulate, acutish, 2 cm. long, 6 to 8 mm. broad, somewhat pruinose; inflorescences several, 10 to nearly 20 cm. tall, erect, laxly cymose-paniculate, with 6 to 12 nodding flowers; peduncle slender, 2 mm. thick below; bracts numerous, readily detached, to 12 mm. long, 3 mm. broad, oblong, spreading; pedicels slender, to 15 mm. long, sometimes bracteolate; sepals free nearly to base, unequal, longest 3 mm. long, ovate-orbicular, obtusish; corolla cylindric, to 9 mm. long and 5 mm. thick near base; petals thin, obscurely keeled and scarcely hollowed at base within; stamens shorter than petals; nectaries thin, sharp-edged, 1 mm. wide. Flowers from May on. Description from locally grown plants.

Color. Leaves deep lichen-green tinged vinaceous-brown, tips maroon; peduncle vinaceous; bracts hermose-pink; sepals like leaves; corolla geranium-pink to rose-doree; inside and edges of petals mars-yellow; carpels pinard-yellow.

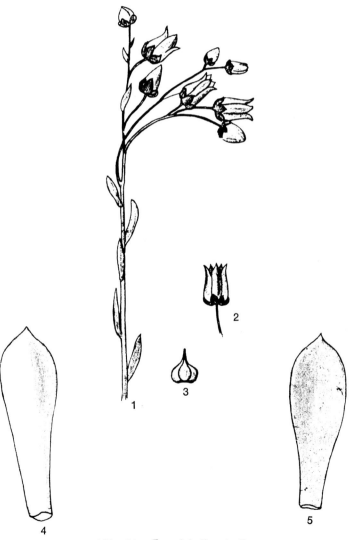

Abb. 31. E. pulchella, A. B.

Figure 20. 4. *Echeveria pulchella* Berger. Parts all natural size. From the original publication (Gartenflora, volume 53, page 204, figure 31).

Figure 21.   4. *Echeveria pulchella* Berger. Plant grown in Washington (Rose green-house plant 990); received from Alwin Berger, La Mortola, Italy. Photograph from the U.S. National Herbarium, no. 469.

TYPE. None designated. Neotype: Gartenflora, volume 53, page 206, figure 30, 1904.

OCCURRENCE. Mexico. Puebla: vicinity of Tehuacan. Veracruz: Boca del Monte; near Perote.

COLLECTIONS. Mexico. Puebla: vicinity of Tehuacan, *Purpus,* 04/R-945 (US); on limestone hill near Limon on road to Perote, *Walther,* 59 (CAS). Veracruz: near Perote. *Cultivated*: Hort. Belg., 1866/362 (BR); La Mortola, *Berger,* R/998 (US, type of *E. pusilla*); Soldena Gardens, *F. G. Floyd,* 351 (BH).

REMARKS. Dr. C. H. Uhl of Cornell has determined the haploid chromosome number of *E. amoena* to be between 56 and 64, in cultivated material. The exact source of my garden plants is uncertain, but probably was some European nursery or botanic garden. Field collections are scarce and in part at least may pertain to the very similar *E. microcalyx*. The latter has slightly larger leaves, reaching a length of 45 mm.; these are more conspicuously pruinose, the caudex is longer, and the scape may reach a height of 20 cm. I have received material from Tehuacan, with no more definite locale, that was identical with my garden plants. Among the latter I have found a form rather smaller in all parts. Berger's *E. pusilla* is a later synonym, as he himself recognized. *Echeveria pulchella* and *E. expatriata* are probably European garden hybrids having *E. amoena* for one parent.

4.   **Echeveria pulchella** Berger.
      (Figures 20–21.)

    Echeveria pulchella BERGER, Gartenflora, vol. 53, p. 206, 1904; BRITTON AND ROSE, N. Amer. Fl., vol. 22, p. 26, 1905; POELLNITZ, *in* Fedde Repert., vol. 39, p. 252, 1936.

    ILLUSTRATIONS. Gartenflora, vol. 53, p. 204, fig. 31, 1904; photograph 469/990 (U.S.) [see figure 21] (also at GH, NY, MO).

Stem evident, to 6 cm. tall, branching at base; leaves many, green, not at all glaucous, oblong-spathulate, 35 mm. long or more, to 15 mm. broad, convex beneath, slightly concave above, thick, strongly mucronate, upcurved; inflorescences two or three, erect, to 20 cm. tall, cymose-paniculate, with two or three branches; peduncle ascending; bracts less readily detached than in related species, obovate-oblong, appressed, curved, 12 to 15 mm. long; branches rather rigid, ascending, 5- or 6-flowered; pedicels stout, 5 mm. long, sometimes bracteolate; upper bracts linear-oblanceolate, upcurved; sepals broad, deltoid-ovate, not over 4 mm. long, thick, appressed, united at base for half their length, with indistinct sutures; corolla to 8 mm. long, 6 mm. in basal diameter, 4 mm. wide at mouth; petals erect, thin, scarcely hollowed within at base; stamens shorter than petals; nectaries narrowly lunate, to 2 mm. wide. Flowers from April on. Description from plants cultivated in Golden Gate Park, San Francisco, originally imported from R. Graessner, Perleberg, Germany.

Color. Leaves biscay-green, often tinged red in sun, not at all glaucous; peduncle etruscan-red; bracts as the leaves; sepals light brownish olive to etruscan-red; corolla scarlet; petals pale orange-yellow within; styles turtle-green.

TYPE. *Berger,* 1904/990, cultivated at La Mortola (MEXU,NY,US, type).

OCCURRENCE. No definite locality is on record for Mexico; presumably this is a hybrid.

COLLECTIONS. *Cultivated*: flowered, Washington, D.C., 08–09/R-990, received in 1904 from A. Berger, La Mortola, Italy (US, type; MEXU,NY); Italy, *Berger,* 04/, flowered in Washington, 09/900.

REMARKS. While both Rose and Poellnitz retain this as a valid species, no field collections are known, so that its hybrid nature may be suspected. Berger does not state the source of his material, which may well have been a volunteer garden hybrid. The absence of any glaucous bloom, coupled with a dark red corolla, would seem to point to *E. amoena* and *E. linguaefolia* as possible parents. James West raised numerous seedlings of *E. pulchella,* all of them essentially alike.

5.   **Echeveria expatriata** Rose.
     (Figure 22.)

> *Echeveria expatriata* ROSE, *in* Britton and Rose, N. Amer. Fl., vol. 22, p. 26, 1905; POELLNITZ, *in* Fedde Repert., vol. 39, p. 253, 1936.
> *Echeveria cochlearis* Hort., BERGER, *in* Engler, Nat. Pflanzenf., ed. 2, vol. 18a, p. 481, 1930.

Stem short but evident, at times to 10 cm. tall, branching below and forming dense mats; leaves densely rosulate, clavate, oblong-obovate, acutish to ob-

Figure 22. 5. *Echeveria expatriata* Rose. Plant flowering in Washington, from Simon Freres, Paris, (6543). Photograph from the U.S. National Herbarium.

tuse, thick, flattened above, slightly upcurved, to 4 cm. long, 9 mm. broad, inflorescences one or two, widely spreading to decumbent, to 30 cm. long, cymose-paniculate; peduncle slender, less than 3 mm. thick at base; lower bracts readily detached, oblong-ovate, semiterete, obtusish, to 17 mm. long; panicle compact, becoming more open at maturity, with as many as six branches, these unilateral rather than secund; upper bracts linear-oblong, nearly terete, obtuse, 5 mm. long or less, sometimes present also on the ultimate pedicels; pedicels slender, to 8 mm. long, deflexed; sepals somewhat unequal, longest 4 mm. long, thick, ovate, acute, appressed except the slightly spreading tips, connate at base but with distinct sutures; corolla campanulate, to 8 mm. long, 4 mm. in basal diameter, to 8 mm. wide at mouth; petals thin, keeled, acute, with faint basal hollow, slightly outcurved; stamens longer than carpels, nearly equaling petals; nectaries narrowly lunate, to 1.75 mm. wide. Flowers from February on. Description from plants cultivated locally.

Color. Leaves bice-green, somewhat glaucous; peduncle ochraceous-salmon above; sepals light bice-green; nectaries whitish.

TYPE. Flowered in Washington, D.C., in 1904, the plants from New York Botanical Garden where they had been originally received from Simon Freres, Paris (US, no. 399775).

OCCURRENCE. Known only from cultivated material of uncertain origin; most likely a hybrid (see remarks below).

COLLECTIONS. *Cultivated*: Washington, D.C., (US, type); New York Bot. Gard., /6543 (MO,NY,US); Missouri Bot. Gard., 1898/57; Cornell University greenhouses, *C. Sands,* 32 (BH); Knickerbocker Nursery, San Diego, 36 (BH); Soldena Gardens, Pasadena, *Floyd,* 35 (BH); garden of Victor Reiter, San Francisco, *Walther* (CAS).

REMARKS. Rose, Berger, and Poellnitz all treat this as a valid species, even though no Mexican locality is known. Material received from Simon Freres of Paris, that flowered at the New York Botanical Garden in October, 1904, clearly belongs here; it was received as *E. cochlearis.* A hybrid of that name was catalogued by J. B. A. Deleuil of Marseilles (Rue Paradis) in 1875 (as quoted in La Belg. Hort., 1875, p. 370) and stated to be a cross of *E. linguaefolia* and *E. atropurpurea,* which scarcely constitutes a valid publication. The resemblance to *E. linguaefolia* is obvious in the decumbent, many-branched inflorescence and the pale petals, but little can be seen here of *E. atropurpurea* (Baker) Morren, said to have been its other parent.

6.   **Echeveria affinis** E. Walther.
       (Figures 23–26.)

   Echeveria affinis E. WALTHER, Cactus and Succ. Jour. Amer., vol. 30, no. 4, p. 105, 1958.
   ILLUSTRATIONS. WALTHER, *op. cit.,* pp. 106, 107, figs. 54, 55, 1958; Nat. Hort. Mag., vol. 38, no. 1, p. 56, 1959.

Plants glabrous; stem evident only in age, mostly simple, but ultimately budding below; rosettes dense; leaves numerous, broadly oblanceolate, shortly acuminate, to 5 cm. long and 2 cm. broad, beneath strongly convex, nearly flat above, somewhat upcurved above middle; inflorescences two or three, to 15 cm. tall; peduncle erect, stout; lower bracts few, oblong, acute, to 2 cm. long, ascending-spreading; inflorescence a flat-topped cyme with three to five spread-

Figure 23.   6. *Echeveria affinis* E. Walther. Flowering plant, × 0.75. Plant photographed in San Diego 11 August 1960; collected near Los Angeles, Durango, Mexico (Moran and Kimnach 7619).

ing branches but without an elongated central axis; each branch with five to seven flowers; pedicels to 8 mm. long; sepals appressed, subequal, ovate-deltoid to oblong-lanceolate, turgid, acute at the somewhat incurved tips; corolla urceolate-campanulate, bluntly pentagonal, 10 mm. long, to 8 mm. wide at the spreading petal-tips, petals with small, but definite basal hollow within and apiculate tips; stamens 8 to 9 mm. long; carpels 8 mm. long, with slender styles; nectaries 1 mm. wide, narrowly lunate-reniform. Flowers from August on.

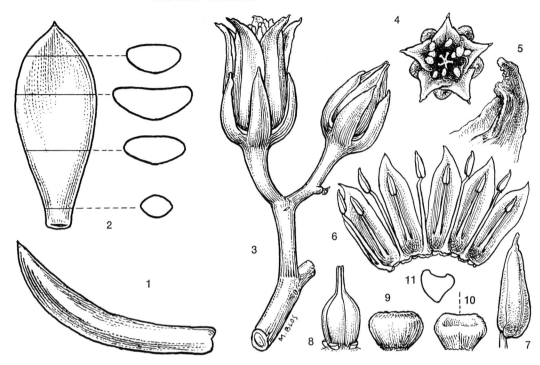

Figure 24. 6. *Echeveria affinis* E. Walther. Explanation: (1, 2) leaf, × 1; (3, 4) flowers, × 3; (5) apex of petal, greatly enlarged; (6) petals and stamens, × 3; (7) anther, greatly enlarged; (8) carpels, × 3; (9-11) nectary, × 15. Drawing by Mrs. May Blos, 24 August 1956; plant of the type collection (UCBG 54.1241-1).

Figure 25. 6. *Echeveria affinis* E. Walther. Inflorescence, × 0.5. Plant flowering in San Diego 1 August 1964; collected near Los Angeles, Durango, Mexico (Moran and Kimnach 7619).

Description from living plant grown in Golden Gate Park, San Francisco, received from the University of California Botanical Garden.

Color. Leaves brownish olive, becoming almost black in full sun, beneath cosse-green; peduncle olive-buff, to corinthian-red above; bracts lettuce-green, to oil-green at tips; sepals scheeles-green, to light jasper-red at anthesis; corolla scarlet-red; petals inside eugenia-red; carpels whitish; styles straw-yellow, as are the nectaries.

TYPE. From Mexico without definite locality, cultivated in Golden Gate Park, San Francisco, *Walther*, in 1957 (CAS, no. 403156).

OCCURRENCE. Mexico.

COLLECTIONS. *Cultivated:* Golden Gate Park, San Francisco, *Walther,* in 1957 (CAS, type), U.S. Agricultural Research Service, Glenn Dale, Md., no. 197677, from Sinaloa, Mexico (CAS).

REMARKS. My original material, furnished me through the courtesy of Mr. Paul C. Hutchison of the University of California Botanical Garden, came without any data as to its exact source. No doubt this is closely related to *E. craigiana,* but differs as stated under that species. According to Dr. C. H. Uhl of Cornell, the chromosome number is $n = 30$.

In cultivation, plants of *E. affinis* may at times develop a fasciated stem, forming a crest with smaller, very crowded leaves. This may be recorded here as *E. affinis* cultivar 'Crest'.

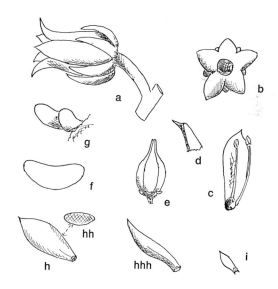

Figure 26. 6. *Echeveria affinis* E. Walther. Explanation: (a) flower, × 2; (b) flower from below, × 2; (c) inside of petal, × 2; (d) apex of petal, × 8; (e) carpels, × 2; (f) nectary, front view, × 16; (g) nectary, side view, × 16; (h) leaf, × 0.4; (hh) leaf, cross-section, × 0.4; (hhh) leaf, side view, × 0.4; (i) bract, × 2. From the original publication (Cactus and Succulent Journal, volume 30, page 107, figure 55).

7.   **Echeveria craigiana** E. Walther.
(Figures 27–29.)

Echeveria craigiana E. WALTHER, Cactus and Succ. Jour. Amer., vol. 24, no. 1, p. 28, 1952.
ILLUSTRATIONS. WALTHER, *op. cit.*, pp. 28, 29, figs. 11–13, 1952.

Plant glabrous; stem short or none, branching only in age; rosettes very dense; leaves 30 to 40, thick, semiterete, linear-oblong, 8 to 11 cm. long, to 2 cm. broad, above flat, beneath rounded and faintly keeled near apex, acute and shortly subulate-aristate, not papillose but faintly glaucous, upcurved from the middle; inflorescences two or three, to over 50 cm. tall; peduncle stout, erect, to 10 mm. thick at base; bracts few, somewhat spreading, semiterete, oblong, acute, aristate-mucronate, to 5 cm. long and 10 mm. broad, faintly keeled near apex both above and below, at base shortly spurred, readily detachable; panicle elongate, with many short, angularly spreading branches, these at times 2-branched; pedicels to 2 cm. long, rigid, bracteolate when young, only slightly thickened below calyx; sepals much connate at base, slightly but distinctly

Figure 27.   7. *Echeveria craigiana* E. Walther. From the original publication (Cactus and Succulent Journal, volume 24, page 28, figure 11).

Figure 28. 7. *Echeveria craigiana* E. Walther. From the original publication (Cactus and Succulent Journal, volume 24, page 29, figure 12).

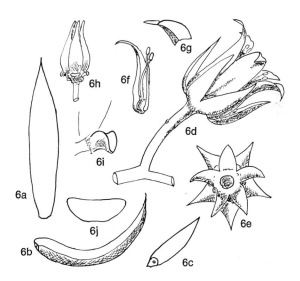

Figure 29. 7. *Echeveria craigiana* E. Walther. Explanation: (6a) leaf, × 0.4; (6b) leaf, side view, × 0.4; (6c) bract, × 0.4; (6d) flower, × 2; (6e) flower from below, × 2; (6f) inside of petal, × 2; (6g) apex of petal, × 4; (6h) carpels, × 2; (6i) nectary, side view, × 8; (6j) nectary, front view, × 8. From the original publication (Cactus and Succulent Journal, volume 24, page 29, figure 13).

spreading above, subequal, longest to 9 mm. long, deltoid-oblong, acute, connivent after anthesis; corolla tubular-campanulate, to 11 mm. long, to 13 mm. wide at mouth when fully open, basal diameter 7 mm.; petals bluntly keeled, at base gibbose and with distinct cavity within, strongly recurved at apex; carpels 8 mm. long; stamens slightly longer; nectaries 2 mm. wide, thick, transversely trapezoid. Flowers October and November. Description from living plant, the type, grown in Golden Gate Park, San Francisco.

Color. Leaves sorghum-brown to natal-brown, grass-green at shaded base or in shade, slightly glaucous; peduncle pale pinkish cinnamon to light russet-vinaceous; bracts dark olive-buff, to army-brown above; pedicels light corinthian-red; sepals rainette-green to light corinthian-red; corolla rose-doree, inside jasper-red; carpels whitish; styles orange-vinaceous; nectaries whitish.

TYPE. Barranca de Rio Urique, Chihuahua, Mexico, *Craig and Lindsay,* 39/3 (CAS, no. 324971).

OCCURRENCE. Mexico. Barranca de Rio Urique (branch of Rio Fuerte), at lower level back from Barranca among pines and ferns, southwest Chihuahua.

COLLECTIONS. Mexico: Chihuahua: Barranca de Rio Urique, *Craig and Lindsay,* 39/3 (CAS, type); *R. Flores,* (UCBG,51.1088); Sierra Canelo. Rio Mayo, *Gentry,* 36/2872 (F,GH,UC); Sierra Charuco, Rancho Byerly, slopes of igneous rock, pine-oak forest, 5,000 to 8,000 feet, *Gentry,* 48/115, (AHFH); Recubich, *J. Knobloch,* 38/5517 (F,MO). *Cultivated:* garden of V. Reiter, San Francisco (CAS, clonotype).

REMARKS. The Sierra Tarahumare in southwestern Chihuahua, where the species is found, approaches closer to the range of the genus *Dudleya* than that of any other species. *Echeveria chihuahuaensis* and *E. paniculata* also occur here, of which the first differs in its very pale gray, flatter, red-tipped leaves and a strictly secund inflorescence. *Echeveria paniculata* has a very condensed caudex, flat, thin, green leaves, very short pedicels, and a strongly pentagonal corolla. In leaf shape, *E. craigiana* recalls the recently discovered *E. tolimanensis* from Hidalgo, but in that the leaves are decidedly grayish pulverulent, the inflorescence is secund, and the sepals are widely spreading to reflexed. It is of interest to note the chromosome numbers, as determined by Dr. Uhl of Cornell, are $n = 30$ in *E. craigiana, E. affinis, E. microcalyx* and *E. tolimanensis,* as well as in *E. elatior* and *E. subalpina,* the last two not being related to the present species.

The irregular inflorescence with occasionally bracteolate pedicels, the thin scarcely keeled petals, and the appressed sepals argue for placing this species in the series Paniculatae, where it seems to fit better than anywhere else. Its nearest ally is *E. affinis* from Sinaloa, which differs in its flatter leaves and lower, distinctly cymose inflorescence.

Series 2. Urceolatae E. Walther

Echeveria, ser. Urceolatae E. Walther, Leafl. West. Bot., vol. 9, pp. 2, 4, 1959.
Urbinia Rose, *in* Britton and Rose, Bull. New York Bot. Gard., vol. 3, p. 11, 1903.
Echeveria, sect. Urbinia (Rose) Berger, *in* Engler Nat. Pflanzenf., ed. 2, vol. 18a, p. 476, 1930.
Echeveria, ser. Urbiniae E. Walther, Cactus and Succ. Jour. Amer., vol. 7, p. 60, 1935; Poellnitz, *in* Fedde Repert., vol. 39, p. 270, 1936.

(No Latin diagnosis.)

Rosettes stemless, simple or becoming cespitose; leaves numerous, crowded, thick and turgid, with cuticle thick, more or less transparent, often with large subepidermal cells creating an alabaster-like appearance, margins often pellucid-hyaline, color frequently whitish or amber, rarely green, occasionally mottled or lurid; inflorescence of one to three secund racemes; peduncle mostly slender, normally with few, narrow, scattered, appressed bracts; pedicels slender, sometimes turbinately thickened below calyx; sepals generally small, unequal, acute, appressed to spreading or more rarely reflexed; corolla globose-urceolate to cylindroid or conoid; petals mostly thin, with shallow basal nectar cavity, scarcely keeled, color pale to bright rose, sometimes tipped green in bud; nectaries small, thin; styles greenish; ripe follicles widely spreading.

Exception. *Echeveria purpusorum* has large nectaries and thick petals with a deep basal cavity.

Typical species. *Echeveria agavoides* Lemaire.

Remarks. In establishing the genus *Urbinia,* Rose recognized the distinctive characters of its type species, *E. agavoides.* Only a slight broadening of his concept serves to bring within the confines of this quite natural group a number of other clearly related species. I do not feel that *Urbinia* can possibly be maintained as a separate genus, nor can I justify treating it as either a subgenus or a section of *Echeveria.* A clearer view of the species relations within the genus will follow from treatment of the various species groups as series.

Under Article 31, of the International Code of Botanical Nomenclature, it is stated that "for subsections and lower subdivisions the epithets are preferably plural adjectives," hence I here substitute the series Urceolatae as correct, in place of section Urbinia, Berger, or my own previously used series Urbiniae.

The series Urceolatae is a quite natural one, its species having much more in common than with species of other groups. Aside from the rotundate corolla, with thin scarcely angled, or hollowed petals, and the thin nectaries, the leaves too display a distinctive quality in their turgidity and frequently hyaline epidermis and margins. Anomalous only is *E. purpusorum* with its mottled foliage, its thick petals deeply hollowed within at base, and broadly truncate nectaries.

Echeveria cuspidata has been much misunderstood and seems more properly placed in the series Secundae.

Key to the Species

A. Inflorescence usually with 2 or more branches, only rarely simple.
  B. Leaves nearly as thick as wide, subterete-clavate, aristate-tipped, gray-green, glaucous, occasionally amber-tinged; sepals spreading to reflexed. Barranca de Toliman, Hidalgo. . . . . 9. *E. tolimanensis*
  B. Leaves much broader than thick, thinner, not aristate; sepals spreading to ascending.
    C. Leaves usually amber colored, scarcely ever slightly grayish or glaucous; inflo-

rescence mostly with 3 or more branches, less often 2-branched, never simple. San Luis Potosi, etc. . . . . 8. *E. agavoides*
    D. Leaves uniformly amber colored, usually without red edges or apices.
        E. Rosettes with few or no offsets. . . . . 8a. *E. agavoides* var. *agavoides*
        E. Rosettes freely soboliferous. . . . . . 8b. *E. agavoides* var. *prolifera*
    D. Leaves usually with conspicuous red edges and apices.
        E. Rosettes freely soboliferous; sepals very small, linear, free to base; inflorescence usually 3-branched. . . . . . 8c. *E. agavoides* var. *corderoyi*
        E. Rosettes usually simple even when old; sepals broader, connate at base; inflorescence with 2 to 5 branches. . . . 8d. *E. agavoides* var. *multifida*
  C. Leaves mostly gray, whitish or lurid, not amber-colored; inflorescences usually 2-branched, rarely simple or 3-branched.
    D. Leaves lurid, highly colored; corolla 6 to 7 mm. long; imperfectly known. Tovar, near Tepehuanes, Durango. . . . . 13. *E. tobarensis*
    D. Leaves gray- to whitish-green; corolla 11 to 14 mm. long.
        E. Leaves thinnish, long-acuminate, pulverulent. Parras, etc., Coahuila.
                                  14. *E. parrasensis*
        E. Leaves thick and turgid, shortly acuminate to mucronate; gray-green.
           F. Leaves narrowly oblong, heavily tinged carmine on whitish ground; sepals deltoid, appressed, decurrent into turbinate pedicel. Cultivated at Guadalajara, Jalisco; Michoacan. . . . . 12. *E. colorata*
           F. Leaves broader, obovate-cuneate, only edges and mucro red; sepals broad or narrow, to spreading, not prominently decurrent into pedicel.
              G. Leaves broad, very white, with edges and mucro dark red; sepals elongated, ascending-spreading; corolla to 14 mm. long. Near Ceracaqui, etc., Chihuahua. . . . . 10. *E. chihuahuaensis*
              G. Leaves narrower, pale whitish green, edges and mucro slightly or not red; sepal short, deltoid, scarcely spreading; corolla 10 mm. long. Cultivated, source unknown. . . . . . . 11. *E. lindsayana*
A. Inflorescence normally a simple raceme, rarely or not branching.
  B. Petals thick, with deep basal nectar cavity within, scarlet tipped yellow; nectaries broad, truncate; corolla globose; leaves dark green mottled brown; inflorescence occasionally forked below middle. Puebla-Oaxaca border. . . 24. *E. purpusorum*
  B. Petals thin, with shallow nectar-cavity, scarcely keeled; corolla mostly pale rose and yellow; nectaries usually thin, narrow; leaves generally whitish or yellowish green.
    C. Leaves green or amber-colored, neither glaucous nor whitish.
        D. Leaves amber-colored, oblong-obovate, to 8 cm. long, acute. At present known only in cultivation. . . . . 20. *E. gilva*
        D. Leaves lettuce-green, truncate, shortly mucronate, slightly or not flattened above near apex, 4 cm. long, to 3 cm. broad. Valle de Bravo, Estado de Mexico.
                                   21. *E. goldiana*
    C. Leaves gray-green to whitish or alabaster colored.
        D. Apex of petals strongly recurved at anthesis; corolla yellow or orange-yellow; leaves 13 to 15 mm. wide.
           E. Corolla orange-yellow; petal tips acutely subulate; leaves obovate, not red-edged. Near Actopan, Hidalgo. . . . . 22. *E. halbingeri*
           E. Corolla bright yellow; petal tips obtusely mucronate; leaves narrowly oblong-oblanceolate, red-edged. Beristain, Hidalgo. . . . 23. *E. pulidonis*
        D. Apex of petals only slightly spreading; corolla rose-colored at base, yellow or greenish at apex; leaves mostly broader.
           E. Leaves gray-green, strongly acuminate-cuspidate.
              F. Leaves narrowly oblong-oblanceolate, rarely over 15 mm. broad; rosettes freely cespitose even in young plants; pedicels scarcely turbinate. Hidalgo. . . . . 17. *E. sanchez-mejoradae*
              F. Leaves broadly obovate, to 35 mm. wide, only slightly narrowed to base; rosettes belatedly cespitose; pedicels strongly turbinate. Guanajuato.
                                  19. *E. hyalina*
           E. Leaves alabaster-white, thick and turgid, mucronate to apiculate, acute or shortly acuminate.
              F. Leaves thickest just below apex; corolla broadly conical at anthesis; pedicels turbinate; nectaries broad, obliquely truncate.
                G. Leaves more or less purple-tinged, with rounded apex and hyaline margins. San Luis Potosi. . . . . 16. *E. potosina*
                G. Leaves clear white, with apex truncate and margins scarcely hyaline.
                                18. *E. albicans*

F. Leaves thickest towards middle, thinner towards apex, acute; corolla cylindroid-urceolate; pedicels mostly slender, not turbinate; nectaries narrow. . . . . 15. *E. elegans*

    G. Sepals uniformly connate without sutures. . . . 15a. *E. elegans* var. *elegans*

    G. Most of the larger sepals with distinct sutures at base where they adjoin the smaller sepals.

        H. Inflorescence to over 20 cm. (to 40 cm.) tall, erect, with 12 to 14 flowers. Nuevo Leon. . . . . . 15d. *E. elegans* var. *simulans*

        H. Inflorescence lower, mostly spreading, with 8 to 12, or fewer, flowers.

            I. Leaves to 7 cm. long, to 3 cm. broad, strongly upcurved above the middle. Hacienda del Carmen, Hidalgo.

                        15b. *E. elegans* var. *hernandonis*

            I. Leaves shorter, narrower, probably nearly straight. Tuxpan, Jalisco. . . . . 15c. *E. elegans* var. *tuxpanensis*

8.   **Echeveria agavoides** Lemaire.

    (Figures 30–31.)

    Echeveria agavoides LEMAIRE, Ill. Hort. 10, misc. 78, no. 2, 1863; BERGER, *in* Engler Nat. Pflanzenf., ed. 2, vol. 18a, p. 476, 1930; E. WALTHER, Cactus and Succ. Jour. Amer., vol. 7, p. 60, 1935; POELLNITZ, *in* Fedde Repert., vol. 39, p. 259, 1936.
    Cotyledon agavoides BAKER, *in* Saunders Refug. Bot., vol. 1, no. 25, pl. 67, 1869.
    Echeveria yuccoides ED. MORREN, La Belg. Hort., vol. 25, p. 168, 1874.
    Urbinia agavoides (Lemaire) ROSE, *in* Britton and Rose, Bull. New York Bot. Gard., vol. 3, p. 12, 1903; BRITTON AND ROSE, N. Amer. Fl., vol. 22, p. 32, 1905.
    Urbinia obscura ROSE, *loc. cit.*; BRITTON AND ROSE, *loc. cit.*
    Echeveria obscura (Rose) POELLNITZ, *in* Fedde Repert., vol. 39, p. 259, 1936.
    ILLUSTRATIONS. Saunders Refug. Bot., vol. 1, pl. 67, 1869; Flore des Serres, vol. 19, pl. 2003, 1873; Gard. Mag., 1873, p. 237.

Plants glabrous; stem short or none; rosettes usually solitary until late, but sometimes freely cespitose; leaves few, crowded, thick and turgid, neither pulverulent nor mottled, but occasionally red-edged above, 3 to 8 cm. long, to 3 cm. broad near base, ovate-deltoid, sharply acuminate, edges rounded and hyaline, cuticle wax-like, subepidermal cells large and conspicuous; inflorescences usually several, mostly 2-branched, branches secund-racemose; peduncle slender; bracts mostly few and small, early deciduous; each branch with five to eight flowers; pedicels slender, slightly turbinate below calyx; sepals 5 mm. long or less, somewhat spreading, connate at base; corolla not pentagonal, conoid-urceolate, 10 to 12 mm. long, narrowed to mouth; petals thin, scarcely hollowed within at base, slightly spreading at apex; nectaries thin, sharp-edged. Flowers from March on. Description based on living plants from locality mentioned.

Color. Leaves deep crysolite-green; peduncle old-rose; sepals buffy olive; corolla begonia-rose, to orange-buff above, mustard-yellow inside; styles spinach-green.

TYPE. None designated. Neotype: Saunders Refugium Botanicum, volume 1, plate 67, 1869.

OCCURRENCE. Mexico. San Luis Potosi, etc. (Hidalgo, Presa de Madero).

COLLECTION. Mexico. San Luis Potosi, *Palmer,* 02/15873 (NY).

REMARKS. *Echeveria agavoides* has been in cultivation since 1863 (according to La Belg. Hort.) and was well illustrated by Baker in Saunders' *Refugium Botanicum (loc. cit.).* It is still widely cultivated today, even if it has never been very common because of the paucity of offsets. A well-grown single rosette may reach a diameter of nearly one foot.

Figure 30.   8. *Echeveria agavoides* Lemaire. Leaves stated to be and flowering plant evidently also natural size; flower enlarged. Plant raised by W. W. Saunders in Reigate, England, "from Northern Mexican seeds." From Baker's monograph (Saunders Refugium Botanicum, volume 1, plate 67). This plate is designated neotype for the species.

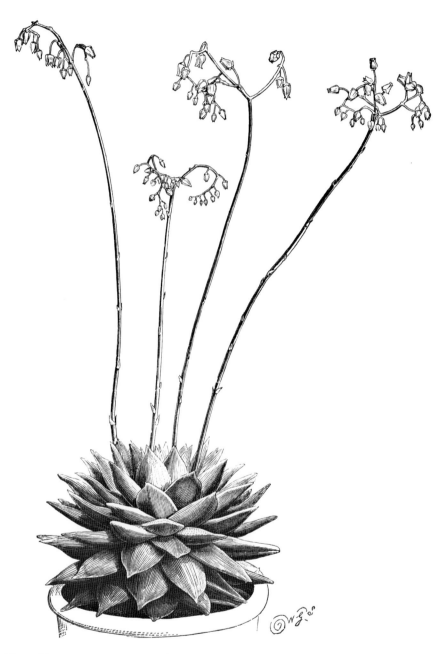

Figure 31.   8c. *Echeveria agavoides* Lemaire var. *corderoyi* (Baker) Poellnitz. Drawing from a photograph received from Mr. Corderoy. From an article by J. G. Baker (Gardeners' Chronicle, new series, volume 19, page 373, figure 56).

In 1937 I saw this in its native habitat near San Luis Potosi, where it grew in numbers at the Hacienda de San Francisco. In semishade at the base of the steep sides of a barranca, it grew with xerophytic ferns and *Yucca australis*. A large proportion of these plants were distinct in having bright red margins and tips; this form is now sold locally and needs to be named, as *Echeveria agavoides* cultivar 'Red edge.' Another, rather rare form is fasciated, forming a dense crest with numerous narrow, smaller leaves; this would be *E. agavoides* cultivar 'Crest.'

Echeveria (Urbinia) obscura was based on an aberrant inflorescence with an abnormal number of rather larger lower bracts; but next year the plant returned to normal *E. agavoides*. Similar variants are known in other species.

8b.   **Echeveria agavoides** var. **prolifera** E. Walther, new.

Echeveria agavoides var. *prolifera* E. Walther, var. nov. Rosulae acaulescentes, copiose surculosae; foliis numerosis, confertis, oblongo-oblanceolatis, 10–12 cm. longis, crassis, acuminatis, flavo-viridibus; inflorescentiis 15 cm. altis; pedunculis tenuibus, ascendentibus vel patentibus; bracteis paucis, adpressis, linearibus, usque ad 8 mm. longis; ramis 3, secundo-racemosis 8- vel 9-floris; pedicellis 10 mm. longis, tenuibus, nec turbinatis; sepalis inaequalibus, patentibus, deltoideis vel ovatis, acutis, leviter connatis ad basin; corollis urceolatis usque ad 16 mm. longis, roseis.

Plants glabrous; rosettes to over 25 cm. in diameter, stemless but usually freely offsetting; leaves numerous and crowded, to 30 or more in each rosette, 10 to 12 cm. long, to 30 mm. wide, turgid, subtriquetrous, oblong-oblanceolate, nearly flat above, acuminate-aristate, ascending, inflorescences three or more; peduncle slender, spreading to ascending, to over 15 cm. long; bracts few, appressed, linear-lanceolate, acuminate, 6 to 8 mm. long; branches usually three, secund-racemose, with eight or nine flowers each; pedicels slender, to 10 mm. long, not turbinate; sepals very unequal, deltoid to ovate, acute, slightly connate at base, spreading; corolla narrowly urceolate, to 16 mm. long; nectaries rather broad, obliquely truncate, to 2 mm. wide. Flowers from April on.

Color. Leaves pale dull green-yellow; peduncle pompeian-red; bracts russet-vinaceous; corolla rose-doree to peach-red above, inside capucine-orange; carpels baryta-yellow; styles cosse-green; nectaries pinard-yellow.

TYPE. From plant grown in Golden Gate Park, San Francisco, originally found in cultivation at Mexico City in the garden of Sr. C. Halbinger (CAS, no. 304230).

OCCURRENCE. Mexico, without any definite locality.

COLLECTION. *Cultivated:* Golden Gate Park, San Francisco, *E. Walther*.

REMARKS. The present variety has proven to be very successful in cultivation locally, hence needs a name even if no definite locale is on record. It clearly belongs to *E. agavoides*, which differs in having fewer broader leaves and more deltoid sepals much more connate below. Var. *corderoyi* differs in having broader gray leaves (to 65 mm. long and 35 mm. wide) and corolla not exceeding 9 mm. in length. In foliage color, var. *prolifera* resembles *E. gilva,* which latter has a simple raceme, a larger corolla, and larger sepals.

The varietal name refers to the numerous proliferous offshoots emitted by each rosette.

8c.   **Echeveria agavoides** var. **corderoyi** (Baker) Poellnitz.
(Figure 31.)

Echeveria agavoides var. *corderoyi* (Baker) POELLNITZ, *in* Fedde Repert., vol. 39,
p. 258, 1936.
Cotyledon corderoyi BAKER, Gardeners' Chronicle, new ser., vol. 1, p. 599, 1874.
Echeveria corderoyi (Baker) ED. MORREN, La Belg. Hort., vol. 24, p. 259, 1874;
BERGER, *in* Engler Nat. Pflanzenf., ed. 2, vol. 18a, p. 476, 1930.
Urbinia corderoyi (Baker) ROSE, *in* Britton and Rose, Bull. New York Bot. Gard.,
vol. 3, p. 12, 1903; BRITTON AND ROSE, N. Amer. Fl., vol. 22, p. 32, 1905.
ILLUSTRATION. Gardeners' Chronicle, new ser., vol. 19, p. 373, fig. 56, 1883.

Glabrous, acaulescent; leaves 60 to 70 in a dense rosette that is 7 to 8
inches broad and 3 to 4 inches deep, ovate, 2 to 2½ inches long, 1¼ inches
broad at middle, ½ inch thick, quite flat on the face in the upper half, rounded
on the back, produced into a firm, lanceolate mucro, both sides a very pale
whitish green, smooth and rather shining; flower stems three or four to a rosette, the scape below the cyme 15 to 18 inches long, terete, with only a few
minute, scariose, bractlike leaves; cyme trichotomous, with 15 to 20 flowers
on long, red, flexuose branches; bracts minute, lanceolate; pedicels ½ to ¾
inch long, bright red; calyx rotate, ¼ inch broad, with lanceolate *divisions
reaching quite down to the pedicel;* corolla urceolate, ⅜ inch long, bright red
at base, yellow upwards, the lanceolate divisions three times at long as the
campanulate tube. (After Baker, *loc. cit.*)
TYPE. Cultivated by J. Corderoy, 4/74.
OCCURRENCE. Mexico.
REMARKS. *Echeveria agavoides* var. *corderoyi* was named after Mr. Justus
Corderoy, Didcot, a succulent grower of the times. It comes close to var. *agavoides,* from which it differs in having more numerous, smaller, narrower,
grayer leaves, a 3-branched inflorescence with 15 to 20 flowers, sepals free to
the base, and a corolla 9 mm. long. The closest relation to var. *corderoyi* would
seem to be my var. *prolifera,* found in cultivation at Mexico City in 1934.
This last has numerous proliferous offshoots, amber-colored leaves at times to
12 cm. long or more, and a corolla attaining a length of 16 mm.
Some Mexican material referred to this variety from the vicinity of Parras
and Saltillo in Coahuila and variously labeled *E. cuspidata* or *E. turgida,* is
herein treated as *E. parrasensis* (see no. 14).

8d.   **Echeveria agavoides** var. **multifida** E. Walther, new.

Echeveria agavoides var. *multifida* E. Walther, var. nov. *E. agavoides* affinis, sed differt: rosulis paucis, foliis ovatis, latissimis ad basin, rubro-marginatis apicibus, separatis difficile; inflorescentiis saepe 4- vel 5-ramosis; sepalis
deltoideis, connatis ad basin; corollis cylindraceis.
Rosettes usually solitary even when old; leaves numerous, as many as 50 in
each rosette, crowded, broadly ovate, shortly acuminate, to 8 cm. long or
more, 3 to 4 cm. broad or more, shallowly concave above, beneath rounded
and faintly keeled, sessile, difficult to detach without breaking; inflorescences
to 25 cm. tall; peduncle slender, erect-ascending, bracts appressed, racemes
two to five on each peduncle, secund-racemose, strongly nodding before anthe-

sis, with about 12 flowers each; pedicels slender, to 9 mm. long or more, turbinate below calyx; sepals unequal, longest 3 to 4 mm. long, deltoid, acute,
ascending to appressed, connate and decurrent at base; corolla conoid-cylindroid, scarcely pentagonal, 9 mm. long, 6 mm. in diameter near base; petals
somewhat spreading at tips, scarcely hollowed, not keeled, thin, bluntly mucronate; carpels 8 mm. long; nectaries thin, very oblique, scarcely over 1 mm.
wide. Flowers March and April.

Color. Leaves amber-colored, with margins near apex deep pompeian-red;
peduncle carmine; pedicels brazil-red; sepals pompeian-red to Hays-maroon;
corolla scarlet-red to rose-doree below, light orange-yellow at tips and inside;
styles apple-green; nectaries nearly white.

TYPE. Collected at the University of California Botanical Garden, *E. Walther,* April 8, 1959 (CAS, no. 413922).

PARATYPE. *Parry and Palmer,* 1878/233, in part (mounted with type of
E. humilis, (US)).

OCCURRENCE. Mexico. San Luis Potosi: Hacienda de San Francisco.

REMARKS. Typical *E. agavoides* has leaves without any such red edges and
its inflorescence is usually only 2-, rarely 3-branched. When I visited the locality cited above I knew nothing of its inflorescence and its frequent 4- or
5-branched habit. While this plant is sufficiently distinct to require definition,

Figure 32. 9. *Echeveria tolimanensis* Matuda. Flowering plant, × 0.4. Plant photographed in San Diego 27 March 1964; collected in the Barranca de Toliman, Hidalgo,
Mexico, the type locality (Moran 10044).

Figure 33. 9. *Echeveria tolimanensis* Matuda. Inflorescence, × 1.7. Plant flowering in San Diego 9 March 1963; collected in the Barranca de Toliman, Hidalgo, Mexico, the type locality (Moran 10044).

especially since it is in cultivation, it is scarcely different enough from *E. agavoides,* as previously known, to be described as a species. Since I published its original discovery, commercial dealers have placed it on sale.

9.   **Echeveria tolimanensis** Matuda.
    (Figures 32–33.)

> *Echeveria tolimanensis* (*"tolimanense"*) Matuda, Cactaceas y Suculentas Mexicanas, vol. 3, p. 31, 1958.
> Illustrations. *Op. cit.,* vol. 3, p. 31, fig. 19, 1958.

Stem short but ultimately evident, usually simple and unbranched; leaves numerous, crowded, thick and turgid, semiterete, narrowly lanceolate to linear-oblong, rounded beneath, above slightly flattened, upcurved to the usually long-aristate apex, 5 to 12 cm. long, 15 to 20 mm. broad, to 13 mm. thick, more or less pruinose; inflorescences 2- or 3- branched; peduncle slender, flexuose, spreading to ascending; bracts fugacious, linear-subulate, subtriquetrous, acute, to 13 mm. long; branches secund, with five to seven nodding flowers each; pedicels slender, to 6 mm. long or more, scarcely turbinate below calyx; sepals unequal, longest to 5 mm. long, deltoid, acute, spreading to reflexed at anthesis; corolla narrowly cylindroid-urceolate, 11 to 12 mm. long, 7 mm. in basal diameter; petals narrow, distinctly spreading at apex, gibbose at base, with more or less evident nectar-cavity within; nectaries oblique, trapezoid-reniform. Flowers March to July. Description from plants cultivated locally long before discovery of definite habitat in Mexico.

Color. Leaves variable, asphodel-green to light grape-green, but more or less pruinose and hence pale olive-gray, sometimes tinged more or less reddish; peduncle congo-pink; bracts deep grape-green; sepals jade-green; corolla coral-pink at base, above orange to light ochraceous-salmon, inside primuline-yellow; carpels ivory-yellow to pale chalcedony-yellow; styles apple-green to pinard-yellow; nectaries whitish to ochraceous-salmon.

TYPE. *Matuda* no. 32637 from Barranca de Toliman, Hidalgo, Mexico (MEXU).

OCCURRENCE. Mexico. Hidalgo: Barranca de Toliman, etc.

COLLECTIONS. Lower portion of nearly sheer calcareous north-facing cliffs, on dry rocky slopes of the Barranca de Toliman, somewhat above mines on road from Zimapan to Mina Loma del Toro and Balcones, 5,000 feet, *Moore and Wood*, 48/4399 (BH). *Cultivated:* Golden Gate Park, San Francisco, *E. Walther*, 1943 (CAS).

REMARKS. I have had this remarkable new species under observation for several years and am grateful to Professor Matuda for placing it on record with a definite locality. With its turgid leaves, 3-branched, secund racemes, and small sepals, it clearly belongs in the series Urceolatae, even if therein it is somewhat anomalous in having well developed nectar cavities and rather broad truncate nectaries. The long narrow leaves, with their aristate tips, and the slender corolla, with reflexed sepals, are distinctive. When grown in a damp greenhouse, its leaves change radically, becoming shorter, thicker, oblong-elliptic, about 6 cm. long by 2 cm. broad, nearly straight and glaucous rather than pruinose, but always with the distinctive setiform tips. In flowers, etc., this phase agrees with plants grown out of doors.

In its long slender corolla, this species resembles *E. chihuahuaensis,* but the latter has much flatter, broader, and shorter leaves and ascending sepals.

My original plants came to me from the late Dr. M. Morgan of Richmond, California, who presumably had them from F. Schmoll, Cadereyta, Queretaro.

The chromosome number is recorded by Dr. Uhl of Cornell to be $n = 30$.

10. Echeveria chihuahuaensis Poellnitz.

Echeveria chihuahuaensis POELLNITZ, *in* Fedde Repert., vol. 38, p. 29, 1935; *op. cit.,* vol. 39, p. 251, 1936.

Glabrous, stemless, with few or no offsets except in age; leaves numerous, densely crowded, as many as 50 or more, obovate-oblong to obovate-spathulate, or oblong, 4 to 6 cm. long, 3 to 4 cm. broad, sometimes narrower, at apex rounded to shortly acuminate, cuspidate-mucronate, mucro red, blade glaucous-white, relatively thin even though fleshy, above flat or shallowly concave, beneath rounded or faintly keeled, thickest just below apex; inflorescences several, as many as six, simple or 2-branched (3- to 5-branched) (Poellnitz), to 20 cm. tall; peduncle erect; bracts appressed, linear-oblanceolate, at apex acute and occasionally hooked, to 3 cm. long; branches secund-racemose, with five to eight flowers each; pedicels slender, to 14 mm. long, slightly thickened below calyx; sepals very unequal, longest to 8 mm. long, deltoid to lanceolate-oblong, acute, appressed or ascending; corolla narrowly cylindroid, about twice as long as thick, to 14 mm. long, 7 mm. in basal diameter, 5 mm. wide at mouth; petals scarcely keeled, within with shallow basal hollow, slightly spreading at tips; nectaries thin, oblique, 1.5 mm. wide. Flowers from March on. Description from living plants received from Craig and Lindsay, grown at Strybing Arboretum, Golden Gate Park, San Francisco.

Color. Leaves light cress-green, but conspicuously glaucous, mucro and sometimes edges pomegranate-purple; peduncle eugenia-red; bracts dark greenish glaucous tinged vinaceous-lilac; pedicels old-rose; sepals pompeian-red and glaucous; corolla rose-doree, to peach-red above, inside orange-chrome; carpels sulphur-yellow; styles pinard-yellow; nectaries empire-yellow.

TYPE. *R. Endlich,* 1232, in the valley of the Rio Colorado, 2,300 m. elevation, 16 April 1906, Chihuahua (B).

OCCURRENCE. Mexico. Chihuahua: valley of the Rio Colorado at confluence of Rio Fuertes; east of Ceracaqui up canyon from El Cajon.

COLLECTION. Mexico. Chihuahua: east of Ceracaqui up canyon from El Cajon, *Craig and Lindsay,* 39/9, living plants flowered in Golden Gate Park, San Francisco (CAS).

REMARKS. The original type specimen was very scanty and immature, and was matched with the Craig and Lindsay plants with some hesitation. Other species from this part of Mexico are *E. paniculata,* which would differ in having fleshy roots, strictly sessile flowers, and an angular corolla; also *E. craigiana;* which has very narrow, thick, brownish, aristate-tipped leaves, and appressed sepals. Poellnitz' comparison with *E. schaffneri* might perhaps pertain to *E. maculata* Rose, both of which differ in having sessile flowers, an angular corolla, and a much more eastern range.

The following is Dr. Lindsay's account of the plant he and Dr. Craig brought to me (Cactus and Succ. Jour. Amer., vol. 15, p. 73, 1943). At Ceracaqui, on Easter Sunday, "early . . . an Indian came into camp carrying some attractive Echeverias from tall "picachos," or rocky crags, nearby. The leaves were a beautiful blue-green, tinged in pink, and the plants were in full flower, each bearing several delicate coral blossom-stalks. These plants may be *E. cuspidata* or possibly *E. corderoyi,* but in either case would mean a decided extension of range."

Locally, the present item has frequently been misnamed *E. cuspidata,* but that species has a usually simple raceme, more spreading sepals, and a broader corolla. Its leaves are thinner, longer, and the range is much more eastern. The imperfectly known *E. tobarensis* from northern Durango needs to be considered because its type locality, Tovar near Tepehuanes, is not much over 100 miles distant. Its leaves have more strongly acuminate apex, are more highly colored; it has a mostly 2-branched raceme and a corolla not over 7 mm. long. In its slender corolla *E. chihuahuaensis* resembles *E. tolimanensis* from Hidalgo, but that species has narrow subterete leaves with long-aristate tips and reflexed sepals.

In the series Urceolatae, *E. chihuahuaensis* is anomalous in its cylindroid corolla, but foliage and nectaries are quite typical of the series. Of the numerous locally raised seedlings, all were substantially uniform. However, some plants of the original collection differed in having rather narrower leaves. According to the original collector, R. Endlich, this is called "Siempreviva" by local residents, while the Tarahumare Indians know it as "Mec."

11. **Echeveria lindsayana** E. Walther, new species.

Echeveria lindsayana E. Walther, sp. nov., pertinens ad ser. Urceolatis, *E. chihuahuaensi* affinis, glabra, acaulescens; rosulis paulum surculosis, foliis numerosis, valde confertis, obovatis vel oblongo-obovatis crassis, conspicue rubro-mucronatis, 5–9 cm. longis, 3–4 cm. latis, pallide viridibus vel albescentibus, leviter glaucescentibus; inflorescentiis 3, usque ad 50 cm. altis, saepe bifidis prope basin; pedunculis tenuibus, 4 mm. crassis ad basin; bracteis distantibus, adpressis, ovato-lanceolatis, acuminatis, usque ad 13 mm. longis, caducis; ramis 2, secundo-racemosis, usque ad 7-floris, nutantibus; pedicellis usque ad 13 mm. longis, tenuibus, leviter turbinatis; sepalis brevissimis, ovato-deltoideis, acutis, subaequalibus, usque ad 3 mm. longis, adpressis, valde connatis ad basin; corollis usque ad 10 mm. longis, 5 mm. diametro ad basin, 7 mm. in fauce, cylindraceis; petalis tenuibus, apice patentibus, roseis et flavis; nectariis 3 mm. latis, subreniformibus, obliquis.

Plant glabrous, acaulescent; rosettes simple when young, but ultimately becoming cespitose; leaves numerous, crowded, obovate to oblong, at apex from shortly acuminate and mucronate to truncate, quite thick, 5 to 9 cm. long, 3 to 4 cm. broad, obscurely keeled beneath near apex; inflorescences three or more, to 50 cm. tall, often 2-branched at middle, sometimes fasciated; peduncle slender, to 4 mm. thick at base; bracts few, distant, appressed, ovate-lanceolate, acute to acuminate, to 13 mm. long, caducous; branches usually two, secund-racemose, with seven flowers each, strongly nodding before anthesis; pedicels slender, to 13 mm. long, slightly turbinate below calyx; sepals very short, ovate-deltoid, acute, subequal, to 3 mm. long, appressed, strongly connate at base; corolla to 10 mm. long, 5 mm. in basal diameter, 7 mm. wide at mouth, cylindroid; petals thin, spreading at their tips, neither keeled nor deeply hollowed; nectaries oblique, subreniform, 3 mm. wide. Flowers from April on.

Color. Leaves water-green, tinged light purplish vinaceous near apex, only the mucro brazil-red; peduncle light pinkish cinnamon; bracts apple-green, to nopal-red at apex; sepals courge-green; corolla grenadine-pink; petals at tips and inside light orange-yellow; carpels above mineral-green; nectaries clear dull yellow.

TYPE. *E. Walther,* 8 April 1959, cultivated in Strybing Arboretum, Golden Gate Park, San Francisco (CAS, no. 413947).

COLLECTIONS. *Cultivated*: Victor Reiter's garden, San Francisco, *E. Walther,* 24 February 1959; Strybing Arboretum, *E. Walther,* 13 March 1959.

REMARKS. In leaf form, and to some extent in color, this new species does resemble *E. chihuahuaensis,* with which it has so long been confused. However, the plants of that species, brought from near Ceracaqui by Dr. Lindsay in 1939, are clearly distinct in their much whiter leaves, with more prominent red margins and mucro; the flowers have much longer unequal sepals; the corolla is cylindrical and up to 15 mm. long. *Echeveria cuspidata* is another species with which our present novelty has been confused, but in that the leaves are thinner, glaucous, and scarcely white; its inflorescence is always simple, with the corolla pentagonal; it is native to the eastern Sierra Madre Oriental.

While the source of the present item is as yet unknown, I feel certain that ultimately its Mexican habitat will be discovered. In naming it for Dr. George Lindsay, I acknowledge the many services towards a better knowledge of cacti and succulents performed by him.

12. **Echeveria colorata** E. Walther, new species.

Echeveria colorata E. Walther, sp. nov., pertinens ad ser. Urceolatis, glabra, acaulescens, rosulis paulum surculosis; foliis valde confertis, angusto-oblongis, usque ad 10 cm. longis et 3 cm. latis, crassis, acutis vel breviter acuminatis, albidis puniceo-tinctis; inflorescentiis usque ad 30 cm. altis, bifidis; pedunculis usque 4 mm. crassis ad basin, flexuosis; bracteis adpressis, lineari-lanceolatis, acuminatis, usque ad 12 mm. longis; ramis secundo-racemosis; pedicellis usque ad 14 mm. longis, valde turbinatis; sepalis inaequalibus, deltoideis vel ovato-deltoideis, acutis, usque ad 5 mm. longis, adpressis, valde connatis et decurrentibus ad basin; corollis subcylindraceis, usque ad 12 mm. longis, 7 mm. diametro prope basin, rubris; nectariis usque ad 2 mm. latis, tenuibus, obliquis, flavidis. *E. chihuahuaensi* affinis, sed differt foliis angusto-oblongis puniceo-tinctis, sepalis adpressis deltoideis vel anguste deltoideis-ovatis decurrentibus et pedicellis valde turbinatis.

Glabrous, stemless, rosettes simple when young, giving out offsets belatedly; leaves crowded, about 25 in number, elliptic-oblong, acute or shortly acuminate, to 10 cm. long and 3 cm. broad, thick, evenly upcurved, nearly flat above, beneath rounded and keeled, with an obscure ridge above near one edge; inflorescence to 30 cm. tall, 2-branched; peduncle flexuose, to 4 mm. thick at base; bracts appressed, linear-lanceolate, acuminate, rounded beneath, concave above; branches secund-racemose; pedicels to 14 mm. long, strongly turbinate below calyx; sepals unequal, very thin, longest 5 mm. long, deltoid to ovate-deltoid, acute, appressed, connate at base and decurrent to petiole; corolla cylindroid, to 12 mm. long, 7 mm. in diameter near base, 5 mm. at mouth; petals neither keeled nor hollowed, but strongly connate with sepals and pedicels at base; carpels 8 mm. long, slender; nectaries narrow, oblique, to 2 mm. wide. Flowers from April on.

Color. Leaves yellowish oil-green to whitish, strongly tinged carmine above; peduncle oxblood-red; pedicels pompeian-red; sepals kildare-green; corolla peach-red to coral-red; petals orange inside; carpels whitish below, above apple-green; nectaries mustard-yellow.

Type. *E. Walther,* 2 April 1959, from plant cultivated at the University of California Botanical Garden (57.794) (CAS, no. 413924). This plant had been received from Señor Zabaleta from cultivated plants at Guadalajara, Jalisco, Mexico.

Remarks. Several living plants were sent me by Sr. Zabaleta of Guadalajara, where this is cultivated in various gardens. My own material has so far failed to flower, but in the warmer Botanical Garden at the University of California flowers were produced for the first time in April, 1959. In the series Urceolatae this comes with the species having 2-branched inflorescences and leaves whitish in basic coloration. Of these the closest relations are *E. chi-*

huahuaensis, E. lindsayana, E. tobarensis, and *E. parrasensis* of which *E. tobarensis* is imperfectly known, but should have broader leaves and a shorter corolla. *Echeveria parrasensis* has thinner leaves, rarely over 6 cm. long, sepals much less connate, and pedicels only slightly turbinate. Both *E. chihuahuaensis* and *E. lindsayana* have broader, relatively shorter leaves with red mucros, but are otherwise clear whitish green, and their sepals are scarcely decurrent.

Until the lost *E. tobarensis* is recollected from its type-locality, no certainty exists that our concept of this is correct, and that *E. colorata* might not have to be reduced to a synonym.

13.   **Echeveria tobarensis** Berger.

> *Echeveria tobarensis* BERGER, *in* Engler Nat. Pflanzenf., ed. 2, vol. 18a, p. 476, 1930; POELLNITZ, *in* Fedde Repert., vol. 39, p. 259, 1936.
> *Urbinia lurida* ROSE, Contrib. U. S. Nat. Herb., vol. 13, p. 301, 1911; BRITTON and ROSE, N. Amer. Fl., vol. 22, p. 541, 1918. Not *E. lurida* Haworth, 1831.

Description, quoted from Rose, *loc. cit.* "Leaves clustered in a dense rosette, very thick, ovate, acuminate, glabrous, purple or lurid in color, 3 to 4 cm. long, 15 to 25 mm. broad at widest point; flowering stem 25 cm. long, 2-branched in only specimen seen; stem-leaves small, bract-like, scattered; sepals small, ovate, acute; corolla 6 to 7 mm. long; petals acute, erect except the small, out-turned tip; carpels distinct to the base. . . . Only four specimens were obtained, of which two reached Washington, D.C., in good condition, one of them flowering April 22, 1908. From this the accompanying illustration was made. This plant died soon afterwards, while the only remaining plant has not done well and probably will soon disappear. This species is smaller than any of the other three species of *Urbinia,* and has much more highly colored leaves."

TYPE. *Palmer,* 248, in a box canyon near Tobar, 28 May 1906, Durango (US).

REMARKS. Of several distinct plants from this part of Mexico, none quite agrees with the above description. The illustration mentioned by Dr. Rose seems to have been mislaid, and so cannot help me. The type specimen is most scanty, and fully covered by Dr. Rose's description. I have seen examples of *E. agavoides,* in its native habitat, depauperate because of their environment, which might be indistinguishable from *E. tobarensis* as described above. *Echeveria chihuahuaensis* varies with leaves often narrower or more highly colored. Attached to the above-mentioned type specimen is a letter, in Dr. Palmer's hand, reading as follows:

"Echeveria: Four plants from holes in sides of box cañon near Tobar. There was no soil, the plants had slight roots to hold to rocks, one had a flower stem with flowers of a dark red, this broke from the plant, and in the effort to secure it I slippèd, fell, and received several contusions and a sprained wrist, left hand, and had to be carried by man-power out of the cañon, then put on a horse to ride to Tobar."

14. **Echeveria parrasensis** E. Walther.
   (Figures 34–38.)

   Echeveria parrasensis E. WALTHER, Cactus and Succ. Jour. Amer., vol. 31, p. 99, 1959.
   Echeveria cuspidata J. A. PURPUS, Kakteenkunde, 1907, p. 184; not *E. cuspidata* Rose.
   ILLUSTRATIONS. Kakteenkunde, *loc. cit.;* Cactus and Succ. Jour. Amer., vol. 31, figs. 32, 33, 1959.

Stem short, long remaining simple, in age to 8 cm. tall and 2 cm. thick, densely covered with the persistent dry leaves among which many slender roots, offsets few or none; leaves numerous, 40 to 100 or more, crowded, obovate-cuneate to oblong-oblanceolate, 5 to 6 cm. long, 20 to 30 mm. broad, at base narrowed to 12 mm., nearly flat above, beneath rounded and obscurely keeled near apex, the latter strongly acuminate-cuspidate, with tip of mucro dark red; inflorescence to 25 cm. tall, usually 2-branched, in cultivation sometimes 3-branched; peduncle slender, to 3 mm. thick; bracts numerous, to 30 or more, closely appressed, subtriquetrous, lanceolate, acuminate, 10 to 15 mm. long; racemes secund, 8 to 15 cm. long, with 6 to 15 flowers each; pedicels slender, 6 to 12 mm. long, slightly turbinate below calyx; sepals unequal, longest 5 mm. long, ovate-deltoid, acute, connate at base, appressed to slightly spreading above; corolla to 11 mm. long, urceolate, gibbose below, to 7 mm. in

Figure 34. 14. *Echeveria parrasensis* E. Walther. Rosette, × 0.85. Plant photographed in San Diego 14 May 1961; collected above Puerto Flores, Coahuila, Mexico (Moran 6294, a cited collection).

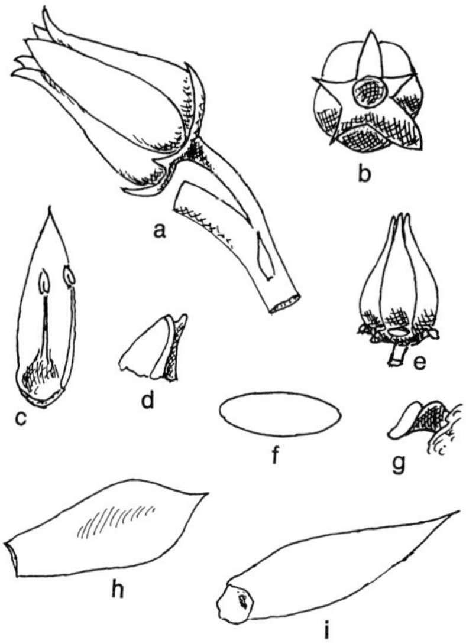

Figure 35. 14. *Echeveria parrasensis* E. Walther. Explanation: (a) flower, × 2; (b) flower from below, × 2; (c) inside of petal, × 2; (d) apex of petal, × 8; (e) carpels, × 2; (f) nectary, front view, × 8; (g) nectary, side view, × 8; (h) leaf, × 0.4; (i) bract, × 2. From the original publication (Cactus and Succulent Journal, volume 31, page 99, figure 32).

Figure 36. 14. *Echeveria parrasensis* E. Walther. Plant from above Puerto Flores, Coahuila (Moran 6294). From the original publication (Cactus and Succulent Journal, volume 31, page 97).

Figure 37. 14. *Echeveria parrasensis* E. Walther. Plant from above Puerto Flores, Coahuila, Mexico *(Moran 6294)*. From the original publication (Cactus and Succulent Journal, volume 31, page 100, part of figure 33).

Figure 38. 14. *Echeveria parrasensis* E. Walther. From the original publication (Cactus and Succulent Journal, volume 31, page 100, part of figure 33).

basal diameter, 5 mm. at mouth, nearly circular in cross-section, at most obscurely angled; petals not keeled, with quite shallow basal hollow and small, subapical mucro; carpels 7 mm. long; nectaries oblique, narrowly elliptic, to 1.75 mm. broad. Flowers from March on, based largely on R. Moran, 58/6294 (UCBG).

Color. Leaves light bice-green, but pulverulent and so light celandine-green; peduncle light pinkish cinnamon; bracts biscay-green, as are the sepals; corolla scarlet to strawberry-pink; carpels whitish below, with styles deep turtle-green; nectaries chartreuse-yellow.

TYPE. *C. A. Purpus,* 04/R: 965, collected near Parras, Coahuila, Mexico (US, no. 431439).

OCCURRENCE. Mexico: Coahuila.

COLLECTIONS. Mexico. Coahuila: Saltillo, *Palmer,* 02/R-509 (MEXU); Patagalana, on limestone rocks southeast of Parras, *Purpus,* 05/1332 (F,GH, MO,UC,US); Cañon of the big waterfall, Chayo Grande, 24 miles southeast of Saltillo, *Palmer,* 04/42 (CAS,GH,US). *Cultivated:* Puerto Flores, Coahuila, 22 miles from Saltillo, on new route 75, *R. Moran,* 57/6294 (CAS,CU, SD,UCBG).

REMARKS. This species has long remained unrecognized because of its superficial similarity to *E. cuspidata* which is from the same part of Mexico. The latter differs in having relatively thinner, broader, blunter leaves, an inflorescence that is always a simple secund raceme, and larger sepals and larger corolla. My concept of *E. cuspidata* is based on living plants I collected near El Tunal, which agreed perfectly with the very clear watercolor of the typeplant prepared by the late Frederick Walpole. *Echeveria turgida* Rose from Viesca, Coahuila, differs in its thinner bluntly truncate leaves, its simple raceme, longer spreading sepals, and a pentagonal corolla, as clearly shown by Walpole's watercolor of the type plant. Both *E. cuspidata* and *E. turgida* belong in the series Secundae, whereas *E. parrasensis* must go in the series Urceolatae. Here it would come near the imperfectly known *E. agavoides* var. *corderoyi* (Baker) Poellnitz, which was described as having "sepals free to base," while Baker's illustration depicts a 3-branched raceme, etc.

C. A. Purpus sent living plants to Dr. Rose, to A. Berger at La Mortola (of which last a sketch by his hand is in the U. S. National Herbarium), and also to his brother, then director of the botanic garden at Darmstadt. A picture and description of the last, as *E. cuspidata*, appeared in Kakteenkunde, *loc. cit.*

When in Parras in 1937, I failed to locate any trace of this, and only the rediscovery by Dr. Reid Moran enables me to settle the matter finally.

15. **Echeveria elegans** Rose.

(Figures 39–42.)

Echeveria elegans Rose, *in* Britton and Rose, N. Amer. Fl., vol. 22, p. 22, 1905; Poellnitz, *in* Fedde Repert., vol. 39, p. 238, 1936, *in part only. Not E. elegans* Berger (which is *E. harmsii* F. Macbride).
Echeveria perelegans Berger, *in* Engler Nat. Pflanzenf., ed. 2, vol. 18a, p. 474, 1930.
Illustrations. Cactus and Succ. Jour. Amer., vol. 6, p. 138, figs. A4, A6, p. 163, 1935; Nat. Hort. Mag., vol. 14, no. 2, pp. 173, 174, 1935.

Rosettes stemless, globose, cespitose, and freely soboliferous; leaves thick and turgid, but thinnish at apex, alabaster white, oblong-obovate, 3 to 6 cm. long, 1 to 2 cm. broad, convex beneath, above flat or slightly concave, up-curved, apex acute and mucronate, surface texture crystalline in appearance, edges somewhat hyaline; inflorescences three or more, 10 to 15 cm. tall, simply racemose; lower bracts few, deltoid-lanceolate, acute, appressed except the outcurved tips, 10 to 12 mm. long; flowers six to ten; pedicels slender, to 6 mm. long, scarcely turbinate; sepals unequal, longest to 5 mm. long, spreading, ovate-deltoid to lanceolate, acute, much connate at base; corolla broadly co-noid-urceolate, to 12 mm. long and 8 mm. in diameter at base; petals thin, scarcely keeled, erect but slightly spreading at tips, with shallow basal hollow; nectaries thin, very oblique. Flowers from March on. Description of material long cultivated in California gardens.

Color. Leaves lettuce-green but more or less pruinose and hence pale glaucous-green, mucro rarely somewhat reddish; peduncle old-rose; bracts as leaves, turning to old-rose in age; sepals old-rose to light grayish vinaceous; corolla begonia-rose to eosine-pink with bloom; petals at tips oural-green in bud, there becoming later pale yellow-orange; inside light cadmium; carpels baryta-yellow; styles cosse-green.

Type. *Rose,* 1901/960, in mountains above Pachuca (US, no. 399884).

Occurrence. Mexico. Hidalgo; widely cultivated at Pachuca, Omitlan, etc.

Collections. Mexico. Hidalgo: mountains near Pachuca, *Rose,* 01/960 (US, type). *Cultivated:* La Mortola, *A. Berger* in 1907 (NY, as *E. cuspidata,* annotated in Berger's hand "kann kaum richtig sein"); garden of Mrs. Jenkins, San Francisco, *E. Walther* in 1929 (CAS).

Remarks. When *Oliveranthus* Rose is merged with *Echeveria* DeCandolle, the specific name *"elegans"* has to be conserved for the species first receiving the epithet in the genus *Echeveria. Oliveranthus elegans* so becomes *Echeveria harmsii* Macbride and the new name, *E. perelegans* Berger is superfluous.

Under *E. elegans,* Poellnitz publishes the var. *kesselringiana,* which appears identical with a plant received from Mexico, without any definite locality, which herein is treated as a valid species, *i.e., E. albicans.* The latter differs from *E. elegans* as stated under no. 18.

Closely related to *E. elegans* is *E. potosina* which differs in its narrower leaves thickest near apex and usually with a distinct purplish tinge in sun, its broader, obovate, scarcely spreading bracts, and its somewhat broader corolla.

Figure 39.   15. *Echeveria elegans* Rose. Plant of the type collection, flowering in Washington. Photograph from the U.S. National Herbarium, no. 190.

Dr. Rose's type material may have come from cultivated plants, for *E. elegans* is much cultivated in Mexico, as in Pachuca in front of my hotel, in various parks and squares, where it is often planted in fancy designs of alligators, tortoises, etc., a practice that may antedate the Conquest. One such famous planting is the spectacular "fence of conchas" near Omitlan (Cactus and Succ. Jour. Amer., vol. 6, p. 138, fig. A6, 1935), where I was informed that the real home of *E. elegans* was near a prominent peak known as "Penas de Jacal."

Cultivated locally is a form with fasciated stems and crested rosettes; on reverting to type its leaves may retain for some time the biconvex shape they have in the crest. I record this as *Echeveria elegans* cultivar 'Crest.'

15b. **Echeveria elegans** var. **hernandonis** E. Walther, new.
(Figures 40–41.)

Echeveria elegans var. hernandonis E. Walther, var. nov. Affinis *E. eleganti* sed differt: foliis valde curvatis, usque ad 7.5 cm. longis et 3 cm. latis; inflorescentiis brevibus, usque ad 12 cm. altis, laxe patentibus, 8–10-floris; calyce suturis ad basin sepali longissimi.

Freely soboliferous even when young; rosettes subglobose, with few (12) to many (25) leaves, these with crystalline epidermis and hyaline margins, glaucous-pulverulent, obovate-oblong, to 75 mm. long and 30 mm. broad, thickest just above middle, noticeably upcurved to apex, this finely mucronate, shallowly concave above, convex beneath, not keeled; inflorescences one to three, secund-racemose, 12 cm. tall or less; peduncle laxly spreading-ascending; bracts about eight, recurved, narrowly-oblanceolate, acuminate, aristate-apiculate, at base spurred, to 20 mm. long; raceme rarely with more than eight flowers; pedicels to 10 mm. long, slightly turbinate; sepals very unequal, smaller 4 mm. long and oblong, the larger to 10 mm. long, elliptic-oblong to oblanceolate, acute, the base of the largest with distinct sutures at junction with the adjoining smaller sepals; nectaries narrowly-lunate, oblique, 2 mm. wide. Flowers from April on.

Color. Leaves light cress-green, greenish glaucous; peduncle corydalis-green; bracts mytho-green, glaucous; pedicels light vinaceous fawn; sepals as bracts; corolla eosine-pink below; petals at tips and inside chalcedony-yellow; carpels whitish; nectaries and styles apple-green.

TYPE. *E. Walther,* 1 May 1959, cultivated in Golden Gate Park, San Francisco, from plants collected at Hacienda del Carmen near Omitlan, Hidalgo, Mexico (CAS, no. 414551).

OCCURRENCE. At present known only from above type locality in Mexico.

REMARKS. When describing *E. elegans,* Dr. Rose stated that it was collected "in the mountains above Pachuca," but all material I had been able to find in this part of Mexico was in cultivation, as in the small park fronting my hotel in Pachuca, or at the farmstead at Omitlan with its famous "fence of conchas." So I was greatly interested when Sr. Hernando Sánchez-Mejorada, in company with several other prominent members of the La Sociedad Mexicana de Cactologia, drove me to the vicinity of the Hacienda del Carmen. Located along the edges of a stream, here cutting a deep chasm through the basic rocks, the hacienda nowadays specializes in raising goats, an ill omen for *Echeveria*-hunters. However, on one particularly steep outcrop, forming a

Figure 40. 15b. *Echeveria elegans* Rose var. *hernandonis* E. Walther. Inflorescence, × 2. Plant flowering in San Diego 6 June 1964; collected at El Carmen, Hidalgo, Mexico, the type locality (Moran 10076B).

sheer cliff too much even for goats, several large clumps of the *Echeveria* had been able to survive in a plant association including *Quercus* spp., *Arbutus glandulifera, Crataegus pubescens, Fuchsia minutiflora, Sedum confusum,* and *S. diversifolium.* With some difficulty, and the use of a long pole to poke the plants off the cliff face, an undertaking not without risk, I finally got a close-up of what I felt sure was *Echeveria elegans.* Each clump appeared to be a single seedling, its roots growing in a mat of sphagnum moss, and of course no flowers were present, because it was December. In San Francisco a full year elapsed before the plants had recovered enough to flower again, and when they did, it was clear that this was not the typical *E. elegans* of Dr. Rose. In fact, it had much in common with var. *simulans,* previously known only from its type locality near Monterrey, but distant nearly 400 miles. Since von Poellnitz had seen fit to reduce *E. simulans* to a synonym of *E. elegans,* I feel that a more adequate concept of these forms would follow their treatment as varieties.

In choosing a varietal name I wish to show my appreciation of the hospitality shown me by Sr. Hernando Sánchez-Mejorada, of Mexico City, Velasco and Los Mochis.

The unusual sutures at the base of the largest sepal appear to be both constant and distinctive. They are found also in var. *simulans* and my new var. *tuxpanensis,* but in only very few other echeverias.

15c. **Echeveria elegans** var. **tuxpanensis** E. Walther, new.

Echeveria elegans var. tuxpanensis E. Walther, var. nov. Affinis *E. eleganti* sed differt: foliis usque ad 35 mm. longis et 10–12 mm. latis; inflorescentiis 15–20 cm. altis, 8–12-floris; pedicellis usque ad 10 mm. longis, turbinatis; sepalis inaequalibus, longissimo suturis ad basin; corollis 12–14 mm. longis.

Leaves oblong-oblanceolate, cuneate, acute to shortly acuminate, 30 to 35 mm. long, 10 to 12 mm. broad; inflorescence simply racemose, 15 cm. tall, with 10 to 12 flowers; pedicels slender, to 10 mm. long, turbinate beneath calyx; sepals unequal, the longest to 8 mm. long and with distinct sutures at base, deltoid to ovate-lanceolate, acute to acuminate; corolla 12 to 14 mm. long; petals apparently thin, neither keeled nor much hollowed within at base; at tips erect or scarcely spreading.

TYPE. *G. Hart Schiff and Purpus,* Rose 04/961 on rocks in cañon near Tuxpan, Jalisco, Mexico. (US, type; NY, isotype.)

Figure 41.   15b. *Echeveria elegans* Rose var. *hernandonis* E. Walther. Flowering plant, × 0.75. Plant photographed in San Diego 16 May 1964; collected at El Carmen, Hidalgo, Mexico, the type locality (Moran 10076).

OCCURRENCE. Known so far only from above collection.

REMARKS. I have not been able to study living plants of this new variety. The original material was misfiled under *E. turgida,* as "cotype," but that is quite another species, belonging to a different series, with much longer spreading sepals, different, truncate, and mucronate leaves, and an angular corolla. The peculiar sutures at the base of the largest sepals are distinctive, and exactly like those found in *E. elegans* var. *simulans,* and var. *hernandonis.*

This variety occurs so close to Guadalajara, it may even be in cultivation there.

15d. **Echeveria elegans** var. **simulans** (Rose) Poellnitz.
(Figure 42.)

> *Echeveria elegans* var. *simulans* (Rose), POELLNITZ, *in* Fedde Repert., vol. 39, p. 239, 1936.
> *Echeveria simulans* ROSE, *in* Britton and Rose, N. Amer. Fl. vol. 22, p. 22, 1905.
> ILLUSTRATIONS. Photograph no. 1843 (US) [See figure 42].

Plant glabrous, stemless; rosettes scarcely globose, to over 10 cm. in diameter, belatedly cespitose; leaves many, crowded, ascending turgid, but thinnish near the acute, mucronate apex, to 7 cm. long and 4 cm. broad, whitish; inflorescences to seven, usually simply racemose, rarely 2-branched; scape 20 to 40 cm. tall; lower bracts 15 to 20 mm. long, appressed, oblanceolate, acute; flowers 12 to 14; pedicels to 10 mm. long or more, turbinately thickened below calyx; sepals very unequal, longest to one-third the length of corolla, deltoid-ovate to lanceolate, more or less appressed, connate at base, but often with distinct sutures evident, largest sepal occasionally spurred and decurrent at base; corolla conoid-urceolate, to 15 mm. long and 10 mm. in diameter at base, obscurely or not angled; petals thin, with shallow basal hollow and slightly spreading tips; nectaries thin, very oblique. Flowers from April on. Description from material cultivated locally, presumably a clonotype.

Color. Leaves biscay-green to greenish glaucous; peduncle and pedicels coral-pink; bracts and sepals vetiver-green; corolla rose-pink, mustard-yellow at apex, inside light cadmium above, pale vinaceous below; styles pale greenish yellow.

TYPE. *Pringle,* 03/R-767, from near Monterrey, flowered in Washington, D.C., 1904–1905 (US, no. 399882).

OCCURRENCE. Mexico. Nuevo Leon; near Monterrey in Sierra Madre Oriental.

COLLECTIONS. Mexico, Nuevo Leon; near Monterrey, *Pringle,* 03/R-767 (US, type; GH), *Runyon,* 23/30 (US); Caja Pinta, near Monterrey, *Pringle,* 06/10168 (G,GH,MEXU,NY,P,PH,UC,W); Cañon de los Charcos, above Alamar, 15 miles southwest of Galeana, *C. H. and M. T. Mueller,* 34/318 (FM,GH); S. F. Cañon, southwest of Pueblo Galeana, *Mueller,* 34/318 (GH); Diente Cañon, 12 miles south of Monterrey, *C. H. and M. T. Mueller,* 34/262 (BH,GH). *Cultivated:* Golden Gate Park, San Francisco (from Mesa de Chipinque), *E. Walther* in 1937 (CAS).

REMARKS. *Echeveria elegans* would appear to differ sufficiently in its smaller and more globose rosettes, producing more numerous offsets even when still small, in its smaller leaves which often are narrower and more erect, in its lower scape with fewer flowers, the smaller corolla, more spreading sepals, pedi-

Figure 42. 15d. *Echeveria elegans* var *simulans* (Rose) Poellnitz. Plant flowering in Washington; collected near Monterrey, Nuevo Leon, Mexico, by Robert Runyon in 1923. Photograph from the U.S. National Herbarium, no. 1843.

cels that are not turbinate, and petals tipped green in bud. *Echeveria hyalina* has green-tipped petals and its leaves are more cuneate at base, more cuspidate at the apex, and conspicuously pellucid at the edges.

In 1937 I was able to visit the type locality as described by C. G. Pringle in his diary (Helen Burns Davis, *Life and Work of Cyrus Guernsey Pringle,* 1936, pp. 231, 232), where I re-collected this. It grew in company with *Sedum palmeri,* in oak woods at the base of the topmost cliffs, along a foot trail not far from the road's end at Chipinque Mesa.

16. **Echeveria potosina** E. Walther.
   (Figures 43–47.)

Echeveria potosina E. WALTHER, Cactus and Succ. Jour. Amer., vol. 7, p. 61, 1935;
   POELLNITZ, *in* Fedde Repert., vol. 39, p. 267, 1936.
ILLUSTRATIONS. Cactus and Succ. Jour. Amer., vol. 7, p. 71, 1935.

Rosettes stemless, dense, ultimately cespitose; leaves narrowly obovate-cuneate, to 6 cm. long and 2 to 3 cm. broad, very turgid, thickest near apex, shortly mucronate, with hyaline margins, nearly flat above, beneath rounded or subcarinate towards tip, margins hyaline; inflorescence 30 to 40 cm. tall, usually a simple raceme; peduncle stout, erect; lower bracts appressed, obovate, acute to acuminate, to 2 cm. long; raceme strongly nodding in bud, with 6 to 16 or more flowers; pedicels 6 mm. long, conspicuously turbinate-thickened below calyx; sepals ovate-deltoid, very short, longest to 5 mm. long, scarcely extending beyond corolla, appressed; corolla urceolate, scarcely pentagonal, 12 to 13 mm. long, 9 mm. in basal diameter; petals erect, only slightly spreading at tips, thin, with basal hollow ill defined; nectaries oblique, thinnish, narrowly reniform. Flowers from March to June. Description from the living type plant.

Color. Leaves olive-gray to sage-green, often tinged vinaceous-drab, especially towards apex; bracts as the leaves, but tinged benzo-brown; pedicels hermosa-pink; sepals as the bracts; corolla begonia-rose, with petal tips turtle-green; styles deep turtle-green; nectaries pinard-yellow.

TYPE. Living plant received from Romeo and Posselt, San Luis Potosí (CAS, no. 234167).

OCCURRENCE. Mexico; without any definite locality.

COLLECTIONS. *Cultivated:* Golden Gate Park, San Francisco, *Walther* in 1957 (CAS).

REMARKS. Closest to *E. potosina,* both geographically and otherwise, is no doubt *E. elegans. Echeveria potosina* would appear to be amply distinct in its rather narrower leaves decidedly thickest just below the apex, the frequent purplish tinge, the broader bracts, the distinctly turbinate pedicels, and the shorter, more deltoid sepals. *Echeveria albicans* also comes near this but differs in having broader leaves never purple-tinged, often 2-branched inflorescence, longer sepals, and a somewhat broader corolla, which is not or scarcely green-tipped. Its nectaries appear rather broader, less oblique, and more truncate. There is little doubt that here we have one of a connected series of very similar species; and only further field work can determine whether these are mere local forms or varieties.

The specific name refers to the state whence the original material came.

Figure 43. 16. *Echeveria potosina* E. Walther. Flowering plant, × 0.6. Plant photographed in San Diego 4 June 1964; part of the type collection (UCBG 51.1356).

Figure 44. 16. *Echeveria potosina* E. Walther. Rosette, approximately × 0.4. From the original publication (Cactus and Succulent Journal, volume 7, page 71, upper left).

Figure 45. 16. *Echeveria potosina* E. Walther. From an article by Eric Walther (American Horticultural Magazine, volume 39, page 84).

Figure 46. 16. *Echeveria potosina* E. Walther. Rosette, natural size. Plant grown in San Diego; part of the type collection (UCBG 51.1356).

Figure 47. 16. *Echeveria potosina* E. Walther. Inflorescence, × 1.5. Plant flowering in San Diego 4 June 1964; part of the type collection (UCBG 51.1356).

17. **Echeveria sanchez-mejoradae** E. Walther, new species.
(Figures 48–49. Plate 1, upper; see page 213.)

Echeveria sanchez-mejoradae E. Walther, sp. nov., pertinens ad ser. Urceolatis, glabra, acaulescens, rosulis caespitosis; foliis numerosis, confertis, lineari-
oblanccolatis, longc attenuatis ad basin, aristato-apiculatis, leviter recurvatis,
subcarinatis, usque ad 6 cm. longis et 15 mm. latis, viridibus, leviter vel non
glaucis; inflorescentiis 3–5, altissimis, usque ad 50 cm. altis, simplicibus, secundo-racemosis; pedunculis erectis, sed flexuosis; bracteis distantibus, oblan-
ceolatis, aristato-acutis, usque ad 20 mm. longis, subtriquetris; floribus 10,
patentibus; pedicellis usque ad 9 mm. longis; sepalis valde inaequalibus, usque
ad 11 mm. longis, acutis, patentibus vel adscendentibus, deltoideo-lanceolatis;
corollis urceolatis, carneis basi, flavo-viridibus apice, 11 mm. longis, 8 mm.
diametro basi, 5 mm. fauce; petalis non carinatis, paulum excavatis; carpellis
7 mm. longis; nectariis anguste lunatis, obliquis, usque ad 2 mm. latis.

Plants glabrous, stemless, cespitose, with even small, young plants consisting of two or more rosettes; leaves numerous, crowded, linear-oblanceolate
to obovate-cuneate, long-attenuate to base, at apex aristate-apiculate, slightly
recurved, obscurely keeled beneath, to 6 cm. long and 15 mm. broad; inflorescences three to five, sometimes to 50 cm. tall, simply secund-racemose; peduncle
slender, flexuose; bracts distant, oblanceolate, aristate-acute, subtriquetrous,
to 20 mm. long; flowers 10, spreading; pedicels to 9 mm. long; sepals very unequal, longest to 11 mm. long, acute, spreading to ascending, deltoid to lanceolate; corolla urceolate, 11 mm. long, 8 mm. in basal diameter, 5 mm. at mouth;
petals not at all keeled, nor hollowed; carpels 7 mm. long; nectaries narrowly
lunate, oblique, 2 mm. wide. Flowers from March on. Description from greenhouse plant.

Color. Leaves spinach-green, not glaucous; peduncle light yellowish olive;
bracts as leaves, but tinged army-brown; pedicels vinaceous-fawn to army-
brown; sepals as bracts; corolla jasper-pink at base, javel-green above; petals
inside javel-green; carpels light lumiere-green; styles apple-green; nectaries light
lumiere-green.

Type. Cultivated by Victor Reiter and collected by E. Walther on 31
March and 5 May 1959, from plants originally collected by E. Walther along
road from Venados to Zacualtipan, Hidalgo, Mexico (CAS, nos. 414603 and
414549).

Collections. Hidalgo, Mexico: barranca walls above Metzquititlan on
road to Zacualtipan, altitude 1,600 to 1,800 m., *Moore, 47/2868* (BH,GH,
US). *Cultivated:* in Victor Reiter's garden from Cumbre de Banco, Hidalgo,
E. Walther, 1 May 1959 (CAS); Golden Gate Park Nursery, *E. Walther,* 22
April 1959 (CAS).

Remarks. Within the series Urceolatae this comes near such other simply
racemose species as *E. hyalina,* with dark gray-green leaves devoid of any glaucous coating. *Echeveria hyalina* differs in having leaves usually rather broader,
with markedly pellucid margins, more turbinate pedicels, and shorter sepals.
Echeveria potosina has grayer leaves distinctly thickened near the apex, corolla
more strongly urceolate, nectaries broader, and both bracts and leaves broader.

In choosing its specific name I desire to express my appreciation of the

Figure 48. 17. *Echeveria sanchez-mejoradae* E. Walther. Flowering plant, × 0.9. Plant photographed in San Diego 16 April 1961; part of the type collection (UCBG 59.403).

hospitality and help extended me by Sr. Hernando Sánchez-Mejorada, during my two visits to Mexico in 1957 and 1959. Without his guidance this novelty might have remained unrecognized for another 10 years.

Figure 49. 17. *Echeveria sanchez-mejoradae* E. Walther. Inflorescence, × 2.0. Plant flowering in San Diego 16 April 1961; part of the type collection (UCBG 59.403).

18. **Echeveria albicans** E. Walther.
(Figures 50–52.)

Echeveria albicans E. WALTHER, Cactus and Succ. Jour. Amer., vol. 30, p. 147, 1958.
Echeveria elegans var. *kesselringiana* POELLNITZ, *in* Fedde Repert., vol. 39, p. 239, 1936.
Echeveria alba Hort. Calif.
ILLUSTRATIONS. Cactus and Succ. Jour. Amer., vol. 30, figs. 82, 83, 1958.

Plants glabrous, conspicuously pruinose; rosettes stemless, ultimately cespitose; leaves closely imbricated, crowded, obovate-oblong, 3 to 5 cm. long, 15 to 25 mm. broad, thick and turgid, thickest just below apex, upcurved, obtuse to truncate, with small, slender, whitish apiculus, not purple-tinged but wholly white, margins scarcely pellucid; inflorescence mostly simple, rarely 2-branched, to 25 cm. tall; peduncle erect or ascending; lower bracts numerous, 8 to 15 mm. long, appressed, occasionally enlarged and aggregated into an aerial rosette, normally lanceolate, acute, with upcurved apiculus; pedicels slender, to 14 mm. long, conspicuously turbinately-thickened below calyx; sepals unequal, strongly connate at base, longest to 10 mm. long, deltoid to linear-oblong, acute to cuspidate, scarcely spreading; corolla broadly conoid to urceolate, 14 to 18 mm. long, 10 to 12 mm. in basal diameter; petals erect or slightly spreading at tips; basal nectar cavity shallow; nectaries narrowly oblong-trapezoid, somewhat obliquely truncate. Flowers from May to August.

Color. Leaves kildare-green, glaucous-pruinose and hence pale olivine; peduncle grape-green and pruinose; corolla begonia-rose or alizarine-pink, to old-

Figure 50.   18. *Echeveria albicans* E. Walther. Flowering plant, × 0.75. Plant photographed in San Diego 25 June 1964; part of the type collection (UCBG 52.1882).

Figure 51. 18. *Echeveria albicans* E. Walther. From the original publication (Cactus and Succulent Journal, volume 30, page 147, figure 82).

rose at base, viridine-yellow to light yellow-green at apex, inside at top oil-yellow; carpels viridine-yellow; styles apple-green; nectaries strontium-yellow.

TYPE. Plants grown in Golden Gate Park, originally received from F. Schmoll, Cadereyta, Mexico (CAS, no. 408987).

OCCURRENCE. Mexico, presumably; without definite locality.

COLLECTIONS. *Cultivated:* Golden Gate Park, San Francisco, *Walther*, type (CAS); clonotype, University of California Botanical Garden, UCBG-52.1882, *P. Hutchison* in 1957 (UC).

REMARKS. This novelty has been cultivated in California collections for some time, and appears identical with those grown in European botanic gardens as *E. elegans* var. *kesselringiana.* Poellnitz' name is of uncertain status, for no type was preserved, and application to our local material seems inadvisable. Plants of *E. elegans* var. *kesselringiana* were raised from seeds sold by H. Winter of Frankfurt a.M. in 1932 *(Ritter 532),* while my material came from a Mexican dealer. I am certain that here we have a distinct species which clearly differs from *E. elegans* in its broader, blunter, thicker leaves that are thickest just above the middle and have a more slender apiculus with less pellucid margins. It also differs in having a more whitish color in its pedicels which usually are more decidedly turbinate below the calyx, in its more unequal strongly ascending sepals, and in a broader, more gibbose, conoid-urceolate corolla to 14 mm. long and to 10 mm. thick in which the petals are scarcely spreading at the greenish tips, and in that the nectaries are broader and obliquely truncate-trapezoid.

Echeveria elegans var. *simulans* has narrower acuminate leaves with a stouter mucro, a cylindroid corolla to 15 mm. long, yellowish at apex, and narrow nectaries; *E. potosina* differs in its longer, narrower, usually purple-tinged leaves, its urceolate corolla 12 mm. to 13 mm. long by 9 mm. in diameter, nectaries obliquely truncate, and finally, in *E. hyalina* the leaves are thinner, have a conspicuously hyaline margin and subtruncate strongly cuspidate-acuminate apex, spreading sepals, a conoid-urceolate corolla 11 mm. by 8 mm., and truncate-oblique nectaries.

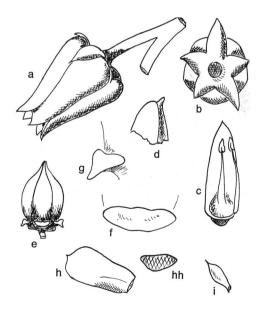

Figure 52. 18. *Echeveria albicans* E. Walther. Explanation: (a) flower × 2; (b) flower from below, × 2; (c) inside of petal, × 2; (d) apex of petal, × 8; (e) carpels, × 2; (f) nectary, front view, × 8; (g) nectary, side view, × 8; (h) leaf, × 0.4; (hh) cross-section of leaf, × 0.4; (i) bract, × 0.8. From the original publication (Cactus and Succulent Journal, volume 30, page 148, figure 83).

19. **Echeveria hyalina** E. Walther.
(Figures 53–54.)

Echeveria hyalina E. WALTHER, Cactus and Succ. Jour. Amer., vol. 30, pp. 43, 44, 1958.
ILLUSTRATIONS. Cactus and Succ. Jour. Amer., vol. 30, figs. 24, 25, 1958.

Glabrous; rosettes stemless, belatedly cespitose; leaves numerous, densely crowded, obovate-cuneate, or sometimes narrower and acuminate, cuspidate, to 6 cm. long and 35 mm. broad, whitish crystalline, rather thin, with sharp, hyaline margins; inflorescence a simple raceme; scape to 30 cm. tall or more, slender, flexuous, ascending; lower bracts linear-oblanceolate, acuminate, to 14 mm. long, appressed; flowers 14 to 20, strongly nodding in bud; pedicels to 10 mm. long, turbinately thickened below calyx, becoming erect after anthesis; sepals very unequal, longest to 5 mm. long, deltoid, spreading, much connate at base; corolla urceolate, scarcely pentagonal, 11 mm. long, 8 mm. in basal diameter; petals slightly spreading at tips; nectaries obliquely reniform. Flowers

Figure 53. 19. *Echeveria hyalina* E. Walther. From the original publication (Cactus and Succulent Journal, volume 30, page 43, figure 24).

January and February. Description from living material found in the garden of Sr. C. Halbinger, Mexico City.

Color. Leaves pale turtle-green, but somewhat glaucous and hence pale medici-blue, at tips usually tinged dark vinaceous-gray; peduncle laelia-pink; sepals buffy-olive; corolla old-rose below, above pale flesh-color, light paris-green at apex, inside bice-green above, to pale pinkish below; carpels pale chalcedony-yellow; styles apple-green; nectaries as the carpels.

TYPE. Cultivated in Golden Gate Park, San Francisco (CAS, no. 234168).

OCCURRENCE. Guanajuato, Mexico.

COLLECTIONS. Mexico. Guanajuato: Santa Rosa de Limon, on road between Guanajuato Gto. and Dolores Hidalgo, *Wiggins,* 55/13225 (DS). *Cultivated:* Golden Gate Park, *Walther,* in 1936, type (CAS); University of California Botanical Garden, UCBG:55.364–1, grown from *Wiggins* no. 13225 (CAS). Wiggins material, as flowered in the University of California Botanical Garden, has a rather smaller corolla, agrees otherwise. In this material $n = 32$.

REMARKS. When first met with in the Mexico City garden of my friend Christian Halbinger, this was thought to be *E. cuspidata*, which differs, however, in having leaves neither crystalline nor hyaline at edges. In this the leaves are also decidedly thinner and distinctly glaucous-pruinose, the sepals are longer and broader, the corolla is longer, and its petals are light coral-red to the apex. Actually*, E. hyalina* appears to be closest to *E. elegans* var. *simulans*, but differs from the latter in its broader leaves more strongly cuspidate at apex, its more spreading sepals, and its corolla greenish at the apex.

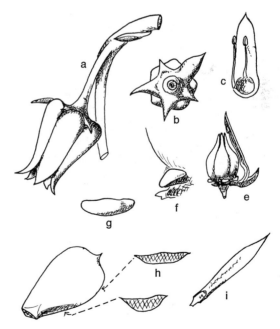

Figure 54. 19. *Echeveria hyalina* E. Walther. Explanation: (a) flower, × 2; (b) flower from below, × 2; (c) inside of petal, × 2; (e) carpels, × 2; (f) nectary, side view, × 8; (g) nectary, front view × 8; (h) leaf with two cross-sections, × 0.4; (i) bract, × 2. From the original publication (Cactus and Succulent Journal, volume 30, page 44, figure 25).

20. **Echeveria gilva** E. Walther.
(Figure 55.)

Echeveria gilva E. WALTHER, Cactus and Succ. Jour. Amer., vol. 7, p. 61, 1935;
POELLNITZ, *in* Fedde Repert., vol. 39, p. 268, 1936.
ILLUSTRATIONS. Cactus and Succ. Jour. Amer., vol. 7, p. 71, 1935.

Rosettes densely cespitose; leaves to 30 or more, obovate-oblong, 5 to 8 cm. long, 20 to 25 mm. broad, thick and turgid, shortly acute and apiculate, somewhat concave above, beneath convex and obscurely keeled near apex, amber-colored, not at all glaucous, of crystalline-appearing texture, edges hyaline; inflorescences two or three, simply racemose, rarely 2-branched, to 25 cm. tall; lower bracts few, linear-lanceolate, acute, outcurved above, 15 to 20 mm. long; flowers about 12; pedicels 5 to 7 mm. long, slender, but turbinately thickened below calyx; sepals deltoid-ovate, acute, the longest to 5 mm. long, ascending-spreading, much connate at base; corolla conoid-urceolate, to 9 mm. long, 7 mm. in basal diameter, scarcely pentagonal; petals somewhat spreading above, thin, basal hollow shallow; nectaries oblique, thin, narrowly trapezoid. Flowers from March on. Description from locally grown plants.

Color. Leaves kildare-green tinged carmine, usually amber-colored in effect, not at all glaucous; peduncle eugenia-red to flesh-pink, pedicels eugenia-red;

Figure 55. 20. *Echeveria gilva* E. Walther. Flowering plant, approximately × 0.4. From the original publication (Cactus and Succulent Journal, volume 7, page 71).

sepals eugenia-red; corolla geranium-pink, petals with keel spectrum-red, inside and at apex light viridine-yellow; styles peacock-green; nectaries nearly white.

TYPE. Cultivated locally (CAS, no. 223895).

OCCURRENCE. Not certainly known, perhaps of garden origin.

REMARKS. The plant here described has been widely cultivated in California gardens. Since no Mexican locality is on record, this may be suspected to be of hybrid origin, a theory supported by information I have from Dr. Uhl of Cornell that meiosis is irregular. As far as I know, no attempt has been made to grow this from seed, which might prove its true nature, and perhaps its parentage.

In leaf color, *E. gilva* resembles *E. agavoides,* but the latter has a branched inflorescence with smaller flowers, more acuminate, broader leaves, and is very slowly soboliferous. If *E. agavoides* should prove to be one parent of this garden plant, attention needs to be called to some hybrids on record.

In the 1870's a French horticulturist, M. Deleuil of Marseilles, raised and named a large number of *Echeveria* hybrids. From his list I selected two, representing crosses with *E. agavoides* as one parent, *i.e., E.* × *aciphylla (E. agavoides* × *E. globosa)* and *E.* × *laetivirens (E. agavoides* × *E. glauca).* He offers no descriptions, so no one can be certain as to whether one of these might not be our *E. gilva,* plants of which somehow found their way to California and have persisted here since.

21. **Echeveria goldiana** E. Walther.
(Figures 56–57.)

Echeveria goldiana E. WALTHER, Cactaceas y Suculentas Mexicanas, vol. 4, p. 27, 1959.
ILLUSTRATIONS. *Loc. cit.,* figs. 15, 16, 1959.

Plant glabrous, stemless, with offsets none or produced belatedly; rosettes densely leafy; leaves to 40 or more, broadly obovate-cuneate, very turgid, beneath rounded and not keeled, above shallowly convex and only slightly flattened near apex, the latter truncate and minutely mucronate, to 4 cm. long, 25 mm. wide near apex, less than 15 mm. broad at base; inflorescences two or three, each a simple, secund raceme; peduncle to 40 cm. tall, slender, erect, with 10 to 12 bracts, these linear-lanceolate, acuminate, flat above, beneath rounded, slightly spreading to recurved, to 14 mm. long; flowers 8 to 10, strongly nodding in bud; pedicels slender, to 15 mm. long, somewhat turbinate below calyx; sepals very unequal, longest to 10 mm. long and lanceolate, the others much shorter, deltoid, acute; corolla conoid-urceolate, 13 mm. long and to 9 mm. broad near base, only 4 mm. in diameter at mouth; petals not keeled and only slightly hollowed within at base, with small, subulate apiculus below tips; carpels 7 mm. long; nectaries to 2 mm. broad, reniform, oblique. Flowers from March on. Description from plants flowering in garden of Victor Reiter, San Francisco.

Color. Leaves lettuce-green, shining, not at all glaucous; peduncle smoke-gray; bracts lettuce-green to light brownish drab, as are the sepals; corolla begonia-rose, near apex viridine-yellow; carpels white; styles cosse-green; nectaries pinard-yellow.

Figure 56.   21. *Echeveria goldiana* E. Walther. From the original publication (Cactáceas y Suculentas Mexicanas, volume 4, page 28, figure 16).

TYPE. From flowering plant collected 11 March 1959, in garden of Victor Reiter in San Francisco, originally found near Valle de Bravo, Estado de Mexico, Mexico, and received from Sr. Dudley B. Gold of Mexico City (CAS, no. 413601, not "413901").

OCCURRENCE. Mexico. Valle de Bravo, Edo. de Mexico.

REMARKS. While this new species clearly belongs in the series Urceolatae, in view of its habit, turgid leaves, thin petals, small nectaries, etc., it stands quite alone in that group by reason of its wholly green leaves, rather long, widely spreading sepals, and conoid corolla. The single plant seen so far was in the private collection of Sr. Dudley B. Gold of Mexico City, who generously donated it for my studies. Sr. Gold, esteemed member of the Sociedad Mexicana de Cactologia, was my host and guide on several most fruitful field trips in Mexico. He is one of the most enthusiastic collectors and students of cacti and succulents that I have ever met, so it has been most proper to dedicate the present novelty to him.

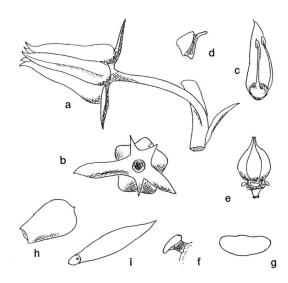

Figure 57. 21. *Echeveria goldiana* E. Walther. Explanation: (a) flower, × 2; (b) flower from below, × 2; (c) inside of petal, × 2; (d) apex of petal, × 8; (e) carpels, × 2; (f) nectary, side view, × 8; (g) nectary, front view × 8; (h) leaf, × 0.4; (i) bract, × 2. From the original publication (Cactáceas y Suculentas Mexicanas, volume 4, page 27, figure 15).

22. **Echeveria halbingeri** E. Walther.

(Figures 58–59. Plate 1, lower; see page 213.)

Echeveria halbingeri E. WALTHER, Cactus and Succ. Jour. Amer., vol. 30, p. 89, 1958.

ILLUSTRATIONS. Cactus and Succ. Jour. Amer., vol. 30, figs. 46, 47, 1958.

Plants glabrous, rather small; rosettes stemless, belatedly cespitose; leaves about 30, densely crowded, thick and turgid, obovate, to 25 mm. long and 13 mm. broad, subtriquetrous in upper half, at apex obtuse but minutely aristate-apiculate; inflorescences two or more, simply racemose; scape to 12 cm. tall, slender, erect or weakly spreading; bracts linear-lanceolate, to 10 mm. long, ascending, triquetrous, sharply keeled, shortly acuminate; flowers six to nine; pedicels 6 mm. long, somewhat turbinate below calyx; sepals unequal, longest 6 mm. long, ascending to rotately spreading at anthesis; corolla about 12 mm. long if one discounts the strongly recurved petal-tips, more or less urceolate-campanulate; petals conspicuously subulate-apiculate at apex, with distinct basal hollow within; nectaries 0.7 mm. wide, narrowly elliptic, very oblique. Flowers from July on. Description from living plants grown at the Strybing Arboretum, Golden Gate Park, San Francisco.

Color. Leaves biscay-green but somewhat glaucous and hence asphodel-green; sepals bice-green to asphodel-green; corolla orange-rufous to deep chrome, inside pale orange; carpels light greenish-yellow; styles oil-yellow; nectaries sulphur-yellow.

TYPE. Plant cultivated in the Strybing Arboretum in Golden Gate Park, San Francisco, and collected 24 July 1941; originally from Hidalgo, Mexico (CAS, no. 289374).

OCCURRENCE. Mexico. Hidalgo: south of Actopan near kilo 104.

COLLECTIONS. Mexico. Hidalgo: south of Actopan, west of highway at kilo 104, El Arenal, summit of red sandstone peak, Cerro de las Canteras; *H. E. Moore,* 46/1542 (GH). Perhaps also: Dist. Pachuca; open meadow in fir forest near Zerezo, below Parque Nacional El Chico, altitude 3,000 m.; *H. E. Moore,* 47/2806 (BH).

REMARKS. In dedicating this to Sr. Christian Halbinger of Mexico City, I wish to recognize the many services and untiring cooperation I have received in organizing my field trips and obtaining plants from various sources. *Echeveria halbingeri* is anomalous in our series Urceolatae by reason of its strongly recurved petal tips, but in other respects, as foliage, nectaries, it has much more in common with *E. elegans* than, say, with *E. secunda.* The recent discovery of *E. halbingeri,* native in Hidalgo, by Dr. H. E. Moore of the Bailey Hortorium, justifies my publication of this from garden material.

Figure 58. 22. *Echeveria halbingeri* E. Walther. From the original publication (Cactus and Succulent Journal, volume 30, page 89, figure 46).

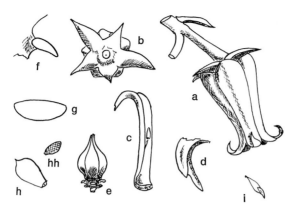

Figure 59. 22. *Echeveria halbingeri* E. Walther. Explanation: (a) flower, × 2; (b) flower from below, × 2; (c) petal, × 2; (d) apex of petal, × 8; (e) carpels, × 2; (f) nectary, side view, × 8; (g) nectary, front view, × 8; (h) leaf, × 0.4; (hh) cross-section of leaf, × 0.4; (i) bract, × 8. From the original publication (Cactus and Succulent Journal, volume 30, page 90, figure 47).

23. **Echeveria pulidonis** E. Walther, new species.
      (Figure 60.)

Echeveria pulidonis E. Walther, sp. nov., pertinens ad ser. Urceolatis, glabra, acaulescens, rosulis simplicibus (semper ?), usque ad 8 cm. diametro; foliis confertis, adscendentibus, oblongo-oblanceolatis, cuneato-attenuatis ad basin, apicibus minutissime mucronatis, turgidis, supra planis, subtus convexis vel carinatis, usque ad 5 cm. longis et 15 mm. latis, viridibus, non glaucis; inflorescentiis valde patentibus vel decumbentibus, usque ad 18 cm. altis, simplicibus, 10-floris; pedunculis tenuibus, 3 mm. crassis basi; bracteis 6, adpressis, lineari-lanceolatis, acutis, usque ad 15 mm. longis; racemis valde nutantibus ante anthesin; pedicellis usque ad 6 mm. longis, turbinatis sub calycibus; sepalis inaequalibus, usque ad 6 mm. longis, patentibus, acutis, deltoideis; corollis valde urceolatis, gibbosis basi, usque ad 10 mm. longis, 8 mm. diametro basi, 8 mm. fauce; petalis citrinis, valde recurvatis apicibus, apice obtuse mucronata, obtuse carinatis, vix excavatis; carpellis 6 mm. longis, pallide viridibus; nectariis usque ad 2.5 mm. latis, tenuibus, valde obliquis.

Plants glabrous; rosettes stemless, solitary at least when young, 8 cm. or more in diameter; leaves numerous, to 25 or more, spreading to ascending, narrowly obovate-oblong to oblong-oblanceolate, long-attenuate to base, turgid, nearly flat above, beneath convex and obscurely keeled, at apex minutely mucronate, to 5 cm. long and 15 mm. broad; inflorescences ascending-spreading to decumbent, to 18 cm. tall; peduncle slender, 3 mm. thick near base, with about six appressed, linear-lanceolate, acute bracts to 15 mm. long; racemes simple, secund, strongly nodding in bud, with 10 or more flowers; pedicels to 6 mm. long, slender but decidedly turbinate below calyx; sepals unequal, longest to 6 mm. long, spreading, deltoid or ovate-deltoid, acute; corolla bluntly pentagonal, strongly urceolate, conical in bud, to 10 mm. long, 8 mm. in diameter near base, 8 mm. at mouth; petals gibbose at base, the apex strongly

out- and recurved, bluntly mucronate, scarcely hollowed within at base; carpels 6 mm. long; nectaries to 2.5 mm. wide, thin, strongly oblique. Flowers
from April on. Description from single plant received from Sr. Miguel Pulido
of Mexico City, 1959.

Color. Leaves bice-green, with edges and mucro morocco-red, not puberulent or glaucous; peduncle dark olive-buff; bracts olivine; corolla lemon-yellow,
both inside and out; carpels chalcedony-yellow below, primrose-yellow above,
as are the nectaries.

TYPE. *E. Walther,* 29 April 1959, from plant in Victor Reiter's collection
(CAS, no. 414555). This plant had been received from Sr. Miguel Pulido of
Mexico City in 1959. Sr. Pulido collected it in Hidalgo, Mexico, at Beristain,
30 kilos from Necaxa on lateral road leading to Zacatlan.

REMARKS. The present novelty is notable because of its bright yellow corolla, a color unusual in the genus *Echeveria,* otherwise known only in *E. lutea*

Figure 60. 23. *Echeveria pulidonis* E. Walther. Flowering plant, natural size. Plant
photographed in San Diego 28 March 1965; probably part of the type collection.

and *E. maculata.* Its closest relation would appear to be *E. halbingeri,* also from Hidalgo, which differs in its shorter, broader, more turgid leaves devoid of any red edges, and its longer, more slender corolla, more orange in color, with subulate mucros at the similarly outcurved tips. Both species have the crystalline texture of their epidermis, even if less prominent than in some other species of the series Urceolatae. I owe my living material to the courtesy of Señor Miguel Pulido of Mexico City, who collected it in its native habitat, and to whom the species is dedicated.

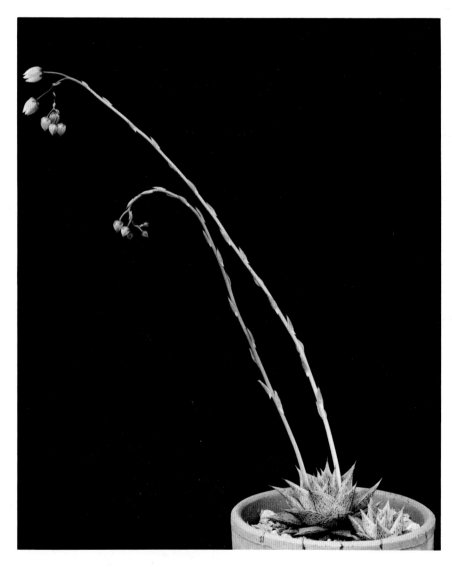

Figure 61. 24. *Echeveria purpusorum* Berger. Flowering plant, × 0.4. Plant photographed in San Diego 20 April 1967; of unknown origin (Moran 12283).

24. **Echeveria purpusorum** Berger.

(Figures 61–64.)

Echeveria purpusorum BERGER, *in* Engler Nat. Pflanzenf, ed. 2, vol. 18a, p. 476, 1930; POELLNITZ, *in* Fedde Repert., vol. 39, p. 259, 1936.

Urbinia purpusii ROSE, Contrib. U.S. Nat. Herb., vol. 13, p. 302, 1911; BRITTON AND ROSE, N. Amer. Fl., vol. 22, p. 541, 1918.

ILLUSTRATION. Van Laren's Succulents, fig. 96, 1934.

Rosettes usually with very short or no stem and without offsets; leaves crowded, thick, and turgid, ovate-acuminate, somewhat recurved at tips, flat

Figure 62.   24. *Echeveria purpusorum* Berger. Rosette with young floral stem, natural size. Plant grown in San Diego; of unknown origin (Moran 12283).

above, rounded beneath, with an evident median keel-line on both surfaces, 3 to 4 cm. long, 2 cm. broad, 1 cm. thick, cuticle unusually thick, epidermal cells opaque, stomata relatively few on both sides; inflorescence simply racemose; scape to 20 cm. tall, erect; lower bracts few, ovate, acute, appressed, thick, to 15 mm. long, with hyaline basal spur; flowers six to nine; pedicels to 12 mm. long; sepals appressed, ovate-deltoid, subequal, acute, their free portion about 2 mm. long; corolla globose-urceolate, to 12 mm. long, greatest diameter 9 mm., about 4 mm. in diameter at mouth at anthesis; petals exceptionally thick for the series Urceolatae, deeply hollowed within at base, but scarcely keeled; nectaries large and thick for the series, truncate-reniform, 2 mm. wide. Flowers May and June. Description from plants cultivated locally.

Color. Leaves spinach-green, but more or less closely marked or spotted brown with numerous scattered cell groups having dark, eugenia-red cell sap; peduncle cinnamon-rufous; bracts as leaves, but more kildare-green; sepals elm-green; corolla rose-doree at base, to scarlet-red above, on outside of tips and within empire-yellow; styles apple-green; stigmas Hays-maroon; nectaries buff-yellow, as is also the corresponding basal portion of the carpels.

Figure 63.   24. *Echeveria purpusorum* Berger. Inflorescence, ×
2. Plant flowering in San Diego 20 April 1967; of unknown origin
(Moran 12283).

TYPE. Collected in southern Mexico by C. A. and J. A. Purpus in 1909 in the Sierra Mixteca, on the border of Oaxaca and Puebla (US, no. 615402).

COLLECTIONS. Mexico. Sierra Mixteca, on border of Oaxaca and Puebla, *C. A. and J. A. Purpus* in 1909 (type). *Cultivated:* Soldena Gardens, Pasadena, *Floyd,* 35 (BH).

REMARKS. In many ways this is one of the most distinctive of any species of *Echeveria.* Its unusual foliage closely simulates that of some South African *Haworthia* of the Liliaceae. As yet we know little about the natural habitat of *E. purpusorum,* but from the xerophytic aspect of the species I assume it to be quite hot and dry.

Cultivated plants are quite uniform, no doubt owing to vegetative propagation from a single original import. Any evident departures from the typical material, as described above, may be suspected to be due to garden hybridization, whether accidental or intentional. Numerous hybrids are listed, as by Berger, Gossot, and Poellnitz.

No comparisons are required here, for this species stands quite alone in its curiously mottled leaves, very small sepals, quite globose, scarlet corolla, and large nectaries.

Figure 64. 24. *Echeveria purpusorum* Berger. From an article by Eric Walther (American Horticultural Magazine, volume 39, page 88).

Series 3. SECUNDAE (Baker) Berger

Echeveria, ser. Secundae (Baker) BERGER, in Engler, Nat. Pflanzenf. ed. 2, vol. 18a, p. 473, 1930; E. WALTHER, Cactus and Succ. Jour. Amer., vol. 7, p. 70, 1935; E. WALTHER, Leafl. Bot., vol. 9, pp. 2, 4, 1959.
Cotyledon, Secundae BAKER in Saunders Refug. Bot., vol. 1, Analytical Table, [p. 1], 1869.

Plants glabrous, small to medium-sized; rosettes usually cespitose, dense, stem short or none; leaves many, crowded, thinnish or slightly turgid, 3 to 17 cm. long, mostly somewhat glaucous, rarely wholly green; inflorescences secund-racemose, usually simple, rarely 2-branched; peduncle slender, erect; bracts mostly few, small, narrow, acute, appressed; pedicels evident, bractless, mostly slender, elongated, not turbinate; sepals unequal, spreading to ascending, longest at least half as long as corolla; corolla 8 to 16 mm. long, somewhat pentagonal, straight or urceolate; petals slightly spreading at tips, hollowed within at base; styles greenish; nectaries thick, broadly truncate.

TYPICAL SPECIES. *Echeveria secunda* Booth.

REMARKS. Baker included two species of *Pachyphytum,* as well as *Echeveria bracteolata* and *E. strictiflora,* in his series Secundae. After elimination of these extraneous elements, the remaining species with the several recent additions constitute a quite natural group. The series Secundae connects the series Urceolatae, on the one hand, with the series Angulatae, Retusae, and Gibbiflorae, on the other. The simple racemes, long pedicels, and subangular corolla are distinctive.

Chromosome numbers for *n* range from 26 to 30 and 32.

I have seen most members of this series in their native habitat, and have had all of them in cultivation under substantially uniform conditions. The key characters here utilized appear the best available, but further field collecting may yet yield intermediate forms making possible reduction of some of these "species" to varieties.

KEY TO THE SPECIES

A. Leaves deep green, not at all glaucous. . . . . 35. *E. byrnesii*
A. Leaves always more or less glaucous, pruinose or gray-green.
  B. Leaves 6 cm. long or less; corolla scarcely over 13 mm. long.
    C. Pedicels to 12 mm. long; sepals to more than half as long as corolla, widely spreading; leaves turgid to edges. Viesca, Coahuila. . . . . . . 31. *E. turgida*
    C. Pedicels 4 to 10 mm. long, rarely longer; sepals less than half the length of the corolla; leaves either thickened in middle, or with thin edges.
      D. Leaves rather thick, especially at midline, usually distinctly keeled beneath, concave above, at apex mucronate to acute or acuminate.
        E. Leaves gradually tapering to the acute or acuminate apex, greenish or at most slightly glaucous; pedicels sometimes over 10 mm. long.
          F. Inflorescence mostly 2-branched, rarely simple; corolla 10 mm. long; nectaries not over 1 mm. broad; leaves flat above, at apex straight, acuminate. . . . . 29. *E. meyraniana*
          F. Inflorescence usually simple, unbranched; corolla 13 mm. long or more; nectaries larger; leaves more or less concave above, at apex more or less upcurved.
            G. Leaves less deeply concave, less upcurved at the acute apex; pedicels over 15 mm. long; sepals ascending. . . . . . 25. *E. secunda*
            G. Leaves conspicuously concave and acuminate with apex upcurved; pedicels about 6 mm. long; sepals widely spreading.
                28. *E. cornuta*

E. Leaf apex abruptly rounded or truncate, mucronate to shortly cuspidate; leaves more or less glaucous; pedicels long or short.

    F. Peduncle strict, erect, at times to over 30 cm. tall; pedicels often short; sepals ascending; corolla straight, cylindroid-pentagonal, the petals erect.

            26. *E. elatior*

    F. Peduncle laxly ascending, to 20 cm. tall; pedicels to 10 mm. long or more; sepals widely spreading; corolla conoid, the petals connivent.

            27. *E. reglensis*

  D. Leaves thinnish, sharp-edged, scarcely keeled, flat or nearly so, at apex acute or mucronate. . . . . 30. *E. pumila*

    E. Leaves oblanceolate-cuneate, acute, rarely over 15 mm. broad.

            30a. *E. pumila* var. *pumila*

    E. Leaves obovate-cuneate, apex rounded or truncate and mucronate, to 2 cm. broad. . . . . 30b. *E. pumila* var. *glauca*

B. Leaves mostly longer, over 5 cm. long; corolla often over 13 mm. long.

  C. Leaves relatively broad, less than 4 times as long as wide, at apex acute or mucronate; rosettes freely offsetting.

    D. Leaves many, crowded, at apex rounded or truncate, mucronate.

            34. *E. alpina*

    D. Leaves relatively fewer, laxly rosulate, at apex deltoid-acute or shortly acuminate-cuspidate.

      E. No sepal more than one third as long as corolla. South of Saltillo, Coahuila.

            32. *E. cuspidata*

      E. Longest sepals half as long as corolla or longer. Toluca. 33. *E. tolucensis*

  C. Leaves relatively long and narrow, apex acuminate; rosettes sparingly cespitose.

    D. Leaves oblanceolate-linear, scarcely over 20 mm. broad, flat, glaucous, normally red only at tips; corolla 12 mm. long or less. Mt. Orizaba.

            36. *E. subalpina*

    D. Leaves oblong-oblanceolate, 25 to 40 mm. broad, concave above, red-edged; corolla 14 to 18 mm. long. . . . . . . 37. *E. lozani* (ser. 4, Retusae)

25. **Echeveria secunda** Booth.

(Figure 65.)

Echeveria secunda BOOTH, Miscell. Notices *in* Edward's Bot. Reg., vol. 24 (new ser., vol. 1), p. 59, 1838; BRITTON AND ROSE, N. Amer. Fl., vol. 22, p. 22, 1905; POELLNITZ, *in* Fedde Repert., vol. 39, p. 243, 1936.
Echeveria spilota KUNZE, Hort. Hal., 1853, p. 20.
Cotyledon secunda BAKER *in* Saunders Refug. Bot., vol. 1, no. 14, sub pl. 60, 1869.
ILLUSTRATIONS. Bot. Reg., vol. 26 (new ser., vol. 3), pl. 57, 1840; Maund's Bot. Gard., vol. 13, no. 1167.

Description by Booth, *loc. cit.:* E. secunda; foliis rosulato-confertis cuneatis mucronatis pinguibus glaucis, racemo secundo recurvo, floribus longe pedunculatis.

"Stem very short, creeping. Leaves numerous, concave, spathulate, and spreading, sessile, thick and fleshy, crowded, and loosely arranged round the stem as a common axis. With the exception of a few in the center, which are much smaller than the others, the whole are similar in size and form, varying from 2 to 2½ inches in length, and rather more than 1 inch in breadth at the widest part near the apex, from which they gradually taper toward the base, and end at the point in a small mucro. Their color is a glaucescent green, covered with a fine bloom, which easily rubs off on being touched. The outer edges and mucro have a brownish tinge. Flower stem round, about a foot high, glaucous pink, rising from one side of the mass of leaves, and terminating in a unilateral, deflexed, raceme, of about 10 or 12 flowers. Bracteas small and fleshy, ovate-acuminate, tinged with pink at the point. Pedicels of the earlier flowers about an inch long, or less, diminishing gradually both in size and length

Figure 65. 25. *Echeveria secunda* Booth. Flowering plant, slightly reduced. Plant grown at the Royal Horticultural Society, London; received from Sir Charles Lemon, who was also the source of the type plant. From an article by J. Lindley (Edwards's Botanical Register, volume 26, plate 57). This plate is designated neotype for the species.

towards the extremity of the raceme. Taking the point where they join the stem, as a centre, it will be found that each pedicel forms, as near as possible, an angle of about 33 degrees with the stem. Calyx five-leaved, rotate, spreading, the segments thick and fleshy, lanceolate, acute. Tube upwards of half an inch in length, gibbous at the base, which is a bright yellowish red, narrowing upwards to the mouth, which is acutely five-toothed, a little recurved, and of a deep yellow. Filaments 10, five attached half way down the petals, and the other five at the base opposite each division of the calyx, but all of the same length. Anthers erect, deep yellow. Styles five, short, and compressed together, pale, shining green. Ovarium five-celled, with numerous seeds in each, and having a small fleshy process at the base, intermediate with the segments of the calyx.

"Plants of this curious succulent were received by Sir Charles Lemon, Bart., M.P., in 1837, and again in 1838, from Mr. John Rule, Superintendent of the Real del Monte Mines in Mexico, of which country it is believed to be a native. Treated like other succulents, in a pot of coarse gravelly soil, and subjected to a high temperature, with very little water, it has been found to thrive very well, and flowered in the stove at Carclew in June, 1838."

Color-notes, from plate 57, volume 26, Botanical Register, 1840. Leaves fluorite-green, edges and mucro deep corinthian-red; peduncle cinnamon; corolla old-rose; at apex pinard-yellow.

TYPE. None designated. Neotype: Botanical Register, volume 26, plate 57, 1840.

OCCURRENCE. Mexico. Hidalgo; mountains east of Pachuca, etc.

COLLECTIONS. Mexico. Hidalgo: Pachuca, *Purpus,* 05/206 (NY); Sierra de Pachuca, *Rose,* 01/626–260 (US). *Cultivated:* Berger Herb., 1931/50 (NY); *A. Berger* (drawing, NY); Herb. C. Bumps no. 82 (BR).

REMARKS. Of special interest as the first member of the series Secundae to become known, *E. secunda* is a name often misapplied to related forms. Whatever the ultimate status of the latter, here we must clearly define typical *E. secunda,* as follows: leaves thickish, especially at the strongly keeled center line, but with thin, sharp edges, concave above, at apex acute or strongly mucronate, 5 cm. long or less, only slightly glaucous; pedicels to 15 mm. long; sepals less than half the length of the corolla; corolla not over 13 mm. long.

I made special efforts to find typical *E. secunda* near Real del Monte, without being able to match Booth's species exactly. Nearest approaches to his plant are *E. elatior* and *E. cornuta.* The first of these grows quite near Real del Monte, but differs from typical *E. secunda* in its leaf apex (abruptly rounded or truncate, mucronate to cuspidate), its more glaucous leaves, and its shorter pedicels. *Echeveria cornuta* from northern Hidalgo has leaves with a strongly acuminate, upcurved apex, pedicels about 6 mm. long and sepals widely spreading.

As more field collections, preferably of living material, become available, my knowledge of the true relationships of these forms will become more accurate.

26. **Echeveria elatior** E. Walther.

(Figure 66.)

Echeveria elatior E. WALTHER, Cactus and Succ. Jour. Amer., vol. 7, p. 72, 1935.
ILLUSTRATIONS. Cactus and Succ. Jour. Amer., vol. 7, p. 71, 1935; vol. 6, p. 165 figs. 4, 5, 1935 (habitat).

Rosettes cespitose, with numerous offsets; leaves glaucous, to 45 mm. long and 22 mm. broad, turgid, thickest at midline and there somewhat keeled, obovate-cuneate, apex rounded and mucronate, somewhat concave above; inflorescences two or three, simply secund-racemose; peduncle straight, erect, to 30 cm. tall or more; bracts few, obovate-acute, appressed, to 15 mm. long; flowers 9 to 12; pedicels relatively short, often only 4 mm. long, more rarely to over 10 mm. long; sepals ascending, less than half as long as corolla, subequal, longest 6 mm. long, deltoid-ovate, acute; corolla straight, cylindroid-pentagonal, 11 to 12 mm. long, 7 mm. in basal diameter; petals only slightly spreading at tips; stigmas elongated; nectaries oblique, 1.5 mm. wide or less. Flowers from June on.

Color. Leaves parrot-green, but dark greenish glaucous with bloom; peduncle dark vinaceous to corinthian-pink; bracts serpentine-green, glaucous, at tips dragon's-blood-red; sepals mytho-green; corolla scarlet, rose-doree at base, empire-yellow at tips; petals inside empire-yellow; carpels martius-yellow; styles lettuce-green; nectaries pale greenish yellow.

TYPE. Plant cultivated in Golden Gate Park, San Francisco, from El Chico near Pachuca, Hidalgo, Mexico, where it was collected in October 1934, by E. Walther (CAS, no. 292475, *not* no. "223899" as given in the original publication).

OCCURRENCE. Mexico. Hidalgo: Sierra de Pachuca, Pueblo Nuevo, Peña del Cuervo, Peñas Ventano, etc.

COLLECTIONS. Mexico. Hidalgo: Sierra de Pachuca, *Pringle* 98/2256 (MEXU), *Rose and Haugh,* 99/4458 (US), *Rose and Painter,* 03/737 (US); National Park, eight miles east of Pachuca, *Hitchcock and Stanford,* 40/7234 (US), *Rose,* 01/626–260 (US); fir forest near Zereyo, Parque Nacional El Chico, *Moore,* 47/2806 (GH); southwest of Pachuca, southeast of Epazoyucan, *Moore,* 47/3061 (GH). *Cultivated:* Golden Gate Park, San Francisco, from El Chico near Pachuca, *Walther,* 34/10 (type); drawing by A. Berger in 1906 from a plant from Pachuca, *Purpus,* 05/206, cultivated at La Mortola.

REMARKS. *Echeveria elatior* appears amply distinct in its blunt grayish glaucous leaves, tall erect peduncle, short pedicels, ascending sepals, and straight corolla with erect petals. I retain it as a distinct species, to clearly elucidate the variations of several closely related forms revolving around the classical *E. secunda.*

Figure 66. 26. *Echeveria elatior* E. Walther. Flowering plant, approximately × 0.2. From the original publication (Cactus and Succulent Journal, volume 7, page 71).

The natural habitat of *E. elatior* is on rocky pinnacles that rise from a dense forest of pine, fir, cypress, and juniper, where summer rains are abundant and winter frosts common. Growing nearby were *Sedum confusum, S. moranense, S. diversifolium, Fuchsia minutiflora*, and *Penstemon campanulatus*. In cultivation at the Strybing Arboretum, Golden Gate Park, San Francisco, this species has proven quite successful.

27. **Echeveria reglensis** E. Walther, new species.

Echeveria reglensis E. Walther, sp. nov., similis *E. secundae,* sed foliis saepe obtuso-truncatis mucronatis, sepalis patentibus; planta glabra acaulescens, caespitosa; foliis glaucescentibus, 35–50 mm. longis, 18–22 mm. latis, obovato-cuneatis, crassis, margine tenuibus, paulo carinatis; pedunculis usque ad 20 cm. altis; pedicellis 8–10 mm. longis; sepalis usque ad 8 mm. longis; corolla 12–13 mm. longa, conoidea, petalis conniventibus.

Rosettes stemless, freely soboliferous, densely leafy; leaves 25 or more, upcurved, thick, concave above, rounded beneath and faintly keeled, obovate-cuneate, abruptly rounded to the cuspidate-mucronate apex, 35 to 50 mm. long, 18 to 22 mm. broad, more or less glaucous; inflorescences two to three, simple, secund-racemose; peduncle slender, often laxly ascending, to 20 cm. tall; bracts few, often only three, oblong-obovate, acute, appressed, 15 mm. long or less; flowers 6 to 12; pedicels 8 to 10 mm. long or more; sepals widely spreading, subequal, longest to 8 mm. long, ovate-deltoid to lanceolate, acute; corolla conoid-urceolate, bluntly pentagonal, 12 to 13 mm. long, 8 to 9 mm. in basal diameter, but often only 4 to 7 mm. in diameter at mouth; petals erect or slightly connivent, somewhat spreading at tips; nectaries transversely elliptic, 2 mm. wide. Flowers from June on. Description from plants grown in Golden Gate Park, San Francisco.

Color. Leaves bice-green, with bloom deep glaucous-green, mucro deep hellebore-red; peduncle testaceous; bracts mignonette-green tinged vinaceous-fawn; sepals as leaves; corolla scarlet, rose-doree at base, petal tips apricot-yellow, inside ochraceous-orange to apricot-yellow; styles chrysolite-green.

Type. Santa Maria Regla, Hidalgo, Mexico, *E. Walther* in October 1934 (CAS, no. 234663).

Occurrence. Mexico. Hidalgo: Santa Maria Regla, on basalt-columns below waterfall; still extant in 1957.

Remarks. This new species differs from typical *E. secunda* in its abruptly rounded leaf apex, the more glaucous leaves, widely spreading sepals, and connivent petals. Comparisons of this with other relatives of *E. secunda* are all based on plants in cultivation growing under quite similar conditions.

28. **Echeveria cornuta** E. Walther, new species.

Echeveria cornuta E. Walther, sp. nov., pertinens ad ser. Secundas; glabra, acaulescens, caespitosa; foliis viridibus vel paulum glaucescentibus, crassis, valde convexis subtus, apice cornutis, acuminatis; inflorescentiis simplicibus, secundifloris; pedicellis usque ad 6 mm. longis; sepalis patentibus; corollis usque ad 13 mm. longis, conoideo-urceolatis, rubris.

Rosettes cespitose, densely leafy; leaves upcurved, oblanceolate to obovate-cuneate, distinctly acuminate with hornlike apex, rounded beneath and somewhat keeled, concave above, thick and fleshy, to 5 cm. long and 22 mm. broad, scarcely glaucous; inflorescences to five or more, simple, secund-racemose, to 30 cm. tall; bracts obovate-oblong, subtriquetrous, keeled, apex with hooked mucro, to 2 cm. long; racemes with 12 or more flowers; pedicels about 6 mm. long; sepals unequal, longest 6 mm. long, ovate-deltoid, acute, widely spreading or even somewhat reflexed in cultivated plants; corolla conoid-urceolate, to 13 mm. long and 9 mm. in basal diameter; petals slightly spreading at tips; nectaries truncate, transversely reniform. Flowers from June on.

Color. Leaves above light cress-green, slightly glaucous, beneath kildaregreen; peduncle deep corinthian-red; bracts as the leaves, but tinged pompeianred; sepals as the bracts, but even more deeply brownish vinaceous; corolla coral- to jasper-red; petals at edges apricot-yellow; styles cosse-green; nectaries buff-yellow.

Type. Collected 15 miles southwest of Jacala, Hidalgo, Mexico, *Hitchcock and Stanford,* 40/6983 (US, no. 1820940).

Paratype. Dist. Zimapan, between Encarnación and Mt. Caugandho, *Moore and Wood,* 48/4356 (BH).

Occurrence. Mexico. Northern Hidalgo, etc.

Remarks. Of the several plants collected alive in Hidalgo, the present ones come closer perhaps than any other to *E. secunda* Booth, as described by Booth and pictured in the Botanical Register, volume 26, plate 57, 1840. However, it appears to differ in the strongly hooked tips of the rather narrower thicker leaves, uncinate bracts, shorter pedicels, and the more widely spreading sepals. The plants I found in 1935 were growing along the trail leading from the International Highway north of Zimapan, to the village of Encarnacion. With the fog lingering among the pines and oaks, and a cool breeze blowing, the scene here had a San Francisco and very home-like aspect. The plants unfortunately became lost before a type specimen could be preserved, so that only now can I publish this species. No further collections are known to me beyond the types listed above.

29. Echeveria meyraniana E. Walther.
(Figures 67–68.)

Echeveria meyraniana E. WALTHER, Cactaceas y Suculentas Mexicanas, vol. 4, p. 29, 1959.
ILLUSTRATIONS. Cactaceas y Suculentas Mexicanas, vol. 4, pp. 29, 30, figs. 17, 18, 1959.

Plant glabrous, stemless, cespitose; leaves numerous, densely rosulate, variable in shape, broadly obovate to oblong-oblanceolate, to 65 mm. long, 20 mm. broad or more, acuminate at the upcurved apex, above nearly flat. below rounded and distinctly keeled; inflorescences several, to 15 cm. tall, usually 2-branched; branches secund-racemose, each with about 11 flowers; peduncle slender, erect; its bracts seven or eight, readily detached, appressed, ovate, subtriquetrous, uncinate-mucronate, keeled beneath, to 14 mm. long; pedicels very slender, to 7 mm. long and 1 mm. in diameter; sepals ascendingspreading, subequal, longest to 5 mm. long, deltoid to linear, shortly acuminate; corolla bluntly pentagonal, cylindroid-urceolate, about 10 mm. long, 8 mm. in basal diameter, 6 mm. wide at mouth; petals narrow, with distinct basal hollow and acute, outcurved apex; carpels 8 mm. long; nectaries small, 1 mm. broad, transversely reniform, obliquely truncate. Flowers from February on.

Color. Leaves grass-green to Rinneman's-green, but more or less glaucous; peduncle terracotta; bracts as the leaves; sepals pois-green; corolla begonia-rose to peach-red, inside deep-chrome; carpels neva-green above.

TYPE. Limestone hill across road from Laguna de Alchichica; living plant collected 4 January 1959, flowered in Victor Reiter's garden in San Francisco, *E. Walther* in 1959 (CAS, no. 413900).

OCCURRENCE. Mexico. Eastern Puebla: so far known only from the type locality.

REMARKS. Obviously this species is closely related to *E. subalpina, E. secunda,* and an as yet unpublished species from northern Hidalgo, all of which have rather narrow, long-pointed leaves that are distinctly keeled beneath. It differs, however, in its usually 2-branched raceme, smaller corolla, tiny nectaries, and different leaves. Its leaves are never as long and narrow as those of *E. subalpina,* native not so many miles to the south of Citlaltepetl.

The type locality is a rather dry and sunny limestone hill, just across the highway from the deep-blue lagoon of Alchichica. On the hill in question, *E. meyraniana* grows with *Sedastrum pachucense* and species of *Villadia, Altamiranoa, Agave,* and *Ephedra,* and also with *Echeveria amoena.* Here is a further addition to the list of *Echeveria* species which occur in nature in pairs; and in this case they would seem to have the same flowering season too. Know-

Figure 67. 29. *Echeveria meyraniana* E. Walther. From the original publication (Cactáceas y Suculentas Mexicanas, volume 4, page 30, figure 18).

ing the readiness with which nearly all species of *Echeveria* will intercross in gardens, the question arises whether they do so here, and if not, why not. The plants appeared to be quite abundant, with ample reproduction evidenced by the numerous young seedlings, and were just coming into flower. The readily detached bracts are unusual in the series Secundae, and the corolla is the smallest I have encountered in this group. The inflorescence represents the sole instance where this is 2-branched in this series, and the nectaries are unusually small.

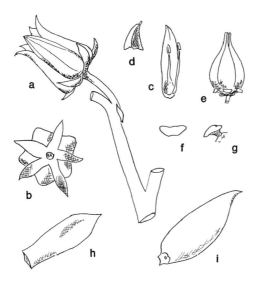

Figure 68. 29. *Echeveria meyraniana* E. Walther. Explanation: (a) flower, × 2; (b) flower from below, × 2; (c) inside of petal, × 2; (d) apex of petal, × 8; (e) carpels, × 2; (f) nectary, front view, × 8; (g) nectary, side view, × 8; (h) leaf, × 0.4; (i) bract, × 2. From the original publication (Cactáceas y Suculentas Mexicanas, volume 4, page 29, figure 17).

30. **Echeveria pumila** Van Houtte.
(Figures 69–71.)

Echeveria pumila Van Houtte, Catalogue, 1846; Schlechtendal, Hort. Hal., vol. 3, p. 20, 1853; Britton and Rose, N. Amer. Fl., vol. 22, p. 21, 1905.
Cotyledon pumila (Van Houtte) Baker, *in* Saunders Refug. Bot. vol. 1, pl. 62, 1869.
Echeveria secunda var. *pumila* (Van Houtte) Otto, Hamb. Gartenztg., vol. 29, p. 9, 1873.
Echeveria glauca var. *pumila* (Van Houtte) Poellnitz, *in* Fedde Repert., vol. 39, p. 246, 1936.
Illustrations. Saunders Refug. Bot., vol. 1, pl. 62, 1869.

Stemless, freely stoloniferous, ultimately forming large clumps; leaves many, crowded, relatively narrow, 5 cm. long or less, scarcely over 14 mm. broad, oblanceolate-cuneate, thinnish and flaccid, but slightly thickened and faintly keeled on midline, at apex deltoid-acute to shortly acuminate, glaucous; inflorescences several, 10 to 15 cm. tall; peduncle slender, ascending-erect; bracts

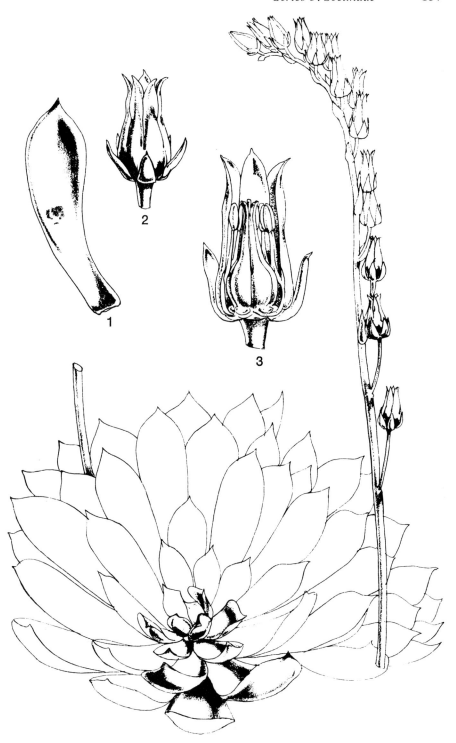

Figure 69. 30. *Echeveria pumila* Van Houtte. Leaf stated to be and flowering plant evidently also natural size; flowers enlarged. Plant grown by W. W. Saunders in Reigate, England; received "from Mons. Van Houtte, of Ghent, many years since." From Baker's monograph (Saunders Refugium Botanicum, volume 1, plate 62). This plate is designated neotype for the species.

few, linear, subtriquetrous, appressed, acute, about 10 mm. long; pedicels 6 mm. long or more; sepals subequal, erect to spreading, deltoid-lanceolate, acute, longest 8 mm. long; corolla cylindroid-urceolate, 10 to 13 mm. long to 7 mm. in diameter near base; petals erect, somewhat spreading at tips. Flowers from June to August. Description based upon material long cultivated locally.

Color. Leaves lettuce-green but glaucous and so glaucous-green; peduncle and pedicels carmine in sun; bracts ecru-olive, to deep corinthian-red at apex; sepals terracotta; corolla scarlet-red, petals lemon-chrome at apex and inside; styles parrot-green.

TYPE. None designated. Neotype: Saunders Refugium Botanicum, volume 1, plate 62, 1869.

OCCURRENCE. Mexico.

COLLECTIONS. *Cultivated:* New York Bot. Gard., *Rose,* 04/11036 (UC); Golden Gate Park, San Francisco, *E. Walther* in 1928 (CAS); North Warren, Pa., *Moldenke,* 43/15067 (BH).

REMARKS. It should be noted that the differences cited are retained in cultivated plants, grown under identical conditions, whether propagated from seeds or divisions. In its narrow leaves, *E. pumila* points to another high mountain species, *E. subalpina* from Mt. Orizaba, but there the leaves are much longer and narrower; and the rosettes are at most sparingly cespitose.

30b. Echeveria pumila var. **glauca** (Baker) E. Walther, new combination.
(Figures 70–71.)

> *Echeveria pumila* var. *glauca* (Baker) E. WALTHER, comb. nov.
> *Cotyledon glauca* BAKER, *in* Saunders Refug. Bot., vol. 1, pl. 61, 1869.
> *Echeveria secunda* var. *glauca* (Baker) OTTO, Hamb. Gartenztg., vol. 29, p. 9, 1873.
> *Echeveria glauca* (Baker) ED. MORREN, La Belg. Hort., vol. 24, p. 161, 1874; BRITTON AND ROSE, N. Amer. Fl., vol. 22, p. 21, 1905; POELLNITZ, *in* Fedde Repert., vol. 39, p. 246, 1936.
> *Echeveria globosa* Hort.
> ILLUSTRATIONS. Saunders Refug. Bot., vol. 1, pl. 61, 1869; Schumann-Rümpler, Sukk., fig. 43; Cactus and Succ. Jour. Amer., vol. 7, p. 167, fig. 11, 1936; Bailey Cycl. Hort., vol. 1, p. 869, fig. 1083, 1927. (as *Cotyledon secunda*).

Rosettes densely cespitose, forming large clusters; leaves numerous, crowded, glaucous, to 5 cm. long, 2 cm. broad, broadly obovate-spathulate, strongly deltoid-mucronate to shortly acuminate, thin to the very edge, flaccid, scarcely or not keeled; inflorescences one or two, simple, secund-racemose, to 15 cm. tall; peduncle slender, ascending to erect; bracts about five, obovate-oblong, to 15 mm. long, acute, slightly spreading; flowers 10 to 12; pedicels to 6 mm. long; sepals unequal, longest 6 mm. long, ascending, turgid, deltoid-ovate, acute; corolla cylindroid-urceolate, pentagonal, rather narrow, to 12 mm. long and 8 mm. in basal diameter; nectaries transversely reniform, to 1¾ mm. wide. Flowers from June on. Description of living material grown in Golden Gate Park, San Francisco, originally from Peñas Cosas, Mexico, D. F.

Color. Leaves cerro-green to dark greenish glaucous, often decidedly pruinose, rarely edged and tipped red; peduncle eugenia-red, to alizarine-pink with bloom; bracts grape-green with nopal-red apex; sepals vetiver-green, tinged army-brown; corolla rose-doree at base, scarlet-red at center, empire-yellow above and on inside; styles lettuce-green; nectaries pale sulphur-yellow.

TYPE. K *ex* Hooker Herb. no. 101, 1856.

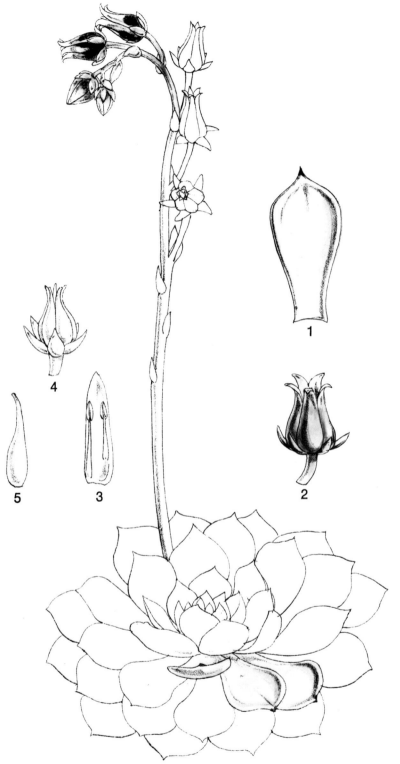

Figure 70. 30b. *Echeveria pumila* Van Houtte var. *glauca* (Baker) E. Walther. Leaf stated to be and flowering plant evidently also natural size; flower and parts enlarged. Plant grown by W. W. Saunders in Reigate, England; received "from Mons. Van Houtte's nursery at Ghent." From the original publication of *Cotyledon glauca* Baker (Saunders Refugium Botanicum, volume 1, plate 61).

Figure 71. 30b. *Echeveria pumila* var. *glauca* (Baker) E. Walther. From an article by Eric Walther (American Horticultural Magazine, volume 39, page 88).

OCCURRENCE. Mexico. Valley of Mexico, Federal District, etc. Serrania de Ajusco, Peñas Cosas, Zempoala Lakes, Popocatepetl. Puebla: Hda. Moria.

COLLECTIONS. Mexico. Federal District: Moulin de Belem, *Bourgeau,* 1865/48 (GH,P); Serrania de Ajusco, *Pringle,* 98/6865 (BR,G,GH,MEXU, PH,UC,US,W), *Matuda,* 50/1921 (F,UC); Santa Fe, *Rose,* 01/624 (MEXU, UC), *Rose,* /920 (GH), *Rose and Painter,* 03/6546 (US), *Carlos Reiche,* 1914 (MEXU); Valley of Mexico, Guadalupe, *Rose and Haugh,* 99/4537 (NY); Zempoala, *L. K. Langman,* 40/2655 (PH); Ixtaccihuatl, *Purpus,* 03/R: 607 (US), near timberline, *Purpus,* 03/R: 605 (US), *Purpus,* 03/R: 604 (US), *Rose,* 05/857 (US). Puebla: Hda. Moria, *Br. Nicolas,* 1910/ (P); Guadalupe, *Br. Nicolas,* 1917/ (P). Without locality: *Hooker,* 1856/101 (K). *Cultivated:* El Salvador, *Salvador Calderon,* 25/2299 (US).

REMARKS. *Echeveria pumila* var. *glauca* differs clearly from *E. secunda* in its thinner, more glaucous, distinctly flaccid leaves; from *E. alpina* and *E. tolu-*

censis in its smaller size, both of leaves and flowers, from var. *pumila* in its broader leaves, and from *E. turgida* in its thin-edged leaves.

This is an old inhabitant of gardens, both here and elsewhere, and has been much used for formal designs, etc. In colder areas the plants are lifted in the fall and stored in cellars or cold-frames where they will escape freezing. This species is surprisingly hardy, ascending to over 10,000 feet altitude in nature, where it always occurs on cliffs and rocks, usually in shade of pines. While in the winter its habitat may become quite dry, in summer there is frequent and ample rainfall.

Of numerous reported hybrids having this for one parent, the best known is undoubtedly *E.* 'Imbricata,' raised by Deleuil of Marseilles in the 1870's, and probably the most widely cultivated *Echeveria.* It is often misnamed either *E. glauca, E. globosa,* or *E. secunda,* but differs from all of these in being larger and in the purplish tinge of its foliage, a heritage from *E. gibbiflora* var. *metallica,* its other parent. Of similar parentage is *E.* 'Glauco-Metallica,' differing in its laxer rosettes with fewer leaves.

A form with a fasciated stem and crested foliage is sometimes grown, under the name *E. glauca* var. *cristata.*

31. **Echeveria turgida** Rose.
(Figure 72.)

Echeveria turgida Rose, *in* Britton and Rose, N. Amer. Fl., vol. 22, p. 21, 1905; op. cit., vol. 22, p. 538, 1918; J. A. Purpus, Monatscht. Kakteenk., vol. 17, p. 148, 1907; Poellnitz, *in* Fedde Repert., vol. 39, p. 243, 1936.
Illustrations. Monatscht. Kakteenk., vol. 17, p. 149, 1907; Moeller's Deutsche Gartenztg., vol. 26, p. 80, 1911.

Rosettes stemless, becoming cespitose; leaves numerous, crowded, upcurved to apex, flat, evenly turgid to the edges, slightly convex beneath but only faintly keeled just below apex, oblong-cuneate, at apex truncate and mucronate, to 5 cm. long and 25 mm. broad; inflorescences two to four, simply secund-racemose; peduncle erect-ascending, to 20 cm. tall, 2 to 3 mm. thick below; bracts few, appressed, oblong-ovate, acute, to 10 mm. long; flowers to 10 or more; pedicels slender, to 12 mm. long; sepals unequal, longest to 10 mm. long, widely spreading, deltoid- to linear-lanceolate, acute; corolla cylindroid-conical, to 12 mm. long, 7 mm. in basal diameter; petals slightly spreading at tips; nectaries lunate, to 2 mm. wide. Flowers from April on. Description from material long cultivated in California gardens.

Color. Leaves biscay-green, strongly pruinose, at edges and mucro Haysrusset; peduncle corinthian-red above; bracts light bice-green, to light jasperred at tips; sepals as the bracts; corolla geranium-pink; petals deep-chrome within; styles light viridine-yellow.

Type. Collected near Viesca, Coahuila, Mexico, *C. A. Purpus,* 04/R-05.962 (US, no. 399652); Walpole nos.107, 108, unpublished.

Occurrence. Mexico. Coahuila; Viesca, not known from any other locality.

Collections. Mexico. Coahuila; Viesca, *Purpus,* 04/R-05.962 (type, US). *Cultivated:* Strybing Arboretum, Golden Gate Park, San Francisco, from Mrs. Dodson, *E. Walther* in 1958 (CAS); Soldena, *Floyd,* 36/ (BH).

Remarks. Plants grown in California agree perfectly with Walpole's water-

Figure 72.   31. *Echeveria turgida* Rose. Flowering plant, slightly reduced. Plant of the type collection, grown by J. A. Purpus at Darmstadt. From an article by J. A. Purpus (Monatsschrift für Kakteenkunde, volume 17, page 149).

color, and undoubtedly are clonotypes. *Echeveria turgida* is readily distinguished in its flattish but thick-edged, pruinose, obtuse, and mucronate leaves, long pedicels, and long widely spreading sepals. It somewhat resembles *E. pumila* var. *glauca,* but is much more pruinose, its leaves have thick edges, and both pedicels and sepals are relatively longer.

Figure 73.   32. *Echeveria cuspidata* Rose. Plant of the type collection, flowering in Washington. Photograph from the U. S. National Herbarium, no. 170.

32. **Echeveria cuspidata** Rose.
(Figure 73.)

> *Echeveria cuspidata* ROSE, *in* Britton and Rose, Bull. New York Bot. Gard., vol. 3,
> p. 9, 1903; BRITTON AND ROSE, N. Amer. Fl., vol. 22, p. 21, 1905; POELLNITZ, *in*
> Fedde Repert., vol. 39, p. 244, 1936.
> ILLUSTRATIONS. Photograph no. 170 (US) [See Figure 73]; Walpole drawing no. 81
> (US).

Rosettes stemless, usually simple, very densely leafy; leaves as many as 100 or more, rather thinnish, grayish green, more or less glaucous-pruinose, but neither crystalline-textural nor hyaline-marginal, ascending, obovate-oblong, to over 6 cm. long and over 35 mm. wide, flat on both sides, beneath obscurely keeled near apex, strongly acuminate-cuspidate; inflorescence a simple, secund raceme; scape to over 40 cm. tall, erect; bracts appressed to ascending, oblanceolate, acuminate, to 16 mm. long; flowers to 15 or more; pedicels to 10 mm. long, or less, somewhat thickened below calyx; sepals unequal, longest 7 to 8 mm. long, oblong-lanceolate, shortly acuminate, sometimes one discrete at base, ascending-spreading; corolla conoid-urceolate, to 14 mm. long, 9 mm. in diameter near base; petals only slightly spreading at tips; nectaries narrow, oblique, 1.5 mm. wide. Flowers from February on. Description of living material collected near San Juan, not far from El Tunal, Mexico, flowered at Golden Gate Park, San Francisco.

Color. Leaves pois-green, with bloom puritan-gray, mucro often dark indian-red; bracts and sepals as leaves, but tinged vinaceous-drab; corolla coral-pink at base, light coral-red above, on inside orange-buff below, to bittersweet-orange above; carpels dull green-yellow above; styles light elm-green; nectaries amber-yellow.

TYPE. Vicinity of Saltillo, Coahuila, Mexico, *Palmer,* 1902/R-509 (US, no. 397916).

OCCURRENCE. Mexico. Coahuila: Canyon southeast of Saltillo (variously known as San Lazaro Canyon, Arteaga Canyon, or the Canyon of the Big Waterfall); Chayo Grande; near El Charro; near San Juan, not far from El Tunal.

COLLECTIONS. Mexico. Coahuila: vicinity of Saltillo, *Palmer,* 02/R-509 (US, type); near Saltillo, *Palmer,* 02/R-570 (R-509?), (GH,US); Canyon de San Lazaro, *Pringle,* 06/13874 (GH,US). *Cultivated:* Washington, D.C., *Palmer,* 04/R-42 (US).

REMARKS. *Echeveria cuspidata* has been much confused (and not only in gardens), with other superficially similar species from the same part of Mexico. My own concept is based largely on Walpole's excellent watercolor of what undoubtedly was Rose's type, and US photograph number 170.

In 1937 I was able to collect living plants, in close agreement with above illustrations and Rose's type. The locality where my, now lost, material was found, was near the tiny village of San Juan, not far from El Tunal, south of Saltillo. Here the species occurred just above a belt of *Pinus cembroides,* with which were associated *Hunnemannia, Mahonia trifoliolata,* and *Salvia regla.* With *E. cuspidata* grew *Agave (Littaea sp.), Dasylirion sp.,* all quite xeric in nature. L. Cutak reports (Cactus and Succ. Jour. Amer., vol. 12, p. 69, 1940) *E. cuspidata* as growing in Arteaga Canyon with *Opuntia, Agave, Hechtia tex-*

ensis, Ferocactus pringlei, and *Mammillaria chinocephala.* I have not seen his material.

Echeveria cuspidata needs to be contrasted with the following species: *E. chihuahuaensis* comes from western Chihuahua, has thicker alabaster-white leaves with bright red margins at apex and a more slender corolla; *E. hyalina,* when first seen, was thought to be *E. cuspidata,* but differs clearly in the hyaline leaf margins without any reddish color at the tips, and a shorter, broader, urceolate corolla. Most often confused with *E. cuspidata* has been *E. parrasensis* from the vicinity of Parras and Saltillo, whence both Purpus and Palmer repeatedly sent home specimens and plants. *Echeveria parrasensis* would differ in having thicker leaves, at least on the centerline, with a more acuminate apex, a usually 2-branched inflorescence, smaller sepals, and a smaller corolla. The illustration in Kakteenk., 1907, figure 185, is of *E. parrasensis,* while J. A. Purpus' description is a compromise.

The species here contrasted all belong in the series Urceolatae, while *E. cuspidata* is much better placed in the series Secundae, in which it would come near *E. turgida.*

33. **Echeveria tolucensis** Rose.

Echeveria tolucensis ROSE, *in* Britton and Rose, N. Amer. Fl., vol. 22, p. 22, 1905.
Echeveria glauca var. *tolucensis* (Rose) POELLNITZ, *in* Fedde Repert., vol. 39, p. 247, 1936.

Rosettes stemless, becoming cespitose, laxly to densely leafy; leaves decidedly glaucous, thinnish and flaccid, scarcely keeled, to 10 cm. long and 3 cm. broad or more, oblanceolate-oblong, at apex deltoid-acute to shortly acuminate, not red-edged; inflorescences one to three, usually simple, in cultivated plants often 2-branched, secund-racemose, to 15 cm. tall or more; peduncle stout, erect; bracts often numerous, obovate-oblong, shortly acuminate, strongly keeled to subtriquetrous, 15 to 25 mm. long, appressed; flowers to 12 or more; pedicels to 10 mm. long; sepals unequal, longest 10 to 12 mm. long, more than half the length of corolla, ovate-deltoid, acute, ascending; corolla distinctly pentagonal, to 15 mm. long, 9 mm. in basal diameter; petals bluntly keeled, gibbose at base, spreading at tips; nectaries transversely elliptic, truncate, 2 mm. wide. Flowers May and June. Description from plant collected near Toluca on Cerro Teresano, Mexico, and grown in the Strybing Arboretum, Golden Gate Park, San Francisco.

Color. Leaves light cress-green, but pruinose and so deep lichen-green; peduncle buff-pink; bracts glaucous-green with corinthian-red mucro; sepals light cress-green; corolla rose-doree below, above and inside empire-yellow; carpels and nectaries sulphur-yellow; styles lettuce-green.

TYPE. Collected at Toluca, Mexico, *Rose and Painter,* 1903/6818 (757) (US, no. 450378).

OCCURRENCE. Mexico. Estado de Mexico: near Toluca, on Cerro Teresano, etc.

COLLECTIONS. Mexico. Toluca, *Rose and Painter,* 03/6818 (type). *Cultivated:* Golden Gate Park, San Francisco, *E. Walther* in 1934, in 1936 (CAS).

REMARKS. In 1934 I found *E. tolucensis* to be frequently cultivated at

Toluca, as at the railroad station and on the Plaza. I could discover only a few plants actually wild, on the Cerro Teresano just outside the town. The species bears a strong resemblance to *E. alpina,* but occurs at much lower elevations, is more glaucous, and has fewer, narrower, more pointed leaves. Plants growing locally frequently have a 2-branched inflorescence.

34. **Echeveria alpina** E. Walther.

Echeveria alpina E. WALTHER, Cactus and Succ. Jour. Amer., vol. 7, p. 70, 1935.
ILLUSTRATIONS. Cactus and Succ. Jour. Amer., vol. 7, p. 71, fig., left center, 1935.

Rosettes cespitose, ultimately with numerous offsets; leaves numerous, crowded, to 6 cm. long and 4 cm. broad, obovate-cuneate, at apex broadly rounded to truncate and mucronate, flat, relatively thin and flaccid, beneath faintly or not keeled, very glaucous; inflorescences to three or more, simple, secund-racemose, to 18 cm. tall; peduncle ascending; bracts few, oblanceolate, subtriquetrous, acute, to 2 cm. long; flowers to 12 or more; pedicels to 8 mm. long; sepals unequal, longest to 12 mm. long, deltoid-oblong, thick, acute, ascending; corolla broad, 14 mm. long by 10 mm. in basal diameter, conoid-urceolate; petals spreading at tips; nectaries thick, truncate, lunate-reniform, to 2.75 mm. broad. Flowers from May on. Description from living plants collected at Peñas de Tomasco, 1934, grown at Golden Gate Park, San Francisco.

Color. Leaves light grape-green, but somewhat pulverulent and so deep greenish glaucous; peduncle avellanous; bracts kildare-green; pedicels glass-green; sepals light cress-green; corolla light coral-red to apricot-yellow; inside of petals empire-yellow above, pinkish vinaceous below; carpels dull green-yellow; styles lumiere-green; nectaries barium-yellow.

TYPE. Heilprin and Baker, Ixtaccihuatl, elevation 14,200 feet (PH). Isotype: US, no. 62394, photograph and fragments.

OCCURRENCE. Mexico. Estado de Mexico: Ixtaccihuatl. Hidalgo: near Real del Monte, Peñas Cargadores. Puebla: Peñas de Tomasco, etc.

COLLECTIONS. Mexico. Estado de Mexico: Ixtaccihuatl, 14,200 feet, *Heilprin and Baker* (PH, type); Ixtaccihuatl, meadows and ledges above tree-line, 3,850 m., *Moore and Wood,* 48/4528a (BH); Ixtaccihuatl, above timberline, *Moore,* 46/1247 (BH); Cueva del Negro, Popocatepetl, *E. K. Balls,* 38B–4191 (UC). Hidalgo: 55 miles southeast of Mexico City, *J. N. Weaver,* 42/745 (GH). *Cultivated:* Golden Gate Park, San Francisco, from Peñas de Tomasco, *E. Walther* in 1934, from Peñas Cargadores, *E. Walther* in 1934.

REMARKS. My specific name was based upon a note by Dr. Rose, attached to the type at Philadelphia, and would seem quite appropriate in view of the habitat. Closest relations of *E. alpina* would seem to be *E. tolucensis* and *E. byrnesii;* of these the latter is wholly bright green, while the former differs in having fewer, longer, narrower, and more deltoid-mucronate leaves. Depauperate plants may resemble *E. pumila* var. *glauca,* but in that the corolla is decidedly smaller and narrower, its leaves are smaller, and it more freely offsets. *Echeveria alpina* is frequently cultivated in Mexico City, as in the Alameda, and at the Casa de Lago in Chapultepec Park. While looking for this species in 1957 on Ixtaccihuatl, I could find it only in a window-box at the hostel near Cortez' Pass, where the attendant told me that it was known as "Rueda de la Fortuna," or "Wheel-of-Fortune."

Except for the lack of any purplish tinge and the simple inflorescence, *E. alpina* might well be mistaken for *E.* 'Imbricata,' our most commonly culti-vated *Echeveria,* a hybrid of French origin.

35. **Echeveria byrnesii** Rose.

Echeveria byrnesii Rose, *in* Britton and Rose, N. Amer. Fl., vol. 22, p. 20, 1905.
Echeveria secunda var. *byrnesii* (Rose) Poellnitz, *in* Fedde Repert., vol. 39, p. 244, 1936.
Illustrations. Cactus and Succ. Jour. Amer., vol. 6, p. 139, fig. 5, 1935.

Rosettes stemless, ultimately cespitose; leaves bright, shining green, not at all glaucous, to 9 cm. long or more, 35 mm. broad or more, oblong-obovate-cuneate, mucronate, keeled beneath near apex, otherwise thin and flat; inflo-rescences usually simple, secund-racemose, to 13 cm. tall or more; peduncle stout, erect; bracts few, deltoid, subtriquetrous, acute, to 25 mm. long; flowers 12 or more; pedicels about 5 mm. long, stout; sepals subequal, longest 10 mm. long, ovate-deltoid, acute, spreading-ascending; corolla broadly conoid-urceo-late, to over 14 mm. long, over 12 mm. in basal diameter, or nearly as thick as long; petals bluntly keeled, hollowed within at base, only slightly spreading at tips; carpels stout; nectaries transversely reniform, oblique, 1.5 mm. wide. Flowers from June on. Description from living plants collected by E. K. Balls in 1938.

Color. Leaves parrot- to lettuce-green; peduncle corinthian-red; bracts courge-green tinged pompeian-red in upper half; pedicels light grape-green, sepals as bracts; corolla scarlet-red; petals at tips and inside empire-yellow; carpels pale green-yellow; styles neva-green; nectaries whitish.

Type. Nevado de Toluca, *Rose and Painter*, 1903/7991 (US, no. 451612).

Occurrence. Mexico, Estado de Mexico: Nevado de Toluca, Ojo del Agua, etc.

Collections. Mexico, Estado de Mexico: Nevado de Toluca *Rose and Painter,* 03/7991 (US, type), 03/6818 (MEXU); Ojo del Agua, *Balls and Gourlay* in 1938; Tultenango Canyon, *Rose,* 03/918 (US). *Cultivated:* Gold-en Gate Park, San Francisco, *E. Walther* in 1934 (CAS).

Remarks. This species was named in honor of Mr. Edward M. Byrnes, Superintendent of Grounds and Gardens at Washington, D.C., who grew Dr. Rose's extensive collection of Crassulaceae, amounting to well over 1,075 potted specimens. He is perhaps best known through the genus *Byrnesia,* now included in *Graptopetalum.* Within the series Secundae, *E. byrnesii* is unique in its plain green foliage, without any trace of glaucous coating.

When in Toluca in 1934 I found this cultivated in the Plaza, and later just below timberline at what presumably was the type locality. Here it grew in shady pine-woods, on outcropping rocks in dripping-wet moss, at about 11,800 feet. The plants did not survive to flower, so that the above description is based on the subsequent collection, at the same locality, by E. K. Balls.

The chromosome number, according to Dr. Uhl, is $n = 32$.

36. **Echeveria subalpina** Rose and Purpus.
(Figure 74.)

Echeveria subalpina ROSE AND PURPUS, Contrib. U.S. Nat. Herb., vol. 13, p. 45, 1910;
BRITTON AND ROSE, N. Amer. Fl., vol. 22, p. 538, 1918; POELLNITZ, *in* Fedde Re-
peit., vol. 39, p. 245, 1936.
Echeveria akontiophylla WERDERMANN, *in* Fedde Repert., vol. 30, p. 53, 1932.
ILLUSTRATIONS. Contrib. U.S. Nat. Herb., vol. 13, pl. 11, 1910; photograph no. 612
(US) [See figure 74.]; Cactus and Succ. Jour. Amer., vol. 6, p. 187, 1935.

Rosettes stemless, with few or no offsets; leaves usually very long and narrow, to more than four times as long as wide, scarcely over 20 mm. broad, but
7 to 14 cm. long, thin, flat, faintly keeled beneath, at apex upcurved, long-acu-

Figure 74. 36. *Echeveria subalpina* Rose and Purpus. Plants grown in Washington;
collected by C. A. Purpus in 1908 at Esperanza, Puebla, Mexico, the type locality.
Photographs from the U.S. National Herbarium, no. 523 and no. 612.

minate, somewhat reddish, but not red-edged, even if at times red-blotched as the result of insect injury; inflorescences three or four, mostly simple, rarely 2-branched, to 30 cm. tall, secund-racemose; peduncle slender, erect or ascending; bracts few, ascending, deltoid-lanceolate, uncinate-acuminate, subtriquetrous, concave above, to 2 cm. long; racemes 12- to 20-flowered; pedicels 6 to 8 or even 22 mm. long; sepals subequal, widely spreading, longest to 7 mm. long, deltoid-lanceolate, acuminate; corolla 10 to 12 mm. long, 8 mm. in basal diameter, bluntly pentagonal; petals often more or less widely spreading to recurved at tips; nectaries transversely-ellipsoid, to 2 mm. wide. Flowers from June to August. Description from cultivated plants.

Color. Leaves parrot-green, but glaucous and hence deep greenish glaucous, mucro tinged indian-red; peduncle testaceous; bracts vinaceous-drab; pedicels light grayish vinaceous; sepals celandine-green in bud, later vinaceous-brown; corolla spectrum-red, begonia-rose towards base, at tips and inside light orange-yellow; carpels pale green-yellow; styles lettuce-green; nectaries sulphur-yellow.

TYPE. Mexico: subalpine regions of Mt. Orizaba, *C. A. Purpus* (US, no. 592489).

OCCURRENCE. Puebla: vicinity of Esperanza, San Antonio Atzitzatlan. Vera Cruz: near Fortin.

COLLECTIONS. Mexico. Puebla. Esperanza, *Purpus* (US, type), *Purpus,* 11/5366 (F,NY,UC,US); Pico de Orizaba, *E. K. Balls,* 38/B-5325 (K,UC, US); San Antonio, *Balls and Gourlay,* 38/B-4511 (K,UC). Vera Cruz: Zamapan, Fortin, *Purpus,* 06/500 (US). *Cultivated:* Golden Gate Park, San Francisco, from Esperanza, *E. Walther* in 1934, in 1957 (CAS).

REMARKS. Normally, *E. subalpina* is too distinct to be confused with any other species, but some dried material has been mislabeled *E. heterosepala.* The latter is distinct in its shorter broader leaves and very short pedicels, as well as in its greenish corolla.

The optimum locale of *E. subalpina* would seem to be high elevations on Mt. Orizaba, and its occurrence near Esperanza probably represents the lower limit of its range into a region of greatly reduced rainfall. During the rainless winter the plants here curl up into tight balls of mostly dried leaves, with only the very center of the rosettes still alive. Then the plants are hard to find in their refuge under *Opuntia, Agave,* etc., where they are safe from the ubiquituous goats. In cultivation, of course, the plants never assume such an extreme xerophytic appearance. In 1934, the time of my first visit, *E. subalpina* shared this ground with *E. rubromarginata,* but on returning in 1957 the latter had completely disappeared.

Series 4. Retusae E. Walther

Echeveria, ser. Retusae E. Walther, Leafl. West. Bot., vol. 9, pp. 3, 4, 1959.
Cotyledon, Gibbiflorae Baker, *in* Saunders Refug. Bot., vol. 1, Analytical Table [p. 2], 1869, *pro parte.*
Echeveria, ser. Gibbiflorae (Baker) Berger, *in* Engler Nat. Pflanzenf., ed. 2, vol. 18a, p. 474, 1930 emend.

Plants usually glabrous, very rarely puberulous or ciliate-margined; small to medium-sized; stem often evident, but short, simple or sometimes stoloniferous from base; leaves either numerous and crowded, or few, relatively small, not over 15 cm. long nor over 7 cm. broad, obtuse, retuse to acute, somewhat narrowed to base but scarcely petiolate, entire or lacerate, sometimes ciliate when young or puberulous when old, green or glaucous, or tinged or edged with red; inflorescence cymose-racemose, mostly with 2 to 4 branches, less often simple or subpaniculate; peduncle mostly stout, erect, with numerous broad and flat bracts; pedicels evident, 3 mm. long or more; sepals ascending or spreading; corolla medium sized, rarely large, scarlet or crimson, to coral- or rose-red; petals bluntly keeled, hollowed within at base; styles mostly dark; nectaries thick.

Typical species. *Echeveria fulgens* Lemaire.

Remarks. Members of this series resemble species of the series Gibbiflorae, but rarely have more than three branches in their inflorescence and their leaves are usually smaller. Anomalous is *E. semivestita* with its puberulous foliage, but its flowers are wholly glabrous. It is undoubtedly best placed here. *Echeveria stolonifera* has never yet been found wild in Mexico, and no doubt is a garden hybrid. (See "Remarks" under that species.) Depauperate species of the series Gibbiflorae may be looked for here; I have tried to allow for them too.

Key to the Species

A. Leaves relatively narrow-petioled, to 4 times as long as broad or more, often red-edged.
  B. Leaves glabrous, at first copper-colored; rosettes stemless or nearly so; inflorescence with 1 to 3 branches. Etzatlan, Jalisco. . . . . 37. *E. lozani*
  B. Leaves green with red edges, sometimes puberulent; stem evident; inflorescence with 3 to 9 branches. Hidalgo, San Luis Potosi and Tamaulipas. . . 45. *E. semivestita*
    C. Leaves puberulent with appressed hairs; inflorescence glabrous.
        45a. *E. semivestita* var. *semivestita*
    C. Leaves and inflorescence wholly glabrous. . 45b. *E. semivestita* var. *floresiana*
A. Leaves relatively shorter and broader, rarely more than 3 times as long as wide.
  B. Stem freely branching, even when short; rosettes more or less clustered.
    C. Leaves larger, to 10 cm. long and to over 6 cm. broad; flowers numerous on elongated branches. Jalisco. . . . . 38. *E. sayulensis*
    C. Leaves small, 5 cm. long or less; flowers few, on short branches. Possibly a garden hybrid. . . . . 39. *E. stolonifera*
  B. Stem usually evident and simple; rosettes mostly solitary.
    C. Pedicels rather short, 1 to 2 mm. long (species in Ser. 5, Gibbiflorae).
      D. Leaves cuneate-attenuate to base. . . . . . . 51. *E. rubromarginata*
      D. Leaves long-petioled. . . . . 56. *E. acutifolia*
    C. Pedicels slender, elongated, to over 4 mm. long.
      D. Stem usually evident; leaves numerous, 5 to 9 cm. long, deeply concave above, acute; inflorescence 2- or 3-branched.
        E. Leaves with undulate margins; corolla to 25 mm. long. Oaxaca, Chontal District. . . . . 40. *E. scheerii*
        E. Leaf-margins not undulate; corolla 12 mm. long. Oaxaca, Sierra de Juarez.
                  41. *E. juarezensis*
      D. Stem usually very short or none, or leaves longer, or flat, or obtuse; inflorescence occasionally simple, or with 2 or 3 branches.

E. Leaves more or less glaucous, obtuse or retuse, often lacerate-margined. Michoacan to Oaxaca. . . . . 42. *E. fulgens*

E. Leaves green, scarcely or not glaucous, occasionally tinged reddish, sometimes acute, mostly entire.

 F. Leaves mostly less than 8 cm. long, acute, entire; inflorescence often reduced to a single branch; pedicels slender. Guatemala.

                 43. *E. steyermarkii*

 F. Leaves to 10 cm. long or more, obtuse to retuse; inflorescence mostly with 2 or 3 branches. Morelos. . . . . 44. *E. obtusifolia*

37. **Echeveria lozani** Rose.

Echeveria lozani Rose, *in* Britton and Rose, N. Amer. Fl., vol. 22, p. 23, 1905; Poellnitz, *in* Fedde Repert., vol. 39, p. 248, 1936.

Glabrous; stemless or nearly so, in old plants stem may reach a length of 5 cm.; leaves few, 8 "forming a dense rosette, lying flat upon the ground . . ." (according to Rose), narrowly oblong-oblanceolate or strap-shaped, 10 to 15 cm. long or more, 2 to 4 cm. broad at widest point, flattened and rather thickish except at base, but here narrowed into long very thick and somewhat channeled petiole 10 mm. broad, acute, the central ones copper-colored; inflorescence 30 to 45 cm. tall, a short panicle; bracts few, linear to oblong or oblanceolate, to 35 mm. long; panicle mostly rather short, with three to seven short, several-flowered branches (two to four flowers each), pedicels stout, to 10 mm. long; sepals unequal, ovate, acute, spreading, longest to 11 mm. long, nearly as long as corolla; corolla 10 to 15 mm. long, light copper-colored, petals acute, only slightly spreading at tips. Description based on the type collection and original description.

Type. *Pringle and Lozano,* 1903/11890, mountains above Etzatlan, near Guadalajara, Jalisco, Mexico (US, no. 460734). Isotypes: CAS, GH, MEXU.

Occurrence. Not known from any other locality than the type.

Collections. Mexico. Jalisco: mountains above Etzatlan, *Pringle and Lozano,* 03/11890 (US, type; CAS,GH,MEXU), *Pringle,* 04/8810 (CAS,G, GH,NY,P,PH,US).

Remarks. Plants grown under this name in California collections do not match any specimens of the type collection. The garden material in question is most likely of hybrid origin, and is referred to, under hybrids, as *E.* 'Plicatilis.' Recently received material, from uncertain source, may turn out to be typical *E. lozani* Rose.

38. **Echeveria sayulensis** E. Walther, new species.

Echeveria sayulensis E. Walther, sp. nov., pertinens ad ser. Retusas; caulibus brevibus; rosulis multifoliatis, caespitosis; foliis glauco-viridibus, obovatis, obtusis, apiculatis, usque ad 14 cm. longis et 7 cm. latis; inflorescentiis 2- vel 3-ramosis, ramis secundis, usque ad 15-floris; pedicellis usque ad 12 mm. longis; sepalis patentibus, usque ad 12 mm. longis; corollis usque ad 17 mm. longis, carneis.

Glabrous, stem short, freely soboliferous; rosettes to over 25 cm. in diameter; leaves numerous, crowded, obovate-spathulate, obtuse and mucronate, nearly flat, thinnish, obscurely keeled beneath, to 14 cm. long and 7 cm. broad, narrowed to 2 cm. at base; inflorescences numerous, to 36 cm. tall, usually 2-branched; peduncle slender, ascending; bracts oblong-oblanceolate, to 5 cm. long and 15 mm. broad, shortly aristate-mucronate at tips; each secund-racemose branch with 12 to 15 flowers; pedicels to 12 mm. long; sepals unequal, longest to 12 mm. long, narrowly deltoid-lanceolate, acute, widely spreading; corolla to 17 mm. long, about 10 mm. in basal diameter; petals bluntly keeled, with small but deep nectar-cavity within at base; carpels 10 mm. long, nectaries transversely reniform, to 3 mm. wide. Flowers from December on.

Color. Leaves bice-green, more or less glaucous; lower bracts pea-green with bloom, shamrock-green without; peduncle above cinnamon-rufous, to avellanous with bloom intact; sepals deep lichen-green; corolla geranium-pink; petals inside and at exposed edges buff-yellow; carpels seafoam-yellow; styles turtle-green; nectaries pale grass-green.

TYPE. From plants cultivated in the Strybing Arboretum, Golden Gate Park, San Francisco. These plants were received through Sr. C. Halbinger of Mexico City from Sayula, near Guadalajara, Jalisco, Mexico (CAS, no. 354986).

REMARKS. In its general aspect, this new species combines characters of the series Secundae with those of the series Gibbiflorae. My material is not definitely known from the wild, and may be of garden origin, with the possibility that we are here dealing with a hybrid, its parents possibly having been species of the groups mentioned above. As more forms of *Echeveria* are collected in the various parts of its natural range, it is not unlikely that some of these newly discovered variants will prove to be intermediates between the various series which I have adopted here. It by no means follows that there is need to postulate hybridization in nature to explain the intermediate nature of this and other forms. Incidentally, as found by Dr. Charles Uhl of Cornell, the chromosome number of *E. sayulensis* is $n = 43 + 1$, "slightly irregular."

Frequently the stems of *E. sayulensis* will become fasciated; the resultant crested form may bear the name, cultivar 'Cristata.'

Owing to the extreme ease with which this may be propagated, it would appear inevitable that it should become widely spread in local gardens, and so of course it needs a name. I hope that presently a definite locality in Mexico will be established.

Freely offsetting species in the series Retusae are *E. stolonifera,* which has very much smaller leaves and flowers, and *E. lozani,* which has narrower, pointed, red-edged leaves, fewer offsets, and few flowers.

39. **Echeveria stolonifera** (Baker) Otto.
(Figure 75.)

> *Echeveria stolonifera* (Baker) OTTO, Hambg. Gartenztg., vol. 29, p. 9, 1873; BRITTON AND ROSE, N. Amer. Fl., vol. 22, p. 24, 1905; POELLNITZ, *in* Fedde Repert., vol. 39, p. 249, 1936.
> *Cotyledon stolonifera* BAKER, *in* Saunders Refug. Bot., vol. 1, pl. 63, 1869.
> *Echeveria pfersdorffii* Hort. ex ED. MORREN, La Belg. Hort., vol. 24, p. 163, 1874.
> *Echeveria mutabilis* Hort., *in part.*
> ILLUSTRATIONS. Saunders Refug. Bot., vol. 1, pl. 63, 1869.

Rosettes densely cespitose in age; stem and its branches slender, 5 to 10 cm. long above ground; leaves numerous, crowded, to 5 cm. long, deeply con-

Figure 75. 39. *Echeveria stolonifera* (Baker) Otto. Plant about natural size; flower en-larged. Plant grown by W. W. Saunders at Reigate, England; received "from Mexico a few years since." From the original publication (Saunders Refugium Botanicum, vol-ume 1, plate 63). This plate is designated lectotype for the species.

cave above, obscurely keeled beneath, acute to shortly acuminate, glabrous, grayish green; inflorescences three or more to each rosette, 6 to 10 cm. tall; bracts numerous, leaflike, to 25 mm. long, spreading, acuminate; branches secund, short, few-flowered, usually two in number; pedicels 6 to 8 mm. long; sepals to 10 mm. long, spreading, subterete, oblanceolate to deltoid-linear, acute; corolla 14 mm. long or less, 9 mm. in diameter, narrowed to apex. Flowers from June on. Description from plants cultivated locally, apparently distributed by Dr. Rose.

Color. Leaves and bracts courge-green, slightly glaucous at least when young; corolla coral-red to old-rose, inside apricot-yellow; styles lime-green; stigmas etruscan-red.

TYPE. None designated. *Lectotype*: Saunders Refugium Botanicum volume 1, plate 63, 1869.

OCCURRENCE. Stated to have come from Mexico, but no definite locality is known.

COLLECTIONS. *Cultivated*: flowered at New York Botanical Garden, *Rose, 04/498* (CAS); flowered at New York Botanical Garden, from A. Berger, La Mortola, *Rose, 991* (photo. no. 2093).

REMARKS. Among the numerous species of *Echeveria* planted in the Strybing Arboretum, Golden Gate Park, San Francisco, *E. stolonifera* was definitely absent, and yet, after some years, several plants that were clearly identical with Baker's species made their appearance. These volunteers undoubtedly were hybrids, from parents growing close by. Of these putative parents, I nominate *E. glauca* and *E. grandifolia* as having been most likely responsible. Both of these were grown in England prior to 1869, so that this supposed origin of *E. stolonifera* is at least not impossible. For the present I follow the precedent set by Rose, Baker, and Poellnitz, of listing this among the species rather than the hybrids.

In habit and foliage, *E. stolonifera* shows some resemblance to *E. scheerii,* the latter only recently rediscovered in Oaxaca, Mexico, but that species is larger in all its parts, especially in the corolla which may reach a length of 25 mm.

40. **Echeveria scheerii** Lindley.
(Figures 76–77.)

> *Echeveria scheerii* LINDLEY, Bot. Reg., vol. 31, (new ser., vol. 8.) pl. 27, 1845; BRITTON AND ROSE, N. Amer. Fl., vol. 22, p. 25, 1905; POELLNITZ, *in* Fedde Repert., vol. 39, p. 257, 1936.
> *Cotyledon scheerii* (Lindley) BAKER, *in* Saunders Refug. Bot., vol. 1, no. 19, 1869.
> ILLUSTRATION. Bot. Reg., vol. 31, pl. 27, 1845.

Glabrous; stem evident, to 10 cm. tall, sparingly or not branching; leaves closely rosulate, obovate-cuneate, 9 cm. long by 4 cm. broad, narrowed into a petiole 10 mm. wide at base, above deeply concave through upturning of margins; at apex acutely mucronate, glaucous; inflorescences two or more, to 50 cm. tall or more; branches two or three, secund-racemose, each with six or seven flowers; peduncle stout, erect; bracts narrowly ovate, acute, to 4 cm. long, ascending; upper bracts much reduced, linear; pedicels slender, to 13 mm. long; sepals unequal, longest to 18 mm. long, linear-deltoid, acute, widely spreading; corolla cylindric-campanulate, strongly pentagonal, to 25 mm. long, 14 mm. in diameter near base, 18 mm. wide at mouth when fully open; petals

Figure 76. 40. *Echeveria scheerii* Lindley. Leaf and inflorescence, probably natural size. From the original publication (Edwards's Botanical Register, volume 31, plate 27).

narrow, sharply keeled on back with prominent basal hollow within; carpels 16 mm. long, of which the styles comprise 7 mm., stamens 10 to 12 mm. long; nectaries obliquely reniform, truncate, to 3 mm. wide. Flowers from May to November. Description from living plant grown in the Strybing Arboretum, Golden Gate Park, San Francisco, originally collected by Thomas MacDougall from the Chontal District, Mexico.

Color. Leaves biscay-green edged corinthian-red; corolla bittersweet orange to geranium-pink below, inside apricot-yellow; styles acajou-red; nectaries baryta-yellow.

TYPE. Specimen from plant cultivated in garden of Horticultural Society, London (CGE).

OCCURRENCE. Mexico: Chontal District, southeastern Oaxaca.

COLLECTIONS. *Cultivated*: Horticultural Society, London (CGE, type); Golden Gate Park, San Francisco, from plants collected in the Chontal District, Oaxaca, Mexico, by MacDougall, *E. Walther* in 1941 (CAS).

REMARKS. This species, long lost to cultivation and known only from the single plate in the Botanical Register, was understandably easy to misinterpret as a form of some other species. Since Mr. Thomas MacDougall's discovery of plants corresponding to *E. scheerii,* no doubt can remain that it is a valid species, quite adequately represented in the figure of the Botanical Register.

Figure 77. 40. *Echeveria scheerii* Lindley. From an article by Eric Walther (Cactus and Succulent Journal, volume 31, page 53, part of figure 28).

Echeveria scheerii is well characterized by its evident, short, simple caudex, rather small, acute, concave leaves, 3-branched inflorescence with large flowers, the corolla reaching a length of 25 mm. In shape, size, and color of corolla alone, *E. scheerii* finds its closest relative in our new *E. longiflora* from Guerrero, which differs in its much stouter caudex, much larger, flattish leaves and tall scapes, which attain a height of 75 cm. or more.

A number of hybrids are recorded with *E. scheerii* for one parent, but we are unable to vouch for these at this remote day.

41. **Echeveria juarezensis** E. Walther.
(Figures 78–79.)

Echeveria juarezensis E. WALTHER, Cactus and Succ. Jour. Amer., vol. 31, p. 52, 1959.
ILLUSTRATIONS. Cactus and Succ. Jour. Amer., vol. 31, pp. 52, 53, figs. 27, 28, 1959.

Plant glabrous; caulescent with stem to 8 cm. tall, usually simple; leaves to 20 or more, crowded in terminal rosettes, obovate-cuneate, acute, and mucronate, thick and rigid, deeply concave above, beneath rounded and somewhat keeled, 5 cm. long and 3 cm. broad; inflorescences two, axillary, of three se-

Figure 78. 41. *Echeveria juarezensis* E. Walther. From the original publication (Cactus and Succulent Journal, volume 31, page 53, figure 28).

cund racemes, to 20 cm. tall; peduncle erect or ascending, to 5 mm. thick near base; lower bracts ascending, oblong-obovate, upcurved, concave above, rounded beneath, mucronate at the upcurved apex, to 25 mm. long and 11 mm. broad; racemes 10 to 12 cm. long, ascending-spreading, with about 12 flowers each; upper bracts as the lower, but 15 mm. long; pedicels slender, to 14 mm. long; sepals ascending to widely spreading at anthesis, subequal, longest 11 mm. long, linear-oblanceolate, acute, convex on both surfaces; corolla pentagonal, conoid-urceolate, to 12 mm. long, 8 mm. in basal diameter; petals apiculate, with distinct basal nectar cavity; carpels 7 mm. long; nectaries oblique, reniform to 2 mm. wide. Flowers from June to August. Description of living plant cultivated at the University of California Botanical Garden, 1958.

Color. Leaves courge-green to lettuce-green, somewhat glaucous; peduncle eugenia-red, as are the pedicels; bracts as leaves but above eugenia-red, glaucous, with edges pomegranate-purple, upper bracts buffy-citrine; sepals light hellebore-green tinged corinthian-red; corolla scarlet; petals light orange-yellow inside; carpels white below, virdine-yellow above; styles oxblood-red.

Type. Plant cultivated in the University of California Botanical Garden (no. 56. 7911), received from Mr. Thomas MacDougall, his no. B–172, said to have been from Ixtepeji, Sierra de Juarez, Oaxaca, Mexico (CAS, no. 409864; isotypes, UC,US).

Occurrence. Known only from the type collection.

Remarks. With the discovery and introduction of a growing number of *Echeveria* species from Mexico, it may become more difficult to delimit closely related species, but on the other hand a much clearer picture is obtained of the organization of the genus as a whole and its probable evolutionary lines. *Echeveria scheerii,* for instance, only quite recently rediscovered in Oaxaca by Mr. MacDougall, formerly was quite isolated without any close relations being known. However, the present plant and it constitute a clear-cut pair. Cultivated plants of *E. scheerii,* growing at the Strybing Arboretum in Golden Gate Park, San Francisco, differ in their larger size, larger, somewhat undulate leaves, and their much larger corolla which may be as much as 25 mm. and bittersweet-orange in color.

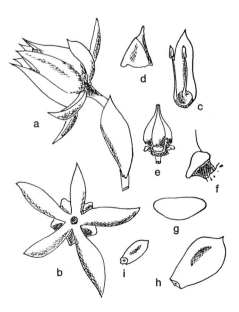

Figure 79. 41. *Echeveria juarezensis* E. Walther. Explanation: (a) flower, × 2; (b) flower from below, × 2; (c) inside of petal, × 2; (d) apex of petal, × 8; (e) carpels, × 2; (f) nectary, side view, × 8; (g) nectary, front view, × 8; (h) leaf, × 0.4; (i) bract, × 0.4. From the original publication (Cactus and Succulent Journal, volume 31, page 52, figure 27).

42. **Echeveria fulgens** Lemaire.
   (Figures 80–82.)

Echeveria fulgens LEMAIRE, Hort. Van Houtte, vol. 1, p. 8, 1845; BRITTON AND ROSE, N. Amer. Fl., vol. 22, p. 25, 1905; POELLNITZ, *in* Fedde Repert., vol. 39, p. 249, 1936.
Echeveria retusa LINDLEY, Jour. Hort. Soc. London, vol. 2, p. 306, 1847.
Cotyledon fulgens (Lemaire) BAKER, in Saunders Refug. Bot., vol. 1, pl. 64, 1869.
ILLUSTRATIONS. Le Jard. Fleur., vol. 3, pl. 244, 1855; Bot. Reg., vol. 33, (new ser. vol. 10) pl. 57, 1847; Saunders Refug. Bot., vol. 1, pl. 64, 1869; Paxton Flower Garden, vol. 3, pl. 73, 1853; Revue Hort., 1876, p. 250; 1882, p. 528; Cactus and Succ. Jour. Amer., vol. 7, p. 183, fig. 15, 1936.

Stem evident, short, or to 30 cm. long, mostly simple; leaves rosulate, comparatively few, always more or less glaucous, obovate-spathulate, 8 to 15 cm. long, 4 to 7 cm. broad, obtuse or retuse, mucronate, above concave, margins often undulate-lacerate, 15 to 25 mm. wide at the petiole-like base; inflorescences two or more, erect or laxly spreading, to 90 cm. tall, but often much less; peduncle stout or slender; lower bracts numerous, broad, obovate, truncate to acutish, to 35 mm. long, ascending; branches two or three, secund-racemose, stiffly spreading or laxly spreading to decumbent, each with 12 or more flowers; pedicels stout or slender, 2 to 6 mm. long; sepals unequal, deltoid to linear-lanceolate, acute to shortly acuminate, longest to 10 mm. long, ascending-spreading; corolla broadly urceolate to narrowly conoid-campanulate, to 15 mm. long, to 11 mm. in basal diameter, less than 8 mm. at mouth; petals slightly spreading at tips, with pronounced basal cavity within; nectaries short, truncate, reniform, 2 to 2.5 mm. wide. Flowers from November to January.

Color. Leaves cress-green, always more or less glaucous, often edged with indian-red; peduncle corinthian-red; bracts as the leaves; sepals celandine-green with bloom; corolla peach-red; petals inside pale orange-yellow at base, above xanthine-orange; carpels martius-yellow; styles maroon, to carmine below; nectaries baryta-yellow.

TYPE. None designated. Neotype: Illustration in Le Jardin Fleur. volume 3, plate 244, 1855.

OCCURRENCE. Mexico. Durango, Jalisco, Michoacan (Angangueo), Oaxaca, Est. de Mexico (Tenancingo).

COLLECTIONS. Mexico. Mexico: Temascaltepec, Casitas, *Hinton*, 33/5363 (GH,NY); Cumbre de Tejupilco, *Hinton,* 32/2300 (GH). Durango: Palmer, 06/635–812 (NY), the same flowered at New York, 09/25951 (US). Jalisco: Sierra Madre Occidental, Real Alto, La Bufa, *Y. Mexia,* 27/1602 (UC). Michoacan: Morelia, Campanario, *Arsene,* 10/5148 (GH), *Arsene,* 12/9932 (F,GH,MO), Jardin de College, *Arsene,* 11/6099 (G,GH,MO,P,US); Cumbre Cruz, *Hinton,* 36/8985 (US); Rincon del Carmen, *Hinton,* 32/2695 (GH, NY); Pantoya, *Hinton,* 32/2858 (GH); Coalcoman, S. Torricellos, *Hinton,* 32/2695 (GH,K,NY); Barrelosa, *Hinton,* 41/5748 (F); Zitacuaro, Zirahaute, *Hinton,* 38/13502 (GH,K,US). Oaxaca: Sierra de San Felipe, *Pringle,* 06/13865 (US), *Conzatti,* /1385 (US). *Cultivated*: Strybing Arboretum, Golden Gate Park, San Francisco, *E. Walther,* 58/CAS (from Sierra de San Felipe); Ithaca, from *A. Berger,* 16/R:1000 (BH).

REMARKS. On the type-sheet of *E. retusa,* in the Lindley Herbarium at Cambridge, England, is mounted a copy of the plate (vol. 3, pl. 244, 1855) in Le Jardin Fleur., presumably by Lindley himself, and undoubtedly at a date sub-

Figure 80. 42. *Echeveria fulgens* Lemaire. Raised from seeds from near Angangueo, Michoacán, Mexico; part of the type collection of *E. retusa* Lindley. From an article by J. Lindley (Edwards's Botanical Register, volume 33, plate 57).

Figure 81. 42. *Echeveria fulgens* Lemaire. Presumably part of the type collection. From an article by Charles Lemaire (Jardin Fleuriste, volume 3, plate 244). This plate is designated neotype for the species. (The photograph used for this figure was provided by the History of Medicine and Rare Book Collection, Bio-Medical Library, University of Minnesota.)

Figure 82.   42. *Echeveria fulgens* Lemaire. Plant grown by W. W. Saunders in Reigate, England; origin unknown. From Baker's monograph (Saunders Refugium Botanicum, volume 1, plate 64).

sequent to his publication of *E. retusa*. In retaining *E. retusa* as distinct, Britton and Rose's concept of *E. retusa* as stemless is not tenable, as far as my observations go. I found *E. fulgens* to be quite variable in nature, with young plants of course taking time to develop an evident caudex. Both Berger and Poellnitz reduce *E. retusa* to synonymy.

Echeveria fulgens varies in habit of growth, with the peduncle often becoming decumbent, with the corolla at the same time being narrower, the sepals shorter and more acute. These variants occur with the normal form and are probably genetic in origin; but it was not possible to correlate the characters mentioned with any geographical separation.

Echeveria obtusifolia, the nearest relation to *E. fulgens,* differs in little but the absence of any glaucous coloration and exhibits a similar variation in its inflorescence and shape of corolla. It never approaches *E. fulgens* in leaf color but is always clear deep green.

Echeveria fulgens has been widely cultivated in Europe, by commercial florists, etc., as a winter-flowering pot-plant, and has given rise to a number of forms that have been given various names there. Not one of the latter has any botanical standing. Several hybrids are reported.

The chromosome number is $n = 160$–180 (according to Dr. Uhl).

43. **Echeveria steyermarkii** Standley.

Echeveria steyermarkii STANDLEY, Field Mus., Bot. Ser., vol. 23, no. 4, p. 160, 1944; STANDLEY AND STEYERMARK, Fieldiana, Botany, vol. 24, p. 409, 1946.

Plants glabrous; stem none, or short, to 5 cm. long and 10 mm. thick; rosettes usually solitary, leaves 12 to very many, crowded, often long-persistent when dried, oblong-obovate to oblong-spathulate or oblanceolate, entire, at apex rounded to acute, apiculate or shortly cuspidate-mucronate, 15, 40, 70 or even 150 mm. long, 10, 15, 20 or to 55 mm. broad, cuneate to base, petiole typical of series Gibbiflorae and Retusae, to 10 mm. broad in largest specimen; largest dried leaves show three parallel, longitudinal veins; inflorescences one or several, 5 to 20 cm. tall, of a simple, or sometimes 2-branched secund raceme; peduncle slender, less than 2 mm. thick at base, 10 to 18 cm. long, erect or spreading to decumbent; bracts to 20 mm. long, appressed, linear to oblong, sessile, acute; racemes with three to five flowers each (or more?), pedicels 5 to 15 mm. long, somewhat turbinate below calyx; sepals unequal, 4 to 8 mm. long, free to base or somewhat connate, spreading to reflexed at anthesis, ovate-oblong, to deltoid, acute; corolla to 11 mm. long, to 8 mm. thick near base when pressed; petals narrowly lanceolate, erect, keeled on back, slightly spreading at the acuminate apex. Description compiled from all available specimens.

Color. Leaves green, tinged purplish or rose; sepals green; corolla red or rose-red, or vermilion, or reddish yellow with yellow margins to petals.

TYPE. *Steyermark,* 42/43145 (F), Guatemala, Dept. Zacapa, between Santa Rosalia de Marmol and San Lorenzo.

OCCURRENCE. Guatemala: epiphytic or on rocks, 1300 m. to 3700 m. altitude.

COLLECTIONS. Guatemala. Dept. Zacapa: between Santa Rosalia de Marmol and San Lorenzo, *Steyermark,* 42/43145 (F, type; US, isotype, with inflorescence paniculate, 10-branched, branches 3- to 5-flowered, and with leaves 8x4 cm., acutish). Dept. Solola: Volcan Santa Clara, *Steyermark,* 42/46910 (F); Volcan Toliman, slopes above San Lucas, *Steyermark,* 42/47603 (F). Dept. San Marcos: between Sibinal and Ichiguan, *Steyermark,* 36507 (F). Dept. Huehuetenango: below La Libertad, above Cañon of Paso del Boqueron, *Steyermark,* 51204 (F). Dept. Quetzaltenango, at 8,300 feet altitude, *Skutch,* 34/798 (US).

REMARKS. The above description covers all available material which was collected at several distinct stations in Guatemala, often at considerably different elevations. The specimens from lower levels appear to be larger, with larger leaves and scapes. An epiphytic habitat, such as appears to be normal for this species, may well result in rather depauperate plants.

One sheet carries the note "fulgens?", in pencil, apparently by Dr. Steyermark, and I agree that that species is rather closely related to *E. steyermarkii.* It differs, however, in having leaves that are usually glaucous, obtuse to retuse and often lacerate-margined, and a 2- or 3-branched inflorescence with larger flowers. *Echeveria obtusifolia* Rose, quite close to *E. fulgens,* has green leaves sometimes tinged red, but they are usually larger, obtuse, and the flowers too are larger. Very similar is *E. stolonifera,* but that would appear to be a garden-hybrid. *Echeveria scheerii* comes perhaps nearest to *E. steyermarkii,* but differs in having broader deeply concave leaves and much larger flowers in 3-branched racemes.

I regret that no living material has been available for study.

44. **Echeveria obtusifolia** Rose.
(Figure 83. Plate 2; see page 216.)

Echeveria obtusifolia ROSE, *in* Britton and Rose, Bull. New York Bot. Gard. vol. 3, p. 8, 1903; BRITTON AND ROSE, N. Amer. Fl., vol. 22, p. 24, 1905; POELLNITZ, *in* Fedde Repert., vol. 39, p. 242, 1936.
Echeveria scopulorum ROSE, *in* Britton and Rose, N. Amer. Fl., vol. 22, p. 25, 1905.
Echeveria obtusifolia var. *scopulorum* (Rose) POELLNITZ, *in* Fedde Repert., vol. 39, p. 242, 1936.
ILLUSTRATIONS. M. E. Eaton, US 1648, unpublished; photograph of *Pringle,* 1904/R: 11061, US, [see figure 83].

Stem evident but short; leaves always wholly green, few, rosulate, oblong obovate-cuneate, concave above, rounded and mucronate at apex, 4 to 8 cm. long; inflorescences one to four, to 35 cm. tall, with two or three secund-racemose branches; peduncle usually stout, erect, or sometimes spreading, to 8 mm. thick at base, more or less glaucous; bracts numerous, ascending to spreading, oblong, acute, to 2 cm. long, rather thick, somewhat convex on both surfaces; each branch with 9 to 11 flowers; pedicels slender, 5 mm. long, sepals lanceolate, acute, unequal, longest to 6 mm. long, widely spreading; corolla broadly or narrowly urceolate, to 13 mm. long, 8 mm. thick at base or more, at mouth to 10 mm. when fully open; nectaries reniform, to 2 mm. wide. Flowers from October to December.

Color. Leaves lettuce-green edged morocco-red; peduncle eugenia-red, somewhat glaucous; bracts and sepals as the leaves; corolla grenadine; styles spectrum-red at base, nearly black above.

Figure 83. 44. *Echeveria obtusifolia* Rose. Plant grown in Washington; collected at the type locality in 1904 by C. G. Pringle (Rose 11061). Photograph from the U.S. National Herbarium, no. 214.

TYPE. *Pringle,* 99/7734, bluffs, mountain cañon above Cuernavaca (US); isotype (MEXU).

OCCURRENCE. Mexico. Morelos: vicinity of Cuernavaca; on road between Huitzilac and Zempoala lakes, on rocks on edge of pine woods.

COLLECTIONS. Mexico. Morelos: bluffs of mountain cañon above Cuernavaca, *Pringle,* 99/7734 (US, type; MEXU, isotype), *Pringle,* 04/11061 (BH, CAS,MEXU,NY,US); Tres Marias, *Goldman* 03/R-633 (US, type of *E. scopulorum*).

REMARKS. *Echeveria obtusifolia* is very close to *E. fulgens,* but seems to differ sufficiently in the total absence of any glaucescence. Aside from this, both species are found to be quite variable in the field, and no valid characters are available for maintaining *E. scopulorum* even as a variety. The description takes into account the several forms, from several sources, that have been grown locally.

45. **Echeveria semivestita** Moran.
(Figures 84–91.)

Echeveria semivestita MORAN, Cactus and Succ. Jour. Amer., vol. 26, p. 60, 1954.
ILLUSTRATIONS. Cactus and Succ. Jour. Amer., vol. 26, pp. 174, 175, figs. 112, 113, 1954.

Description as amended by the author. Plants puberulent or glabrous; stem evident but short, usually simple; leaves rosulate, narrow, oblanceolate, acute, 10 to 14 cm. long, 15 to 30 mm. broad, concave above, faintly keeled beneath, narrowed to subterete base, dark green, usually edged red or purplish, puberulent or glabrous; inflorescence paniculate, with three to nine secund-racemose, often short branches, to 55 cm. tall, each branch with six to nine flowers or fewer; peduncle puberulent below, above papillose, or quite glabrous; lower bracts 30 to 55 mm. long, puberulent or glabrous obovate-oblong, straight or recurved; pedicels 1 to 7 mm. long, often very short; sepals glabrous, unequal, longest 11 to 15 mm. long, green to purplish or bluish glaucous, pruinose; corolla glabrous, 13 mm. long, coral-pink to jasper-red, inside yellowish or light coral-red; styles green or jasper-red; nectaries 1 to 2 mm. wide, white or yellowish.

TYPE. Collected by R. J. Taylor near Pan American Highway 25 miles north of Zimapan, Hildalgo, Mexico (UC, no. 985641).

OCCURRENCE. Mexico. Hidalgo and Nuevo Leon.

COLLECTIONS. Mexico. Hidalgo: near Pan American Highway 25 miles north of Zimapan, *R. J. Taylor,* cult. (UC, type); Puerto de La Zorra, near kilo 284 on highway northeast of Jacala, *Moore,* 47/3417 (BH); near Cherimoya, between Jacala and Santa Ana along road between kilo 294 and kilo 296, *Moore and Wood,* 48/3953 (BH). Nuevo Leon: Sierra Madre Oriental, Puerto de Santa Ana, *C. H. and F. T. Mueller* in 1929 (GH).

Figure 84.   45. *Echeveria semivestita* Moran. Flowering plant, approximately × 0.35. From an article by J. R. Brown (Cactus and Succulent Journal, volume 26, page 175, figure 113).

Figure 85.   45. *Echeveria semivestita* Moran.   Inflorescence,   ×1.   Photograph by J. R. Brown.   From the Cactus and Succulent Journal, volume 26, page 174, fig. 112.

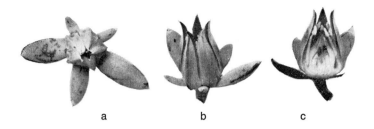

a   b   c

Figure 86. 45. *Echeveria semivestita* Moran. Flowers, slightly enlarged. Photograph by J. R. Brown. From the Cactus and Succulent Journal, volume 26, page 176, figure 114.

Figure 87. 45. *Echeveria semivestita* Moran. Leaves, natural size. Photograph by J. R. Brown. From the Cactus and Succulent Journal, volume 26, page 176, figure 115.

45b. **Echeveria semivestita** var. **floresiana** E. Walther.
(Figures 88–91.)

Echeveria semivestita var. *floresiana* E. WALTHER, Cactus and Succ. Jour. Amer., vol.
   30, p. 109, 1958.
ILLUSTRATIONS. Cactus and Succ. Jour. Amer., vol. 30, pp. 108, 109, figs. 56, 57, 1958.

Similar to var. *semivestita* except that plants are wholly glabrous in all
their parts; caudex evident with age, usually simple; leaves often minutely
undulate at lower margins; lower bracts straight, ascending, 30 to 35 mm. long;
nectaries to 2 mm. wide.

Color. Leaves light cress-green, edged dark corinthian-purple, beneath
rainette-green tinged dull indian-red; peduncle deep chrysolite-green; bracts
as the leaves but somewhat paler; pedicels onionskin-pink; sepals light celandine-green to vinaceous-brown, glaucous; corolla jasper-red, somewhat glaucous, inside light coral-red; carpels and scales pale yellowish; styles jasper-red.

TYPE. Cultivated in Strybing Arboretum, Golden Gate Park, San Francisco (CAS, no. 332306). Originally collected by R. Flores along road from
Antigua Morelos to San Luis Potosi, about 10 miles from Antigua Morelos in
the eastern or semitropical side of the mountains, on moss-covered rocks in
company with *Agave attenuata. Echeveria rosea* grew here too, on trees.

OCCURRENCE. San Luis Potosi and Tamaulipas, Mexico.

COLLECTIONS. Mexico. San Luis Potosi: collected along International
highway, between San Luis Potosi and Antigua Morelos by R. Flores (type).
Tamaulipas: near border of Nuevo Leon, Dulces Nombres, *Meyer and Rogers,*
48/2872 (MO); Sierra del Tigre, above Gomez Farias, Rancho del Cielo,
Dressler, 57/1837 (MO).

REMARKS. The material of var. *floresiana* was furnished by Mr. R. Flores,
now of Salinas, who found it during one of his various collection trips to
Mexico. In its paniculate inflorescence with numerous secund branches, and in
its relatively few leaves, these plants clearly come within series Retusae. Without flowers it may recall *E. schaffneri* (series Angulatae), which differs in its
strictly sessile flowers and fewer branches.

Echeveria maculata (series Mucronatae) is somewhat similar too, but has
fusiform roots, a very short caudex, and flowers often borne singly on the
upper pseudopedicels. It should be noted here that the airline distance between the respective type localities is less than 100 miles.

Figure 88.   45b. *Echeveria semivestita* Moran var. *floresiana* E. Walther.   Flowering plant, × 0.75.   Plant photographed in San Diego 24 July 1960; collected at El Platanito, near the type locality, in San Luis Potosi, Mexico (Moran and Kimnach 7814).

Figure 89.   45b. *Echeveria semivestita* Moran var. *floresiana* E. Walther. Inflorescence, × 2. Plant flowering in San Diego 24 July 1960; from El Platanito, near the type locality, in San Luis Potosi, Mexico (Moran and Kimnach 7814).

Figure 90.   45b. *Echeveria semivestita* var. *floresiana* E. Walther. From the original publication (Cactus and Succulent Journal, volume 30, page 108, figure 56).

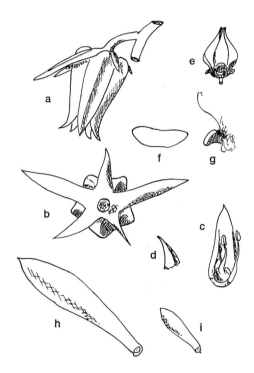

Figure 91.   45b. *Echeveria semivestita* Moran
var. *floresiana* E. Walther. Explanation: (a)
flower, × 2; (b) flower from below, × 2; (c)
inside of petal, × 2; (d) apex of petal, × 8;
(e) carpels, × 2; (f) nectary, front view, × 8;
(g) nectary, side view, × 8; (h) leaf, × 0.4;
(i) bract, × 0.4. From the original publication
(Cactus and Succulent Journal, volume 30,
page 109, figure 57).

Series 5. GIBBIFLORAE (Baker) Berger

Echeveria, ser. Gibbiflorae (Baker) BERGER, *in* Engler, Nat. Pflanzenf. ed. 2, vol. 18a, p. 474, 1930, *pro parte;* E. Walther, Leafl. West. Bot., vol. 9, pp. 3, 4, 1959.
Cotyledon, § Gibbiflorae BAKER, *in* Saunders Refug. Bot., vol. 1, Analytical Table ....[p. 2], 1869, *pro parte.*
Echeveria, ser. Grandes E. WALTHER, Cactus and Succ. Jour. Amer., vol. 30, p. 40, 1958.

Plants usually glabrous except occasionally when quite young, large to very large; stem stout, mostly unbranched, often rather tall in age; leaves mostly rather few, medium-sized to large, often with a distinct petiole which is thick, channeled above, keeled beneath, and narrowly winged at edges; inflorescence always paniculate, with an elongated rachis and three or more secund-racemose branches; lower bracts relatively large, resembling the leaves but smaller; pedicels short, or to 10 mm. long; sepals unequal, ascending to spreading, deltoid to linear or oblanceolate, mostly acute; corolla 15 to 22 mm. long or more, cylindroid-urceolate to campanulate, pentagonal, rose-red to scarlet and yellow, more or less glaucous-pruinose; petals bluntly keeled, with prominent basal hollow within; nectaries large, thick, truncate; styles dark, red to nearly black.

TYPICAL SPECIES. *Echeveria gibbiflora* DeCandolle.

REMARKS. With its large leaves, large, compound inflorescence with secund branches, pedicellate flowers, and dark colored stigmas, this series stands out from all others except the series Retusae. The species of that series may be viewed as reduced versions of the series Gibbiflorae, or the reverse may be the case. Its member species are much confused, both in the literature and in herbaria. To study them adequately, living plants grown under uniform conditions are essential.

KEY TO THE SPECIES

A. Caudex short or none; leaves crowded, sessile, scarcely petioled, acute; nectaries sometimes scarlet.
   B. Nectaries yellow; leaves hazel-brown, more or less red-edged; upper rim of petal cavity with two fingerlike projections spreading horizontally. Sinaloa, Durango, Jalisco, etc. . . . . 48. *E. dactylifera*
   B. Nectaries scarlet-red; leaves silvery-pruinose or green, red-edged; upper rim of petal cavity not appendaged.
      C. Leaves silvery-pruinose. Tultenango Cañon. . . . . 46. *E. subrigida*
      C. Leaves bright green, scarcely glaucous. San Luis Potosi, Hidalgo.
                                            47. *E. palmeri*
A. Caudex usually evident, sometimes tall, mostly simple; leaves few, rarely crowded, generally distinctly petioled; nectaries mostly pale.
   B. Leaves with conspicuous, sharply defined red margins.
      C. Leaves dark green, scarcely glaucous, margins often finely undulate. Morelos, Cuernavaca. 54. *E. crenulata*
      C. Leaves more or less glaucous, or gray-green to pale green or purple-tinged.
         D. Leaves narrowly obovate to broadly oblanceolate, acute, subsessile. Puebla, Veracruz. . . . . 51. *E. rubromarginata*
         D. Leaves broadly obovate to orbicular, apex rounded, base petioled. Southern Puebla to Oaxaca. . . . . 55. *E. gigantea*
   B. Leaves without sharply defined red marginal line.
      C. Leaves dark brownish green, not at all glaucous, often ciliate-pubescent when young. Morelos, near El Parque. . . . . 50. *E. fimbriata*
      C. Leaves more or less glaucous or gray-green to pale green, occasionally purplish tinged.
         D. Base of caudex emitting numerous spreading to decumbent offshoots; leaves very pale, yellowish green. Oaxaca. . . . . 53. *E. pallida*

D. Stem mostly simple, unbranched; leaves dark green to gray-green or purple-tinged.
   E. Corolla long and narrow, to 22 mm. long, nearly twice as long as thick, pinkish, not at all yellowish; inflorescence 3-branched. Guerrero.
                                                                52. *E. longiflora*
   E. Corolla shorter, 16 mm. long or less, relatively thicker, often red and yellow.
      F. Upper bracts and sepals turgid, subterete; leaves thick, obtuse. Guerrero, Iguala, etc.   .   .   .   .   49. *E. grisea*
      F. Bracts and sepals thinnish, flat; leaves acute to obtuse and mucronate.
         G. Pedicels mostly short, 3 to 5 mm. long; sepals narrow, more or less ascending.
            H. Leaves and lower bracts narrow, acute. Oaxaca.
                                                                56. *E. acutifolia*
            H. Leaves and lower bracts broader, obovate, obtuse to truncate and mucronate.   .   .   .   .   57. *E. violescens*
         G. Pedicels mostly longer, to 10 mm. long; sepals broader, widely spreading.
            H. Leaves and lower bracts broader, obovate to orbicular, at apex rounded and mucronate. Morelos.   .   .   .   .   58. *E. gibbiflora*
            H. Leaves and bracts narrower, oblanceolate to narrowly obovate, acute. Federal District, Esto. de Mexico.   .   .   59. *E. grandifolia*

46.   **Echeveria subrigida** (Robinson and Seaton) Rose.

(Figures 92–93.)

Echeveria subrigida (Robinson and Seaton) ROSE, *in* Britton and Rose, Bull New York Bot. Gard., vol. 3, p. 10, 1903; BRITTON and ROSE, N. Amer. Fl., vol. 22, p. 23, 1905; POELLNITZ, *in* Fedde Repert., vol. 39, p. 250, 1936, *in part*.
Cotyledon subrigida ROBINSON AND SEATON, Proc. Amer. Acad. Arts and Sci., vol. 28, p. 105, 1893; N. E. BROWN, Bot. Mag., pl. 8445, 1912.
Echeveria angusta POELLNITZ, *in* Fedde Repert., vol. 39, p. 247, 1936.
ILLUSTRATIONS. Bot. Mag., pl. 8445, 1912; Cactus and Succ. Jour. Amer., vol. 6, p. 139, fig. 4, 1935; vol. 8, p. 19, figs. 22, 23, 1936; vol. 17, p. 83, fig. 54, 1945; vol. 31, p. 42, fig. 18, 1959.

Stem usually quite short, simple, to 5 cm. thick; leaves rather few, about 15, but densely rosulate, oblong-oblanceolate, 15 to 25 cm. long, 5 to 10 cm. broad, scarcely petioled, but at base narrowed to width of 4 cm. or less, thick, rigid, acute or shortly acuminate, edges somewhat upturned and often finely undulate-crenulate, conspicuously white-pruinose; with red margin and mucro; inflorescences one or two, sometimes to 100 cm. tall, narrowly paniculate; peduncle erect, stout, to 15 mm. thick at base; bracts few, slightly spreading, obovate, acuminate, 30 to 55 mm. long; branches as many as 12, each with one to seven flowers; pedicels stout, 2 to 5 mm. long; sepals subequal, longest to 25 mm. long, deltoid-lanceolate, acuminate, ascending; corolla urceolate, pentagonal, to 25 mm. long, 14 mm. or more in diameter at base, to 20 mm. wide at mouth when fully open; petals keeled, with pronounced basal hollow within; carpels to 18 mm. long; stamens 16 to 18 mm. long; nectaries truncate, reniform, to 4 mm. broad, red. Flowers from August to October. Description from plants collected at the type locality by the author in 1934.

Color. Leaves water- to light grape-green without bloom, but strikingly white-pruinose, tinged light purplish vinaceous, edged and tipped pompeian-red; bracts deep bluish glaucous, to dark vinaceous-brown at edges and apex; sepals deep heliotrope-gray to dull indian-purple; corolla hermosa-pink, but scarlet without bloom; petals inside grenadine-red to buff-yellow, chateney-pink at base; carpels whitish to javel-green; styles scarlet to maroon; nectaries spectrum-red.

Figure 92. 46. *Echeveria subrigida* (Robinson and Seaton) Rose. Plant at the type locality, in Tultenango Cañon, State of Mexico, 25 July 1966 (Moran 13420).

TYPE. *Pringle,* 1892/4326, ledges, Tultenango Cañon (GH, type; BR,F,-MEXU,P,PH,UC,US,W).

OCCURRENCE. Mexico. State of Mexico, on cliffs along railroad between Solis and Tultenango.

COLLECTIONS. Mexico. State of Mexico: ledges, Tultenango Cañon, *Pringle,* type; *Pringle,* 02/9778 (GH,NY,US). *Cultivated:* Golden Gate Park, San Francisco, *E. Walther* in 1934 (CAS).

REMARKS. *Echeveria subrigida* is one of the most distinct of all *Echeveria* species, because of its silvery, narrow, acute subsessile leaves, tall inflorescences with numerous, few-flowered branches, its very large corolla, and last but not least, its unique scarlet nectaries. In most of these points it is very close to *E. palmeri* Rose, from San Luis Potosi, Hidalgo, Durango, and Jalisco, but its silvery foliage serves to distinguish *E. subrigida* from *E. palmeri.* For further discussion, see *E. palmeri.*

Echeveria angusta Poellnitz clearly belongs here; apparently Poellnitz knew *E. subrigida* only from herbarium specimens. His citation of Ehrenberg's material from the barrancas near Regla, Hidalgo, probably represents confusion with *E. mucronata* or one of its allies.

Echeveria subrigida appears to be frequently cultivated in European collections; I saw it in numerous botanic gardens in 1957.

Figure 93.   46. *Echeveria subrigida* (Robinson and Seaton) Rose. Plant grown at Kew; received in 1905 from Dr. J. N. Rose as *E. palmeri* Rose. From an article by N. E. Brown (Curtis's Botanical Magazine, volume 138, plate 8445).

47. **Echeveria palmeri** Rose.

Echeveria palmeri ROSE, *in* Britton and Rose, Bull. New York Bot. Gard., vol. 3, p. 10, 1903; BRITTON AND ROSE, N. Amer. Fl. vol. 22, p. 24, 1905. *Not E. palmeri* (Watson) Nelson and Macbride, which is *Dudleya palmeri* (Watson) Britton and Rose.
Echeveria rosei NELSON AND MACBRIDE, Bot. Gaz., vol. 56, p. 477, 1913.
Echeveria subrigida (Robinson and Seaton) POELLNITZ, *in* Fedde Repert., vol. 39, p. 250, 1936, *in part.*

Plants glabrous; stem short or none, simple; leaves few, about 15, crowded, sessile, elliptic-oblong to obovate, to 15 cm. long or more, 6 to 7 cm. broad, narrowed to 2 cm. at extreme base, shallowly concave above, convex beneath, acute, bright green with red edges; inflorescence usually solitary, 30 to over 50 cm. tall, narrowly paniculate; peduncle stout, erect to ascending; bracts obovate-elliptic, 2 cm. long, ascending, the mucro sometimes subapical; branches six to nine (usually six or seven) relatively short, sometimes with only a single flower; pedicels 5 to 15 mm. long or less, stout; sepals ascending or widely spreading to recurved, subequal, longest to 14 mm. long, deltoid-lanceolate, acute; corolla urceolate to cylindroid-pentagonal, 22 to 27 mm. long or more, about 16 mm. thick near base, 16 mm. wide at open mouth; petals keeled, hollowed at base within; nectaries truncate, reniform, to 4 mm. wide, scarlet red. Flowers in December and January. Description from plants collected by the author in 1935 near Encarnacion and grown in Golden Gate Park, San Francisco.

Color. Leaves light bice-green, with narrow maroon edges and mucro, not at all glaucous; sepals cress-green edged maroon; corolla orange on back of petals, geranium-pink at base, scarlet to carmine on keel and at apex, inside orange-buff; styles maroon to nopal-red; nectaries scarlet-red.

TYPE. *Palmer,* in 1902, high mountains above Alvarez, San Luis Potosi, Mexico (US, no. 397548).

OCCURRENCE. Mexico. San Luis Potosi; Hidalgo.

COLLECTIONS. Mexico. San Luis Potosi: *Palmer* (US, type); Sierra de Alvarez, *Orcutt,* 25/1770 (US). Hidalgo: Encarnacion, flowered in Golden Gate Park, San Francisco, *E. Walther* in 1935 (CAS).

REMARKS. That *E. palmeri* is closely related to *E. subrigida* is certain, but the extremely silvery pruinose coating of the leaves, sepals, and bracts, characteristic of the latter in its type locality at Tultenango Cañon, is quite constant in cultivated plants, while it is never found in *E. palmeri,* whether in cultivation or in the wild. The two species agree in the unique color of the nectaries, not found in any other members of the genus. At anthesis, these brightly colored nectaries would be readily visible to pollinating agents such as hummingbirds.

48. **Echeveria dactylifera** E. Walther, new species.
(Figures 94–95.)

Echeveria dactylifera E. Walther, sp. nov. pertinens ad ser. Gibbifloras, glabra, caudicibus brevibus vel nullis; foliis oblongo-ellipticis, acutis, leviter conduplicatis, avellaneis, rubro-marginatis, 25 cm. longis, 9 cm. latis, crassis, carinatis, inflorescentiis usque ad 100 cm. altis, paniculatis, pedunculis validis, erectis; bracteis oblongo-ellipticis, acutis, usque ad 7 cm. longis, 2 cm. latis;

Figure 94.   48. *Echeveria dactylifera* E. Walther. Flowering plant about 6 miles west of El Palmito, Sinaloa, Mexico, near the type locality, 3 November 1959 (Moran and Kimnach 7617).

ramis numerosis, brevibus, paucifloris; pedicellis usque ad 2 cm. longis, leviter turbinatis sub calyce; sepalis inaequalibus, usque ad 2 cm. longis, deltoideis vel obongo-ovatis, acutis, connatis ad basin, adscendentibus; corollis urceolatis, usque ad 30 mm. longis, 17 mm. diametro ad basin, 15 mm. in fauce, roseis;

petalis obtuso-carinatis, ad basin excavatis et 2 appendicibus dactyloideis or-
natis; antheris usque ad 6 mm. longis; carpellis usque ad 25 mm. longis; nectariis lunatis, usque ad 4 mm. latis, flavidis.

Glabrous, stemless or nearly so; rosettes mostly simple, with rather few,
crowded, sessile leaves, these elliptic-oblong, acute, somewhat cuneate towards
the thick, keeled base but not petiolate, blade folded upwards from the midrib,
to 25 cm. long or more, to 9 cm. broad; inflorescence solitary, to 100 cm.
tall, strict, erect, paniculate, with many short, secund, few-flowered branches;
lower bracts narrowly oblong-elliptic, flat, acute, to 7 cm. long and 2 cm.
broad; pedicels slender, to 20 mm. long, somewhat thickened below calyx;
sepals unequal, longest to 20 mm. long, deltoid to oblong-ovate, acute, flattish,
connate at base, the largest sometimes pseudocarinate at base, ascending; corolla narrowly urceolate, pentagonal, to 30 mm. long, 17 mm. in basal diameter, 15 mm. at mouth; petals bluntly keeled, their tips hooded and apiculate,
the basal hollow short, its upper rim produced into two fingerlike processes at
base of epipetalous filaments, these fingers recurved in front of filament base,
and there bearing three or more bright red dots; anthers to 6 mm. long; carpels
25 mm. long; styles long and slender, somewhat outcurved above; stigmas
obliquely truncate; nectaries narrowly lunate, to 4 mm. wide. Flowers from
December on. Description from greenhouse-grown plant.

Color. Leaves hazel above, with edges pompeian-red, lower surface rainette-green tinged alizarine-pink; lower bracts japan-rose, peduncle and pedicels
old-rose with bloom; sepals deep vinaceous-lavender; corolla alizarine-pink

Figure 95. 48. *Echeveria dactylifera* E. Walther. Rosette of plant about 6 miles west
of El Palmito, Sinaloa, Mexico, near the type locality, 3 November 1959 (Moran and
Kimnach 7617).

with bloom; petals inside buff-yellow above, edges minutely dotted coral-red; styles oxblood-red, to brazil-red towards base; carpels whitish; nectaries maize-yellow, never scarlet.

TYPE. From plant cultivated by Victor Reiter, San Francisco, originally received from Sr. Dudley B. Gold, Mexico City. Native along road from Mazatlan to Durango, near Sinaloa-Durango boundary (CAS, no. 412759).

PARATYPE. *Gentry, 39/5307* (MO,NY,US), from Sierra Tres Picos, Durango.

OCCURRENCE. Mexico. Sierra Madre Occidental in Jalisco, Sinaloa, and Durango.

COLLECTIONS. Mexico. Jalisco: Bolaños, *Rose,* in 1897 (US). Sinaloa: Balboa, *Ortega,* 23/5040 (UC); 55 miles east of Villa Union, *Lindsay,* 55/2569 (UCBG/55.363, living plant). Durango: Sierra Tres Picos, on rocks in oak forest (paratype cited above). *Cultivated:* garden of Victor Reiter, San Francisco, *E. Walther,* in 1959 (CAS, type).

REMARKS. This novel species, the finger-bearing *Echeveria,* is clearly related to *E. subrigida* and *E. palmeri,* both of which have a more eastern range, have bright scarlet nectaries, differently colored foliage, and lack the remarkable fingerlike appendages on the upper rim of the nectar-cavity. These processes are quite unlike those found in *Pachyphytum,* occasionally in abnormal plants of *Echeveria,* and in *E. heterosepala* and *E. longissima.* The nectaries of *E. dactylifera* are clear yellow, lacking the bright scarlet color of the other two species, but some of this red pigment is represented by several minute red dots near the tips of said fingers. At first noted on dissecting fresh flowers of locally cultivated material, I also found these appendages in *Gentry, 39/5307,* on boiling out a corolla.

The new species is highly ornamental, promises to be fairly hardy, and should become more widely known since it has recently been reimported by Bettencourt and Taylor. Some seed has been produced locally, so that the plants are not wholly self-sterile.

49. **Echeveria grisea** E. Walther.
     (Figures 96–98.)

> *Echeveria grisea* E. WALTHER, Cactus and Succ. Jour. Amer., vol. 9, p. 165, 1938.
> *Echeveria campanulata* POELLNITZ, *in* Fedde Repert., vol. 39, p. 256, 1936; *not* Kunze, which is *E. grandifolia.*
> ILLUSTRATIONS. Cactus and Succ. Jour. Amer., vol. 9, pp. 165, 166, 1938; US photograph no. 210. [See figure 97].

Stem evident, usually short, unbranched, 2 to 3 cm. thick; leaves about 12, forming a lax rosette, 10 to 15 cm. long, 5 to 8 cm. broad, broadly obovate-spathulate, at apex rounded and minutely mucronulate, thick, flat or very slightly concave above, more or less undulate at edges, at base narrowed into short petiole 18 mm. wide; inflorescences one or two, to 50 cm. tall, paniculate, with three to five short, often few-flowered branches; peduncle stout, erect; bracts numerous, ascending, oblong-obovate, mucronate, to 5 cm. long, 2 cm. broad, turgid, subterete at base; rachis of flowering branches angularly divaricate, occasionally 2-branched; upper bracts linear, terete, very turgid; pedicels stout, to 4 mm. long or less; sepals subequal, longest to 7 mm. long, widely spreading, turgid and terete, linear-ovate, obtusish; corolla conoid-urceolate, to 13 mm. long, 9 mm. in basal diameter, 6 mm. wide at mouth; petals thick and fleshy, nearly straight, bluntly keeled, with prominent basal hollow inside; stamens 7 mm. long; nectaries narrowly lunate-reniform, to 2.5 mm. broad. Flowers December and January. Description from living plants cultivated in Golden Gate Park, San Francisco.

Color. Leaves corydalis-green to asphodel-green, pruinose, occasionally spotted deep purplish vinaceous; bracts as the leaves; sepals light celadine-green; corolla shrimp-pink outside at base, at edges and tips of petals strawberry-pink, inside pale seashell-pink; styles victoria-lake to carmine.

TYPE. Collected in Cañon de la Mano, near Iguala, Guerrero, Mexico, *E. Walther,* 35/1 (CAS, no. 251051).

OCCURRENCE. Mexico. On shady cliffs, Guerrero; on lava, Michoacan.

COLLECTIONS. Mexico. Guerrero: Cañon de la Mano (flowered in Golden Gate Park, San Francisco), *E. Walther,* 1935/1 (CAS, type); Petatlan-Chilapa, *Nelson,* 94/2153 (US); Iguala, *Holway,* 03/R:689 (US). *Michoacan:* Uruapan, on lava field, *Pringle,* 05/10129 (F,GH,MEXU,NY,P,PH, US,W), *Pringle,* 91/3766.

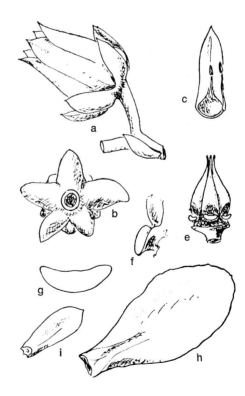

Figure 96. 49. *Echeveria grisea* E. Walther. Explanation: (a) flower, × 2; (b) flower from below, × 2; (c) inside of petal, × 2; (e) carpels, × 2; (f) nectary, side view, × 8; (g) nectary, front view, × 8; (h) leaf, × 0.4; (i) lower bract, × 0.4. From the original publication (Cactus and Succulent Journal, volume 9, page 165).

Figure 97. 49. *Echeveria grisea* E. Walther. Plant grown in Washington; collected by E. W. D. Holway in 1903 near Iguala, Guerrero, Mexico (Rose greenhouse plant 689). Photograph from the U. S. National Herbarium, no. 210.

Figure 98.   49. *Echeveria grisea* E. Walther.   Explanation: Upper left, flowering branch, approximately × 1.5; upper right, flowering plant, approximately × 0.15; lower left, Cañon de la Mano, with Señora Halbinger; lower right, rosette, approximately × 0.4. From the original publication (Cactus and Succulent Journal, volume 9, page 166).

REMARKS. Dried material of *E. grisea* is difficult to distinguish from that of either *E. fulgens* or *E. obtusifolia*. Both of these have thinner, often lacerate-margined leaves, flatter bracts, and thinner sepals, and in neither is the rachis of the panicle angular-divaricate. Holway's 1903 collection from near Iguala *(Rose, 689)* was seen by Poellnitz, and by him quite adequately described, but under the name *E. campanulata* D. G. Kunze, which last is refererable to *E. grandifolia* Haworth. This cañon has been a favorite collecting ground for visiting botanists, Rose, Pringle, Holway, etc. Its vegetation is rather tropical, as witnessed by such plants as *Achimenes* and *Begonia uni-*

folia. Atop the cliffs grows *Sedum dendroideum,* and *Thompsonella platy-phylla* occurs on hot dry rocks at the edge of the railroad tracks. *Echeveria grisea* prefers the shady cliffs, here composed of marble. Since the altitude is only about 2,400 feet, it is doubtful whether *E. grisea* will prove to be very hardy.

Specimens from Uruapan are needed to determine whether they truly belong here.

50. **Echeveria fimbriata** C. H. Thompson.
(Figure 99.)

> *Echeveria fimbriata* C. H. THOMPSON, Trans. Acad. Sci. St. Louis, vol. 20, no. 2, p. 20, 1911; BRITTON AND ROSE, N. Amer. Fl., vol. 22, p. 538, 1918. (Mentioned by neither Berger nor Poellnitz.)
> ILLUSTRATIONS. Trans. Acad. Sci. St. Louis, vol. 20, pls. 8, 9; Cactus and Succ. Jour. Amer., vol. 6, p. 139, figs. 1, 2, 1935; vol. 27, p. 123, fig. 86, 1955.

Stem to over 50 cm. long and to 3 cm. thick, usually simple; leaves rather few, laxly rosulate, obovate-spathulate, to 20 cm. long (in the wild), in cultivation rarely exceeding 15 cm., to 6 to 7 cm. broad, narrowed to less than 20 mm. at the petiole-like base, at apex rounded and mucronate, above flat or shallowly concave, not at all glaucous, when young ciliate and pubescent, the unique trichomes appear to be quite solid and are outgrowths of the cuticle, the longest to 1 mm. long, 0.09 mm. thick, straight or curved, blunt-tipped, colorless, usually lost at maturity when the hyaline margins may become somewhat fimbriate-lacerate; inflorescence mostly solitary; panicle to 60 cm. tall, of two or three laxly drooping, secund racemes; peduncle to 10 mm. thick at base, above slender; bracts few, ascending, to 4 cm. long and 18 mm. broad, obovate-oblong, acute, thick, prominently spurred at base; racemes each with 8 to 12 flowers; pedicels to 10 mm. long, slender; sepals ascending-spreading, subequal, longest to 9 mm. long, linear-deltoid, acute to acuminate; corolla cylindroid-pentagonal, to 15 mm. long, 11 mm. in diameter at base, 10 mm. at mouth; petals thick, deeply hollowed within at base, above slightly spreading; nectaries reniform, truncate, to 2 mm. wide. Flowers from November to January. Description from plants cultivated in Golden Gate Park, San Francisco, collected at the type locality by the author, 1934.

Color. Leaves calla-green tinged benzo-brown; bracts as leaves but tinged deep purplish vinaceous, spur eugenia-red; peduncle buffy-citrine; sepals light hellebore-green to light grayish blue-violet; corolla spectrum-red, to alizarine-pink with bloom; inside light ochraceous-buff; styles vandyke-red at tips, old-rose below; nectaries sulphur-yellow.

TYPE. *Trelease* 1905, MO:674 (3/3), from the Sierra de Tepoxtlan near San Juanico, Tlacotenco, Morelos, Mexico. *Clonotype:* US, no. 149472. *Topotype: E. Walther* in 1959, garden of V. Reiter (CAS).

OCCURRENCE. Known only from the type locality.

REMARKS. When present, the unique trichomes suffice to identify this species; in their absence it may be distinguished from similar green-leaved echeverias as follows: *Echeveria obtusifolia* has a shorter caudex, smaller leaves, more numerous bracts, shorter pedicels, and a broader, often erect corolla; *E. crenulata* from Cuernavaca is much larger, its leaves have a prominent red margin, its panicle is larger, with more numerous and shorter branches, bearing fewer flowers and a larger corolla.

Figure 99. 50. *Echeveria fimbriata* C. H. Thompson. Rosette and inflorescence, × 0.75 (natural size in the original). From the original publication (Transactions of the Academy of Science of St. Louis, volume 20, plates 8 and 9).

At its type locality, *E. fimbriata* grows on damp, shady cliffs, which are the habitat also of *Sedum longipes, Pinguicula caudata,* and *Begonia gracilis;* in dense woods of *Clethra, Arbutus,* and *Quercus;* and with *Monochaetum pringlei, Eupatorium areolatum.* All plants of *E. fimbriata* seen appeared to be quite alike, with numerous seedlings springing up in the damp moss covering the cliffs. All of these seedlings exhibited the remarkable trichomes described above.

In cultivation, *E. fimbriata* has proven to be rather tender and very susceptible to insect injury. Cuttings root readily, and the young plants, grown in the greenhouse, invariably develop the characteristic hairs.

51. **Echeveria rubromarginata** Rose.

(Figures 100–102.)

> *Echeveria rubromarginata* Rose, *in* Britton and Rose, N. Amer. Fl., vol. 22, p. 23, 1905; Poellnitz, *in* Fedde Repert., vol. 39, p. 249, 1936.
> *Echeveria gloriosa* Rose, Contrib. U.S. Nat. Herb., vol. 13, p. 295, 1911; N. Amer. Fl., vol. 22, p. 538, 1918.
> *Echeveria nuda* Botteri Ms., no. 390.
> *Echeveria palmeri* Hort. Calif. *in part* (?).
> Illustrations. Contrib. U.S. Nat. Herb., vol. 13, pls. 50, 51, 1911 (as *E. gloriosa*), *op. cit.*, pl. 12 only (as *E. gigantea*) 1910; Cactus and Succ. Jour. Amer., vol. 6, pp. 186, 187, 1935; Nat. Hort. Mag., vol. 15, no. 1, pp. 94, 95, 1936; photograph no 209, (US) [see figure 100].

Stem evident in age, but mostly rather short, usually simple; leaves obovate or broadly oblanceolate, 11 to 17 cm. long, 7 to 9 cm. broad, obtusish and mucronate to acute, flat or shallowly concave above, glaucous; inflorescences one or two, paniculate, to over 100 cm. tall; peduncle erect, stout, to 12 mm. thick near base; bracts ascending, obovate-oblong, to 6 cm. long, to 23 mm. broad, acute or shortly acuminate, flat, thickest near base; branches 6 to 12 each with five flowers; pedicels short, usually 1 to 2 mm. long, rarely longer; sepals very unequal, longest to 13 mm. long, ascending, deltoid- to linear-lanceolate, shortly acuminate; corolla urceolate, pentagonal, to 14 mm. long, 11 mm. in diameter at base, 8 mm. at mouth; petals bluntly keeled, hollowed within at base; nectaries reniform truncate, to 4 mm. wide; occasionally red-dotted. Flowers September and October. Description from cultivated plants collected at Esperanza in 1934.

Color. Leaves light elm-green, tinged vinaceous-purple, edged oxblood-red, glaucous; peduncle pinkish vinaceous with bloom; bracts light hellebore to glaucous-green; sepals pearl-blue with bloom, deep brownish drab without it; corolla pinkish vinaceous in bud, scarlet without bloom; petals inside apricot- to chrome-yellow; carpels yellowish; nectaries whitish, sometimes red-dotted; styles maroon; stigmas black.

Type. Mexico. On rocks near Orizaba, *C. A. Purpus,* 1903/R:930 (US no. 399848).

Occurrence. Mexico. Veracruz: near Orizaba, Arroyo Seco, Alta Luz, rocky slopes at 5000 to 6000 feet. Puebla: near Puebla along Rio Atoyac, Amatlan, Mayorazgo, Acatzingo, Manzanillo, Tepeaca, Hacienda Batan, Totimehuacan, on edge of lava flow near Esperanza.

Collections. Mexico. Veracruz: on rocks, near Orizaba, *Purpus,* 03/R: 930 (US, type; BH,GH), *Purpus,* 07/25214 (NY); Orizaba, *Botteri,* 390 (GH,US,photo; as *E. nuda);* on road to Veracruz, *Arsene,* 07/1844 (P,US); Cerro Borrego, near Orizaba, *Bourgeau,* 1866/3027 (P); Orizaba, *F. Meyer,* 04/11015 (US). Puebla: on rocks, Rio de Santa Lucia, *Purpus,* 07/423 (US, no. 615398, type of *E. gloriosa);* near Esperanza, *Rose,* 04/937 (BH); near Puebla, *P. Maury,* 1884/1103 (NY); Mayorazgo, *Arsene,* 07/10056 (US), *Arsene and Nicholas,* 11/6177 (GH,NY,US); Hacienda Batan, *Arsene,* 07/

Figure 100. 51. *Echeveria rubromarginata* Rose. Plant of the type collection, grown in Washington (Rose greenhouse plant 930). Photograph from the U. S. National Herbarium.

1881 (US); Acatzingo, *Arsene and Amable,* 07/10057 (GH,US); Hacienda Moria, *Nicholas* in 1908 (P); Manzanillo, *Nicholas* in 1911 (P); Necaxa, *Brockway* in 1905 (US). *Cultivated: E. Walther* in 1934 (CAS).

REMARKS. *Echeveria rubromarginata* ranges widely in Puebla and adjoining parts of Veracruz, growing along banks of streams, in dry arroyos, and on lava flows. In 1934 I found it abundant near San Antonio Atzizitlan, in company with *E. subalpina,* but not a single specimen was to be found in 1957. In such a wide-ranging species some variation must be expected, as the more luxuriant specimens seen on the edge of the lava flow near Esperanza. Careful comparison of these plants with the type of Rose's *E. gloriosa* leaves as sole difference the rather shorter pedicels of the latter, scarcely adequate for maintenance of a distinct species.

Echeveria fulgens Lemaire, sometimes miscalled *E. rubromarginata* has obtuse to retuse leaves with often lacerate margins, obtuse bracts, and a much lower inflorescence with fewer branches and longer pedicels. *Echeveria grisea* E. Walther, from near Iguala, differs in its lead-colored leaves, smaller inflorescence with at most three branches, its turgid terete bracts and sepals, and a smaller corolla. *Echeveria palmeri* Rose has a much larger corolla, longer pedicels, and dark scarlet nectaries *(E. rubromarginata* has at most a mere suggestion of pink color in its nectaries). Plants grown in California gardens under the name *E. palmeri* may have descended from *E. rubromarginata,* but differ in their broader leaves, an inflorescence with fewer, longer branches, longer pedicels, subequal sepals, and larger corolla. At present I know of no authentic material of *E. rubromarginata* in cultivation anywhere.

Figure 101. 51. *Echeveria rubromarginata* Rose. Plants in the plaza at Puebla, Mexico. From an article by Eric Walther (Cactus and Succulent Journal, volume 6, page 186).

Figure 102. 51. *Echeveria rubromarginata* Rose. Rosette, × 0.4; flowering plant, × 0.1. From the original publication of *E. gloriosa* Rose (Contributions from the U. S. National Herbarium, volume 13, plate 50 and plate 51).

52. **Echeveria longiflora** E. Walther.
(Figures 103–104.)

Echeveria longiflora E. WALTHER, Cactus and Succ. Jour. Amer., vol. 31, pp. 101, 102, 1959.
ILLUSTRATIONS. Cactus and Succ. Jour. Amer., vol. 31, pp. 101, 102, figs. 34, 35, 1959.

Plants glabrous, with evident, stout, normally simple stem; leaves few, large, to over 15 cm. long and over 8 cm. broad, obovate-orbicular, at apex obliquely obtuse, apiculate to acutish, at base narrowed into broad channeled, keeled and narrowly winged petiole; inflorescences one or two, to 75 cm. tall or more, paniculate, with nearly always three elongate, horizontally spreading branches; peduncle stout, erect; lower bracts oblong, to 6 cm. long, mucronate; pedicels short, or to 15 mm. long; sepals very unequal, shortly deltoid to linear-lanceolate, acute, longest to 12 mm. long, widely spreading to slightly recurved; corolla long and relatively narrow, to 22 mm. long, 13 mm. broad near base, 10 mm. in diameter at mouth; petals bluntly keeled, obtuse; carpels to 17 mm. long; styles long and slender; nectaries oblique, transverse-rhomboid, 3 mm. wide. Flowers from January on.

Color. Leaves vetiver-green, more or less glaucous, tinged light vinaceous-drab; bracts as the leaves but mineral-gray with bloom, tinged light cinnamon-drab; pedicels bluish glaucous; sepals grayish lavender with bloom intact, to light vinaceous-lilac; corolla pale vinaceous-lilac at base, to old-rose above with bloom, never yellow-orange, inside and at edges above pale flesh-color; carpels seafoam-yellow, styles indian-lake; nectaries straw-yellow.

TYPE. From a living plant grown in the Strybing Arboretum, Golden Gate Park, San Francisco, originally received from Sr. C. Halbinger, Mexico City, the type collected by E. Walther in 1950 (CAS, no. 354990).

OCCURRENCE. Mexico. Guerrero, without definite locality.

COLLECTIONS. *Cultivated:* Strybing Arboretum, *E. Walther,* 25 January 1950 (CAS); garden of V. Reiter, San Francisco, *E. Walther* in 1958 (CAS), in 1959 (CAS).

REMARKS. The present plant further illustrates the diversity existing within the formerly broad concept of *E. gibbiflora.* In its series, the species is notable for the exceptionally long and rather narrow corolla, which lacks any trace of yellow or orange coloration. A corolla, similar in shape and color, is found in *E. scheerii* Lindley from Oaxaca, which has only recently been rediscovered by Mr. Thomas MacDougall. Here too the inflorescence is usually 3-branched, but the plant is much smaller and has a shorter stem, its leaves are smaller, more crowded, deeply concave above with margins strongly undulate, and the inflorescence is much smaller and lower.

The stumps of old plants of *E. longiflora,* decapitated for rejuvenation, produce numerous sprouts from dormant axillary buds, which become readily detached and root freely.

Figure 103. 52. *Echeveria longiflora* E. Walther. From the original publication (Cactus and Succulent Journal, volume 31, page 101, figure 34).

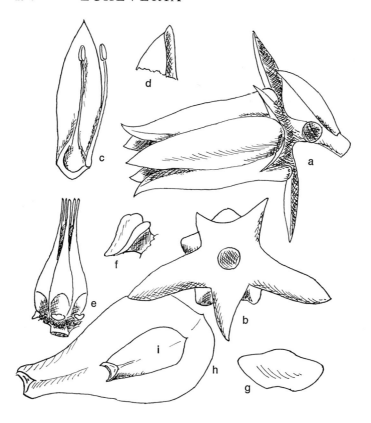

Figure 104. 52. *Echeveria longiflora* E. Walther. Explanation: (a) flower, × 2; (b) flower from below, × 2; (c) inside of petal, × 2; (d) apex of petal, × 8; (e) carpels, × 2; (f) nectary, side view, × 8; (g) nectary, front view, × 8; (h) leaf, × 0.4; (i) upper bract, × 2. From the original publication (Cactus and Succulent Journal, volume 31, page 102, figure 35).

53. **Echeveria pallida** E. Walther.

(Figures 105–106.)

Echeveria pallida E. WALTHER, Cactus and Succ. Jour. Amer., vol. 10, pp. 14, 15, 1938.

ILLUSTRATIONS. Cactus and Succ. Jour. Amer., vol. 10, pp. 14, 15, 1938.

Stem to 10 cm. tall and 3 cm. thick, at first simple, but ultimately giving off numerous branches from below that take root, forming large clusters; leaves laxly rosulate, obovate-spathulate, to over 15 cm. long and 9 cm. broad, at apex rounded and mucronate, shallowly concave above; petiole to 25 mm. wide, deeply channeled above, sharply keeled beneath; inflorescence single, to 50 cm. tall; peduncle erect, to 15 mm. thick at base; lower bracts numerous, spreading, obovate, mucronate, to 6 cm. long and 35 mm. broad, thick at the spurred base; panicle with eight or more secund-racemose branches, these occasionally 2-branched, strongly nodding in bud, each with five or more flowers; upper bracts exceptionally broad, ovate, acute, to 12 mm. wide and 20 mm. long, not recurved; pedicels stout, noticeably thickened below calyx, 6 mm.

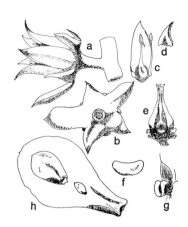

Figure 105. 53. *Echeveria pallida* E. Walther. Explanation: (a) flower, × 1; (b) flower from below, × 1; (c) inside of petal, × 1; (d) apex of petal, × 4; (e) carpels, × 1; (f) nectary, front view, × 4; (g) nectary, side view, × 4; (h) leaf, × 0.2; (i) lower bract, × 0.2; (j) upper bract, × 0.2. From the original publication (Cactus and Succulent Journal, volume 10, page 14).

long or less, sepals much connate at base, almost completely covering base of corolla, very unequal, longest to 14 mm. long, short- or oblong-deltoid, often keeled, acute; corolla cylindric, somewhat campanulate above, pentagonal, 16 mm. long, 12 mm. in diameter near base, to 16 mm. in diameter at mouth when fully expanded; petals bluntly keeled, hollowed inside at base; carpels slender, tapering from base to apex; nectaries truncate, reniform, to 2 mm. wide. Flowers December and January.

Color. Leaves asphodel-green, to corydalis-green, rarely or not tinged vinaceous-russet at edges; bracts light elm-green, slightly glaucous; pedicels light vinaceous-lilac with bloom, acajou-red without; sepals kildare-green in bud, later vinaceous-lilac, glaucous; corolla scarlet-red, alizarine-pink with bloom; petals inside palest maize-yellow, finely lined with scarlet near top; styles amaranth-purple, to dahlia-purple above; nectaries whitish.

Type. From plant found in cultivation in Mexico City and grown in Golden Gate Park, San Francisco (CAS, no. 251053).

Occurrence. Mexico. Chiapas: cultivated at Cintalapa, at Tuxtla Gutierrez, and at Ocozocoaultla (as stated in letter from Mr. Thomas MacDougall).

Collections. *Cultivated:* flowered in Golden Gate Park, San Francisco, *E. Walther* in 1937 (CAS); garden of Mrs. Schultz, Richmond, California, *P. C. Hutchison* (UCBG).

Remarks. *Echeveria pallida* is quite distinct from related species in the unique basal offshoots produced in age, which ultimately lead to the formation of widespread colonies. It further differs from similarly broad- and round-leaved species in the very pale-green leaf color, without any trace of purple-tinged or red edges. The exceptionally broad sepals are quite unlike those of *E. gibbiflora* and *E. crenulata.* In *E. gigantea,* which too has rather broad sepals, the leaves are quite dark gray-green with red edges, the bracts are narrower, and the corolla is deep red without any trace of yellow.

Echeveria pallida, chromosome number, $n = 54$, originally was found in a commercial nursery in Mexico City, without any information available as to its native habitat. Mr. Thomas MacDougall wrote me, 12 May 1947: *"Echeveria pallida* was collected from cultivation in Cintalapa, Chiapas. This I have also seen cultivated, at Tuxtla Gutierrez and Ocozocoaultla, Chiapas."

Mr. Don B. Skinner of Los Angeles has raised an interesting hybrid between *E. pallida* and *E. gigantea* and named it *Echeveria* 'Blue-Boy.'

Figure 106. 53. *Echeveria pallida* E. Walther. Explanation: Upper left, flowering plant, approximately × 0.15; upper right, one bifid branch, approximately × 0.8; lower left, rosette, approximately × 0.25; lower right, panicle in bud, approximately × 0.35. From the original publication (Cactus and Succulent Journal, volume 10, page 15).

54. **Echeveria crenulata** Rose.

> *Echeveria crenulata* Rose, Contrib. U.S. Nat. Herb., vol. 13, p. 295, 1911; Britton and Rose, N. Amer. Fl., vol. 22, p. 539, 1918; Poellnitz, *in* Fedde Repert., vol. 39, p. 256, 1936.
> Illustration. Cactus and Succ. Jour. Amer., vol. 7, p. 138, fig. A5 (habitat), 1936.

Stem to over 10 cm. tall, sometimes budding from near base; leaves rather few, rhomboid-obovate, to over 10 cm. long, 7 cm. broad or more, strongly mucronate to acute, narrowed to width of 2 cm. at base; margins flat, or strongly and finely undulate, scarcely crenulate, not at all glaucous; inflorescences one to four, to over 50 cm. tall; peduncle stout, erect; lower bracts numerous, ascending, obovate-cuneate, mucronate to acutish, to 5 cm. long, at base narrowed into stout petiole; panicle with nine or more short, secund-racemose branches, each with 4 to 12 flowers; the bracts subtending these branches usually borne some distance above base of branch, instead of being borne on peduncle as is normally the case in the genus; pedicels to 10 mm. long; sepals unequal, linear-deltoid to oblanceolate, longest to 10 mm. long, acute, widely spreading, to recurved; corolla urceolate, pentagonal, to companulate above, to 18 mm. long, 12 mm. in basal diameter, at times to 16 mm. wide at mouth; petals bluntly keeled on back, with prominent basal hollow inside, spreading above the middle; nectaries subrotund, truncate, to 4 mm. broad. Flowers from November on. Description based upon living plants collected at Cuernavaca, 1934.

Color. Leaves elm-green tinged fawn-color, edged dark vinaceous-brown, at most only very slightly glaucous; peduncle corinthian-red, glaucous; bracts as leaves; sepals light purple-drab; corolla alizarine-pink to ochraceous-buff, inside naples-yellow; styles carmine, to maroon at tips; nectaries nearly white, faintly tinged pinkish.

TYPE. Collected by *Rose* and *Painter,* 1903/797, 790, in barranca near Cuernavaca (US, no. 454957).

OCCURRENCE. Mexico. Morelos: along banks and streamsides, and on ruined walls at Cuernavaca.

COLLECTIONS. Mexico. Morelos: barranca near Cuernavaca, *Rose and Painter,* 03/790–797 (US, type), *Rose,* 05/1348 (BH,NY), *Bourgeau,* 1865/1379 (P,UC). *Cultivated:* Washington, D. C., *Rose,* 03/19304, photograph; garden of V. Reiter, San Francisco, *E. Walther* in 1931 (CAS); Huntington Botanical Gardens, *E. Walther* in 1929 (CAS).

55. **Echeveria gigantea** Rose and Purpus.
(Figures 107–111.)

> *Echeveria gigantea* ROSE AND PURPUS, Contrib. U.S. Nat. Herb., vol. 13, p. 46, 1910; BRITTON AND ROSE, N. Amer. Fl., vol. 22, p. 539, 1918; POELLNITZ, *in* Fedde Repert., vol. 39, p. 254, 1936.
> ILLUSTRATIONS. Contrib. U.S. Nat. Herb., *loc. cit.,* pls. 13, 14 (not pl. 12 which is *E. rubromarginata* Rose); Möller's Deutsche Gärtenzt., vol. 26, pp. 73, 74, 1911, *in part* (?); Cactus and Succ. Jour. Amer., vol. 21, pp. 163, 164, figs. 105, 106, 1949 (habitat).

Stem to 50 cm. tall, simple, erect; leaves 15 to 20, broadly obovate-spathulate, 15 to 20 cm. long, 8 to 10 cm. broad, at apex rounded emarginate and apiculate, at base narrowed to 25 mm. wide petiole, above flat or shallowly concave; inflorescence mostly single, to 100 or even 200 cm. tall, paniculate, with seven or more secund-racemose branches; peduncle erect, with conspicuous bulge at base of each branch; bracts numerous, ascending, oblong-spatulate, thick, to 10 cm. long, obtusish to acute; branches with 7 to 16 flowers each, nodding in bud; upper bracts oblong, acute, recurved, to 7 mm. broad; pedicels 2 to 8 mm. long; sepals very unequal, longest to 15 mm. long, deltoid to lanceolate-oblong, acuminate, broadly connate at base, spreading to recurved; corolla urceolate, pentagonal, 12 to 17 mm. long, 9 to 11 mm. thick at the gibbose base, to 12 mm. in diameter at mouth; petals somewhat spread-

Figure 107.   55. *Echeveria gigantea* Rose and Purpus. Plant on a dry wall in Tlaxiaco, Oaxaca, Mexico. From an article by T. MacDougall (Cactus and Succulent Journal, volume 21, page 164, figure 106).

ing above, bluntly keeled on back, hollowed within at base; nectaries truncate, reniform, to over 3 mm. wide, ripe follicles widely spreading. Flowers from December to February. Description based on clonotype cultivated at Huntington Botanical Gardens, San Marino, California.

Color. Leaves courge-green to grape-green, edged corinthian-purple, scarcely glaucous; peduncle pompeian-red, with bloom pale rosalane-purple; bracts light elm-green, edged and tinged with vinaceous-brown; sepals indian-red; corolla rose-red, to rose-color with bloom, pomegranate-purple without bloom, not at all yellow inside; styles carmine below, to dark-purple at tips.

TYPE. *Purpus,* 07/414, Cerro de la Yerba, near San Luis Atolotitlan, southern Puebla (US, no. 592488; isotypes, BH,F,GH,NY,US; clonotype, CAS).

OCCURRENCE. Mexico: Puebla, on border of Oaxaca (type); Oaxaca; 5 kilos southeast of Tlaxiaco, on dry walls and limestone ridges at 7000 to 8000 feet.

Figure 108.   55. *Echeveria gigantea* Rose and Purpus. Flowering plant, ✕ 0.6. Plant photographed in San Diego 2 October 1960; collected near Huitzo, Oaxaca, Mexico (Moran 6380, a cited collection).

Figure 109.   55. *Echeveria gigantea* Rose and Purpus. Inflorescence, × 0.5. Plant flowering in San Diego 11 December 1960; collected 14 miles southeast of Huajua-pan, Oaxaca, Mexico (Moran 6372, a cited collection).

Figure 110. 55. *Echeveria gigantea* Rose and Purpus. Flowering branch, × 1.5. Plant flowering in San Diego 11 December 1960; collected near Huitzo, Oaxaca, Mexico (Moran 6380, a cited collection).

COLLECTIONS. Mexico. Puebla: at type locality; Cerro Grande, near Zapotitlan, south of Tehuacan, *Cox,* 58, flowered in Golden Gate Park, San Francisco, *E. Walther* in 1958 (CAS). Oaxaca: barranca 14 miles southeast of Huajuapan, 1850 m., *R. Moran,* 6372, in 1957 (SD); grassy hillside, 5 miles northwest of Huitzo, 2050 m., *R. Moran,* 6380, in 1957 (SD). *Cultivated:* La Mortola, *Berger,* /R–07/468 (NY,US); Huntington Botanical Gardens, San Marino, *E. Walther* in 1929 (CAS, clonotype).

REMARKS. Unfortunately plate 12 (Cont. U. S. Nat. Herb. *loc. cit.),* was mislabeled and helped in confusing *E. gigantea* with *E. rubromarginata* Rose. The latter differs in its shorter caudex, narrower and more pointed leaves, shorter flowering branches with fewer flowers, shorter pedicels, shorter sepals, and a smaller differently colored corolla. Of the several species with such broad, orbicular leaves, *E. crenulata* differs in these being deep green, as are the bracts, in its often shorter and fewer-flowered branches, in its sepals narrower at base and there only slightly connate, and in its red and yellow corolla. In both *E. gibbiflora* and *E. pallida,* the leaves are devoid of any red margins and the lower bracts are broader.

The original plant seen at the Huntington Botanical Gardens would appear to have been a clonotype, originally sent out by Dr. Rose. It suffered from

Figure 111. 55. *Echeveria gigantea* Rose and Purpus. Plant of the type collection, grown in Washington. Photograph from the U. S. National Herbarium, no. 478; also in the original publication.

some unidentified leaf fungus. Living plants imported more recently through Sr. Halbinger and Dr. Cox do not differ noticeably from the type. Numerous seedlings have been raised locally, but few or none are true to name, in view of the readiness with which this crosses with any other nearby *Echeveria*.

56. **Echeveria acutifolia** Lindley.

(Figures 112–113. See pages 214, 215.)

Echeveria acutifolia LINDLEY, Bot. Reg. new ser., vol. 5, pl. 29, 1842; BRITTON AND ROSE, N. Amer. Fl., vol. 22, p. 24, 1905; POELLNITZ, *in* Fedde Repert., vol. 39, p. 254, 1936.
Cotyledon acutifolia (Lindley) BAKER, *in* Saunders Refug. Bot., vol. 1, no. 34, 1869.
Cotyledon devensis N. E. BROWN, Bot. Mag., pl. 8104, 1906.
Echeveria holwayi ROSE, Contrib. U.S. Nat. Herb., vol. 13, p. 295, 1911; BRITTON AND ROSE, N. Amer. Fl., vol. 22, p. 539, 1918.
ILLUSTRATIONS. Bot. Reg., vol. 5, new ser., pl. 29, 1842; Bot. Mag., pl. 8104, 1906; Jour. New York Bot. Gard., vol. 44, p. 522, 1943 (as *E. gibbiflora*); photograph no. 260, (US) [see figure 112].

Stem ultimately to 30 cm. tall or more, simple; leaves to 30 cm. long, to 8 cm. broad or more, oblong-obovate, at apex obliquely-obtuse and mucronate, less often somewhat acute, at base contracted into long petiole, this channeled above and winged at margins, the latter often undulate; inflorescence to 100 cm. tall, paniculate; peduncle erect; bracts numerous, oblong-oblanceolate, 3 to 10 cm. long, keeled, acutish, ascending; branches 9 or more, strongly nodding in bud, each with 10 to 12 flowers; pedicels 3 to 5 mm. long; sepals subequal, longest to 10 mm. long, linear-lanceolate, flattish, acute, ascending; corolla urceolate, pentagonal, to 13 mm. long, 10 mm. in diameter near base, 8 mm. at mouth; petals with deep basal hollow within; carpels short; nectaries truncate, transverse-reniform, to 1.5 mm. wide. Flowers from November to January. Description based on plant from Huntington Botanical Gardens, San Marino, California, presumably a clonotype of Rose's *E. holwayi*.

Color. Leaves courge-green tinged, deeply purplish vinaceous, or etruscan-red, more or less glaucous; peduncle often deep hellebore-red or nopal-red above; bracts as leaves, but in sun often with numerous merging red spots that consist of single or grouped epidermal cells containing red cell-sap (anthocyan); sepals hydrangea-red, but glaucous and hence purplish-lilac; corolla rose-red, but alizarine-pink with bloom; petals inside rose-red to orange-buff, lined red near apex; styles bordeaux, to black at tips.

TYPE. *Hartweg, 749,* from garden at Oaxaca, Mexico (CGE).

OCCURRENCE. Mexico. Oaxaca: Las Sedas; Sierra de Clavellina; San Sebastian los Fustes; Sierra de Juarez.

COLLECTIONS. Mexico. Oaxaca: in garden, Oaxaca, *Hartweg, 749* (CGE, type); Mixteca Alta, *Galeotti, 1840/2813* (BR); Las Sedas, *Conzatti, 07/2029* (F,GH,US); Sierra de Clavellinas, *C. L. Smith, 94/861* (US); Sierra de Juarez, Ixtlan, Ixtepeji, *T. MacDougall B-161* (UCBG-56.800); San Sebastian las Fustes, *T. MacDougall B-175* (UCBG-56.796); Oaxaca, *Holway, 03/693* (US, type of *E. holwayi;* CAS,GH,BH, clonotypes). *Cultivated:* Huntington Bot. Gard., San Marino, *E. Walther* in 1932 (US).

REMARKS. If *E. acutifolia* remained relatively unknown, as shown by the synonyms cited, this undoubtedly was because of the poor condition of both the illustration in the Botanical Register and the type specimen. Only by careful comparison of the striking distinctive coloration did I manage to recognize *E. acutifolia* in Rose's *E. holwayi* and *Cotyledon devensis* of the Botanical Magazine. Incidentally, the type of *E. holwayi* Rose which is US, no. 399680, *E. W. D. Holway,* Oaxaca in 1903, flowered in Washington, D. C., 1905 and

1909 (Rose, p. 693). The plant I studied at the Huntington Gardens undoubtedly came from this material. Under his remarks on *C. devensis* in the Botanical Magazine, N. R. Brown casts doubt on the reputed origin of *C. devensis* as a hybrid between *E. glauca* and *E. gibbiflora,* supposed to have come from Dickson's Nursery, of Chester. In the Kew Herbarium I saw a letter from Dickson's, Chester, dated February 22, 1906, which states "we are unable to trace having supplied the plant referred to and regret . . . that we can give no information about it as we have no knowledge of it."

Echeveria acutifolia resembles *E. grandifolia,* but the latter has much less brightly colored leaves and flowers, its leaves are usually straight and nearly always acute, and it has more elongate flowering branches, longer and more spreading sepals, and a larger corolla.

Plants grown locally have not proven very frost resistant, not surprising in view of their source; they often further suffer from an as yet unidentified leaf-spot disease, as does *E. gigantea.*

57. **Echeveria violescens** E. Walther.

(Figures 114–116. See pages 218, 219, 222.)

> *Echeveria violescens* E. WALTHER, Cactus and Succ. Jour. Amer., vol. 30, p. 40, 1958.
> *Echeveria gibbiflora* var. *metallica* Hort.; neither Baker nor Lemaire.
> ILLUSTRATIONS. Cactus and Succ. Jour. Amer., vol. 30, pp. 40–42, figs. 21–23, 1958; Smithsonian Scient. Ser., vol. 11, pl. 21 (as *E. gibbiflora* var. *metallica*), 1931.

Stem to 60 cm. tall, in vigorous plants branched in age; leaves 10 to 15, laxly rosulate, obovate-spathulate, at apex rounded to emarginate, mucronate, at base narrowed into petiole to 20 mm. broad, blade with edges folded upwards and often undulate; inflorescence one or many, often branched below into several erect panicles, 50 to 90 cm. tall; peduncle erect or ascending; lower bracts many, obovate-cuneate, 2 to 5 cm. long, flat, at apex truncate, mucronate; ultimate branches often short, lowermost sometimes with only one or two flowers each, strongly nodding in bud; upper bracts oblong-obovate, cuneate, acute; pedicels 2 to 4 mm. long, stout; sepals ascending, very unequal, longest to 10 mm. long, ovate-deltoid to oblong-oblanceolate, acute or shortly acuminate; corolla broadly urceolate, pentagonal, 12 to 14 mm. long, 9 to 11 mm. thick at base, 8 to 10 mm. at mouth; petals ovate-lanceolate, acuminate, spreading above, thick and deeply hollowed within at base, upper rim of cavity prominently transverse; stamens shorter than carpels, the epipetalous ones scarcely dilated at base; carpels short; nectaries transversely rhomboid-reniform, to over 2 mm. wide. Flowers from December to February. Description from living plant obtained from E. O. Orpet, Santa Barbara, California.

Color. Leaves vetiver-green, glaucous, tinged vinaceous-lilac; peduncle oxblood-red; bracts and sepals vinaceous-drab; corolla geranium-pink with bloom, or rose-red to deep pink, inside rose-pink above; styles nopal-red, to maroon at tips, nectaries whitish.

TYPE. From plant cultivated in Botanic Garden, Washington, D. C., supposedly from Saltillo, Coahuila, Mexico (US, no. 399949).

OCCURRENCE. Mexico. No definite locality is on record so far.

COLLECTIONS. *Cultivated:* flowered in Washington, D. C., *Palmer,* 05/399,660, supposedly from Saltillo, Coahuila (US, type; UC), *Rose,* 04/606 (BH); garden of Victor Reiter, San Francisco, *M. S. Jussel,* in 1933 (CAS).

REMARKS. A well grown plant of *E. violescens* is a truly colorful spectacle when in flower and an ornament to any garden sufficiently frost free to permit its unblemished development. My living material of this new species is traceable to Dr. Rose's collection at Washington, D. C., and is clearly identical with the illustration cited above. This watercolor was prepared by the late F. A. Walpole, (no. 524), one of a series Dr. Rose contemplated using for illustrating a monograph of the Crassulaceae.

Echeveria violescens appears distinct from *E. gibbiflora* var. *metallica,* as we understand the latter, in its broader, blunt-pointed bracts and rose-colored corolla, the last without any trace of yellow either inside or out. *Echeveria grandifolia* Haworth differs in having longer, narrower, more pointed leaves and bracts, and a red and yellow corolla. *Echeveria gigantea* Rose and Purpus agrees in having a red corolla without any trace of yellow, but there the leaves are a deep dull green with prominent red margins, and the sepals are much longer and more connate at base.

I am confident that sooner or later this species will be found in Mexico, too, even if rumors of its occurrence in Valle Bravo probably refer to another species.

Several hybrids are said to have been raised with this as one parent, but none seems to be extant at present.

58. **Echeveria gibbiflora** DeCandolle.
(Figures 117–119. See pages 223, 226, 227.)

Echeveria gibbiflora DECANDOLLE, Prodromus, vol. 3, p. 401, 1828.
Cotyledon gibbiflora (DeCandolle) BAKER, *in* Saunders Refug. Bot., vol. 1, no. 23, 1869, *in part.*
ILLUSTRATIONS. DeCandolle, Mem. Crass., pl. 5, 1828; Cactus and Succ. Jour. Amer., vol. 6, p. 150, figs. C1, C2, 1935; vol. 7, p. 167, figs. 8, 9, 10, 1936.

Stem stout, to 30 cm. tall, 5 cm. thick, simple; rosettes laxly few-leaved; leaves 15 or more, broadly obovate-orbicular, to over 25 cm. long and 15 cm. wide, narrowed at base into short petiole 25 mm. broad, at apex rounded and mucronate or acutish, shallowly concave above, margins often undulate crenulate, obscurely keeled beneath; inflorescence mostly solitary, paniculate, to over 100 cm. tall, with nine or more, about 12-flowered branches; peduncle stout, erect; bracts obovate-cuneate, to 10 cm. long and 45 mm. broad, thick at base, at apex rounded and acutish-mucronate; upper bracts linear, below calyx; sepals spreading to ascending, unequal, longest to 11 mm. long, deltoid-lanceolate, acute, the basal sinus revealing the gibbose base of the petals; corolla cylindric, pentagonal, slightly campanulate apex, to 16 mm. long, 10 mm. in diameter near base, 9 mm. at mouth; petals only slightly spreading above, bluntly keeled on back, deeply hollowed within at base; nectaries transversely ellipsoid, to 3 mm. wide. Flowers from October to January. Description from plants collected in Mexico at kilo 86, between Mexico City and Cuernavaca and grown in Golden Gate Park, San Francisco.

Color. Leaves light yellowish olive to rainette-green, more or less glaucous, tinged vinaceous-gray to vinaceous-lilac; peduncle pale rosalane-purple with bloom; bracts grayish olive tinged vinaceous-lavender to deep plumbago-blue; sepals deep dull lavender; corolla alizarine-pink with bloom, scarlet without this; petals inside light buff, to light jasper-red above; carpels and nectaries chartreuse-yellow; styles carmine to maroon.

TYPE. None designated. Neotype: DeCandolle, Mémoire Sur la Famille des Crassulacees, plate 5, 1828.

OCCURRENCE. Mexico. Morelos: at kilo 86 along railroad from Mexico City to Cuernavaca; also along new toll road at Kilos 50 to 60 on lava; Sierra de Tepoxtlan; San Juanico Tlacotenco; cultivated at Tepoxtlan.

COLLECTIONS. Mexico. Estado de Mexico: barranca between Tlacotepec and Zacoalpan, *P. Maury,* 1890/4977 (NY). Morelos: Cetela de Volcan, Cuautla, *P. Maury,* 90/4872 (NY); El Parque, *C. H. Thompson* in 1946 (MO); Pedregal above Cuernavaca, kilo 86 on R-road, flowered in Golden Gate Park, San Francisco, *E. Walther* in 1935 (CAS). *Cultivated*: A. Blake garden, Berkeley, *Bracelin* in 1942 (CAS); Washington, D. C., Botanic Garden, 03/529 (US); Golden Gate Park, San Francisco, *Baldwin,* 37/H-168 (BH); Knickerbocker Nursery, San Diego, California, 36/(BH).

REMARKS. When DeCandolle founded the new genus *Echeveria* in 1828, he included therein four species, of which one is a *Dudleya.* The others are: *Echeveria coccinea,* which had been in cultivation in Europe for about 30 years; *E. teretifolia,* known only from a rather poor drawing of a flowering branch; and the present species, also known then only from a drawing by Sr. A. Echeverria. However inadequate this drawing might be, it clearly represents a plant with very broad, rounded, and obtuse leaves and bracts. Looking for such a form near Mexico City finally led to the rediscovery of the true *E. gibbiflora* growing by thousands along the railroad at kilo 86, between Mexico City and Cuernavaca. Nowadays this colony is of easy access by auto, for the new toll road to Cuernavaca passes right through this area. Seedlings, abundant on the lava rocks, vary somewhat in color of leaf, but otherwise are very uniform and do not show any transitions to *E. grandifolia.* Plants associated with *E. gibbiflora* at this spot include *Pinus montezumae, Garrya macrophylla, Agave (Littaea)* sp., *Hechtia* sp., *Eryngium* sp., *Dahlia coccinea, Lopezia mexicana, Bocconia arborea, Notholaena* sp., *Cheilanthes* sp., *Pellaea sagittifolia, Adiantum* sp., and *Begonia* sp.

Ruins of the church at San Juanico Tlacotenco, not far away, were covered with numerous plants of this species at the time of my visit in 1934, when I also found this cultivated at El Parque and in Tepoxtlan. The flowers bloom at Christmas, and are utilized for decorating wayside crosses, etc.

When cultivated locally together, *E. gibbiflora* and *E. grandifolia* retain their distinctive characters. Similar broad round leaves are found in *E. crenulata,* in which they are deep green with red edges; in *E. gigantea,* in which they are lead-colored with red margins; and in *E. pallida,* in which they are a very pale yellowish green (and in which, also, numerous offshoots are produced from the base of the stem).

Several aberrant forms of *E. gibbiflora* have been placed on record in the past and given varietal names. They are here recognized as cultivars, as follows:

1. 'Metallica.' Leaves to 18 cm. long by 13 cm. broad, orbicular, obtuse and mucronate, when young a decided purplish-lilac edged with glaucous-green. *Echeveria metallica* Lemaire, Ill. Hort., volume 10, page 81, 1863; *Cotyledon gibbiflora* var. *metallica* (Lemaire) Baker in Saunders, Refug. Bot., volume 1, plate 65, 1869; *Echeveria gibbiflora* var. *metallica* (Lemaire) Ed. Morren, La Belg. Hort., volume 24, page 160, 1874.

2. 'Decora.' Leaves variegated white, rose, and green. *Echeveria gibbiflora* var. *decora* Rodigas.

3. 'Wavy-leaf.' Leaves with finely undulate margins. *Echeveria gibbiflora* var. *crispata* Hort.

Numerous hybrids have been reared, having *E. gibbiflora* for one parent. One of these is probably the most commonly cultivated *Echeveria* in California, *i.e. E.* 'Imbricata.'

59. **Echeveria grandifolia** Haworth.
   (Figures 120–121. See pages 230, 231.)

> *Echeveria grandifolia* HAWORTH, *in* Taylor's Phil. Mag., vol. 4, p. 262, 1828; SWEET, Brit. Fl. Gard., vol. 3, pl. 275, 1838; LEMAIRE, Ill. Hort., vol. 10, misc. p. 80, no. 16, 1863.
>
> *Echeveria gibbiflora* LINDLEY, Bot. Reg., vol. 15, pl. 1247, 1829; BRITTON AND ROSE, N. Amer. Fl., vol. 22, p. 25, 1905; BERGER (as var. *typica*) *in* Engler Nat. Pflanzenf., ed. 2, vol. 18a, p. 476, 1930; POELLNITZ, *in* Fedde Repert., vol. 39, p. 255, 1936; *not* DeCandolle.
>
> *Echeveria campanulata* KUNZE, Delect. Sem. Lips., 1842; Linnaea, vol. 17, p. 574, 1843.
>
> *Cotyledon gibbiflora* BAKER, *in* Saunders Refug. Bot., vol. 1, no. 23, 1869, *in part only.*
>
> ILLUSTRATIONS. Sweet, Brit. Fl. Gard., vol. 3, pl. 275, 1838; Bot. Reg., vol. 15, pl. 1247, 1829; Cactus and Succ. Jour. Amer., vol. 6, no. 10 (cover), April, 1935; Cactaceas y Suculentas Mexicanas, vol. 3, p. 33, fig. 20, 1958.

Stem to 25 cm. tall or more, rarely branched below; rosettes lax; leaves few, 12 to 15, large, to 30 cm. long and 12 cm. broad, broadly oblanceolate, usually flat, or with margins upcurved and sometimes undulate, acute and mucronate at base narrowed into long petiole to 2 cm. wide which is channeled above and keeled beneath; inflorescences three or more, to 100 cm. tall or more, paniculate, sometimes compound; peduncle stout, to over 15 mm. thick near base, mostly erect; bracts numerous, oblong-obovate, shortly acuminate, to 4 cm. long ascending; branches 10 to 12, each with eight or more flowers, strongly nodding in bud; pedicels 3 to 6 mm. long; sepals unequal, longest to 15 mm. long but often much shorter, deltoid to linear-lanceolate, acute, ascending to recurved; corolla cylindroid, to campanulate above, pentagonal, 12 to 14 mm. long, 9 to 10 mm. in diameter at base, to 12 mm. wide at mouth, narrowed to 8 mm. at neck; petals keeled on back, prominently hollowed at base within; carpels slender; anthers oblong; nectaries reniform, truncate, to 2 mm. wide. Flowers from October to December. Description from plants cultivated locally which agree with Mexican material seen.

Color. Leaves light cress-green to biscay-green, glaucous; peduncle pompeian-red; bracts light purple-drab to deep purplish vinaceous; sepals like bracts; corolla jasper-red with bloom, scarlet-red without this; petals inside buff-yellow lined red above; styles carmine to maroon above; stigmas greenish; nectaries white.

TYPE. None designated. Neotype: Sweet's plate 275, British Flower Garden, volume 3, 1838.

OCCURRENCE. Mexico. Federal District: Barranca de Aqueducto near Santa Fe, Cañada de Contreras, along road to Toluca at Tetelpan, barranca near Villa Obregon, State of Mexico: Toluca, on Cerro Teresano Morelos: epiphytic and on rocks in woods near village of Santa Maria near Cuernavaca. Michoacan: San Jose de Purua.

COLLECTIONS. Mexico. Federal District: Pedregal lava fields, *Bourgeau,* 1378 (P), *Pringle* 99/8017 (BH,GH,NY,P,PH,UC,US); Santa Fe, *Rose, 05/*

704 (GH); Eslava, *Rose,* 03/7155 (F,GH,NY,US). *Cultivated*: Cornell, *Clausen* in 1936 (BH); San Francisco; *Clausen* in 1938 (BH,CAS); Geneva, *Moricand* in 1840 (G); garden of V. Reiter, San Francisco, *E. Walther* in 1931 (CAS).

REMARKS. Both Haworth and Sweet would seem to have been well acquainted with the true *E. gibbiflora* when they published their description of *E. grandifolia,* in the same year in which DeCandolle published the genus *Echeveria,* as well as the drawing, by A. Echeverria, of *E. gibbiflora.* Kunze, too, knew the difference between these species, but appears to have overlooked *E. grandifolia* of Haworth and Sweet, and hence coined the superfluous name *E. campanulata.*

The most notable difference between *E. gibbiflora* and *E. grandifolia* is the shape of leaves and bracts, both of which are distinctly narrower and more pointed in the latter species. This difference applies to cultivated plants as well as to most plants I saw in their native habitat, and is retained when they are grown together in gardens.

Of narrow-leaved species that have a distinct caudex, *E. acutifolia* from Oaxaca differs in its usually more highly colored leaves, peduncle, and bracts, in its linear sepals, and in its smaller bright-red corolla. *Echeveria rubromarginata,* too, has smaller flowers that are almost sessile.

Echeveria grandifolia occurs wild within the limits of Mexico City, as on the well known Pedregal, and appears in no danger of extinction. Its occurrence appears to be governed by the incidence of frost, not unknown at this altitude of over 7500 feet. "Oreja de Cerro" is its local name.

Echeveria grandifolia has long been cultivated in California gardens, and a number of *E. grandifolia* cultivars may be noted here:

1. 'Blister-leaf.' Leaves conspicuously blistered above. *Echeveria carunculata* Hort.

2. 'Crest.' Stem flattened laterally, fasciated. *Echeveria cristata* Hort.

3. 'Green-leaf.' Leaves flat, green, scarcely glaucous and only slightly purplish. *Echeveria viridis* Hort.

Series 6. ANGULATAE E. Walther

Echeveria, ser. Angulatae E. WALTHER, Cactus and Succ. Jour. Amer., vol. 7, p. 69, 1935; Leafl. West. Bot., vol. 9, pp. 2, 4, 1959.

Glabrous; stem short or none, with few or no offsets; leaves densely rosulate, often rather few, mostly thick and turgid, small to medium-sized, frequently more or less deeply concave above; inflorescence with one to three secund branches; peduncle stout, erect, with few to many bracts, these usually appressed to ascending, thick, often subterete; pedicels short or none, rarely elongate, bractless; sepals stout, mostly spreading, half the length of the corolla or more; corolla sharply pentagonal; petals thick, deeply hollowed within at base; nectaries large, thick.

TYPICAL SPECIES. *Echeveria teretifolia* DeCandolle.

REMARKS. *Echeveria teretifolia* is known to us only from a drawing of a fragmentary specimen without any basal leaves. I regret that it has not been possible to identify it positively but still I can safely designate it the type of the series Angulatae. Anomalous by reason of their small thick leaves that are scarcely hollowed above are *E. humilis, E. tenuis, E. bifida,* and *E. heterosepala.* The last-mentioned species may occasionally develop petal appendages resembling those found in the genus *Pachyphytum,* but this would appear to be an abnormality.

KEY TO THE SPECIES

A. Inflorescence mostly simple, unbranched.
    B. Flowers distinctly pedicellate.
        C. Leaves broadly ovate-lanceolate, thick, to over 22 mm. wide. . 60. *E. humilis*
        C. Leaves narrowly oblong-oblanceolate, to 4 cm. long and only 9 mm. broad or less. . . . . 61. *E. angustifolia*
    B. Flowers sessile, pedicels very short or none.
        C. Corolla clear yellow, neither greenish nor reddish, leaves deeply concave above, strongly upcurved at the hornlike apex; sepals sometimes articulated.
                                                69. *E. lutea*
           D. Leaves pale green, as are the bracts and sepals; leaves 7 to 11 cm. long; inflorescence to 75 cm. tall, occasionally 2-branched. . 69a. *E. lutea* var. *lutea*
           D. Leaves fuscous, brownish green, as are the bracts and sepals; leaves to 5 cm. long; inflorescence to 35 cm. tall. . . . . . . 69b. *E. lutea* var. *fuscata*
        C. Flowers reddish or greenish, never clear yellow.
           D. Leaves very thick, short, 6 cm. long or less, above flat or convex.
                                                62. *E. tenuis*
           D. Leaves thin, longer, to 7 cm. long or more, above flat or shallowly concave.
              E. Leaves 4 to 7 cm. long; rachis not brightly colored; corolla greenish, tinged red at maturity. Puebla. . . . . 63. *E. heterosepala*
              E. Leaves 7 to 9 cm. long; rachis bright red at anthesis; corolla red. Texas to Mexico. . . . . 66. *E. strictiflora*
A. Inflorescence with 2 or 3 branches.
    B. Pedicels evident, 2 to 4 or even 6 mm. long, slender. Hidalgo. . . 64. *E. bifida*
    B. Pedicels very short or none, thick; flowers sessile.
        C. Bracts flat, relatively broad, scarcely subterete.
           D. Leaves and bracts bright shining-green with red margins; corolla scarlet; inflorescence 2- or 3-branched. San Luis Potosi, Puebla. . . 68. *E. schaffneri*
           D. Leaves rather dull or pale green, occasionally tinged red or brown.
              E. Rachis above, bracts and sepals bright red at anthesis; sepals ascending; inflorescence more often simple, unbranched. Texas to Mexico.
                                              66. *E. strictiflora*
              E. Rachis, bracts and sepals not highly colored at anthesis; sepals widely spreading, short; inflorescence usually 2-branched. Northeastern Mexico.
                                            67. *E. walpoleana*

C. Bracts narrow, subterete.
    D. Basal leaves unknown; inflorescence 2-branched; pedicels very short; sepals widely spreading; corolla short, broad, red. Mexico (?). . 70. *E. teretifolia*
    D. Basal leaves known.
        E. Leaves deeply hollowed above, apex more or less strongly upcurved.
            F. Corolla red to scarlet; sepals not articulated at base. Ixmiquilpan, Hidalgo. . . . . 71. *E. bifurcata*
            F. Corolla pale, rose or yellowish; one or more sepals articulated at base.
                G. Corolla rose-colored; inflorescence mostly 2- or 3-branched; leaves gray-green. . . . . 72. *E. erubescens*
                G. Corolla bright yellow; inflorescence more often simple, unbranched, or 2-branched; leaves deeply concave above and strongly upcurved at apex. San Luis Potosi. . . . . 69. *E. lutea*
                    H. Leaves pale green. . . . . 69a. *E. lutea* var. *lutea*
                    H. Leaves brownish green. . . . . . 69b. *E. lutea* var. *fuscata*
        E. Leaves flat or nearly so above, apex straight.
            F. Leaves broad, oblanceolate, flat, 6 to 12 cm. long and 10 to 18 mm. broad; stem evident in age; sepals deflexed at anthesis. Hidalgo; Rio de Tolantango. . . . . 65. *E. trianthina*
            F. Leaves very narrow, linear-oblong, to 11 cm. long and scarcely over 10 mm. broad. . . . . 73. *E. tenuifolia*

60. **Echeveria humilis** Rose.

Echeveria humilis Rose, *in* Britton and Rose, Bull. New York Bot. Gard., vol. 3, p. 8, 1903; Britton and Rose, N. Amer. Fl., vol. 22, p. 20, 1905; E. Walther, Cactus and Succ. Jour. Amer., vol. 7, p. 70, 1935; Poellnitz, *in* Fedde Repert., vol. 39, p. 238, 1936.

Stem short, ultimately branched, axis or rosettes somewhat elongated, but leaves crowded, numerous, 4 cm. to 5 cm. or rarely to 7 cm. long, to 22 mm. broad, ovate-lanceolate, acute to acuminate, apex pungent-pointed to aristate, very turgid, thickest near base, strongly convex beneath, both transversely and longitudinally, flatish above, upcurved above the middle, drying very thick and leathery; inflorescences one or two; usually simple, but sometimes 3-branched (G. H. Schaffner, 76/769) (see Bull. NYBG, *loc. cit.*) peduncle erect or somewhat flexuose, to 20 cm. tall; bracts oblong, acute, subterete, to 2 cm. long, appressed; racemes simple, secund, with 12 or more flowers; pedicels short, but evident, 2 to 4 mm. long, slender; sepals very unequal, longest to 9 mm. long, very thick and turgid, deltoid-lanceolate, acute, ascending; corolla urceolate-campanulate, to 13 mm. long, 8 mm. in basal diameter; petals somewhat spreading above, long-apiculate at apex; carpels 6 mm. long; nectaries oblique, transversely reniform, to 2 mm. wide. Flowers from August on. Description of imported plants grown at Strybing Arboretum, Golden Gate Park, San Francisco.

Color. Leaves grape-green to buffy-brown; peduncle grape-green; bracts vinaceous-brown to deep-olive; sepals as bracts, but somewhat glaucous; corolla viridine-yellow in bud, later capucine-buff at base, salmon-orange at apex; petals light orange-yellow inside; styles cosse-green; nectaries pale green-yellow.

Type. *Parry and Palmer* 1878/233, vicinity of San Luis Potosi, Mexico (US, no. 48363).

Occurrence. Mexico. San Luis Potosi; Hidalgo (?).

Collections. Mexico. San Luis Potosi: vicinity of San Luis Potosi, *Parry and Palmer,* 1878/233 (US, type), Schaffner, 79/769 (GH, MEXU, NY), *Purpus,* 05/465 (GH); *Virles,* 1891/1573, 1574 (P).

REMARKS. Parry and Palmer's type sheet originally consisted of mixed material, some of it being *E. agavoides,* which has since been removed. I base the description wholly on living material recently imported. *Echeveria humilis* is closely related to *E. tenuis,* but clearly differs in the evident pedicels and in its narrower, longer, and long-acuminate leaves. The chromosome number is $n=32$.

61. **Echeveria angustifolia** E. Walther, new species.
(Figures 122–123. See pages 234, 235.)

Echeveria angustifolia E. Walther, sp. nov., pertinens ad ser. Angulatas, glaberrima; caudice brevi, erecto, simplici; foliis rosulatis, numerosis, usque ad 30, crassis, angustis, oblongo-oblanceolatis, usque ad 4 cm. longis, 7–9 mm. latis, apice acuminato-pungentibus; scapis usque ad 20 cm. altis; pedunculis erectis, strictis, usque ad 4 mm. crassis ad basin, bracteis paucis instructis; bracteis planis, adpressis, usque ad 10 mm. longis; racemis simplicibus, secundis, 10–15-floris; pedicellis 2–4 mm. longis; sepalis patentibus, usque ad 8 mm. longis, deltoideo-lanceolatis; corollis pentagonalibus, usque ad 11 mm. longis, 6–7 mm. diametro ad basin, rubris.

Glabrous; stem evident, simple, to 3 cm. tall or more, leaves densely rosulate, to 30 or more, narrowly oblong-oblanceolate, to 4 cm. long, but only 7 to 9 mm. broad, thick, rounded beneath, above shallowly concave, somewhat up-curved at the pungent-acuminate apex; scapes two, to 20 cm. tall, erect or ascending; peduncle 3 to 4 mm. thick at base; bracts few and small, four to eight in number, flat, linear-obovate, to 10 mm. long, appressed; racemes simple, secund, with 10 to 15 flowers; pedicels evident, 2 to 4 mm. long or more; sepals widely spreading, longest to 8 mm. long, deltoid-lanceolate, acute; corolla conoid, sharply pentagonal, to 11 mm. long, 6 to 7 mm. in basal diameter, 3 to 4 mm. wide at mouth; petals acuminate, only slightly spreading at tips. Description based solely on the type and US photograph number 719.

Color. Not discernable in the dried type, but corolla dark, reddish.

TYPE. *Purpus,* 05/205 (*Rose,* 05/465), US, no. 888640, collected at San Luis Potosi, San Luis Potosi, Mexico. Illustration: Photograph no. 719 (US). [See figure 122].

OCCURRENCE. Mexico. San Luis Potosi; no exact locale is known.

REMARKS. The type sheet was filed under *E. humilis* Rose, to which species *E. angustifolia* is probably related, but from which it clearly differs in the longer, narrower leaves, less than 10 mm. in width, more distinctly concave above, and much more acuminate. The plant shown in the photograph was obviously grown under glass, and allowances should be made for this when comparing this with field-collected material.

62. **Echeveria tenuis** Rose.

Echeveria tenuis ROSE, *in* Britton and Rose, Bull. New York Bot. Gard., vol. 3, p. 7, 1903; BRITTON AND ROSE, N. Amer. Fl., vol. 22, p. 19, 1905; POELLNITZ, *in* Fedde Repert., vol. 39, p. 239, 1936 (as synonym of *E. peacockii*).

Stem very short or none, usually simple; rosettes with short axis and few, usually less than 10 crowded leaves, these very thick and turgid, thickest below middle, strongly convex beneath, nearly flat above, oblong-ovate, acute, pungent-mucronate to aristate when young, 4 to 6 cm. long, 10 to 15 mm. broad, 10 to 12 mm. thick, not at all glaucous; inflorescence usually solitary, simple, secund, to 25 cm. tall; peduncle laxly ascending or flexuose; bracts few, appressed, thick, semiterete, narrowly deltoid-oblong, to 18 mm. long, acute, at base truncate or with a short, single, rounded spur; racemes with 12 to 15 crowded flowers; upper bracts linear, to 10 mm. long; pedicels slender, but less than 2 mm. long; sepals ascending-upcurved, very thick and turgid at base, terete-triquetrous, linear-deltoid, acute, the longest to 10 mm. long; corolla urceolate-campanulate, to 15 mm. long, 10 mm. in basal diameter, 6 to 7 mm. wide at mouth; petals thick, bluntly keeled, gibbose at base, at apex outcurved and subulate-apiculate; carpels 7 mm. long; nectaries oblique, narrowly transverse-reniform, to 3.5 mm. wide. Flowers from August on. Description based on living plants imported from F. Schmoll, Cadereyta.

Color. Leaves light elm-green tinged dull indian-purple, not at all glaucous; bracts as leaves; sepals brownish olive; corolla ochraceous-salmon, to pale flesh-color at base; petals inside empire-yellow; styles turtle-green.

TYPE. *Rose,* 1897/2640a, on rocks on top of mountain near Monte Escobeda, Zacatecas, Mexico (US, no. 301564).

OCCURRENCE. So far known only from above locality.

COLLECTIONS. Mexico. Zacatecas, the type collection (US). *Cultivated*: Golden Gate Park, San Francisco, *E. Walther* (CAS).

REMARKS. This species differs quite clearly from *E. peacockii* in the total absence of any pruinose coating of foliage and bracts, which of course may not be so readily apparent in dried specimens. Actually, its nearest relation is *E. humilis,* from which it differs in its very short pedicels, less acuminate leaves thickest near the middle, and more ascending sepals.

63. **Echeveria heterosepala** Rose.

(Figures 124–127. See pages 238, 239, 242.)

Echeveria heterosepala ROSE, *in* Britton and Rose, Bull. New York Bot. Gard., vol. 3, p. 8, 1903; BRITTON AND ROSE, N. Amer. Fl., vol. 22, p. 20, 1905; BERGER, *in* Engler Nat. Pflanzenf. ed. 2, vol. 18a., p. 474, 1930.
Pachyphytum chloranthum E. WALTHER, Cactus and Succ. Jour. Amer., vol. 3, p. 12, 1931.
Pachyphytum heterosepalum (Rose) E. WALTHER, Cactus and Succ. Jour. Amer., vol. 7, p. 70, 1935.
ILLUSTRATIONS. Cactus and Succ. Jour. Amer., vol. 3, p. 13, figs. 2–7, photographs, pp. 9, 10, figs. 9, 10, 12, 1931.

Glabrous, stem simple, fusiform, short or to 6 cm. long, mostly subterranean; leaves densely rosulate, rhomboid-lanceolate, acuminate to aristate-mucronate, broadest above the middle, 4 to 7 cm. long, 15 to 20 mm. broad; inflorescence single, simply secund-racemose; peduncle stout, erect, to 45 cm. tall; lower bracts numerous, strongly ascending, 2 to 3 cm. long, oblanceolate, acute, readily detached; raceme with 8 to 15 flowers; upper bracts smaller and more distant than the lower, oblong, thickest near base, curved downward to ascending; pedicels stout, 3 mm. long or less, only rarely to 7 mm. long; sepals unequal, broadly united at base, turgid, ovate-deltoid, acute, longest 5 to 7 mm. long, spreading to ascending; corolla broadly urceolate, pentagonal, to 10 mm. long, relatively broad, 8 mm. in diameter at base and at mouth; petals bluntly keeled, with basal hollow within, the last sometimes bearing two appendages on its upper rim at each side of epipetalous filaments, simulating the

PLATE ONE, UPPER

17. *Echeveria sanchez-mejoradae* E. Walther. Flowers, × 0.3. Plant flowering in San Diego 13 April 1960; collected at Tajo de Caballeros, near the type locality, on the road from Venados to Zacualtipán, Hidalgo, Mexico (Moran & Kimnach 7798).
[See page 108]

PLATE ONE, LOWER

22. *Echeveria halbingeri* E. Walther. Flowers, × 2.7. Plant flowering in San Diego 24 April 1960; part of the type collection (UCBG 57.796). [See page 120]

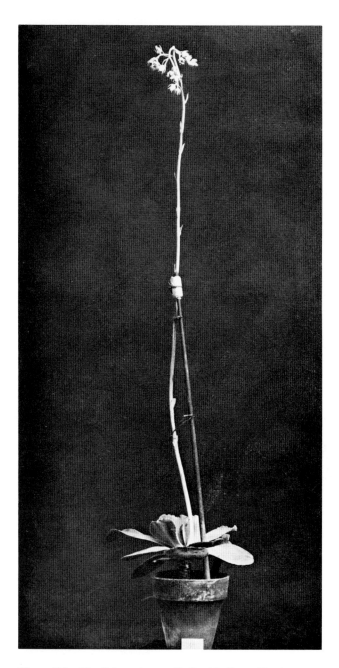

Figure 112. 56. *Echeveria acutifolia* Lindley. Plant grown in Washington; part of the type collection of *E. holwayi* Rose (Rose greenhouse plant 693). Photograph from the U. S. National Herbarium, no. 260. [See page 203]

Figure 113. 56. *Echeveria acutifolia* Lindley. Plant of the type collection, grown at the Royal Horticultural Society, London. From the original publication (Edwards's Botanical Register, volume 28, plate 29). [See page 203]

216

PLATE TWO

44. *Echeveria obtusifolia* Rose. Plant of the type collection of *E. scopulorum* Rose (greenhouse plant *653*), flowering in Washington 19 December 1903. Watercolor painting no. 131 by F. A. Walpole, from the U.S. National Herbarium. [See page 164]

PLATE THREE, UPPER

66. *Echeveria strictiflora* A. Gray. Flowering plant, × 0.3. Plant photographed 18 July 1957 at the U. C. Botanical Garden (52.1677); collected on Emory Peak, Chisos Mountains, Texas. [See page 249]

PLATE THREE, LOWER

64. *Echeveria bifida* Schlechtendal. Inflorescence, × 1.3. Plant flowering in San Diego 22 July 1959; collected in the Barranca de Venados, a cited locality, Hidalgo, Mexico (Moran 6416). [See page 245]

Figure 114.   57. *Echeveria violescens* E. Walther. Plant grown in Washington. Watercolor by F. A. Walpole, titled *E. gibbiflora* var. *metallica* (Smithsonian Scientific Series, volume 11, plate 21). [See page 204]

Figure 115. 57. *Echeveria violescens* E. Walther. From the original publication (Cactus and Succulent Journal, volume 30, page 41, figure 22). [See page 204]

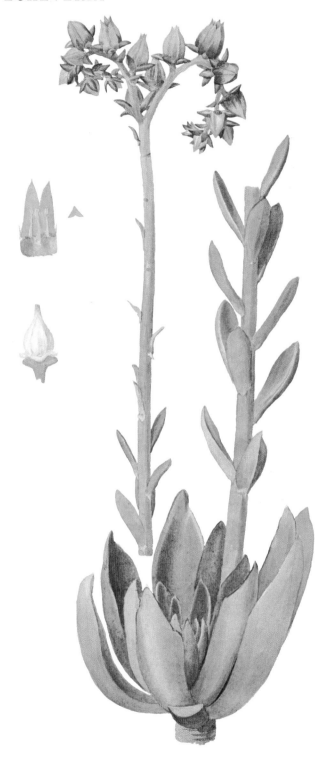

PLATE FOUR

67. *Echeveria walpoleana* Rose. Plant of the type collection (greenhouse plant *506*), flowering in Washington 11 August 1903. Watercolor painting no. 116 by F. A. Walpole, from the U.S. National Herbarium. [See page 252]

PLATE FIVE, UPPER

79. *Echeveria nuda* Lindley. Flowering plant.
× 0.4. Plant photographed in San Diego
2 July 1960; collected at El Paraje, Veracruz, Mexico (Moran & Kimnach 7775).
[See page 278]

PLATE FIVE, LOWER

76. *Echeveria shaviana* E. Walther. Rosettes, × 1.4. Cultivated plants of uncertain
origin, photographed in Berkeley 29 August
1962.[See page 270]

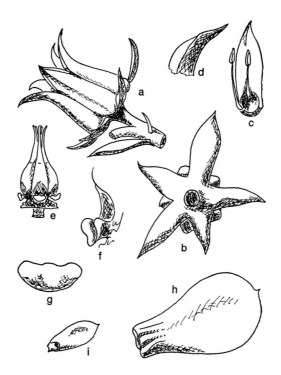

Figure 116. 57. *Echeveria violescens* E. Walther. Explanation: (a) flower, × 2; (b) flower from below, × 2; (c) inside of petal, × 2; (d) apex of petal, × 8; (e) carpels, × 2; (f) nectary, side view, × 8; (g) nectary, front view, × 8; (h) leaf, × 0.12; (i) bract, × 0.4. From the original publication (Cactus and Succulent Journal, volume 30, page 40, figure 21). [See page 204]

Figure 117. 58. *Echeveria gibbiflora* DeCandolle. Plate on which the original description was based, here three-quarters the original size (DeCandolle, Mémoire sur la Famille des Crassulacées, plate 5). This plate is designated lectotype for the species.
[See page 205]

PLATE SIX, UPPER

80. *Echeveria montana* Rose. Inflorescence, × 1.3. Plant flowering in San Diego 11 June 1960; collected in Cañada Estudiante, near the type locality, Oaxaca, Mexico (Moran & Kimnach 7762). [See page 281]

PLATE SIX, LOWER

84. *Echeveria sprucei* (Baker) Berger. Inflorescence, × 1.9. Plant flowering in San Diego 2 April 1960; collected at the type locality by Harry Johnson (UCBG 57.452b). [See page 290]

PLATE SEVEN

87. *Echeveria australis* Rose. Plant of the type collection (greenhouse plant *523*), flowering in Washington 14 December 1902. Watercolor painting no. 69 by F. A. Walpole, from the U.S. National Herbarium. [See page 297]

Figure 118. 58. *Echeveria gibbiflora* DeCandolle. Inflorescence, × 0.5. Plant flowering in San Diego 10 December 1960; collected on the pedregal above Cuernavaca, Morelos, Mexico, a cited locality (Moran 6401). [See page 205]

Figure 119. 58. *Echeveria gibbiflora* DeCandolle. Flowering branch, × 2. Plant flowering in San Diego 13 December 1959; collected on the pedregal above Cuernavaca, Morelos, Mexico, a cited locality (Moran 6401).

[See page 205]

PLATE EIGHT

94. *Echeveria multicaulis* Rose. Plant of the type collection (greenhouse plant *628*), flowering in Washington 22 December 1903. Watercolor painting no. 132 by F. A. Walpole, from the U.S. National Herbarium. [See page 312]

PLATE NINE, UPPER

100. *Echeveria rosea* Lindley. Inflorescence, × 1.4. Plant flowering in San Diego 21 January 1961; collected at Puerto Obscuro, Hidalgo, Mexico (Moran & Kimnach 7813).
[See page 324]

PLATE NINE, LOWER

95. *Echeveria nodulosa* (Baker) Otto. Inflorescence, × 1.8. Plant flowering in San Diego 11 July 1959; collected at Santiago Acatepec, Oaxaca, Mexico (Moran 6356, a cited collection). [See page 313]

Figure 120.   59. *Echeveria grandifolia* Haworth. Plant grown at the Royal Horticultural Society, London; collected by James McRae. From an article by J. Lindley (Edwards's Botanical Register, volume 15, plate 1247). [See page 207]

Figure 121. 59. *Echeveria grandifolia* Haworth. From an article by Eric Walther (American Horticultural Magazine, volume 39, page 86). The plate at the left (Sweet, British Flower Garden, volume 3, plate 275) is designated neotype for the species.

[See page 207]

PLATE TEN

101. *Echeveria atropurpurea* (Baker) Ed. Morren. Plant (Rose greenhouse plant *531*), flowering in Washington 3 January 1903. Watercolor painting no. 73 by F. A. Walpole, from the U.S. National Herbarium. [See page 328]

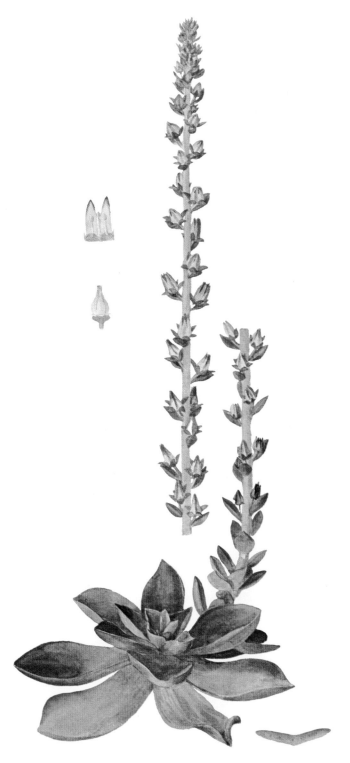

PLATE ELEVEN

108. *Echeveria racemosa* Schlechtendal & Chamisso. Plant flowering in Washington 21 August 1903; collected at Jalapa, Veracruz, Mexico, the type locality (Rose & Hay 6124 = greenhouse plant *316*). Watercolor painting no. 120 by F. A. Walpole, from the U.S. National Herbarium. [See page 340]

Figure 122. 61. *Echeveria angustifolia* E. Walther. Type plant, grown in Washington; collected near San Luis Potosi, Mexico, in 1905 by C. A. Purpus (205). Photograph from the U.S. National Herbarium, no. 719.
[See page 211]

Figure 123. 61. *Echeveria angustifolia* E. Walther. Holotype in the U.S. National Herbarium. [See page 211]

PLATE TWELVE

127. *Echeveria platyphylla* Rose. Plant of the type collection (Rose *6393* = greenhouse plant *202*), flowering in Washington 13 February 1902. Watercolor painting no. 46 by F. A. Walpole, from the U.S. National Herbarium. [See page 378]

PLATE THIRTEEN

133. *Echeveria pulvinata* Rose. Plant flowering in Washington February 1902; collected in Tomellin Cañon, Oaxaca, Mexico, the type locality (Rose *4994* = greenhouse plant *61*). Watercolor painting no. 48 by F. A. Walpole, from the U.S. National Herbarium.

[See page 392]

Figure 124. 63. *Echeveria heterosepala* Rose. Inflorescence, × 2. Plant flowering in San Diego 11 June 1960; collected near Santiago Acatepec, Puebla, Mexico (Moran and Kimnach 7728). [See page 212]

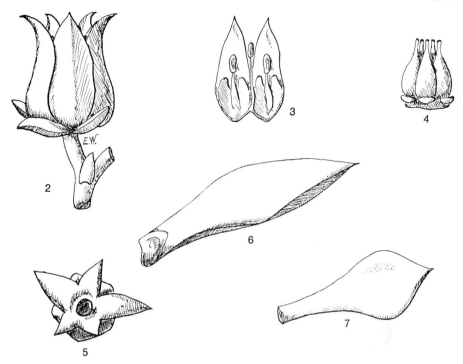

Figure 125. 63. *Echeveria heterosepala* Rose. Explanation: (2) flower, × 3; (3) inside of petals, showing the scale-like appendages, × 3; (4) carpels, × 3; (5) flower from below, × 3; (6) lower bract, × 3; (7) leaf, × 1. From the original publication of *Pachyphytum chloranthum* E. Walther (Cactus and Succulent Journal, volume 3, page 13).

[See page 212]

Figure 126. 63. *Echeveria heterosepala* Rose. Rosette, approximately × 0.7. From the original publication of *Pachyphytum chloranthum* E. Walther (Cactus and Succulent Journal, volume 3, page 10, figure 12).

[See page 212]

PLATE FOURTEEN, UPPER

136. *Echeveria setosa* Rose & Purpus. Flowering plant, × 0.6. Plant photographed in San Diego 20 May 1962; collected at the type locality (Moran & Kimnach 7721).
[See page 398]

PLATE FOURTEEN, LOWER

137. *Echeveria ciliata* Moran. Inflorescence, × 1.4. Plant flowering in San Diego 30 April 1961; collected at the type locality (Moran & Kimnach 7733). [See page 401]

PLATE FIFTEEN, UPPER

138. *Echeveria pringlei* (S. Watson) Rose. Inflorescence, × 1.4. Plant flowering in San Diego 18 November 1964; collected at Experiencia, Jalisco, Mexico, by J. B. Zabaleta (UCBG 53.1156, a cited collection). [See page 402]

PLATE FIFTEEN, LOWER

140. *Echeveria amphoralis* E. Walther. Inflorescence, × 0.8. Plant flowering in San Diego 18 July 1964; collected at kilometer 606, south of Mitla, Oaxaca, Mexico, by H. E. Moore (8176). [See page 406]

Figure 127. 63. *Echeveria heterosepala* Rose. Rosette, × 2. Plant grown in San Diego; collected near Santiago Acatepec, Puebla, Mexico (Moran and Kimnach 7728).
[See page 212]

Figure 128. 64. *Echeveria bifida* Schlechtendal. Flowering plant, ×
0.75. Plant photographed in San Diego 9 July 1960; collected at La
Paila, Barranca de Venados, Hidalgo, Mexico (Moran and Kimnach
7791). Barranca de Venados is a cited locality. [See page 245]

PLATE SIXTEEN, UPPER

142. *Echeveria harmsi* J. F. Macbride. Flowering plant, × 0.6. Cultivated plant of unknown origin (Moran 8362) flowering in San Diego 8 July 1961. [See page 409]

PLATE SIXTEEN, LOWER

143. *Echeveria longissima* E. Walther. Flowering plant, × 0.5. Cultivated plant (Moran 12277) presumably from the original introduction; flowering in San Diego 12 June 1966. [See page 413]

characteristic appendages found in *Pachyphytum,* but often absent; carpels stout, 6 mm. long; ripe follicles widely spreading (Rose, Painter, and Rose, 1905); nectaries transversely elliptic, 2 mm. wide. Flowers from July on. Description from plants grown locally, originally from Esperanza (Eric Walther, 1934).

Color. Leaves light hellebore-green, but somewhat glaucous and hence pea-green, tinged vinaceous-brown; bracts as leaves but more vinaceous-brown; sepals as leaves and bracts; pedicels eugenia-red; corolla in bud apple-green to malachite-green, at anthesis tinged light coral-red on keel, later wholly acajou-red; inside light bice-green to courge-green; carpels lettuce- to peacock-green above, grass-green below; nectaries amber-yellow.

TYPE. *Pringle,* 1895/7499, from calcareous hills near Tehuacan, Puebla, Mexico (US, no. 316777).

OCCURRENCE. Mexico. Puebla: vicinity of Tehuacan, near Esperanza, Cerro de Paxtle, etc.

COLLECTIONS. Mexico. Puebla: the type (US); near Tehuacan, *Rose, Painter and Rose,* 05/10277 (US); near Esperanza, *H. E. Seaton,* 91/333a (F,US), *E. K. Balls,* 38/B-5254 (K,UC,US); Cerro de Paxtle, on limestone, *Purpus,* 07/420 (BH,US). *Cultivated*: *E. Walther* (CAS).

REMARKS. Confusion attending this species has been due, first, to the difficulty of identifying living plants from dried herbarium material, and second, to the remarkable occasional occurrence of petal-appendages which are supposedly confined to *Pachyphytum.* Similarly, abnormal petal-appendages have been observed in at least one specimen of *Echeveria longissima. Pachyphytum,* for its existence as a genus, of course does not depend solely on this one character; nor would we ever consider merging the two genera. While admittedly they are closely related and intercross freely in gardens, they differ sufficiently to be regarded as distinct entities.

Echeveria heterosepala slightly resembles *E. tenuis,* but that differs in having much thicker leaves broadest below the middle, fewer, semiterete bracts, and a corolla which is up to 15 mm. long, salmon-colored, and never green at anthesis.

[This species was discussed, described, and illustrated by Reid Moran in 1960 in Cactaceas y Suculentas Mexicanas vol. 5, pp. 75–80, figs. 41–45, 52 (figs. 41 and 52 in color). Dr. Moran established a new series, Chloranthae, based on this remarkable species (loc. cit., p. 78).—EDITOR.]

64. **Echeveria bifida** Schlechtendal.

(Figures 128–129. Plate 3, lower; see page 217.)

Echeveria bifida SCHLECHTENDAL, Linnaea, vol. 13, p. 411, 1839; BRITTON AND ROSE, N. Amer. Fl., vol. 22, p. 20, 1905; POELLNITZ, *in* Fedde Repert., vol. 39, p. 242, 1936.
Echeveria teretifolia KUNZE, Linnaea, vol. 17, p. 574, 1843; *not* DeCandolle.
Cotyledon bifida (Schlechtendal) HEMSLEY, Biol. Cent. Amer., Bot., vol. 1, p. 388, 1879–1880.

Stem usually short, mostly simple; leaves about 15, laxly rosulate, rather turgid, rhomboid-oblanceolate, subpetiolate, mucronate when young, 4 to 12 cm. long, 10 to 25 mm. broad, rounded beneath, slightly concave; inflorescences one to three, usually 2-branched, rarely simple or 3-branched, but in good soil paniculately many-branched; peduncle erect, 30 to 60 cm. tall; bracts numerous, ascending to erect, narrowly oblong-oblanceolate, compressed-subterete, obtusish, to 3 cm. long or more; racemes with 10 to 14 flowers each; pedicels evident, 2 to 4, or even 8 mm. long; sepals unequal, longest to 10 mm. long, turgid, terete, deltoid-oblanceolate, obtusish, spreading to reflexed; corolla conoid-urceolate, 12 mm. long, 9 to 10 mm. in diameter at base, 4 mm. wide at mouth; petals bluntly keeled, with conspicuous basal hollow inside, much connate below; episepalous filaments flattened radially, nearly 2 mm. at base; nectaries transversely rhomboid-oblong, to 3 mm. wide. Flowers from August on. Description based on plant received from J. Brown of Pasadena, California, 1935.

Color. Leaves fawn-color tinged vinaceous, somewhat glaucous when young; bracts yellowish olive; sepals colored as the bracts; corolla flesh-pink at base, to light salmon-orange above; petals pinkish inside at base, apricot-yellow above, at the apex tipped indian-red; styles turtle-green; nectaries whitish.

Figure 129. 64. *Echeveria bifida* Schlechtendal. Part of inflorescence, × 2. Plant flowering in San Diego 9 July 1960; collected at La Paila, Hidalgo, Mexico (Moran and Kimnach 7791).

TYPE. *Ehrenberg,* 1835/546, collected between Regla and San Bartolo, Hidalgo, Mexico.

OCCURRENCE. Hidalgo, Mexico.

COLLECTIONS. Mexico. Hidalgo: Tlapajahue, *E. W. Keerl,* 1829 (BR).

Cultivated: Barranca de Venados, flowered in Golden Gate Park, San Francisco, *E. Walther,* 58/ (CAS).

REMARKS. Through Mr. Poellnitz' cooperation I was able to obtain a photograph of Ehrenberg's original collection, which was the type of Schlechtendal's description, but which had been mislabeled and misplaced. In 1957, with members of the Mexican Cactus Society, I visited the type locality to gather seeds and living plants, which are undoubtedly *E. bifida,* but distinct from *E. teretifolia* DeCandolle. However imperfect the drawing of the last-mentioned may be, as reproduced by DeCandolle in his "Memoire sur la famille des Crassulacees" it clearly shows the flowers to be sessile.

Actually, *E. bifida* comes near *E. humilis* and *E. tenuis,* both of which have simple racemes and thicker leaves, with those of the last scarcely subpetiolate.

The habitat of *E. bifida* is truly xeric, as may be judged by such associated plants noted on our recent visit as *Cephalocereus senilis, Lemaireocereus dumortieri, Astrophytum ornatum, Ferocactus* sp., *Mammillaria* ssp., *Thelocactus goldii, Hechtia* sp., *Dolichothele longimamma,* and *Pachyphytum longifolium* (?).

65. **Echeveria trianthina** Rose.

(Figure 130.)

Echeveria trianthina ROSE, Contrib. U.S. Nat. Herb., vol. 12, p. 439, 1909; BRITTON AND ROSE, N. Amer. Fl., vol. 22, p. 537, 1918; POELLNITZ, *in* Fedde Repert., vol. 39, p. 237, 1936.

ILLUSTRATION. Contrib. U.S. Nat. Herb., vol. 12, pl. 78, 1909.

Acaulescent, giving off rosettes freely; basal leaves numerous, deep purple and mucronate when young, becoming greenish and losing their mucro, oblanceolate, 6 to 12 cm. long, 10 to 18 mm. broad, very thick, rounded below, concave above; flowering stem 30 to 40 cm. long, naked below; stem leaves narrow, terete or semiterete, acute, 2 to 8 cm. long, erect or ascending; inflorescence at first strongly reflexed, usually 2-branched near the top, rarely 3-branched or simple, the branches 8 to 10 cm. long; pedicels very short, 2 to 3 mm. long, only a little elongating in age; sepals unequal, deflexed in anthesis, but later spreading at right angles to the corolla, terete, acute; corolla-buds ovate, acute; corolla pink; carpels distinct.

TYPE. *Purpus,* 04/R:957, collected on Rio de Tolantongo, Hidalgo, Mexico (US, no. 399673).

OCCURRENCE. Mexico, Hidalgo.

COLLECTIONS. Mexico. Hidalgo: the type (US); Sierra de la Mesa, *Rose, Painter and Rose,* 05/1167 (NY,US); *Purpus,* 05/202 (NY).

REMARKS. Plate 78, cited above, clearly shows an obvious caudex. The short pedicels and evident offsets serve to distinguish this from *E. bifida.* That species and its several allies make few, if any, offsets, and have larger and deeply concave leaves.

Figure 130.   65. *Echeveria trianthina* Rose. Flowering plant, × 0.4. Plant of the type collection, grown in Washington. From the original publication (Contributions from the U. S. National Herbarium, volume 12, plate 78).

66. **Echeveria strictiflora** A. Gray.

(Figures 131–132. Plate 3, upper; see page 217.)

Echeveria strictiflora A. GRAY, Plantae Wrightianae, pl. 1, p. 76, 1850; BRITTON AND ROSE, N. Amer. Fl., vol. 22, p. 19, 1905; POELLNITZ, *in* Fedde Repert., vol. 39, p. 241, 1936.
Cotyledon strictiflora (A. Gray) BAKER, *in* Saunders Refug. Bot., vol. 1, no. 17, 1869.

Stem very short or none, usually simple; leaves sometimes semi-deciduous during winter, about 20, ascending-spreading, rhomboid-oblanceolate, narrowed to base, flat, thinnish, acute, 7 to 9 cm. long, 15 to 20 mm. broad, grayish or glaucous at least when young; inflorescences one to three, simple, secund; peduncle strict, erect, to 20 cm. tall, to 6 mm. thick at base, rarely 2-branched; bracts numerous, ascending, oblong-ovate, acute, 2 to 3 cm. long, flat above, rounded and slightly keeled beneath, at base with 3-pointed spur, but scarcely auriculate, not readily detached; flowering branches strongly nodding in bud, with 10 to 15 flowers; pedicels very short, 1 mm. long, 3 mm. thick; sepals subequal, longest to 13 mm. long, thick, deltoid-oblong, acute, ascending; corolla conoid to urceolate-campanulate, to 15 mm. long, 8 mm. in diameter at base, 5 mm. at mouth, strongly pentagonal; petals nearly straight or slightly spreading at tips, thick, sharply keeled, deeply hollowed within at base; nectaries oblique, transversely-reniform, to 1.5 mm. wide. Flowers from August on. Description based on living plants from Mr. Davis of Marathon, Texas.

Color. Leaves dark olive-buff tinged testaceous above, slightly glaucous when young; upper part of peduncle and rachis a striking begonia-rose; bracts deep lichen-green tipped and spotted with scarlet-red; upper bracts corydalis-green in bud but later jasper-pink; sepals mytho-green to deep greenish glaucous in bud, later vinaceous-tawny to etruscan-red; corolla peach-red above to begonia-rose at base; petals inside capucine-orange above, light orange-yellow at base; styles honey-yellow; nectaries buff-yellow.

TYPE. *Charles Wright,* 1849/228a and b, 1056, "mountains west of the pass of the Limpia," collected on expedition from west Texas to El Paso, May to October, 1849 (G; isotypes, NY,US).

OCCURRENCE. United States: Texas. Mexico: Nuevo Leon, Coahuila, and Chihuahua.

COLLECTIONS. United States. Texas: type collection (GH,NY,US); Chisos mountains, *Havard,* 1883/133 (US); Honeysuckle Canyon, *Warnock,* 37/1004 (GH,US), 40/W-132 (PH), *C. H. Mueller,* 39/8012 (F,PH,US), *Moore and Steyermark,* 31/3336 (GH,PH,UC), *C. H. Mueller,* 30/8012 (GH), 32/115 (GH), *E. G. Marsh,* 35/192 (F), *Ferris and Duncan,* 21/2796 (CAS); Glass mountains, Brewster Co., *V. L. Cory,* 27/1644 (GH); Marathon, *J. R. Parry,* UCBG-55.826 (CAS); Ft. Peña, *Tharp,* 25/3439 (US); Mt. Livermore, *Hinkley,* 35/528 (F); Davis mountains, *Hinkley* in 1936 (GH).

Mexico. Coahuila: General Cepeda, *Palmer,* 04/R-7 (US), *Hinton,* 44/16520 (NY,US); west base of Picacho del Fuste, northeast from Tanque Vaionetta, *I. M. Johnston,* 41/8365 (GH); Cañon de Tinaja Blanca, east slope of Sierra de las Cruces, west of Santa Elena mines, *Stewart,* 41/623 (GH); 1 mile south of Carricilo, *Johnson and Mueller,* 40/164 (GH). Nuevo Leon: near Saltillo on top of bluff, *Palmer,* 02/311 (US); Dulces Nombres,

Figure 131. 66. *Echeveria strictiflora* A. Gray. Flowering plant, × 0.63. Plant photographed in San Diego 24 June 1961; collected at Ft. Peña Colorada, Texas (Uhl 871).

Meyer and Rogers, 48/2872 (BR,G); Lampazos, *Mary Edwards Taylor,* 37/365 (F), Chihuahua: southeast flank of Sierra Rica, Rancho de la Madero, *R. M. Stewart,* 42/2451 (GH); vicinity of Fierro, *Stewart,* 41/774 (GH); Los Organos mountains, *Harde Leseur,* 37/1330 (GH).

REMARKS. *Echeveria strictiflora* is of special interest, for it is the sole species of the genus to extend into the United States and it is the northernmost species, as well. As I saw it growing near Marathon, it inhabits a very dry limestone region with a decidedly xerophytic vegetation. Here the plants seem to prefer a southerly exposure, and thereby escape severe winter cold.

The Mexican localities cited need verification, for dried specimens of *E. strictiflora* are often difficult to separate from the closely related *E. walpoleana.*

The range of the latter supposedly extends to Coahuila, Nuevo Leon, and Tamaulipas, but it should be separable by its leaves which are deeply concave above, as well as by its broader bracts, paler sepals, and more urceolate corolla with its more spreading petal-tips.

In its Texas home, *E. strictiflora* goes under the name "Brewster's Light," from the colorful inflorescence and its native county. The number of chromosomes is $n = 12$.

Figure 132. 66. *Echeveria strictiflora* A. Gray. Inflorescence, × 2. Plant flowering in San Diego 24 June 1961; collected at Ft. Peña Colorada, Texas (Uhl 871).

67. **Echeveria walpoleana** Rose.

(Figures 133–134. Plate 4; see page 220.)

Echeveria walpoleana ROSE, Contrib. U.S. Nat. Herb., vol. 8, p. 295, 1905; BRITTON
AND ROSE, N. Amer. Fl., vol. 22, p. 24, 1905; POELLNITZ, *in* Fedde Repert., vol.
39, p. 241, 1936.

ILLUSTRATIONS. Walpole no. 116, [see plate 4]; US photographs no. 888641, nos. 812,
814, 815, [see figures 133–134].

Stem very short or none, usually simple; rosettes with about 20 crowded
leaves, these spreading to ascending, obovate to lanceolate, narrowed at base,
5 to 9 cm. long, to 20 mm. broad or more, deeply concave or boat-shaped
above, rounded beneath, apex acute, occasionally upcurved; inflorescences
one or two, 30 to 40 cm. tall, in nature to over 90 cm., normally with two, but
in nature with as many as five, secund branches; peduncle erect, stout, to 6
mm. thick at base; bracts ascending, obovate-oblong, thick, but distinctly
flattened, acute, to 2 cm. long; branches with 8 or as many as 15 flowers each;
pedicels stout, not over 1 mm. long; sepals unequal, longest to 10 mm. long,
deltoid-lanceolate, thick, subterete, acute, widely spreading to somewhat downward curving; corolla conoid-urceolate, to 14 mm. long, 10 mm. in diameter at
base, less than 5 mm. wide at mouth, sharply pentagonal; petals narrow, at
tips slightly spreading, sharply keeled on back, at base gibbose and deeply hollowed within; carpels 10 mm. long; stamens unequal, episepalous 8 mm.,
epipetalous 5 mm. long; nectaries broadly triangular-reniform, 2.5 mm. wide.
Flowers from July on. Description from living plants received from Dr. Lowry,
Laredo, Texas.

Color. Leaves mytho- to biscay-green above, courge-green beneath, more
or less spotted morocco-red, scarcely glaucous; bracts as leaves; sepals morocco-red; corolla begonia-rose at base, to peach-red above, spotted scarlet-
red towards apex; petals inside orange-chrome to orange-buff at edges; carpels
cream-buff; styles lettuce-green; nectaries whitish.

TYPE. *Palmer,* 02/R:506, collected at Las Canoas, San Luis Potosi,
Mexico (US, no. 399856).

OCCURRENCE. Mexico. San Luis Potosi, Coahuila, Guanajuato, Nuevo
Leon, and Tamaulipas.

COLLECTIONS. Mexico. San Luis Potosi: Las Canoas, the type (US);
Charcas, *C. L. Lundell,* 34/5573 (GH,US). Coahuila: barranca near Parras,
Purpus, 10/162 (US); Mentlas, north of Saltillo, *Gregg,* 48/531 (GH)
Guanajuato: San Luis de la Paz, *Kenoyer,* 47/2376 (GH). Nuevo Leon: San
Jorge, *Purpus,* 11/136 (US); hills between Soledad and Escondido, *Shreve
and Tinkham,* 40/9608 (GH); limestone loma near Doctor Arroyo, *Shreve
and Tinkham,* 40/9672 (GH); Rancho Resendez, *Harry Taylor Edwards,*
37/365 (MO). Tamaulipas: Gomez Farias, *Palmer,* 07/284 (NY,US);
Sierra de Tamaulipas, *Dressler,* 57/1925 (MO).

REMARKS. Dr. Rose named this species in honor of Frederick A. Walpole,
late botanical artist of Santa Barbara and Washington, D. C., who had prepared numerous drawings, many in watercolor, of *Echeveria* species, etc.
These were intended to serve as illustrations for the monograph of the Crassulaceae, contemplated by Dr. Rose. Unfortunately, only one of these watercolors has ever been published. However, I was able to inspect these drawings
and obtain a much clearer idea of the species in question.

Figure 133.   67. *Echeveria walpoleana* Rose. Plant flowering in Washington, 25 July 1911; collected in 1910 by Dr. E. Palmer in Tamaulipas, Mexico. Photograph from the U. S. National Herbarium, no. 814.

Figure 134. 67. *Echeveria walpoleana* Rose. Plant grown in Washington; collected in August 1910 by C. A. Purpus in a barranca near Parras, Coahuila, Mexico. Photograph from U. S. National Herbarium, no. 815.

Echeveria walpoleana is intermediate, both in range and form, between *E. strictiflora* and *E. teretifolia*. Since the latter is typified by a quite imperfect drawing, it must remain in doubt, but would seem to differ from the present species in having narrower terete bracts. *Echeveria strictiflora* ranges from western Texas into northeastern Mexico, and is often difficult to differentiate when dried. The latter would seem to be adequately distinct by reason of the brilliantly colored rachis, upper bracts, sepals, and corolla, as well as in its rather flatter broader leaves.

68. **Echeveria schaffneri** (S. Watson) Rose.

> *Echeveria schaffneri* (S. Watson) ROSE, *in* Britton and Rose, Bull. New York Bot. Gard., vol. 3, p. 9, 1903; BRITTON AND ROSE, N. Amer. Fl., vol. 22, p. 23, 1905. As to name; both include foreign material, probably *E. maculata*. POELLNITZ, *in* Fedde Repert., vol. 39, p. 240, 1936 [as "E. schaffneri (S. Watson) E. Walther in litt. ad me."].
> *Cotyledon schaffneri* S. WATSON, Proc. Amer. Acad. Arts and Sci., vol. 17, p. 354, 1882.
> *Echeveria teretifolia* var. *schaffneri* (S. Watson) E. WALTHER, Cactus and Succ. Jour. Amer., vol. 7, p. 70, 1935.

Stem usually short, more evident in age, mostly simple; leaves in dense rosettes, widely spreading, oblong-oblanceolate, acute to shortly-acuminate, thinnish, decidedly concave above, 6 to 10 cm. long, to 2 cm. broad, bright green with red margins, not glaucous; inflorescence solitary, 2-branched, to 20 cm. tall; peduncle stout, flexuose-ascending, to 7 mm. thick below; bracts numerous, distinctly flattened, ascending, oblanceolate, acute to acuminate, to 25 mm. long and 7 mm. broad; branches with 4 to 12 flowers each; pedicels stout, less than 2 mm. long; sepals subequal, longest to 8 mm. long, spreading, lanceolate, acuminate, flattened; corolla sharply pentagonal, 14 to 17 mm. long, 10 mm. in basal diameter, 8 mm. wide at mouth; petals sharply keeled, with deep basal cavity; nectaries transversely-lunate, with thick lower edge, to 2 mm. wide. Flowers from January on. Description based on living plants received from E. Oestlund and C. Halbinger.

Color. Leaves biscay-green edged and spotted dahlia-carmine, not at all glaucous or grayish; bracts as leaves; sepals spinach-green; corolla scarlet at base, above and inside light orange-yellow; styles lettuce-green; nectaries maize-yellow edged carmine.

TYPE. *Schaffner,* 1876/768, on sandy hills near San Luis Potosi, Mexico (GH).

OCCURRENCE. Mexico. San Luis Potosi: Tomasopo Cañon and San Luis Potosi. Puebla: Necaxa.

COLLECTIONS. Mexico. San Luis Potosi: San Luis Potosi (GH, type), *Orcutt,* 03/R.643 (US); Tomasopo Cañon, *Pringle,* 90/3508 (GH); flowered, Washington, D. C., *Palmer,* 05/R–627 (US).

REMARKS. In dried material it is difficult to discern whether the bracts are flat or terete, but in *E. teretifolia* they should be quite terete. (Living plants settled that question.) In both *E. paniculata* and *E. maculata,* the inflorescence is an elongated many-branched panicle, with the uppermost branches single-flowered. Both of these species should have fusiform roots, and in *E. maculata* the corolla is pure yellow. In its foliage, *E. schaffneri* is strongly reminiscent of *E. semivestita* var. *floresiana,* but in that plant the inflorescence has numerous short branches, and the leaf margins are minutely undulate.

In its native habitat, this species is said to go under the name "orejo de burro" or donkey's ear. When cultivated in the Cuernavaca garden of our friend, C. Halbinger, this species produced scapes nearly 3 feet tall.

69. Echeveria lutea Rose.
(Figures 135–136.)

> *Echeveria lutea* Rose, Jour. Wash. Acad. Sci., vol. 1, nos. 1, 2, p. 268, 1911; Britton
> and Rose, N. Amer. Fl., vol. 22, p. 537, 1918; Poellnitz, *in* Fedde Repert., vol.
> 39, p. 237, 1936.
> Illustrations. Jour. Wash. Acad. Sci., vol. 1, fig. 1, p. 269, 1911; Möller's Deutsche
> Gärt.-Zeit., 1931, 15; US photograph no. 802 [see figure 135].

Plant glabrous, acaulescent, sparingly or not soboliferous; leaves to 25 in number, oblanceolate, to 11 cm. long and 30 mm. broad, acute to shortly acuminate, thick, deeply hollowed above, with upturned margins and upcurved apex, obscurely keeled beneath, ascending-spreading; inflorescence usually solitary, to 75 cm. tall or less; peduncle stout, erect, to 8 mm. thick at base; bracts numerous, ascending, oblong-linear, semiterete-triquetrous, shallowly concave above, 30 to 65 mm. long, at tips acute with cartilaginous-hyaline mucro; raceme simply racemose or 2-branched, strongly nodding before anthesis, each branch with 12 or more flowers; pedicels very short or none, to 4 mm. in diameter; sepals subequal, longest to 13 mm. long, linear-lanceolate, thick, semiterete, at base articulated, at apex with cartilaginous-hyaline mucro; corolla yellow, pentagonal, conoid-cylindroid, to 17 mm. long, 10 mm. in basal diameter; petals somewhat spreading at tips, the latter acuminate-subulate, basal hollow well developed; carpels 11 mm. long; nectaries reniform, truncate, to 2 mm. wide. Flowers from July on. Description from living plant obtained from Dr. J. Meyrán, of Mexico City.

Color. Leaves cerro-green to light elm-green above, beneath deep grape-green; peduncle and rachis lime-green; bracts light grape-green above, lettuce-green below; sepals courge-green; corolla empire-yellow, inside of petals pinard-yellow; carpels white, styles light bice-green; nectaries straw-yellow.

Type. *C. A. Purpus,* 10/800 (Rose 10/304), Minas de San Rafael, San Luis Potosi, Mexico (US, no. 619743).

Occurrence. Mexico. San Luis Potosi.

Collections. Mexico. San Luis Potosi: Minas de San Rafael, *Purpus,* 10/800–R:10/304 (US, type), *Purpus,* 11/117, with Hechtia (BH), *Purpus,* 11/5353 (UC; inflorescence 2-branched). *Cultivated:* V. Reiter's coll., *E. Walther* in 1958 (CAS).

Figure 135. 69. *Echeveria lutea* Rose. Plant of the type collection, grown in Washington. Photograph from the U. S. National Herbarium, no. 802; also in the original publication.

Figure 136.   69b. *Echeveria lutea* Rose var. *fuscata* E. Walther. Flowering plant, × 0.5. Plant photographed in San Diego 2 July 1960; collected near Las Rusias, Sierra de Alvarez, San Luis Potosí, Mexico (Moran 6338, the type collection).

69b. Echeveria lutea var. **fuscata** E. Walther, new variety.
(Figure 136.)

Echeveria lutea var. fuscata E. Walther, var. nov., pertinens ad ser. Angulatas, glaberrima; caudice brevissimo vel nullo; rosulis solitariis vel caespitosis, foliis fuscatis, canaliculatis, lineari-ellipticis, acutis, apice cornutis, usque ad 5 cm. longis, usque ad 18 mm. latis; inflorescentiis simplicibus, usque ad 35 cm. altis; bracteis numerosis, adscendentibus, angustis, acuminatis, usque ad 30 mm. longis; racemis valde nutantibus, usque ad 12-floris; pedicellis brevissimis; sepalis subaequalibus, usque ad 11 mm. longis, ad basin articulatis et calcaratis, patentibus vel reflexis anthesin; corollis pentagonalibus, flavissimis, usque ad 13 mm. longis, 9 mm. diametro ad basin et 4 mm. ad faucem; nectariis usque ad 1.5 mm. latis, trapezoideo-reniformibus.

Glabrous; stem short or none; rosettes solitary or in two's or three's, with 20 to 50 crowded, ascending to spreading leaves; leaves linear-elliptic or lanceolate, broadest near middle, gradually tapering to the slender, acute, up-curved apex, deeply channelled above, rounded beneath, margins obtuse, 4 to 5 cm. long, 8 to 18 mm. broad, 3 to 5 mm. thick; inflorescence simple, secund, 28 to 35 cm. tall; peduncle 2 mm. thick at base, erect; bracts numerous, ascending, elliptic- to linear-lanceolate, acuminate, nearly flat above, beneath rounded and faintly keeled, 25 to 30 mm. long, 5 mm. broad, 2 mm. thick; raceme with 10 to 12 flowers, strongly nodding before anthesis; pedicels very short, 1 mm. long or less; sepals subequal, to 11 mm. long, one or two of the lower flowers articulated and spurred at base in occasional plants, deltoid-lanceolate, acute to acuminate, widely spreading to somewhat reflexed; corolla strongly pentagonal, urceolate, bigibbose, to 13 mm. long, 9 mm. in diameter near base, narrowed to 4 mm. at mouth; petals very sharply keeled on back, triangular-lanceolate, acuminate, deeply hollowed within at base, at apex with simple acute tips; carpels 9 mm. long; nectaries 1.5 mm. broad, trapezoid-reniform. Flowers from July on. Description from Reid Moran's field notes, in part.

Color. Leaves fuscous, *i.e.* brownish olive, to dark vinaceous-drab beneath; bracts and sepals spinach-green; corolla lemon-chrome, inside lemon-yellow; carpels white; styles spinach-green.

Type. Collected by E. Walther on 21 July 1958, from plant growing in University of California Botanical Garden that was collected by Reid Moran (his no. 6338) in the Sierra de Alvarez, San Luis Potosi, Mexico, on rocks about 4 miles east of San Francisco, on the road from San Luis Potosi to Rio Verde, at about 1900 meters elevation, 10 November 1957 (CAS, no. 409865).

Occurrence. Mexico. San Luis Potosi, known only from the type collection.

Remarks. For a long time *E. lutea* Rose remained quite rare, being known only from the type collection and photo taken from a plant grown at Washington, D. C., in 1910. Now, several forms have been brought into cultivation, most of which agree very well with the type. However, the present plant, which I owe to the courtesy of Dr. Reid Moran of the San Diego Museum of Natural History, is sufficiently distinct to deserve a separate name. It is rather smaller than Rose's type plant, but the most conspicuous character is the leaf color. Several plants have been distributed by the collector, and are growing at the University of California (the type), at Cornell, and in San Francisco.

a

Figure 137. 70. *Echeveria teretifolia* De-Candolle. Plate on which the original description was based (DeCandolle, Mémoire sur la Famille des Crassulacées, plate 6A). This plate is designated lectotype for the species.

70. **Echeveria teretifolia** DeCandolle.

    (Figure 137.)

> *Echeveria teretifolia* DeCandolle, Prodromus, vol. 3, p. 401, 1828; Britton and
>   Rose, N. Amer. Fl., vol. 22, p. 23, 1905; Poellnitz, *in* Fedde Repert., vol. 39,
>   p. 240, 1936. *Not E. teretifolia* D. G. Kunze, which is *E. bifida* Schlechtendal.
> *Sedum teretifolium* Mocino and Sesse, cited by DeCandolle, *loc. cit.*
> *Cotyledon subulifolia* Baker *in* Saunders Refug. Bot., vol. 1, no. 32, 1869.
> *Echeveria subulifolia* (Baker) Ed. Morren, La Belg. Hort., vol. 24, p. 168, 1874.
> Illustration. DeCandolle, "Memoire sur la famille des Crassulacees," pl. 6-A, p.
>   29, Paris, 1828.

Description by DeCandolle, *loc. cit: "E. teretifolia,* foliis teretibus acutis sparsis basi subsolutis, spicis secundis paucifloris . . . *Sedum teretifolium* icon. fl. mex. ined. Flos omnino prioris." The preceding species referred to is *E. coccinea.*

Type. None designated. *Lectotype*: DeCandolle, plate 6-A, 1828.

Occurrence. Mexico, without any definite locality.

Remarks. When A. P. DeCandolle founded his genus *Echeveria* in 1828, he was acquainted with four species, of which one was what we now call *Dudleya caespitosa;* of the others *E. coccinea* was in cultivation at Geneva and had been well illustrated, while the remaining two were known only from drawings made by Sr. D. Atanasio Echeverria. (For a detailed recital of the story of these drawings, see Standley, "Trees and Shrubs of Mexico," Contrib. U. S. Nat. Herb., vol. 23, pp. 13–18, 1920.) *Echeveria gibbiflora* is clearly recognizable, with the orbicular leaves so characteristic of that species, but *E. teretifolia* is represented by only a fragment of the inflorescence, without any of the basal leaves. For lack of the latter it is not possible to identify certainly any of the presently known species with the original *E. teretifolia* De Candolle. Terete bracts, sessile, red-colored flowers with spreading sepals are to be found in *E. bifurcata, E. trianthina, E. erubescens,* and *E. tenuifolia,* any one of which might be *E. teretifolia* of DeCandolle and Echeverria.

71. **Echeveria bifurcata** Rose.

    (Figure 138.)

> *Echeveria bifurcata* Rose, Contrib. U.S. Nat. Herb., vol. 12, p. 439, 1909; Britton
>   and Rose, N. Amer. Fl., vol. 22, p. 537, 1918.
> *Echeveria teretifolia* var. *bifurcata* (Rose) E. Walther, Cactus and Succ. Jour.
>   Amer., vol. 7, p. 70, 1935.
> *Echeveria teretifolia* Poellnitz, *in* Fedde Repert., vol. 39, p. 240, 1936. *Not* De-
>   Candolle.
> Illustration. Contrib. U.S. Nat. Herb., vol. 12, pl. 77, 1909.

Stem short or none, simple; leaves to 25 or more, narrowly rhomboid-oblanceolate, 6 to 15 cm. long, 12 to 20 mm. broad, thick, more or less deeply concave above, the acuminate apex somewhat up-curved; inflorescence one or two, to 50 cm. tall or more, usually 2-branched, more rarely 3-branched, branches secund, with 6 to 20 flowers each; peduncle to 8 mm. thick at base; bracts numerous, ascending, linear-oblong, acute, semiterete, 5 to 8 cm. long; pedicels stout, scarcely 1 mm. long; sepals widely spreading, subequal, longest to 11 mm. long, narrowly deltoid-lanceolate, acuminate, not articulate at base; corolla sharply pentagonal, 12 to 16 mm. long, 10 mm. in basal diameter;

Figure 138. 71. *Echeveria bifurcata* Rose. Flowering plant, ×
0.4. Plant of the type collection, grown in Washington. From the
original publication (Contributions from the U.S. National Herbarium, volume 12, plate 77).

petals sharply keeled, deeply hollowed within at base, the acuminate tips outcurved; stamens half the length of corolla; carpels laterally compressed;
nectaries reniform, to over 2 mm. wide. Flowers from June on. Description
from living plant received from E. P. Bradbury, Fontana, California.

 Color. Leaves lime-green, neither glaucous nor reddish; bracts and sepals
as the leaves; corolla scarlet or grenadine on keel, at base and edges of petals
apricot-yellow; inside deep chrome to salmon color; styles peacock-green;
nectaries maize-yellow.

TYPE. *Rose, Painter and Rose,* 05/649090, from limestone hills near Ix-miquilpan, Hidalgo, Mexico (US, no. 454971).

OCCURRENCE. Mexico. Hidalgo. So far known only from type locality.

COLLECTIONS. Mexico. Hidalgo: the type (US); Jacala, *M. T. Edwards,* 37/807 (F); (?) *Dr. J. Gregg,* 531 (MO). *Cultivated:* garden of V. Reiter, San Francisco, *E. Walther* in 1932 (CAS).

REMARKS. The incomplete nature of the drawing of *E. teretifolia* as published by DeCandolle makes it impossible to identify any known *Echeveria* as *E. teretifolia.* On comparing the two illustrations available, a curious curvature or kink in one of the floral branches will be noted, which is exactly alike in both illustrations. The corolla in our *E. bifurcata* appears to be rather more narrow and the sepals somewhat more ascending than in DeCandolle's figure of *E. teretifolia.*

72. **Echeveria erubescens** E. Walther, new species.

Echeveria erubescens, E. Walther, sp. nov., pertinens ad ser. Angulatas, glabra; caudice brevi; foliis rosulatis, crassis, supra concavis, apicibus cornutis, usque ad 8 cm. longis et 2 cm. latis, viridibus, non glaucis; inflorescentiis bi- vel tri-furcatis, ramis secundis; pedunculis erectis, validis, usque ad 10 mm. diametro ad basin; bracteis numerosis, ascendentibus, subteretibus, usque ad 6 cm. longis, pedicellis brevissimis; sepalis subaequalibus, usque ad 15 mm. longis, subteretibus, ad basin articulatis vel calcaratis; corollis urceolatis, usque ad 17 mm. longis, 11 mm. diametro; petalis crassis, carinatis, excavatis ad basin interiore, roseis, non flavis.

Glabrous; stem evident with age, to 6 cm. tall and to 10 mm. thick, usually simple, crowned by a dense rosette of 20 or more leaves, these thick, turgid, lanceolate, acuminate, to 8 cm. long and 2 cm. broad, rounded beneath, more or less concave above, thickest near middle, tapering to base, apex upcurved; inflorescences one or two, to 50 cm. tall; peduncle erect, stout, nearly 10 mm. thick at base; bracts numerous, ascending, oblong-linear, turgid, subterete, obtuse, and mucronate, to 6 cm. long; branches two or three, secund, each with 12 or more flowers; pedicels short, less than 2 mm. long; sepals subequal, longest to 15 mm. long, in one or more of the lowermost flowers the sepals may at times be articulate and spurred at base (as described by Rose for *E. lutea),* deltoid-lanceolate, acute, subterete, upcurved, ascending; corolla urceolate, gibbose at base, to 17 mm. long, 11 mm. in basal diameter, 7 to 10 mm. at mouth; petals thick, sharply keeled on back, somewhat spreading at tips, acute, with prominent basal hollow within; carpels angular, much hollowed on face; nectaries transversely reniform, 2 mm. wide. Flowers from July on. Description from living plant grown in Golden Gate Park, San Francisco.

Color. Leaves grape-green to olive-lake or congo-pink, not glaucous; bracts grape-green; sepals light bice-green; corolla old-rose, to coral-pink at base, not at all yellow; petals inside salmon-orange above; styles parrot-green; nectaries whitish.

TYPE. *E. Walther* in 1936, cultivated in Golden Gate Park, San Francisco; received from Sr. C. Halbinger, Mexico City, in 1935 (CAS, no. 235487).

OCCURRENCE. Mexico, without definite locality, perhaps Hidalgo, Queretaro or San Luis Potosi.

REMARKS. In its foliage, bracts, and sepals this new species strongly resembles *E. lutea,* but that species more often has a simple unbranched inflorescence and corolla of pure yellow. More extensive field studies may yet reveal connecting links between these forms, but until then they must both be regarded as valid and distinct.

73. **Echeveria tenuifolia** E. Walther, new species.

Echeveria tenuifolia E. Walther, sp. nov., pertinens ad ser. Angulatas, glabra, acaulescens; foliis rosulatis, linearibus, angustis, usque ad 11 cm. longis, 10–12 mm. latis, subteretibus; inflorescentiis trifurcatis; pedunculis validis; bracteis subteretibus, usque ad 5 cm. longis; racemis usque ad 15 cm. longis, nutantibus; pedicellis brevissimis; sepalis patentibus, usque ad 10 mm. longis, teretibus, nec articulatis nec calcaratis; corollis roseis et flavis, usque ad 12 mm. longis, 10 mm. diametro ad basin; petalis carinatis, excavatis ad basin interiore.

Glabrous; stem short or none, rosette simple or with a few offsets; leaves numerous, narrowly linear-oblanceolate, ascending, crowded, thick, semiterete, acute, to 11 cm. long, 10 to 12 mm. broad, 5 to 6 mm. thick; scapes mostly solitary, to 30 cm. tall or more; peduncle stout, erect; lower bracts ascending to spreading, linear-oblong, subterete, acute to acuminate, to 50 mm. long; inflorescence usually 3-branched, its branches to over 15 cm. long, each with 18 or more flowers; pedicels very short, 1 mm. long; sepals spreading, longest 10 mm. long, terete, acute, subequal, not articulate at base; corolla to 12 mm. long, 10 mm. in basal diameter, 6 mm. wide at mouth; petals strongly keeled on back, deeply hollowed within at base; carpels slightly thickened above middle; nectaries narrowly transverse-reniform, 3 mm. wide. Flowers from August on.

Color. Leaves light hellebore-green to light brownish olive, scarcely or not glaucous; bracts light brownish olive; sepals cress-green, somewhat glaucous; corolla peach-red above, primrose-yellow at base; styles lumiere-green; nectaries straw-yellow.

Type. E. Walther in 1948, cultivated in Golden Gate Park, San Francisco, imported from unrecorded locality in Mexico by the late Dr. M. Morgan of Richmond, California (CAS, no. 343069).

Collections. Mexico. Type (CAS). Hidalgo: dry slopes and ledges with scrub thickets, kilo 229 on highway between Zimapan and Jacala, District Zimapan, *Moore and Wood,* 48/4311 (BH).

Remarks. Both Dr. Morgan's plant and another once cultivated at the University of California Botanical Garden were obtained from F. Schmoll of Cadereyta, Queretaro, no locality being stated. My new species appears to be related to *E. teretifolia* DeCandolle of which only a pictured fragment of the inflorescence is known. This *Echeveria* fragment, however, shows sessile flowers with spreading sepals and a broad pentagonal corolla, arranged on a 2-branched, not 3-branched, secund raceme.

Series 7. Pruinosae E. Walther

Echeveria, ser. Pruinosae E. Walther, Leafl. West. Bot. vol. 9, pp. 2, 4, 1959.

Plants glabrous but more or less strongly pruinose; stem usually very short and simple; leaves in dense rosettes, often thick, but flat above; inflorescence simple or branched, branches secund; bracts flat, appressed or spreading; pedicels short or elongated, bractless; corolla strongly pentagonal, orange-colored; petals keeled on back and hollowed at base within, nectaries truncate.

TYPICAL SPECIES. *Echeveria peacockii* Croucher.

REMARKS. The series Pruinosae comes close to the series Angulatae, but differs in the often strongly pruinose leaves, etc. of its species, as well as the broader leaves and bracts.

KEY TO THE SPECIES

A. Pedicels short or none; sepals unequal, scarcely spreading; rosettes only belatedly cespitose.
  B. Leaves numerous, rather thin, below the middle abruptly narrowed into an elongated petiole. Northeast Mexico. . . . .   76. *E. shaviana*
  B. Leaves rather few, thick, closely imbricated, not petioled.
    C. Leaves numerous, relatively thinner, narrower; bracts and sepals narrower.
                                                              74. *E. peacockii*
    C. Leaves few, broad, thick; bracts and sepals broad. South of Tehuacan, Puebla.
                                                              75. *E. subsessilis*
A. Pedicels of at least lowermost flowers elongated, 4 to 12 mm. long, sepals subequal, ascending to widely spreading.
  B. Leaves 3 to 4 cm. long, quite thick, red-tipped; corolla 15 mm. long or less, erect. Cerro Verde, Sierra de Mixteca. . . . .   77. *E. derenbergii*
  B. Leaves 6 to 10 cm. long, thinnish; corolla to 20 mm. long. Northeast Mexico.
                                                              78. *E. runyonii*
    C. Leaves obtuse or emarginate. . . . . . .   78a. *E. runyonii* var. *runyonii*
    C. Leaves acute. . . . .   78b. *E. runyonii* var. *macabeana*

74. **Echeveria peacockii** Croucher.

Echeveria peacockii CROUCHER, Gardeners' Chronicle, new ser., vol. 1, p. 674, 1874; Britton and Rose, N. Amer. Fl., vol. 22, p. 19, 1905.
Echeveria desmetiana ED. MORREN, La Belg. Hort., p. 159, 1874.
Cotyledon peacockii (Croucher) BAKER, Gardeners' Chronicle, new ser., vol. 2, p. 258, 1874.
Cotyledon desmetiana (Ed. Morren) HEMSLEY, Biol. Centr. Amer., vol. 1, p. 389, 1880.
ILLUSTRATIONS. Ill. Hort., vol. 42, p. 93, 1895; Jardin, vol. 11, p. 57, 1897; Florist, p. 121, 1875; Van Laren, Succ., p. 79, fig. 107, 1934.

Stem short or none, rosettes scarcely ever cespitose, except in old specimens; leaves numerous, crowded, to 50 or more, relatively narrow, obovate-spathulate and mucronate, to oblanceolate and acute, narrowed to base, 5 to 6 cm. long, 20 to 35 mm. broad, flat above, rounded and somewhat keeled beneath, always strongly pulverulent; inflorescences to three, simple, secund, to 30 cm. tall or more; peduncle stout, erect; bracts few, appressed, obovate, shortly acuminate, keeled, 18 mm. long, 2-spurred at base, pruinose; flowers to 20 or more; pedicels very short, to 3 mm. thick; sepals appressed, unequal, deltoid-oblong or ovate, acute, longest to 8 mm. long; corolla straight, to 11 mm. long, basal diameter 6 to 7 mm.; petals only slightly spreading at tips, sharply keeled, hollowed within at base; nectaries oblique, reniform to 1.5 mm. wide. Flowers from June on. Description from locally cultivated material.

Color. Leaves rainette-green, but pruinose and hence pale glaucous-blue; peduncle ageratum-blue with bloom, bordeaux without; bracts as leaves; sepals also as leaves but often tinged vinaceous-purple; corolla rose-doree.

TYPE. None designated. (B. Roezl.)

OCCURRENCE. Mexico, with no definite location known.

COLLECTIONS. Mexico. Coahuila: Valle Seco, S. Paila, near General Cepeda, *Hinton, 44/16520* (GH)? *Cultivated:* Garfield Park, Chicago, *Steyermark* in 1939 (F); San Diego, Knickerbocker Nursery, 1936 (BH); garden of Victor Reiter, San Francisco, *E. Walther* in 1931 (CAS); Hort. Thenensis, 1288/11 (BR).

REMARKS. In its strongly pulverulent leaves and bracts, and its quite sessile, sharply pentagonal flowers, *E. peacockii* is quite distinct from all other species, with the exception of *E. subsessilis* Rose. On a visit to Tehuacan I failed to find any trace of *E. peacockii,* but the term "near Tehuacan" may cover a lot of territory. This is a hot and dry region, ideal cactus country, which accounts for the xerophytic character of this species of *Echeveria.*

The chromosome number is stated by Dr. Uhl of Cornell to be $n = 15$.

Numerous hybrids having *E. peacockii* for one parent are on record, but none appears to be extant today.

75. **Echeveria subsessilis** Rose.
(Figures 139–141.)

Echeveria subsessilis ROSE *in* Britton and Rose, N. Amer. Fl., vol. 22, p. 19, 1905;
BERGER, in Engler Nat. Pflanzenf. ed. 2, vol. 18a, p. 473, 1930.
Echeveria peacockii POELLNITZ, *in* Fedde Repert., vol. 39, p. 239, *in part.*
ILLUSTRATIONS. Photograph no. 718 (MO, unpublished); photograph no. 542 (US), [see figure 141].

Usually stemless or nearly so, stem to 15 cm. long, procumbent, without offsets; leaves relatively few, 15 to 20, rather thick, shallowly concave above, beneath rounded and keeled toward apex, broadly oblong to oblong-rhomboid, cuneately narrowed to base, apex rounded to truncate, acutely mucronate, 3 to 5 cm. long, to 35 mm. broad; inflorescences one to three, to 15 cm. tall, simply secund; peduncle stout, erect; bracts appressed, about eight, obovate-oblong, triquetrous, base 2- or 3-spurred, to 20 mm. long, acute; flowers 15 to 20, erect at anthesis; pedicels short and stout, less than 2 mm. long, at least as thick; sepals appressed, very unequal, largest to 10 mm. long and 5 mm. wide, deltoid to oblong-lanceolate, acute, flat; corolla strongly pentagonal, to 11 mm. long, 8 mm. in diameter near base, 5 mm. at open mouth; petals keeled and hollowed within at base, somewhat spreading at tips; nectaries about 2 mm. wide, oblique, elliptic-trapezoid in outline. Flowers from May on. Description from plants flowering in Golden Gate Park, San Francisco, 1958.

Color. Leaves cosse-green, but thickly pruinose and hence light celandine-green to mineral-gray; peduncle pecan-brown; bracts gnaphalium-green, pruinose; sepals mytho-green; corolla strawberry-pink above, to geranium-pink, but hermose-pink with bloom; nectaries white.

TYPE. Collected by Dr. Wm. Trelease, no. 718–719–720, near Tehuacan, Puebla, Mexico (MO, no. 130/04/30).

OCCURRENCE. Mexico. Puebla: Tehuacan; near El Riego; near Salinas on road to Zapotitlan, *D. K. Cox* in 1958.

Figure 139. 75. *Echeveria subsessilis* Rose. Flowering plant, × 0.5. Plant photographed in San Diego 13 June 1961; collected near Santiago Acatepec, Puebla, Mexico (Moran 6355, a cited collection).

COLLECTIONS. Mexico. Puebla: vicinity of Tehuacan, *Trelease,* 04/30 (MO, type); near Tehuacan, *Rose, Painter and Rose,* 05/4741 (US), *Rose,* 04/1018 (MO,US); El Riego, *Rose,* 05/1335 (BH,GH,US); San Luis Atototitlan, *Purpus,* 07/429–R–482 (GH,US); 1.3 miles north of Santiago Acatepec, *R. Moran,* 57/6355 (SD). *Cultivated:* Golden Gate Park, San Francisco (from Salinas, near Tehuacan, from Dr. Cox), *E. Walther,* 58/CAS.

REMARKS. I had seen nothing of this species in cultivation until the receipt of several plants from Salinas, near Tehuacan, from Dr. D. K. Cox. These are quite distinct from the commonly grown *E. peacockii,* but agree very well with both Dr. Rose's description and the photographs at the Missouri Botanical Garden. From typical *E. peacockii* this differs in its broader leaves, bracts, and sepals.

Figure 140.   75. *Echeveria subsessilis* Rose. Inflorescence, × 2. Plant flowering in San Diego 18 June 1960; collected near Santiago Acatepec, Puebla, Mexico (Moran 6355, a cited collection).

Figure 141. 75. *Echeveria subsessilis* Rose. Plant flowering in Washington; collected in 1907 near San Luis Atolotitlan, Puebla, Mexico, by C. A. Purpus. Photograph from the U.S. National Herbarium, no. 542.

76. **Echeveria shaviana** E. Walther, new species.
(Figures 142–143. Plate 5, lower; see page 221.)

Echeveria shaviana E. Walther, sp. nov., pertinens ad ser. Pruinosas, glabra; foliis numerosis, conferte rosulatis, obovato-spathulatis, usque ad 5 cm. longis et 15–25 mm. latis, tenuibus, apice rotundatis et mucronatis, saepe crispato-marginatis, basi longe petiolatis; inflorescentiis usque ad 30 cm. altis; racemis secundis, simplicibus, usque ad 12-floris; bracteis linearibus, acutis, 10–15 mm. longis, adpressis; pedicellis brevissimis; sepalis inaequalibus, adscendentibus, usque ad 9 mm. longis; corollis pentagonalibus, 10–13 mm. longis, carneis.

Plants glabrous; rosettes without evident caudex, apparently simple, ultimately becoming cespitose (?), to 10 cm. in diameter; leaves very numerous, crowded, to 50 or more in each rosette, to 5 cm. long or more, 15 to 25 mm. broad or more, apparently thinnish, flat or at times with margins finely crenulate or strongly undulate-crispate, at base narrowed into long, narrow petiole which may be less than 5 mm. wide for a distance of 15 to 20 mm., at apex triangular-rounded and deltoid-mucronate; inflorescences one or two or more; scape to 30 cm. tall, erect; peduncle 2 to 3 mm. thick at base; bracts to 10 or more, appressed to ascending, linear- to oblong-obovate, acute or shortly acuminate, long-spurred at base, 10 to 15 mm. long; racemes simple secund, to 12 cm. long, strongly nodding in bud, with 12 to 13 or more flowers; pedicels very short, rarely over 2 mm. long; sepals ascending, not appressed, linear- to deltoid-lanceolate, acute, unequal, longest to 9 mm. long; corolla erect at anthesis, 10 to 13 mm. long, 6 to 7 mm. in basal diameter, pentagonal; petals narrow, keeled, the slender tips somewhat spreading. Flowers from June on.

Color. (After Kodachrome by Meyer and Rogers.) Leaves artemisia-green, but more or less glaucous-pruinose; sepals as the leaves, but tinged purplish; corolla rose-color.

TYPE. Collected on limestone in oak-pine woods near Dulces Nombres, elevation 1850 m., Nuevo Leon at border with Tamaulipas, Mexico, *Meyer and Rogers,* 48/2527 (MO, no. 1598523). Isotype (G). Paratype. Mexico. Tamaulipas: Sierra del Tigre, Rancho del Cielo above Gomez Farias, *Dressler,* 57/1838 (MO).

ADDITIONAL COLLECTION. Mexico. Coahuila: near General Cepeda, *Palmer,* 04R:04.7 (?) (US).

REMARKS. This new species is an interesting addition to series Pruinosae, in which it clearly belongs in view of the very short pedicels, angular corolla, and pruinose foliage. It might be considered transitional between *E. runyonii* from northeast Mexico, and *E. peacockii.* The numerous, thin, petioled leaves distinguish *E. shaviana* from *E. peacockii* while in its smaller leaves and smaller corolla it is adequately distinct from *E. runyonii.*

In naming the species we recognize the many services to botany and horticulture performed by the Missouri Botanical Garden, sometimes better known as "Shaw's Garden," as well as the fact that the several collections of this novelty were all made by staff members of the garden.

In view of the highly ornamental nature of *E. shaviana,* it is hoped that its introduction into cultivation may follow soon upon publication of these lines.

Figure 142. 76. *Echeveria shaviana* E. Walther. Flowering plant, × 0.5. Plant grown by Dick Wright at Los Alamitos, California; photographed 10 June 1967; of unknown origin (Moran 13935).

Figure 143. 76. *Echeveria shaviana* E. Walther. Inflorescence, × 2. Plant flowering in San Diego 30 July 1964; of unknown origin (Moran 9895).

77. **Echeveria derenbergii** J. A. Purpus.
(Figure 144.)

> *Echeveria derenbergii* J. A. PURPUS, Monatsch. Kakteenkd., vol. 31, p. 8, 1921; POELLNITZ, *in* Fedde Repert., vol. 39, p. 245, 1936.
> *Echeveria ehrenbergii* auct., Just's Bot. Jahresb.
> ILLUSTRATIONS. Purpus, *loc. cit.,* p. 9; Roeder, Sukk., pl. 30, 2; van Laren, Succulents, p. 80, fig. 110, 1934; Cactus and Succ. Jour. Amer., vol. 9, p. 19, 1937 (mislabeled *E. haageana* Hort.); Desert Plant Life, vol. 20, p. 47, 1948.

Stem short, freely soboliferous and hence rosettes densely cespitose; leaves crowded, obovate-cuneate, mucronate, thick, 3 to 4 cm. long, 20 to 25 mm. broad; inflorescences to four or more, to 10 cm. tall, usually simple, or 2-branched, secund-racemose; peduncle slender, ascending; bracts ascending to appressed, obovate-cuneate, acute or shortly acuminate, keeled beneath, to 15 mm. long; racemes with five or more flowers each; pedicels slender, erect, to

12 mm. long or more, not bracteolate; sepals ascending to spreading, subequal, longest 7 to 10 mm. long, broadly oblanceolate, acuminate, only shortly connate at base; corolla erect, 12 to 15 mm. long, 6 mm. in diameter at base, narrowly campanulate at mouth; petals keeled on back, with small but deep basal hollow within; nectaries ellipsoid, to 1.5 mm. wide. Flowers from April on. Description from plants cultivated in local gardens.

Color. Leaves water-green to light grape-green, glaucous-pulverulent, edges and mucro grenadine-red; peduncle rhodonite-pink; bracts and sepals like leaves; pedicels as peduncle; corolla capucine-yellow, paler toward base, keel and tip of petals grenadine-red, edges light orange-yellow, inside deep chrome to empire-yellow; carpels baryta-yellow above, styles vandyke-red.

TYPE. None designated. Neotype: U. S. Nat. Herb. no. 593195, *Purpus* in 1908, Cerro Verde, Sierra de Mixteca, Oaxaca, Mexico.

OCCURRENCE. Mexico. Eastern Oaxaca: southwestern Sierra de Mixteca near border of Puebla.

COLLECTIONS. Type (US). *Cultivated: E. Walther* in 1943 (CAS).

REMARKS. Discovered on the Sierra de Mixteca in 1908 by C. A. Purpus, this species was named in honor of Dr. J. Derenberg of Hamburg by the

Figure 144. 77. *Echeveria derenbergii* J. A. Purpus. Approximately × 0.7. From an article by Eric Walther (Cactus and Succulent Journal, volume 9, page 19).

brother, J. A. Purpus, in 1921. The species is unique in its thick, small, pruinose leaves borne in dense cespitose rosettes, in its secund-racemose inflorescence with long-stalked, erect, orange-yellow flowers, and in its demonstrated ability to intercross with several species of *Sedum*. Dr. Charles Uhl of Cornell reports its chromosome number as $n = 27$.

A considerable number of hybrids of this species have been raised in recent years, of which several have attained wide popularity. Most promising have been crosses with *E. harmsii,* yielding *Echeveria* 'Victor,' and *E.* 'Derosa,' a German cross with *E. setosa*. The hybrids with *Sedum* are now listed under Sedeveria, with the type being Sedeveria 'Hummelii,' whose other parent was *Sedum pachyphyllum*.

78. **Echeveria runyonii** Rose *ex* E. Walther.
(Figures 145–146.)

> *Echeveria runyonii* ROSE *ex* E. Walther, Cactus and Succ. Jour. Amer., vol. 7, p. 69, 1935.
> ILLUSTRATIONS. US photograph [see figure 145].

Stem short or none; leaves rosulate, upcurved at the base, spathulate-cuneate, flattish, truncate to retuse or acute, very glaucous, 6 to 8 cm. long, 3 to 4 cm. broad; inflorescences two or more, 15 to 20 cm. tall; bracts numerous, appressed, flat, linear-oblong, 2 to 4 cm. long; racemes 2-branched, secund, strongly nodding before anthesis; pedicels to 4 mm. long; sepals spreading, unequal, longest to 15 mm. long; corolla sharply pentagonal, pink

Figure 145.   78. *Echeveria runyonii* Rose. Part of the type collection. Photograph from U.S. National Herbarium sheet no. 1319921.

Figure 146. 78b. *Echeveria runyonii* Rose var. *macabeana* E. Walther. From the original publication (Cactus and Succulent Journal, volume 7, page 71).

to scarlet, glaucous in bud, to 20 mm. long and 10 mm. in diameter; segments erect or slightly spreading—"On account of the short pedicels we should place this near *E. subsessilis*." Description from Dr. Rose's manuscript.

TYPE. *R. Runyon,* 22/R:339, cultivated (US, no. 1319920).

OCCURRENCE. Mexico. Tamaulipas: from cultivation in Matamoros, Victoria, etc.

78b. **Echeveria runyonii** var. **macabeana** E. Walther.
   (Figure 146.)

> *Echeveria runyonii* var. *macabeana* E. WALTHER, Cactus and Succ. Jour. Amer., vol. 7, p. 69, 1935.
> ILLUSTRATIONS. E. Walther, Cactus and Succ. Jour. Amer., vol. 7, p. 71, fig. bottom right, 1935; Nat. Hort. Mag., vol. 26, no. 1, p. 60, 1947.

Stem short; rosettes ultimately becoming cespitose; leaves numerous, up-curved, oblong-spathulate, to 6 cm. long, 25 mm. broad, strongly mucronate to acute at apex; inflorescences two or more, to 20 cm. tall; racemes secund, simple, to 2-branched, or even 3-branched; peduncle erect from the upcurved base; bracts numerous, slightly spreading, oblong-obovate, to 4 cm. long; sepals ascending-spreading, unequal, longest to 11 mm. long, linear- to ovate-lanceolate, acute, free nearly to base; corolla 19 to 20 mm. long, 10 mm. in diameter at base, conic-urceolate, pentagonal; petals rather thick, keeled on back and with deep basal hollow within; styles slender; nectaries thick, trun-cate, lunate-reniform, to 2.5 mm. wide. Flowers from August on. Description of living plant purchased from McCabe Cactus Garden, San Diego, California.

Color. Leaves vetiver-green, but very glaucous and hence pale medici-blue; peduncle light gull-gray; sepals pale violet-plumbaceous; corolla alizarine-pink in bud, later scarlet without bloom; petals within coral-red from numerous fine, crowded red lines; carpels seashell-pink; styles light ochraceous-buff to corinthian-red at tips; nectaries coral-pink from numerous minute red dots.

TYPE. Cultivated material, *E. Walther,* 35/51 (CAS, no. 223894).

OCCURRENCE. Presumably Mexican, but so far known only from gardens.

REMARKS. My variety appears to be the only form of this species in cultivation at this time. Nothing is known as to its origin, and possibly it is a locally raised seedling, the seed having come from a typical plant of *E. runyonii.* However, it is not necessary to presuppose hybridization to account for the slightly different leaf shape.

Series 8. Nudae E. Walther

Echeveria, ser. Nudae E. WALTHER, Cactus and Succ. Jour. Amer., vol. 30, p. 46, 1958 (Latin description); Leafl. West.Bot., vol. 9, p. 4, 1959 in synonym.

Cotyledon, § Racemosae BAKER, *in* Saunders Refug. Bot., vol. 1, 1869, *pro parte*.

Echeveria, ser. Racemosae (Baker) BERGER, *in* Engler Nat. Pflanzenf. ed. 2, vol. 18a, p. 472, 1930, *pro parte*.

Echeveria, ser. Bracteolatae E. WALTHER, Cactus and Succ. Jour. Amer., vol. 30, p. 153, 1958; Leafl. West.Bot., vol. 9, p. 4, 1959.

Echeveria, ser. Australes E. WALTHER, Leafl. West.Bot., vol. 9, pp. 3, 4, 1959, as to type and synonymy; not as to original typification and description (English only), Cactus and Succ. Jour. Amer., vol. 7, p. 39, 1935. [Cf. MORAN, Cactus and Succ. Jour. Amer., vol. 33, p. 138, 1961; MORAN AND MEYRÁN, Cactaceas y Succulentas Mexicanas, vol. 6, p. 82, 1961. Ed.]

Plants glabrous, suffruticose, with evident, erect, often branching stem and small to medium sized leaves, the latter sometimes subrosulate or scattered; inflorescence equilateral, spicate, racemose or subpaniculate; pseudopedicels short or long, always bibracteolate; sepals ascending to spreading, sometimes reflexed; corolla more or less sharply pentagonal; styles short or medium-sized.

TYPICAL SPECIES. *Echeveria nuda* Lindley.

REMARKS. With nearly 20 known species, this is the largest series of the genus. Two groups of species need further study, *i.e.,* those related to *E. quitensis,* many of those published by Poellnitz being very difficult to maintain; and the Mexican species allied to *E. gracilis,* as *E. alata, E. sedoides,* and *E. macdougalii.* Further field collections, especially from South America, are greatly to be desired. In *E. nodulosa* and *E. spectabilis,* with their papillose or muricate leaves, a transition may be seen to the series Echeveria but their trichomes differ widely.

KEY TO THE SPECIES

A. Leaf-epidermis clearly (hand-lens) papillose or muriculately roughened; flowers mostly rather large, to 16 mm. long or more.
  B. Leaves thinner, scarcely keeled, remotely and finely muriculate; corolla to 24 mm. long. Oaxaca. . . . . 96. *E. spectabilis*
  B. Leaves thick, keeled beneath, epidermis finely papillose; corolla 16 mm. long or less. Puebla and Oaxaca. . . . . 95. *E. nodulosa*
    C. Leaves to 7 cm. long, 3 cm. broad; corolla to 14 mm. in diameter; sepals spreading at right angles to corolla. . . . . . . 95a. *E. nodulosa* var. *nodulosa*
    C. Leaves 4 cm. long or less, less than 15 mm. broad; sepals reflexed.
                                 95b. *E. nodulosa* var. *minor*
A. Leaf-epidermis neither papillose nor muriculate; flower often smaller.
  B. Corolla rather large, 16 mm. long or more.
    C. Leaves gray-green or lead-colored. Oaxaca.
      D. Leaves decidedly flattened. . . . . 92. *E. skinneri*
      D. Leaves very thick, subterete to subtriquetrous.
        E. Leaves subterete; pedicels very short; plant low, compact.
                                 90. *E. macdougallii*
        E. Leaves subtriquetrous; pedicels elongated; plants taller, lax.
                                 91. *E. sedoides*
    C. Leaves not gray, but dark or bright green, often with red edges and keel.
      D. Leaves rather narrow; pedicels recurved; sepals reflexed. Ecuador.
                                 84. *E. sprucei*
      D. Leaves broader; pedicels spreading; sepals never reflexed.
        E. Leaves without red margins. Venezuela and Colombia. (Species of ser. Elatae.) . . . . 105. *E. bicolor*
        E. Leaves with red margins and tips. Oaxaca.
          F. Lowermost pedicels with several flowers each. . . 81. *E. viridissima*
         F. Pedicels usually all single-flowered. . . . . 89. *E. alata*

B. Corolla smaller, 10 to 15 mm. long.
  C. Most flowers sessile or nearly so.
    D. Sepals appressed; leaves small, narrow, deeply concave above. Chiapas.
                                                            97. *E. goldmani*
    D. Sepals spreading to ascending.
      E. Leaves broadly lanceolate; sepals widely spreading at least as long as the narrow corolla. Puebla, Veracruz. . . . . 79. *E. nuda*
      E. Leaves obovate; sepals ascending, shorter than the broader corolla. Oaxaca to Guatemala. . . . . 80. *E. montana*
  C. Flowers with evident, often elongated pedicels.
    D. At least the lowermost branches (pedicels) with several flowers each.
      E. Leaves with edges and mucro prominently red-colored.
        F. Corolla with petals spreading from below middle; stems often granular-roughened. Guerrero. . . . . 94. *E. multicaulis*
        F. Corolla urceolate or cylindric; stems mostly smooth.
          G. Leaves thin, flexible; inflorescence often lax to decumbent. Oaxaca.
                                          93. *E. globuliflora*
          G. Leaves thick, rigid; inflorescence sometimes erect. . 88. *E. gracilis*
      E. Leaf-margins usually as green as the rest of the blade.
        F. Leaves decidedly concave above, brownish green, scarcely glaucous; flowers rather distant; sepals short, 3 to 5 mm. long, spreading; corolla salmon. Guatemala. . . . . 86. *E. maxonii*
        F. Leaves nearly flat, gray-green or glaucous; flowers usually crowded; sepals to 13 mm. long, ascending; corolla bright red. Costa Rica, Panama, Honduras. . . . . 87. *E. australis*
    D. All flowers solitary on the pedicels, even below.
      E. Leaves subterete, clavate, obtuse. Ecuador. . . . . 85. *E. johnsonii*
      E. Leaves flat, acute or mucronate.
        F. Pedicels recurved; sepals reflexed. Ecuador. . . . . 84. *E. sprucei*
        F. Pedicels and sepals ascending or spreading, not reflexed.
          G. Leaves scattered, never rosulate, often tinged deep red in sun, thin, flexible. Guatemala, Honduras. . . . . . 82. *E. guatemalensis*
          G. Leaves green, subrosulate to somewhat scattered, thicker.
            H. Leaves 8 cm. long or more; inflorescence to over 40 cm. tall. Venezuela, Colombia. (Species of ser. Elatae.) . . 105. *E. bicolor*
            H. Leaves smaller, shorter; inflorescence lower. Venezuela, Colombia, Ecuador. . . . . 83. *E. quitensis*

79. **Echeveria nuda** Lindley.

(Figures 147–148. Plate 5, upper; see page 221.)

Echeveria nuda LINDLEY, Gardeners' Chronicle, 1856, p. 280; BRITTON AND ROSE, N. Amer. Fl., vol. 22, p. 16, 1905; POELLNITZ, *in* Fedde Repert., vol. 39, p. 223, 1936.
Cotyledon nuda (Lindley) BAKER, *in* Saunders Refug. Bot., vol. 1, pl. 57, 1869.
Echeveria navicularis L. DE SMET, Cat., 1874 (according to Poellnitz, *loc. cit.*).
ILLUSTRATIONS. Saunders Refug. Bot., *loc. cit.*; Cactus and Succ. Jour. Amer., vol. 6, p. 150, figs. C3, C4, 1935.

Stems to 30 cm. tall or more, erect, sparingly branched, smooth and terete; leaves subrosulate or laxly aggregated near end of shoots, obovate-spathulate to oblanceolate, at apex rounded, obtuse and mucronate, to acutish, rather thin and flat, neither papillose nor muriculate, 6 to 13 cm. long, 25 to 50 mm. broad, narrowed to 8 mm. at base; inflorescences several, lateral from below the leaves, to 40 cm. tall or more, equilaterally spicate; peduncle stout, erect, 4 to 10 mm. thick at base; bracts ascending to spreading, obovate, acute, thin, somewhat keeled beneath, shallowly concave above, to 25 mm. long; flowers to 20 or more; lowermost pedicels to 5 mm. long, sometimes 2-flowered, uppermost 2 mm. long or less, with two bractlets; sepals subequal, longest to 9 mm. long, linear-lanceolate, acuminate, widely spreading; corolla sharply pentagonal, about 8 mm. long, 6.5 mm. thick near base; petals sharply keeled, deeply hollowed within at base, at tips erect or widely spreading; stamens un-

Figure 147. 79. *Echeveria nuda* Lindley. Flowering plant evidently natural size; flower and carpels enlarged. Plant grown by W. W. Saunders in Reigate, England; origin unknown. From Baker's monograph (Saunders Refugium Botanicum, volume 1, plate 57). This plate is designated neotype for the species.

Figure 148. 79. *Echeveria nuda* Lindley. Inflorescence, × 1.25. Plant flowering in San Diego 2 July 1960; collected near El Paraje, Veracruz, Mexico (Moran and Kimnach 7775).

equal; styles short; nectaries lunate-reniform; follicles widely divergent even when immature. Flowers from June on.

Color. Leaves sage-green with bloom when young, later cress-green above, below corydalis-green, at edges hellebore-red; peduncle lettuce-green tinged vinaceous; bracts as leaves; sepals lettuce-green; corolla old-rose at base, cosse-green above; carpels pale viridine-yellow; styles spinach-green; nectaries white.

Neotype. Saunders Refugium Botanicum, volume 1, plate 57, 1869.

OCCURRENCE. Mexico. Veracruz: near Orizaba City; Boca del Monte. Puebla: along road from Tehuacan to Esperanza.

COLLECTIONS. Mexico. Puebla: Tehuacan, *P. Maury,* 1885/1091 (NY); Mt. Orizaba, *Wawra,* /955 (W), *Schlumberger,* 1853/138 (BR); Orizaba Railroad, *Purpus and Meyer,* 04/1898 (NY,UC); Boca del Monte, *Arsene,* 07/2141 (MO). Botteri's material, *i.e.* no. 390, from Orizaba belongs to *E. rubromarginata.*

REMARKS. *Botteri* no. 390, referred to *E. nuda* by Poellnitz, if identical with a duplicate in the Gray Herbarium, U.S. photograph no. 399888 is *E. rubromarginata* Rose, having a paniculate inflorescence. Pringle no. 6779, from the vicinity of Tehuacan, belongs to *E. nodulosa,* rather common there in drier locations, and distinct in its minutely papillose leaves. Concededly, *E. nuda* is very close to *E. montana,* even if I do not feel that the latter is merely a variety of *E. nuda. Echeveria montana* appears sufficiently distinct in having broader more obtuse leaves, shorter stouter pedicels, shorter, broader, more ascending sepals, and a larger broader corolla with petals scarcely spreading above. Chromosome numbers: *Echeveria nuda, n*=24; *Echeveria montana, n*=22.

As seen in its native habitat, *E. nuda* appears to prefer rather moister locations, as near Orizaba City and Cerro Borrego, where I found it in damp subtropical woods in company with *Sedum lucidum, Epidendrum radicans,* and *Urera caracasana.* Along the road from Tehuacan to Esperanza, *E. nuda* took refuge among low shrubs, as *Baccharis* spp., and *Salvia* sp. This species had almost completely disappeared there in 1957, when I could find only a single plant. Occasionally this species is an epiphyte, as when I found it growing on an oak, in company with the curious orchid *Hartwegia purpurea.*

Echeveria nuda has proven to be quite hardy in local gardens, but is scarcely ornamental enough to justify its wide cultivation.

80. **Echeveria montana** Rose.

(Figure 149. Plate 6, upper; see page 224.)

Echeveria montana ROSE, *in* Britton and Rose, Bull. New York Bot. Gard., vol. 3, p. 6, 1903; BRITTON AND ROSE, N. Amer. Fl., vol. 22, p. 16, 1905.
Echeveria nuda var. *montana* (Rose) POELLNITZ, *in* Fedde Repert., vol. 39, p. 224, 1936; STANDLEY AND STEYERMARK, Flora of Guatemala, Fieldiana, Botany, vol. 24, pt. 4, p. 409, 1946.

Stem to 50 cm. tall, erect, smooth, sparingly branched above, to 13 mm. thick at base; leaves subrosulate, broadly obovate, obtuse and mucronate, to 7 cm. long and 4 cm. broad, thin, flat or nearly so above, keeled beneath, at base narrowed into subtriquetrous petiole, neither papillose nor roughened-muriculate, ascending, to deflexed when old; inflorescences two or more to each branch, arising from below the leaves, multilaterally spicate, to 60 cm. tall, erect; peduncle to 6 mm. thick at base; bracts numerous, spreading, obovate-cuneate, acute, to 3 cm. long and 2 cm. broad, obliquely keeled beneath; flowers 10 to 20; upper bracts exceeding flowers; pedicels less than 4 mm. long at anthesis, bibracteolate; sepals ascending, subequal, longest to 12 mm. long, deltoid-lanceolate, acute, no more granular than are the flowering stems; corolla broadly urceolate, to 13 mm. long, 10 mm. in diameter near base, pentagonal; petals scarcely spreading at tips, rather broad, obovate-

Figure 149. 80. *Echeveria montana* Rose. Flowering plant, × 0.5. Plant photographed in San Diego 11 June 1960; collected in Cañada Estudiante, near the type locality, in Oaxaca, Mexico (Moran and Kimnach 7762).

oblong, thick, sharply keeled, acute and apiculate, with deep basal hollow within; nectaries oblique, narrowly lunate, to 2.5 mm. wide; follicles become divergent only when fully mature. Flowers from June on. Description from living plant received from Mr. Thomas MacDougall.

Color. Leaves cerro- to parrot-green; bracts spinach-green; peduncle chartreuse-yellow, tinged coral-pink; sepals cress-green, corolla peach-red to scarlet; petals pale lemon-yellow at edges, empire-yellow inside; carpels martius-yellow; styles acajou-red; scales nearly white.

TYPE. *Pringle,* 94/4706, Sierra de San Felipe, Oaxaca, Mexico, on ledges and trees (US, no. 48365).

OCCURRENCE. Mexico: Oaxaca, Sierra de San Felipe (Type); at high elevations between Tehuantepec and Miahuatlan. Guatemala: usually on shaded cliffs, 1800 to 3400 m., Solola; Quetzaltenango; San Marcos; Huehuetenango.

COLLECTIONS. Mexico. Oaxaca: type (US), isotypes (G,GH,MEXU,MO, NY,PH,US,W); Sierra de San Felipe, *Andrieux,* 1831/362 (G). Chiapas: Sierra Madre, Cerro Laguna, Mapastepec (according to no. 2047 *Matuda).* Guatemala. Huehuetenango, *Standley,* 41/81933 (F); Quetzaltenango, *Standley,* 41/86093 (F); *Steyermark,* 40/35766 (F); Volcan Tejumulco, *Steyermark,* 40/34017 (F). *Cultivated:* Golden Gate Park, San Francisco, *E. Walther* in 1940 (CAS).

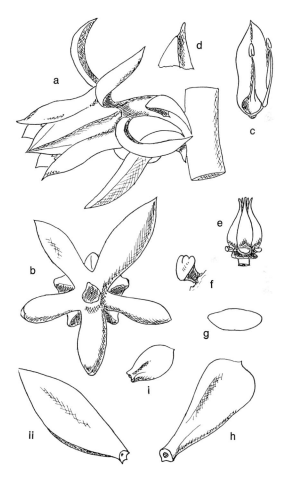

Figure 150. 81. *Echeveria viridissima* E. Walther. Explanation: (a) flower, × 2; (b) flower from below, × 2; (c) inside of petal, × 2; (d) apex of petal, × 8; (e) carpels, × 2; (f) nectary, side view, × 8; (g) nectary, front view, × 8; (h) leaf, × 0.4; (i) bract, × 0.4; (ii) upper bract, × 2. From the original publication (Cactus and Succulent Journal, volume 31, page 22, figure 11).

81. **Echeveria viridissima** E. Walther.
(Figures 150–151.)

Echeveria viridissima E. WALTHER, Cactus and Succ. Jour. Amer., vol. 31, p. 22, 1959.

ILLUSTRATIONS. Cactus and Succ. Jour. Amer., vol. 31, pp. 22, 23, figs. 11, 12, 1959.

Glabrous subshrub with numerous ascending to spreading branches, to 20 cm. tall or more; leaves subrosulate, ascending to spreading, obovate to cuneate, shortly mucronate, flat or shallowly concave above, faintly keeled beneath, to 10 cm. long and 6 cm. broad; inflorescences one or more, arising from below the leaves, erect above, racemose to subspicate in upper portion, subpaniculate in lower part; peduncle stout, 8 to 12 mm. thick at base; bracts numerous, broadly ovate, mucronate, 35 mm. long, ascending to strongly recurved; some of the lowermost pedicels with two or more flowers, uppermost single-flowered, 4 to 8 mm. long, subangular, with two or three bractlets, these recurved; sepals subequal, ascending to recurved, linear-lanceolate, aristate-acuminate, scarcely united at base, longest to 20 mm. long, faintly keeled beneath; corolla pentagonal, bigibbose, to 16 mm. long and 10 to 13 mm. in diameter; petals sharply keeled, deeply hollowed within at base, at apex slightly spreading, acuminate; nectaries transversely-reniform, to 2.5 mm. wide. Flowers from April to November. Description from living material obtained from the University of California Botanical Garden, Berkeley, California.

Color. Leaves biscay-green, in sun tinged indian-red at edges, apex and on lower surface; peduncle to spectrum-red in sun; bracts as the leaves; sepals biscay-green tinged morocco-red at tips in sun; corolla spectrum-red; petals light orange-yellow inside; carpels clear dull green-yellow; styles morocco-red; nectaries apricot-yellow.

TYPE. Collected by E. Walther in 1958 from plants cultivated in University of California Botanical Garden, Berkeley, from material collected by T. MacDougall (no. 51/B–134) at "Guish-gal," San Pedro Mixtepec, elevation 10,000 feet, Oaxaca (CAS, no. 409883). Clonotype: UCBG 56.805.

OCCURRENCE. Known only from the type locality where the plant grew between and on scattered rocks in nearly full light or partial shade from scattered oaks, madroños, etc., accompanied by *Villadia* sp., a fern with "20 leaflets."

COLLECTIONS. Type (CAS); clonotypes, *P. C. Hutchison* in 1959 (CAS, K,MEXU,NY,UC,US).

REMARKS. Notable in its exceptionally bright deep green foliage which often assumes brilliant red tints in the sun, and in its bright red flowers, this novelty promises to become popular in gardens, especially if its promise of hardiness, inferred from its high-mountain origin, is realized. In habit, foliage, and inflorescence, this species recalls *E. bicolor* and *E. montana,* both of which have much paler foliage and less brightly colored flowers. Also these normally bear only a solitary flower on the lowermost pseudopedicels.

"Guish-gal" is Zapotec for *"Fern-twenty,"* the reference being to a fern with approximately twenty leaflets found at the particular locality (as stated by Mr. T. MacDougall in a letter). An attempt to coin a specific name for this Zapotec word was considered, but abandoned as inadvisable.

Figure 151. 81. *Echeveria viridissima* E. Walther. From the original publication (Cactus and Succulent Journal, volume 31, page 23, figure 12).

82. **Echeveria guatemalensis** Rose.

(Figure 152.)

Echeveria guatemalensis Rose, Contrib. U.S. Nat. Herb., vol. 12, p. 395, 1909; Rose, N. Amer. Fl., vol. 22, p. 537, 1918; Poellnitz, *in* Fedde Repert., vol. 39, p. 225, 1936; Standley and Steyermark, Flora of Guatemala, Fieldiana, Botany, vol. 24, pt. 4, p. 407, 1946.

Illustrations. Contrib. U.S. Nat. Herb., vol. 12, pl. 47, 1909.

Plant glabrous, upright shrublet to 25 cm. tall; branching from base; branches slender, sometimes decumbent, becoming woody at base; leaves alternately scattered, not at all rosulate, spreading at right angle to stems, thin, flat, flexible, oblong-oblanceolate to spathulate, 20 to 45 mm. long, 15 to 20 mm. broad, at apex rounded to obtuse and mucronate, at base narrowed to 6 mm. broad petiole, obscurely keeled beneath; inflorescences two or more, arising from between leaves; lower bracts oblong-obovate, to 25 mm. long, not

Figure 152. 82. *Echeveria guatemalensis* Rose. Plant of the type collection flowering in Washington, about × ⅓. Photograph from the U.S. National Herbarium, no. 286; also in original publication.

readily detached; racemes equilateral, with 15 to 20 flowers; pedicels to 9 mm. long, bibracteolate; bractlets linear-lanceolate, 8 mm. long, fugaceous; sepals subequal, longest to 10 mm. long, linear, acute, spreading to ascending; corolla pentagonal, to 12 mm. long, to 12 mm. wide, at anthesis bigibbose; petals sharply keeled on back, lanceolate, long-apiculate, prominently hollowed at base, spreading from near base; nectaries 2 mm. wide, oblique, narrowly transverse-lunate-reniform. Flowers from June on. Description from living plant obtained from Don B. Skinner of Los Angeles, California.

Color. Leaves biscay-green, but in sun deeply tinged old-rose to pompeian-red; peduncle and rachis ocher-red; bracts similar to the leaves, as are the sepals; corolla rose-doree, petals at edges and inside empire-yellow; carpels nearly white at base, above greenish white; styles fawn color; stigmas vinaceous.

TYPE. *W. R. Maxon and Hay,* 05/3726, Volcan de Agua, 2700 to 3000 m., Guatemala (US, no. 399713).

OCCURRENCE. Guatemala: Jalapa; Sacatepequez; Chimaltenango; Solola, Totonicapan; Quetzaltenango; San Marcos. Honduras: near Tegucigalpa. Nicaragua: in Sierra west of Tinotega.

COLLECTIONS. Guatemala: Volcan del Agua, *J. Donnell-Smith,* 92/3633 (US), *Maxon and Hay,* 05/3726 (US, type); Volcan de Santa Maria, *Standley,* 39/67762 (F), *Steyermark,* 40/34053 (NY); Volcan de Santa Clara, *Steyermark,* 42/46297 (F); Santa Elena, *Skutch,* 33/444 (US); Dept. Jalapa, *Kellerman,* 08/8015 (NY); Quetzaltenango, *Skutch,* 34/798 (GH). Honduras: on rocks, 5 kilos southwest of Tegucigalpa, near La Soledad, 1200 m., *A. Molino,* R:47/725 (F). Nicaragua: Cerro de la Cruz, 1200 to 1400 m. in Sierra west of Tinotega, Dept. Tinotega, *Standley,* 47/11104 (F).

REMARKS. In its scattered thin leaves, *E. guatemalensis* recalls *E. pittieri ,* but that species has very short pedicels, appressed sepals, crowded flowers, and leaves without such deep red coloration. Standley's Nicaragua material clearly belongs here.

83. **Echeveria quitensis** (Humboldt, Bonpland and Kunth) Lindley.
(Figure 153.)

Echeveria quitensis (Humboldt, Bonpland and Kunth) LINDLEY, Jour. Hort. Soc., vol. 7, p. 268, 1852; LAGERHEIM, Gartenflora, vol. 42, p. 60, 1893; POELLNITZ, *in* Fedde Repert., vol. 39, p. 230, 1936.

Sedum quitense HUMBOLDT, BONPLAND AND KUNTH, Nov. Gen. Spec., vol. 6, pp. 46, 47, 1823; DECANDOLLE, Prodromus, vol. 3, p. 410, 1828.

Cotyledon quitensis (Humboldt, Bonpland and Kunth) BAKER, *in* Saunders Refug. Bot., vol. 1, no. 5, 1869; SPRENGER, Gartenflora, vol. 42, p. 641, 1893.

Echeveria aequitorialis ROSE ex Poellnitz, *in* Fedde Repert., vol. 38, p. 185, 1935; vol. 39, p. 236, 1936.

Echeveria columbiana POELLNITZ, *in* Fedde Repert., vol. 38, p. 186, 1935; vol. 39, p. 236, 1936.

Echeveria pachanoi ROSE, *in* Poellnitz, *in* Fedde Repert., vol. 38, p. 187, 1935; vol. 39, p. 226, 1936.

Echeveria bicolor var. *turumiquirensis* STEYERMARK, Contribution to the Flora of Venezuela, Fieldiana, Botany, vol. 28, no. 2, p. 244, 1952.

ILLUSTRATIONS. Gartenflora, vol. 42, pl. 1396, 1893; Cott. Gard., p. 164, 1858.

Plant glabrous; stem evident, usually branching, smooth; leaves rosulate, subrosulate to scattered, neither papillose nor muriculate, pale or bright green, rarely glaucous, paler beneath, rather thin, flat, faintly keeled below, oblanceolate to obovate, usually 10 to 60 mm. long, about half as wide, apex obtuse, retuse or rounded, mucronate, base narrowed to 10 mm. or less; inflorescences equilaterally or unilaterally racemose, 10 to 25 cm. tall, with 3 to 20 flowers; peduncle erect; bracts oblong-obovate, acute, to 25 mm. long, flat, faintly keeled; pedicels spreading or ascending, not recurved, 1 to 10 mm. long, bibracteolate, bractlets occasionally to over 15 mm. long; sepals ascending to spreading, not reflexed, rarely appressed (in bud), subequal, longest to 14 mm. long, oblong-oblanceolate, acute, keeled; corolla 8 to 15 mm. long, to 11 mm. in basal diameter, pentagonal, nearly straight, color scarlet and yellow. Description from living plant grown in Golden Gate Park, San Francisco, from seed collected by Miss Ynes Mexía at Ipiales in South Colombia.

Figure 153.   83. *Echeveria quitensis* (Humboldt, Bonpland, and Kunth) Lindley. From an article by Lagerheim (Gartenflora, volume 42, plate 1396).

Color. Leaves lettuce-green above, to biscay-green beneath, edges and mucro maroon; peduncle grape-green; bracts as the leaves; sepals light cress-green, tipped and edged maroon; corolla scarlet, to buff-yellow below; petals inside empire-yellow; carpels pale-greenish yellow; styles vinaceous-brown; nectaries whitish.

TYPE. *Humboldt and Bonpland,* 1802/3096, collected at Quito, Ecuador (P).

OCCURRENCE. Ecuador: Quito, vicinity of city, on walls, etc.; Santa Rosa de Canar; Huigra, Hda. de Licay. Colombia: widely spread, as near Bogota, Paramo de Vetas, Tolima, Cundinamarca, Santander, Cauca, Narino, Ipiales to Layas. Venezuela: Sucre, Cerro Turumiquire. (Note: other Venezuelan material may belong in *E. bicolor.*)

COLLECTIONS. Ecuador: Quito, *Humboldt and Bonpland,* 1802/3096 (P, type); Hda. de Licay near Huigra, *Rose and Rose,* 18/22180 (type of *E. aequatorialis,* US;NY); Santa Rosa de Canar, *Rose and Rose,* 18/22762 (type of *E. pachanoi,* US); Canar, *Camp,* 45/3967 (NY); Huigra, Azuay, *Camp,* 45/1951 (NY,US), *Haught,* 42/3342 (NY,UC,US); Chimborazo, *Camp,* 45/3036, *Penland and Summers* (F,US); Pichincha, above Quito, *E. K. Balls,* 38/5789 (US); Tunguragua, Ambato-Pillaro, *E. K. Balls,* 38/7146 (US); Cuenca, Quebrada de Chushkin, *E. K. Balls,* 39/B–7080 (GH,UC,US); Andes, *F. C. Lehmann,* 1880/153 (US); La Cabuya, region del Sarare, *Cuatrecasas, Schultes and Smith,* 41/12085 (GH). Colombia: Ipiales, *Y. Mexia,* 35/7643a (CAS), *E. K. Balls,* 39/7369 (US); Vetas, *Killip and Smith,* 27/17245 (GH,NY,US); 27/17399 (GH,NY,US); Santander, Rio Surato, Bucaramanga-Jaboncillo, *Killip and Smith,* 27/16380 (PH); Montserrate, near Bogota, *I. F. Holton,* 52/660 (PH). Venezuela (some material seen may belong here, rather than in *E. bicolor).*

REMARKS. Through the courtesy of Dr. Lyman B. Smith, Curator, U.S. National Herbarium, I was enabled to study ample material of this species, collected in recent years in Colombia. Considerable variation is bound to occur in any widespread species, even if much of this may be due to climatic and other environmental factors. Poellnitz' segregates are only too often founded on single, imperfect, and immature specimens, and hence cannot be maintained as valid. I have retained, provisionally at least, *E. sprucei* as a species. *Echeveria sprucei* appears sufficiently distinct in the generally recurved pedicels, reflexed sepals, and often narrower leaves. My new *E. johnsonii,* too, belongs near here, but differs in its clavate subterete leaves.

In the original description, *E. quitensis* is stated to have alternate leaves, but this obviously refers to the floral bracts, for the type specimen is devoid of any basal leaves. DeCandolle gives *E. quitensis* under *Sedum,* but remarks "an *Echeveria* species?"

Bonpland, *loc. cit.,* mentions a form with red-margined leaves, as var. *marginata,* not otherwise known to me. Poellnitz mentions an unpublished var. *gracilior* Sodiro, stated to have smaller, somewhat narrower, more glaucous leaves; I know nothing further of this; it may perhaps be referrable to *E. sprucei.*

84. **Echeveria sprucei** (Baker) Berger.
(Figure 154. Plate 6, lower; see page 224.)

Echeveria sprucei (Baker) BERGER, *in* Engler, Nat. Pflanzenf. ed. 2, vol. 18a, p. 473, 1930.
Cotyledon sprucei BAKER, *in* Saunders Refug. Bot., vol. 1, no. 31, 1869.
Echeveria quitensis var. *sprucei* (Baker) POELLNITZ, *in* Fedde Repert., vol. 39, p. 232, 1936.
ILLUSTRATION. An unpublished pencil drawing by Miss Smith in US Nat. Herb.

Plant glabrous, caulescent, stem simple or sparingly branched; leaves subrosulate or somewhat scattered, oblong-oblanceolate, to 7 cm. long and 2 cm. broad, flat above, somewhat keeled beneath, mucronate, upcurved, gray-green and somewhat glaucous; inflorescences two to three, arising from below the leaves, simply and equilaterally racemose, to 30 cm. tall, sometimes unilateral from one-sided lighting; peduncle slender, ascending; bracts oblanceolate, 3 cm. long or less, flat above, rounded beneath, acuminate; pedicels noticeably recurved, to 6 mm. long (occasionally 18 mm.), bibracteolate; sepals subequal, longest 11 mm. long, lanceolate, acuminate, convex above, flat beneath, strongly reflexed at anthesis; corolla cylindric-campanulate at anthesis, to 14 mm. long, 12 mm. wide at open mouth, 10 mm. near base, pentagonal; petals sharply keeled, deeply hollowed within at base, at apex with minute, subulate mucro; nectaries transversely ellipsoid-trapezoid or reniform, 2.5 mm. wide. Flowers from July on. Description of locally cultivated plants received from Mr. H. Johnson.

Color. Leaves dark greenish glaucous with bloom, deep turtle-green without bloom; peduncle, sepals, and tips and edges of leaves and bracts indian-lake; corolla light coral-red; petals inside warm-buff above, wax-yellow at base; carpels absinthe-green, whitish at base; styles vandyke-red; nectaries whitish.

TYPE. *Spruce,* 1858/5463, collected at Ambato, Ecuador (K; isotype, W).

OCCURRENCE. Ecuador: Andes near Ambato, Ambato towards Pillaro at 10,000 feet; La Magdalena, Quinta de los H. H., Pichincha 2800 m. altitude.

COLLECTIONS. Ecuador: Ambato, *Spruce,* 1858/5463 (K, type; W, isotype), *Pachano,* 18/83 (GH,NY,US), *Rose and Rose,* 18/22395 (US); Ambato, Tunguragua, *Hitchcock,* 23/21703 (GH,US); Ambato towards Pillaro, *E. K. Balls,* 38/B–7164 (UC); vicinity of San Antino and Pomasqui, *Rose and Rose,* 18/23560 (US); Paramo near Volcan Antisana, *Prescott,* 53/997 (NY); Riobamba, *Rimbach,* 35/589 (FM,US). *Cultivated:* Strybing Arboretum, San Francisco, *E. Walther* in 1951 (CAS; from H. Johnson, Ambato).

REMARKS. Baker's type, *i.e.* Spruce no. 5463, differs from the plant described above as follows: leaves narrower, linear-lanceolate, long-acuminate, not at all rosulate, but laxly borne along outer end of branches. I have before me the drawing of Spruce's type by Miss Smith, which differs from Mr. Johnson's Ambato plant mainly in its narrower leaves. A plant formerly grown locally, presumably sent out by Dr. Rose, agrees with Miss Smith's figure, the leaves are distant, alternate, and not at all rosulate.

The specific name commemorates Richard Spruce, famous botanical collector of the Amazon region. While I am aware of the considerable variation to be found in *E. quitensis,* with at least four synonyms requiring reduction based upon depauperate or immature forms or growth forms, *E. sprucei* appears to be sufficiently distinct with its recurved pedicels, reflexed sepals, and usually narrower, more pointed, and often scattered leaves.

Figure 154. 84. *Echeveria sprucei* (Baker) Berger. Flowering plant, × 0.75. Plant photographed in San Diego 14 May 1961; collected by Harry Johnson at Ambato, Ecuador, the type locality (UCBG 57.452b).

85. **Echeveria johnsonii** E. Walther.
(Figures 155–156.)

Echeveria johnsonii E. WALTHER, Cactus and Succ. Jour. Amer., vol. 30, p. 46, 1958.
ILLUSTRATIONS. Cactus and Succ. Jour. Amer., vol. 30, pp. 47, 48, figs. 28, 29, 1958.

Plants glabrous, with evident, usually branching stem to 10 cm. tall or more, erect to somewhat decumbent; leaves scarcely or not rosulate, but crowded along upper end of branches, clavate- to linear-oblong, or oblanceolate, narrowly subterete, or occasionally flattened, obtuse, to acute, minutely apiculate, usually about 35 mm. long, 9 mm. in thickness; inflorescences subspicate, arising from below the leaves, about 10 cm. long, erect or ascending; bracts terete or slightly flattened, linear-oblong, 2 cm. long, obtuse or acute; flowers 10 to 12; pedicels 3 mm. long or less; upper bracts 10 mm. long; bractlets two, somewhat smaller; sepals subequal, ascending to spreading, longest 9 mm. long, linear-oblong, subterete, acute; corolla strongly pentagonal, to 11 mm. long, 9 mm. in diameter at the open mouth; petals sharply keeled, erect or somewhat spreading, inside at base with rather small hollows, tips apiculate; carpels rather slender, 8 mm. long; nectaries lunate-reniform, oblique, about 1 mm. broad. Description from living plant cultivated in the Strybing Arboretum, Golden Gate Park, San Francisco, originally collected in Ecuador at Ibara, by Mr. H. Johnson.

Color. Leaves biscay-green, with faint lines of corinthian-purple at edges

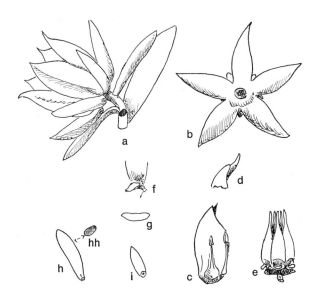

Figure 155. 85. *Echeveria johnsonii* E. Walther. Explanation: (a) flower, × 2; (b) flower from below, × 2; (c) inside of petal, × 2; (d) apex of petal, × 8; (e) carpels, × 2; (f) nectary, side view, × 8; (g) nectary, front view, × 8; (h) leaf, × 0.4; (hh) cross-section of leaf, × 0.4; (i) bract, × 0.4. From the original publication (Cactus and Succulent Journal, volume 30, page 48, figure 29).

Figure 156. 85. *Echeveria johnsonii* E. Walther. From the original publication (Cactus and Succulent Journal, volume 30, page 47, figure 28).

near apex; bracts similar to leaves, upper bracts apple-green, corinthian-purple at apex; sepals similar to bracts; corolla ochraceous-buff, at apex and on keel coral-red, inside light orange-yellow; carpels vetiver-green; styles pompeian-red; nectaries as the carpels.

TYPE. From a plant cultivated in the Strybing Arboretum, Golden Gate Park, San Francisco, *E. Walther* in 1950; originally collected in Ecuador at Ibara (about 100 miles north of Quito) by Mr. H. Johnson (CAS, no. 354989).

OCCURRENCE. Ecuador: Ibara.

REMARKS. In naming this species after Mr. Harry Johnson, I wish to record not merely the fact that this was discovered and introduced into cultivation by him, but also the many services which he has rendered the intelligent cultivation of cacti and succulents during many years.

In its broadest sense, *E. quitensis* is very near *E. johnsonii,* but differs in its usually decidedly flat thinner leaves and bracts generally rather more rosulate; *E sprucei,* too, comes near but is distinct by reason of its deflexed pedicels and reflexed sepals, with leaves usually rather gray or glaucous. The Mexican *E. macdougallii* has subangular leaves and bracts somewhat more grayish in color, its bractlets are much smaller, and its corolla, which reaches a length of 18 mm., is almost straight, scarcely urceolate.

According to Dr. C. H. Uhl of Cornell University, the haploid chromosome number of *E. johnsonii* is 22, the same number also found in *E. sprucei,* and the Mexican *E. montana.* All have much in common and no doubt are closely related.

86. **Echeveria maxonii** Rose.
(Figures 157–158.)

> *Echeveria maxonii* ROSE, Contrib. U. S. Nat. Herb., vol. 12, p. 395, 1909; ROSE, N. Amer. Fl., vol. 22, p. 537, 1918; POELLNITZ, *in* Fedde Repert., vol. 39, p. 234, 1936; STANDLEY AND STEYERMARK, Flora of Guatemala, Fieldiana, Botany, vol. 24, pt. 4, p. 408, 1946.
> *Cotyledon acutifolia* HEMSLEY, Biologia Centrali—Americana, Botany, vol. 1, p. 387, 1880 (as pertains to Salvin and Godman's material from Guatemala); not *Echeveria acutifolia* Lindley.
> ILLUSTRATIONS. Contrib. U. S. Nat. Herb., *loc. cit.,* pl. 48; US photograph no. 8306.

Stems to 30 cm. long (in nature to 80 cm.), stout, erect or decumbent, mostly simple, smooth, terete; leaves laxly rosulate or scattered, not at all glaucous, but epidermis minutely papillose, broadly oblanceolate or spathulate, obtuse and mucronate, or acute, deeply concave above, rounded below, 3 to 10 cm. long, to 3 cm. broad, at base narrowed to 8 mm.; inflorescence usually solitary, to 60 cm. tall, equilaterally racemose, or subpaniculate below; peduncle slender, 3 mm. thick at base, ascending, quite smooth; bracts numerous, ascending, ovate, shallowly concave above, acute to 4 cm. long; flowers to 25; pseudopedicels very slender, lowest often with two or more flowers each, upper single-flowered and bracteolate, 8 to 10 mm. long, glaucous; sepals subequal, longest 5 mm. long, thick, semiterete, oblong-elliptic, free nearly to base; ascending to spreading; corolla 10 mm. long, 6 mm. thick near base; petals oblong, acute, with shallow basal hollow; carpels slender, finely papillose; nectaries globose-reniform, stipitate. Flowers from December on. Description based on living plants from Dr. Rose, presumably clonotypes.

Color. Leaves courge-green to yellowish citrine; peduncle corinthian-red;

bracts as leaves, but often light yellowish olive above, tinged cinnamon at tips; sepals purplish vinaceous; corolla scarlet, coral-red inside; carpels maize-yellow; styles acajou-red.

TYPE. *Maxon and Hay,* 05/3406, collected between Salama and Canoas, Chuacus, Guatemala (US, no. 473390).

OCCURRENCE. Guatemala. Chuacus; Dept. Quetzaltenango, near Zunil, at 1800 to 2100 m., on exposed or shaded rocks, or more often epiphytic, 2200 to 3300 m.; Baja Vera Paz; El Progreso; Totonicapan; Quetzaltenango.

COLLECTIONS. Guatemala: Chuacus (US, type; G); Quetzaltenango, *Maxon and Hay,* 05/3605 (US); Cartago, *Friedrichsthal,* 1841/1422 (W); Dept. Zacapa, along Rio Repallal, *Steyermark,* 42/42483 (F); Baja Vera Paz, *Clover,* 18689 (UCBG–54.1243). *Cultivated:* New York Bot. Gard., *Maxon,* 09/24468 (NY); flowered in Washington, D. C., *Maxon,* 05/242 (US); Soldena Gardens, Pasadena, California, *Floyd* in 1935 (BH).

REMARKS. *Echeveria acutifolia* Lindley, a name sometimes applied to this

Figure 157. 86. *Echeveria maxonii* Rose. Inflorescence, × 2. Plant flowering in San Diego 12 December 1961; collected at Salama, Baja Verapaz, Guatemala (Clover 18689—UCBG 54.1243, a cited collection).

Figure 158.   86. *Echeveria maxonii* Rose. Plant in its natural habitat. From the original publication (Contributions from the U.S. National Herbarium, volume 12, plate 48).

species, belongs to the series Gibbiflorae, and, like its other members, has larger leaves and a large paniculate inflorescence. Of related species with subrosulate leaves, *E. australis* from Costa Rica and Panama has flat, thin, grayish leaves, a more paniculate inflorescence with most pedicels having more than one flower, and sepals often more or less appressed. Most of the other species in question have larger corollas which are more strongly pentagonal and usually have rather larger nectaries.

This is stated to be rather common in Guatemala, where it is known as "Siempreviva." As shown in the illustration cited, it grows in almost solid rock.

87. **Echeveria australis** Rose.
(Figure 159. Plate 7; see page 225.)

> *Echeveria australis* ROSE, *in* Britton and Rose, Bull. New York Bot. Gard., vol. 3, p. 6, 1903; BRITTON AND ROSE, N. Amer. Fl., vol. 22, p. 17, 1905; BRITTON, Addisonia, vol. 1, no. 4, p. 79, 1916; POELLNITZ, *in* Fedde Repert., vol. 39, p. 235, 1936.
> ILLUSTRATIONS. Addisonia, vol. 1, no. 4, pl. 40; Walpole no. 69 [see plate 7]; V. Higgins, unpublished.

Glabrous subshrub to 30 cm. tall; stems smooth, terete, sparingly branching; leaves subrosulate, to crowded, narrowly obovate-cuneate, at apex rounded and mucronate to acute, to 7 cm. long, to over 2 cm. broad, at base narrowed to 7 mm., thinnish, somewhat concave above, keeled beneath, neither papillose nor roughened; inflorescence equilateral, very densely racemose-paniculate, to over 25 cm. long; peduncle erect, to 5 mm. thick at base; bracts numerous, spreading, oblong to obovate-orbicular, to 25 mm. long or more; flowers crowded, to 40 or more; lowest pseudopedicels nearly always with two flowers each rarely single-flowered, upper pedicels often single-flowered, to 5 mm. long, bibracteolate; sepals subequal, longest 8 to 12 mm. long, ascending or spreading, free almost to base; corolla 11 to 14 mm. long, bigibbose, strongly pentagonal; petals thickish, somewhat spreading at tips, with small, but distinct basal hollow within; tapering upwards along stamen; carpels 6 mm. long; nectaries narrowly lunate, with central projection above, 1 mm. wide. Flowers from March on. Description from locally cultivated material.

Color. Leaves lime-green, somewhat glaucous-pruinose and tinged purplish; sepals mignonette-green, tinged purplish; corolla peach-red, inside onion-skin-pink lined with red above; styles oxblood-red.

TYPE. *Pittier, 02/523,* Volcan Irazu, San Jose, Costa Rica (US, no. 397557).

OCCURRENCE. Costa Rica: vicinity of Cartago, Potrero, common on stonewalls; along Rio Reventado north of Cartago; Prov. San Jose, Cerro de Pietra Blanca, above Escasu, common in moist woods; Rio Maria Aguilar near San Jose; vicinity of Santa Maria de Dota; Panama: Prov. Chiriqui, igneous cliffs, valley of Rio Caldero, from Boquete to the Cordillera; Honduras: Dept. Morazan, Zamorana.

COLLECTIONS. Costa Rica: Prov. Cartago, Cartago, *Juan J. Cooper, 87/ 5734* (US), *M. Mart., 96/6498* (GH,US), *Maxon, 06/42* (NY); La Carpintera, above Tres Rios, *L. A. Williams, 40/16149* (F), *Dodge and Thomas, 30/6156* (GH); vicinity of El Alto railroad station, *P. H. Allen, 37/668* (GH); Cerro de Pietra Blanca, above Escasu, *Standley, 24/32327* (US); Rio Maria Aguilar, *Anastasio Alfaro, 24/36021* (US); vicinity of Santa Maria de

Dota, *Standley,* 25/41876 (US); Volcan Iscazu, *Pittier,* 98/13064 (US); Rio Reventado, *Standley and Valerio,* 26/49596 (US); Gorge de Rio Ciruelas, *Pittier and Durand,* 90/2358 (BR); Valle de Los Arcangelos, Volcan Irazu, *Pittier and Durand,* 98/7480 (US); region of Zarcero, *A. C. Smith,* 37/A– 679 (F). Honduras: Dept. Morazan, Zamorana, *J. V. Rodriguez,* 45/3583. (F). Panama: Chiriqui; Valley of Rio Caldero, from Boquete to Cordillera, *E. P. Killip,* 18/3515 (US); etc.

Figure 159.   87. *Echeveria australis* Rose. Plant grown in the New York Botanical Garden; collected by William R. Maxon near Cartago, Costa Rica. From an article by N. L. Britton (Addisonia, volume 1, plate 40).

REMARKS. Here also belong *Donnell-Smith* no. 3633 (sent out as *Sedum bicolor),* as well as his no. 7308 (determined as *Cotyledon peruviana).* Of these the first has much larger leaves, and a taller inflorescence with more numerous flowers, while the latter has flowers always solitary on each pseudo-pedicel. In *Echeveria peruviana* the densely rosulate leaves are larger, longer, borne on a very short stem, and the inflorescence is a simple raceme. In its foliage, *E. australis* bears some resemblance to species of the series Spicatae, as *E. rosea, E. pittieri ,* and *E. chiapensis.* In all of these, the flowers are borne singly on the pedicels, the sepals are appressed, the inflorescence is much congested, and the corolla may be yellow.

Echeveria australis appears to be abundant in western Panama, to judge by the numerous herbarium specimens.

88. **Echeveria gracilis** Rose *ex* E. Walther.
(Figure 160.)

Echeveria gracilis Rose *ex* E. WALTHER, Cactus and Succ. Jour. Amer., vol. 7, p. 40, 1935; POELLNITZ, *in* Fedde Repert., vol. 39, p. 233, 1936.

ILLUSTRATIONS. Cactus and Succ. Jour. Amer., vol. 7, p. 38, fig. bottom right, 1935; US photograph no. 817 [see figure 160].

Plant a glabrous subshrub with short, often decumbent stems 10 cm. long or less; leaves subrosulate or scattered, thick, clavately-thickened below apex, not papillose, oblong-obovate, cuneate, upcurved, 25 to 30 mm. long, 12 mm. broad, to 5 mm. thick; inflorescences two or more, axillary, to 20 cm. or more, tall, ascending, equilaterally racemose, but often one-sided from uneven lighting; peduncle 3 to 4 mm. thick; bracts numerous, ascending, to 20 mm. long, acute; flowers 10 or more; pedicels 10 to 15 mm. long, lowest some-times 2-flowered, bracteolate; sepals subequal, longest to 10 mm. long, linear-oblanceolate, acute, widely spreading to appressed; corolla sharply pentagonal, to 10 mm. long, 6 mm. in diameter at base, 4 to 5 mm. at mouth, distinctly constricted at middle; petals thick, sharply keeled, deeply hollowed within at base; nectaries thick, truncate. Flowers from September on. Description based on locally cultivated plants originally received from Dr. Rose.

Color. Leaves lettuce-green when young, later courge-green with terra-cotta tinge, mucro nopal-red; bracts isabella colored; pedicels alizarine-pink; sepals light brownish vinaceous; corolla scarlet; petals inside orange-buff; carpels light orange-yellow above; styles dark-maroon at tips; nectaries maize-yellow.

TYPE. *C. A. Purpus,* 09/24, collected near Coxcatlan, on rocky slopes at 8000 to 9000 feet, Puebla, Mexico (US, no. 1319967).

OCCURRENCE. Mexico. Puebla: at the type locality. Oaxaca: Maguey Verde, Santa Maria Ecatepec, 5200 feet, collected by Mr. Thomas Mac-Dougall.

REMARKS. *Echeveria gracilis* is one of several southern Mexican species of *Echeveria* having in common a subshrubby habit, thick, fleshy, gray-green leaves, and evident pedicels bearing medium to large flowers with spreading or ascending sepals.

Figure 160.   88. *Echeveria gracilis* Rose. Plant of the type collection, flowering in Washington. Photograph from the U.S. National Herbarium, no. 817.

89. **Echeveria alata** Alexander.
(Figure 161.)

Echeveria alata ALEXANDER, Cactus and Succ. Jour. Amer., vol. 13, p. 136, 1941.
ILLUSTRATIONS. Cactus and Succ. Jour. Amer., vol. 13, pp. 136, 138, figs. 77, 78, 1941.

Plants glabrous, shrubby, branching freely below, branches erect or ascending; leaves scattered, not at all rosulate, oblanceolate, long-attenuate at base, apex rounded and mucronate, to 6 cm. long and 24 mm. broad, thick and fleshy; inflorescences equilaterally racemose, to 20 cm. tall, erect; peduncle stout, somewhat curved; bracts about eight, ascending, obovate, at apex truncate and mucronate to shortly acuminate, 20 mm. long or more; flowers 10 to 12; pedicels 15 to 18 mm. (?) long, with two lanceolate bractlets to 12 mm. long; sepals subequal, longest 11 to 18 mm. long, oblong-lanceolate, acute, strongly ascending; corolla 17 to 22 mm. long, urceolate, sharply 5-angled or 5-winged, basal diameter 13 mm. or more, at mouth 9 mm. wide or more; petals with upper rim of nectar cavity protruding downwards; carpels to 17 mm. long, slender; styles elongated, long-acuminate; nectaries to 2 mm. wide, narrowly transverse-reniform, oblique. Flowers from November on.

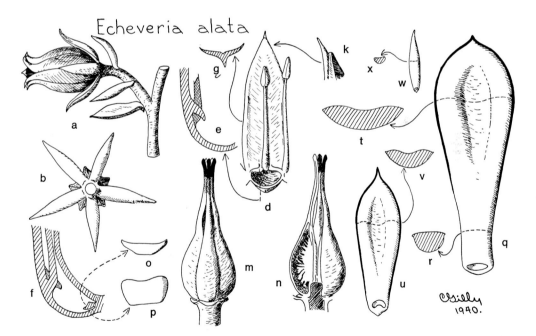

Figure 161. 89. *Echeveria alata* Alexander. Explanation: (a) flower, × 1; (b) flower from below, × 1; (d) inside of petal, × 2; (e) longitudinal section of base of petal (as shown by dotted line on figure d), × 4; (f) median longitudinal section of petal base, × 4; (g) median cross section of petal, × 2; (k) apex of petal, the inner face to the right, × 4; (m) carpels, × 2; (n) longitudinal section of carpels, × 2; (o) nectary, face view, × 5; (p) nectary, dorsal view, × 5; (q) leaf, × 1; (r) cross-section of leaf base, × 1; (t) cross-section of widest part of leaf, × 1; (u) mid-peduncle bract, × 1; (v) cross-section of mid-peduncle bract, × 1; (w) pedicellary bract, × 1; (x) cross-section of pedicellary bract, × 1. From the original publication (Cactus and Succulent Journal, volume 13, page 136, figure 77).

Color: Leaves and bracts lettuce-green edged and tipped indian-red; sepals light elm-green; corolla scarlet below, citron-yellow at apex and free margins; carpels light pinkish cinnamon, whitish at base; styles courge-green.

TYPE. Cultivated at New York Botanical Garden from material collected on rocks and epiphytic on oaks, at Zapotitlan, Tehuantepec, Oaxaca, Mexico, at about 4000 feet elevation, by T. MacDougall, his no. B–16 (NY).

OCCURRENCE. Mexico. Oaxaca: mountains west of Tehuantepec.

REMARKS. My inability to inspect the type of *E. alata* led to some confusion. As illustrated, the down-bent edge of the nectar cavity is conspicuous, but not mentioned by Alexander. In figure 77–n [fig. 161–n] in the longitudinal section of a carpel, the placenta is shown as distinctly lobulate, a condition rare in the genus.

Echeveria macdougallii is also related, but obviously differs in its clavate-subterete leaves and shorter pedicels. There is scarcely any need to mention *E. guatemalensis* here, which has very thin flexible leaves, usually tinged a deep red in the sun, and smaller flowers, rarely exceeding 12 mm. in length.

90. Echeveria macdougallii E. Walther.
(Figures 162–163.)

Echeveria macdougallii E. WALTHER, Cactus and Succ. Jour. Amer., vol. 30, p. 87, 1958.
ILLUSTRATIONS. Cactus and Succ. Jour. Amer., vol. 30, pp. 87, 88, figs. 44, 45, 1958.

Plants glabrous, subshrubby, with numerous ascending or spreading branches, to 12 cm. tall or more; leaves many, subrosulate or closely aggregated along upper portion of stems, spreading to reflexed, oblong-obovate to obovate, cuneate, thick-clavate, more or less subterete or faintly subangular and keeled, bluntly pointed, upcurved, not conspicuously papillose, to 3 cm. long or more, 10 mm. thick; inflorescence spreading or ascending, equilaterally racemose, often less than 10 cm. long; peduncle slender, flexuose; bracts similar to leaves but smaller, 18 to 25 mm. long, widely spreading, obliquely pointed, rather readily detached; flowers often only five, or fewer, less often as many as 10; pedicels 6 mm. long or less, with two linear bractlets that are 2 to 5 mm long, only rarely with more than a single flower; sepals subequal, longest to 10 mm. long, elliptic-oblong, nearly terete, obtusish, ascending to spreading; corolla nearly straight, pentagonal, to 18 mm. long, 12 mm. in basal diameter, 6 to 7 mm. wide at mouth; petals only slightly spreading above when grown outdoors, but often widely flaring when grown in a greenhouse; carpels to 12 mm. long; nectaries narrowly lunate, about 2 mm. wide. Description from living plant grown in Strybing Arboretum, Golden Gate Park, San Francisco.

Color. Leaves oil- to cosse-green, in sun tinged oxblood-red at edges and apex; peduncle chrysolite-green; bracts as the leaves, or more absinthe-green; sepals kildare-green tinged deep corinthian-red; corolla peach-red to spectrum-red on outside, lemon-chrome inside; carpels bittersweet-pink; styles corinthian-purple; nectaries straw-yellow.

TYPE. *T. MacDougall* B–15, collected on rocks at 4000 feet, Cerro Tres Cruces, Tenango, Oaxaca, Mexico (CAS, no. 268566).

OCCURRENCE. Mexico. Oaxaca: known only from the type locality.

REMARKS. I was pleased to dedicate this species of *Echeveria* to its discoverer, Mr. Thomas MacDougall. This is one of several closely related forms, of which the first to become known was *E. gracilis* Rose *ex* E. Walther. This differs from my present species in having distinctly flattened, if thick, leaves, longer pedicels, and shorter flowers, with the flowers often paired on the lowermost pseudopedicels.

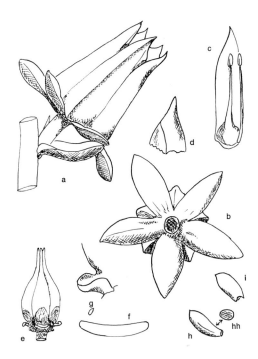

Figure 162. 90. *Echeveria macdougallii* E. Walther. Explanation: (a) flower, × 2; (b) flower from below, × 2; (c) inside of petal, × 2; (d) apex of petal, × 8; (e) carpels, × 2; (f) nectary, front view, × 8; (g) nectary, side view, × 8; (h) leaf, × 0.4; (hh) cross-section of leaf, × 0.4; (i) bract, × 0.4. From the original publication (Cactus and Succulent Journal, volume 30, page 87, figure 44).

Figure 163. 90. *Echeveria macdougallii* E. Walther. From the original publication (Cactus and Succulent Journal, volume 30, page 88, figure 45).

91. **Echeveria sedoides** E. Walther.
    (Figures 164–165.)

Echeveria sedoides E. WALTHER, Cactus and Succ. Jour. Amer., vol. 30, p. 153, 1958.
ILLUSTRATIONS. Cactus and Succ. Jour. Amer., vol. 30, pp. 152, 153, figs. 88, 89, 1958.

Plants glabrous, shrubby, freely branching, becoming 25 cm. tall or more; branches spreading to drooping; leaves scattered, usually rather remote, not at all rosulate, oblong-obovate, quite thick, clavate, subtriquetrous, shallowly convex above, rounded and bluntly keeled beneath, somewhat recurved, obtuse, to 25 mm. long, 10 mm. broad and 8 mm. thick; inflorescences several,

Figure 164. 91. *Echeveria sedoides* E. Walther. From the original publication (Cactus and Succulent Journal, volume 30, page 152, figure 88).

with four to six flowers each, equilaterally racemose; peduncle decurved to ascending; bracts rather few, similar to leaves but smaller, noticeable, recurved, 8 mm. long or less; pedicels elongate, to 20 mm. long, somewhat turbinate below calyx, bibracteolate, bractlets spreading, subterete, to 6 mm. long; sepals subequal, to 9 mm. long, terete, obtuse, widely spreading to reflexed; corolla strongly pentagonal, to 16 mm. long, campanulate, to 12 mm. wide at mouth at full anthesis; petals sharply keeled on back, very thick, with deep basal nectar cavity, apex with thick, blunt mucro; carpels to 8 mm long; nectaries reniform, to 2 mm. wide. Flowers from June on. Description from material through Don B. Skinner, Los Angeles, California.

Color. Leaves cerro-green, maroon at tips, in sun, as are the bracts and sepals; peduncle viridine-green, but tinged corinthian-red; corolla scarlet-red, with edges lemon-chrome; in shade wholly yellow; petals inside apricot-yellow; carpels scheele's-green; styles viridine-green tipped corinthian-red at tips.

Type. A cultivated specimen collected by E. Walther at the University of California Botanical Garden (56/792) from material collected by Mr. T.

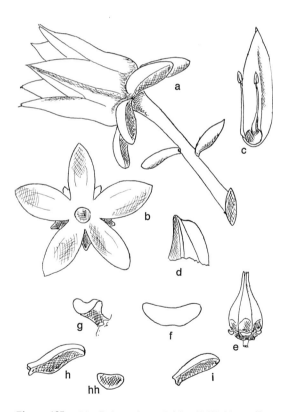

Figure 165. 91. *Echeveria sedoides* E. Walther. Explanation: (a) flower, × 2; (b) flower from below, × 2; (c) inside of petal, × 2; (d) apex of petal, × 8; (e) carpels, × 2; (f) nectary, front view, × 8; (g) nectary, side view, × 8; (h) leaf, × 0.4; (hh) cross-section of leaf, × 0.4; (i) bract, × 0.4. From the original publication (Cactus and Succulent Journal, volume 30, page 153, figure 89).

MacDougall (no. B–171) at Palacio San Bartolo Yautepec, 4500 feet, Oaxaca, Mexico (CAS, no. 409843).

OCCURRENCE. Known only from the type locality.

REMARKS. *Echeveria sedoides* is another of Mr. MacDougall's many interesting discoveries in Oaxaca. As the specific name indicates, it greatly resembles members of the group of Mexican subshrubby *Sedum* species with a lateral inflorescence, at least until its flowers appear. This is one of a number of closely related species near *E. gracilis,* the first of the series to become known. Differences between them are summarized in my key. *Echeveria sedoides* differs from its allies in the large corolla, which is up to 16 mm. long or more, its rather distant thick, subtriquetrous leaves, its pedicels up to 18 mm. long, and its terete widely spreading to reflexed sepals.

92. **Echeveria skinneri** E. Walther, new species.
   (Figures 166–167.)

Echeveria skinneri E. Walther, sp. nov., pertinens ad ser. Nudas, glabra, suffruticosa, ramis adscendentibus, usque ad 30 cm. altis; foliis non rosulatis, crassis, oblongo-obovatis, usque ad 45 mm. longis; inflorescentiis lateralibus, aequilaterali-racemosis, usque ad 30 cm. altis; pedunculis flexuosis; bracteis obovatis, mucronatis, adscendentibus, usque ad 30 mm. longis; floribus 10–17; pedicellis 16–24 mm. longis, bibracteolatis, validis; sepalis aequalibus, patentibus vel reflexis, crassis, ellipticis, obtusis; corollis conoideis, pentagonalibus, 17–20 mm. longis, 14 mm. diametro basi, 8 mm. fauce, coccineis; nectariis usque ad 3 mm. latis, reniformibus.

Glabrous, subshrubby, branching from below to 30 cm. tall or more; branches erect or laxly spreading-ascending, smooth; leaves scattered, not rosulate, 4 cm. long or more, 20 mm. broad, obovate-cuneate, attenuate to 6 mm. broad petiole, thick, fleshy and rigid, shallowly concave above, beneath rounded and keeled, apex rounded and mucronate; inflorescences several, arising laterally from below leaves, 15 to 20 cm. tall; peduncle erect or spreading, to 7 mm. thick, its cortex sometimes rugose; bracts ascending-spreading, oblong-obovate, keeled, mucronate to acute, to 30 mm. long and 12 mm. broad; raceme equilateral, often one-sided due to one-sided lighting, to 15 cm. long or more, with 10 or more flowers; pedicels 10 to 16 mm. long, 2 mm. thick, more or less recurved, bearing two lanceolate, caducous bractlets to 12 mm. long; sepals nearly equal, longest to 10 mm. long, widely spreading to recurved, elliptic-lanceolate, subterete, acute; corolla conoid-urceolate, sharply pentagonal, 17 to 20 mm. long, 14 mm. in basal diameter, 8 mm. wide at mouth; petals erect, scarcely spreading at tips, sharply keeled, with deep basal nectar cavity, 6 mm. broad; nectaries to 3 mm. wide, truncate, narrowly transverse-reniform. Flowers from March to May.

Color. Leaves cerro-green, with edges and tips indian-red; bracts as the leaves; sepals cerro-green above, lettuce-green beneath; corolla scarlet-red, with petals pinard-yellow inside and at overlapping edges; carpels whitish, but faintly tinged rose-red above; base of styles cosse-green, tips maroon; nectaries whitish.

TYPE. *E. Walther,* 27 January 1959, a plant cultivated by Victor Reiter, San Francisco, grown from material collected by Thomas MacDougall (B-204) at 7000 feet altitude, Santo Tomas Quieri, Cerro Madreña, Oaxaca (CAS, no. 413180).

PARATYPES. University of California Botanical Garden (58.851–1), *E. Walther,* 17 March 1959, and 4 April 1959; J. W. Dodson's nursery, Millbrae, California, *E. Walther,* 12 March 1959; all in Calif. Acad. Sci. Herb.

OCCURRENCE. Known only from the type locality in Mexico.

REMARKS. This new species might be mistaken for *E. alata* Alexander, but the latter is clearly distinct in its thinner leaves with more decidedly red margins, apex, and keel, strongly ascending sepals, more urceolate corolla, longer styles, and differently shaped nectaries. I have not been able to make

Figure 166.   92. *Echeveria skinneri* E. Walther. Flowering plant, × 0.4. Plant photographed in San Diego 23 March 1967; part of the type collection (MacDougall B-204).

comparisons with the type of *E. alata.* Actually, this novelty appears nearest to *E. sedoides,* which has smaller, thicker, subtriquetrous leaves, longer pedicels, narrower and thicker bracts, a shorter corolla with petals more spreading at apex, and smaller, more reniform nectaries.

My material of this was first received through Mr. Don B. Skinner, after whom I name this new species with pleasure. Mr. and Mrs. Skinner have long been active in stimulating interest in and knowledge of succulents, and they have been most helpful to me in my studies by furnishing material and data.

Figure 167.   92. *Echeveria skinneri* E. Walther. Flowers, × 2. Plant flowering in San Diego 23 March 1967; part of the type collection (MacDougall B-204).

93. **Echeveria globuliflora** E. Walther.
(Figures 168–169.)

Echeveria globuliflora E. WALTHER, Cactus and Succ. Jour. Amer., vol. 31, p. 24, 1959.
ILLUSTRATIONS. Cactus and Succ. Jour. Amer., vol. 31, pp. 24, 25, figs. 13, 14, 1959.

Plant glabrous, with evident, erect, at first simple stem to 10 cm. tall or more; bark of stem usually roughened; leaves numerous, subrosulately crowded, ascending when young, later spreading, oblong-oblanceolate to obovate-cuneate, mucronate, to acute or shortly acuminate, about 5 cm. long, 15 mm. broad, rather thin even though fleshy, upcurved, somewhat oblique, keeled beneath; inflorescences three to five, arising from between lower leaves, to 25 cm. tall, equilateral, irregularly paniculate-racemose or cymose; peduncle erect to spreading, or even decumbent in shade, 3 mm. thick below; lower bracts not readily detached, obovate-oblong, to 20 mm. long, thick, subtriquetrous, obliquely keeled, acute, or truncate and mucronate, upcurved; lower branches of inflorescence few, short, with two to six flowers each; upper pseudopedicels slender, elongated, to 10 mm. long or more, somewhat thickened below calyx, bearing two slender, linear, terete upcurved bractlets that are often only 1 mm. long; sepals nearly equal, linear-lanceolate, subterete, acute, strongly ascending to appresed, longest 4 to 5 mm. long; corolla globose-urceolate, almost spherical at anthesis but pentagonal, to 10 mm. long, 8 mm. in diameter near

Figure 168.   93. *Echeveria globuliflora* E. Walther. From the original publication (Cactus and Succulent Journal, volume 31, page 24, figure 13).

base, 6 mm. wide at mouth at anthesis; petals keeled, rather broad, folded together above, apex bluntly apiculate, bearing a fine, retrorse bristle-like tip; carpels 6 mm. long, slender; nectaries transversely lunate-reniform, 1 to 1.5 mm. wide. Flowers from May to November. Description from plant received from Scott Haselton, Pasadena, California.

Color. Leaves lettuce- to elm-green, strongly tinged pompeian-red beneath, especially at edges and keel; peduncle acajou-red; bracts as the leaves; pedicels jasper-pink with bloom intact; corolla peach-red, edges of petals light orange-yellow; sepals and upper bracts biscay-green, tipped with sorghum-brown; carpels bright green-yellow, to neva-green above.

Type. *E. Walther,* 6 June 1958, a cultivated plant received from Thomas MacDougall (no. B–79) collected on rocks at about 7000 feet elevation, Cerro Jilotepec, San Pedro Jilotepec, Tehuantepec, Oaxaca, Mexico (CAS, no. 408-986). [Editor's note. The type locality was originally given as "Cerro Arenal, 50 miles west of Tehuantepec."]

Occurrence. Known only from the type locality.

Remarks. This is another novelty introduced from Oaxaca, where it was discovered by the indefatigable collector Mr. Thomas MacDougall. *Echeveria multicaulis* Rose is probably the closest relation, but that species has broader blunter leaves and wide-open campanulate corolla.

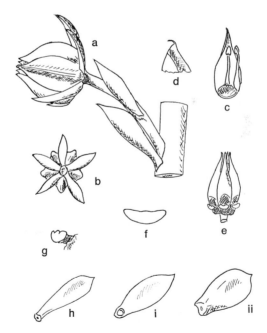

Figure 169. 93. *Echeveria globuliflora* E. Walther. Explanation: (a) flower, × 2; (b) flower from below, × 2; (c) inside of petal, × 2; (d) apex of petal, × 8; (e) carpels, × 2; (f) nectary, front view, × 8; (g) nectary, side view, × 8; (h) leaf, × 0.4; (i) upper bract, × 2; (ii) lower bract, × .8. From the original publication (Cactus and Succulent Journal, volume 31, page 25, figure 14).

94. **Echeveria multicaulis** Rose.

(Figure 170. Plate 8; see page 228.)

Echeveria multicaulis Rose, Contrib. U. S. Nat. Herb., vol. 8, p. 294, 1905; Britton
  and Rose, N. Amer. Fl., vol. 22, p. 16, 1905; Rose, Addisonia, vol. 2, no. 2, p. 23,
  1917; Poellnitz, *in* Fedde Repert., vol. 39, n. 226, 1936.
Illustrations. Addisonia, vol. 2, no. 2, pl. 52, 1917; Gardeners' Chronicle, ser. 3,
  vol. 81, p. 93, fig. 48, 1927; Walpole no. 132 [see Plate 8]; V. Higgins, unpublished (US).

Figure 170.   94. *Echeveria multicaulis* Rose. Plant of the type collection, flowering in
Washington. Photograph from the U.S. National Herbarium, no. 375.

Glabrous subshrub to 25 cm. or even 120 cm. in nature, with numerous spreading branches that are granular-roughened and marked by leaf scars that are irregular hexagons; leaves in rather dense rosettes, obovate-cuneate, at apex rounded to truncate, mucronate, 3 to 4 cm. long, 15 to 30 mm. broad, at base narrowed to 4 mm., relatively thin, flat or slightly concave above, faintly keeled beneath, neither papillose nor glaucous, but deep shining green with red tips and edges; inflorescences one or several, arising from below leaves, an equilateral raceme, spike or thyrse, with 6 to 15 flowers, to 25 cm. tall; peduncle subangular with granular-roughened ridges; bracts numerous, spreading, obovate-orbicular, mucronate, to 25 mm. long; pedicels to 10 mm. long below, shorter above, bracteolate; sepals deltoid-lanceolate, acute, ascending, longest to 6 mm. long; corolla campanulate, decidedly pentagonal, to 10 mm. long or more, 10 mm. wide at mouth, 5 mm. at base; petals spreading from base, sharply keeled, acuminate, with small, but deep basal hollow; carpels abruptly narrowed into the long and slender styles; nectaries transversely-lunate, 1 mm. wide. Flowers from January on. Description based on locally grown plants received from Dr. Rose.

Color. Leaves glossy spinach-green, not at all glaucous, toward apex tinged oxblood-red; upper bracts becoming orange-vinaceous; sepals and bractlets oxblood-red; corolla shining carmine to scarlet; petals at edges and inside light orange-yellow, styles pale corinthian-red; nectaries maize-yellow.

Type. *Nelson* and *Goldman,* 03/R:628, Omiltemi, Guerrero, Mexico (US, no. 399650).

Occurrence. Mexico. Guerrero: Omiltemi; near Chilpancingo; etc.

Collections. Mexico. Guerrero: the type (US,GH). *Cultivated:* Harvard University, 06/628 (clonotype); Cornell University, *Clausen,* 38/H–435 (BH); Soldena Gardens, Pasadena, *Floyd* in 1936 (BH).

Remarks. With its shining, dark-green, rosulate leaves and granular-roughened branches *E. multicaulis* is quite distinct. *Echeveria alata* and *E. guatemalensis* have similarly colored foliage, but in those the leaves are scattered, not rosulate, the corolla is larger and not campanulate, and the branches and peduncles are smooth. *Echeveria gracilis* and *E. macdougallii,* have thicker, subangular, grayish leaves and larger flowers.

Echeveria multicaulis has long been grown in California, proven quite hardy, and deserves to be better known. One hybrid of this has come to my attention, raised by Mr. Walmsley of the Soledad Gardens at San Diego; it clearly shows the parentage of *E. multicaulis,* but nothing is known of the other parent.

95. Echeveria nodulosa (Baker) Otto.
(Figures 171–172. Plate 9, lower; see page 229.)

Echeveria nodulosa (Baker) Otto, Hambg. Gartenztg. vol. 29, p. 8, 1873; Britton and Rose, N. Amer. Fl., vol. 22, p. 17, 1905; Poellnitz, *in* Fedde Repert., vol. 39, p. 225, 1936.
Cotyledon nodulosa Baker, *in* Saunders Refug. Bot., vol. 1, no. 6, pl. 56, 1869.
Echeveria discolor L. de Smet, Cat., 1874; Ed Morren, La Belg. Hort., vol. 24, p. 159, 1874; Poellnitz, *in* Fedde Repert., vol. 39, p. 219, 1936.
Echeveria misteca L. de Smet, Cat., 1874; Ed. Morren, *loc. cit.,* p. 282.
Illustrations. Saunders Refug. Bot., vol. 1, pl. 56, 1869; Addisonia, vol. 3, no. 2, pl. 92, 1918.

Stem evident, to 20 cm. tall, branching in age; leaves, bracts, sepals and outer surface of corolla minutely papillose (under hand lens); leaves subrosulate to scattered, obovate-cuneate, acute, to 5 cm. long, 15 mm. broad, narrowed to 5 mm. at base, thick, shallowly concave above, keeled beneath, upcurved; inflorescences two, arising from below leaves, equilaterally-racemose, to 30 cm. tall; peduncle erect, to 5 mm. thick at base; bracts ascending, obovate, acute, to 3 cm. long; flowers 8 to 12, spreading nearly horizontally; pedicels 5 mm. long or less, bibracteolate at least in bud; sepals widely spreading, subequal, longest 15 mm. long, linear-lanceolate, thick, acute and upcurved at tips; corolla sharply pentagonal, to 16 mm. long and 14 mm. in basal diameter, 13 to 14 mm. wide at mouth; petals thick, sharply keeled, the deep basal hollow with prominent upper rim, at tips outcurved and acuminate-apiculate; base of epipetalous filament dilated; anthers to 4 mm. long in bud; nectaries narrowly transverse-reniform, to 4 mm. wide. Flowers September and October. Description of living plant collected alongside road from Tehuacan to Orizaba.

Color. Leaves absinthe-green, at edges and keel oxblood-red; bracts and sepals like leaves; corolla begonia-rose, petals at edges and tips maize-yellow; styles eugenia-red; nectaries maize-yellow.

Type. None designated. Lectotype: plate 56, Saunders Refugium Botanicum, vol. 1, 1869.

Occurrence. Mexico. Oaxaca: Monte Alban; Reyes, altitude 5800 to 6700 feet; Cerro de San Felipe del Agua. Puebla: abundant on dry limestone hills, along road between Tehuacan and Esperanza.

Collections. Mexico. Oaxaca: Monte Alban, *Rose* 01/6391 (UC), *Rose,* 99/60 (US), *Berger,* Herb., 12/60 (NY); Ixtlan de Juarez, *Krueger and Gillespie,* 40/5, (CAS, GH,MO); Oaxaca, *Conzatti,* 06/25325 (CAS, NY); Cerro de San Felipe, *Conzatti,* 06/188 (GH, var. *minor?);* Yanhuitlan, *R. Moran,* 57/6378 (SD); 14 miles southeast of Huajuapan, *R. Moran,* 57/6373; 5 miles east of Mitla, *R. Moran,* 57/6383 (SD). Puebla: 1 mile north of Santiago Acatepec, *R. Moran,* 57/6356 (SD); limestone hills near Tehuacan, *Pringle,* 97/6779 (CAS,F,G,GH,MEXU,NY,P,PH,UC,US), *Purpus,* 05/1096 (US); El Riego, *Rose* 05/1131 (NY). *Cultivated:* Knickerbocker Nursery, San Diego, in 1936 (BH).

Remarks. Of the synonyms listed above, *E. discolor* de Smet appears to differ only in being stemless; it is not further traceable today. *Echeveria sturmiana* Poellnitz, as described and pictured (Desert Plant Life, vol. 10, p. 226, 1938) is flowerless, and appears to belong here. In habit, size of flower, etc., *E. nodulosa* recalls *E. spectabilis,* but its unique epidermal papillae are quite different from the scattered muriculate outgrowths of the epidermis found in *E. spectabilis.*

Echeveria nodulosa has a wide range on the border between Puebla and Oaxaca, where I saw it in 1934; in 1957 it was very abundant on low limestone hills along the road between Tehuacan and Esperanza. This is a rather dry region with sparse vegetation, which last included also *Sedum stahlii* in quantity, and a single specimen of *E. heterosepala. Echeveria nuda* also occurs here, but always in moister locations. Of other plants directly associated with *E. nodulosa* in this area I may mention *Mimosa, Fouquieria, Nolina, Hechtia, Yucca, Littaea, Opuntia,* and *Pachycereus.*

Figure 171. 95. *Echeveria nodulosa* (Baker) Otto. Flowering plant, × 0.4. Plant photographed in San Diego 24 July 1964; collected southeast of Huajuapan, Oaxaca, Mexico (Moran 6373, a cited collection).

316

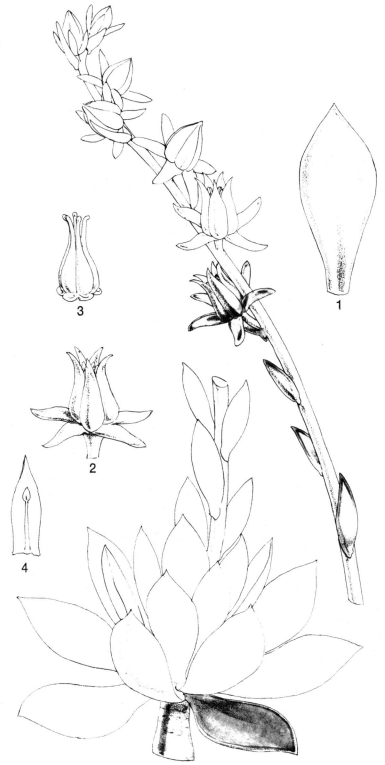

Figure 172. 95. *Echeveria nodulosa* (Baker) Otto. Leaf stated to be and flowering plant evidently also natural size; flower and parts enlarged. Plant grown by W. W. Saunders in Reigate, England, obtained with plants understood to be from Mexico. From the original publication (Saunders Refugium Botanicum, volume 1, plate 56). This plate is designated lectotype for the species.

95b. **Echeveria nodulosa** (Baker) Otto var. **minor** E. Walther, new variety.

Echeveria nodulosa (Baker) Otto var. minor E. Walther, var. nov., similis var. nodulosae sed foliis angustioribus minoribus, sepalis reflexis, corollis tenuioribus.

Stem evident, branching above; leaves somewhat scattered, papillose as in var. *nodulosa* (as are the bracts, sepals, etc.) obovate-cuneate, acute, thick, 4 cm. long, less than 15 mm. broad; inflorescence to 40 cm. tall, equilaterally racemose; peduncle erect; bracts widely spreading, oblong-obovate, to 35 mm. long; flowers to 20; pedicels 5 mm. long or less, 2 mm. thick, bracteolate in bud; sepals reflexed at anthesis, subequal, longest 12 mm. long; corolla urceolate, to 17 mm. long, 12 mm. in diameter or less at base, 7 mm. wide at mouth; petals thick and keeled, deeply hollowed at base; nectaries to 4 mm. wide. Flowers from August on.

Color. Leaves grass- to spinach-green, edged Hay's maroon; bracts as the leaves or more lettuce-green; sepals as leaves; corolla peach-red; petals edged martius-yellow; inside sulphur-yellow; carpels seashell-pink; styles vandyke-red; nectaries whitish.

TYPE. Received from F. Schmoll, Cadereyta, Queretaro, Mexico (CAS no. 258584).

OCCURRENCE. Mexico. No definite locality is on record at present.

REMARKS. Ordinarily *E. nodulosa* appears to be quite uniform in its native habitat, the new variety here described being the sole exception known. It differs in the smaller leaves and the strongly reflexed sepals, but agrees perfectly in the nature of the epidermal papillae.

96. **Echeveria spectabilis** Alexander.
   (Figure 173.)

   Echeveria spectabilis ALEXANDER, Cactus and Succ. Jour. Amer., vol. 13, p. 137, 1941.
   ILLUSTRATIONS. Cactus and Succ. Jour. Amer., vol. 13, pp. 137, 138, figs. 79, 80, 1941.

Subshrub 10 to 60 cm. tall, with numerous ascending branches; epidermis of all exterior parts bearing scattered muriculate papillae; leaves subrosulate, or scattered near end of branches, obovate-spathulate and mucronate, thinnish, not keeled beneath, above flat or shallowly concave, slightly upcurved, 4 to 7 cm. long, 25 to 30 mm. broad, the distinct petiole 10 mm. broad; inflorescence two or more, equilaterally-racemose, to 70 cm. tall; peduncle stout, ascending; lower bracts obovate-oblong, sessile, spreading, to 5 cm. long; flowers to 10 or more, somewhat nodding; pedicels recurved, 10 to 35 mm. long, bearing two slender bractlets to 15 mm. long; upper bracts shorter than the flowers; sepals subequal, longest to 18 mm. long; shorter than corolla, oblong-lanceolate, acute, ascending-spreading, recurved at tips; corolla pentagonal, to 24 mm. long and to 18 mm. in diameter at base, 14 mm. wide at mouth; petals thick, keeled on back, deeply sulcate inside, the deep basal hollow with prominent upper rim; styles slightly longer than ovaries; nectaries narrowly lunate-reniform, to 4 mm. wide. Flowers from July on. Description based on living plants received from Mr. Thomas MacDougall, 1939.

Color. Leaves cerro-green to parrot-green, edged pompeian-red; bracts as leaves, but tending to courge-green; sepals the same, but more spinach-green; corolla scarlet to bittersweet-orange; petals at edges empire- to lemon-yellow, inside pinard-yellow; carpels martius-yellow above; styles light bice-green; nectaries nearly white.

TYPE. Collected by Mr. Thomas MacDougall in 1939, Sierra Juarez, Oaxaca, Mexico (NY).

OCCURRENCE. Mexico. Oaxaca: near Macuiltianguis, pine-slopes of Sierra Juarez.

COLLECTIONS. Type (NY), *Alexander* in 1940 (NY). *Cultivated:* Golden Gate Park, San Francisco, *E. Walther* in 1938, 1941, 1958 (CAS).

REMARKS. I first met with this remarkable species as a dried specimen in Sr. Conzatti's herbarium at Oaxaca in 1937, when it was still nameless. Plants I received from Mr. MacDougall in 1939 flowered shortly afterwards, but Dr. Alexander anticipated my publication, in which I had intended to call this after Sr. Conzatti. In its growth-habit and very large corolla, this comes close to *E. carminea,* but the muriculate papillae are unique. According to Dr.

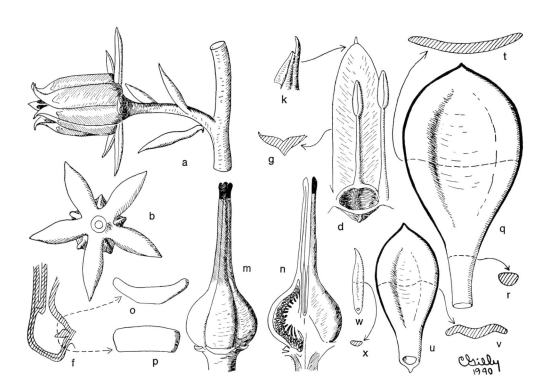

Figure 173. 96. *Echeveria spectabilis* Alexander. Explanation: (a) flower, × 1; (b) flower from below, × 1; (d) inside of petal, × 2; (f) median longitudinal section of petal base, × 4; (g) median cross-section of petal, × 2; (k) apex of petal, the inner face to the left, × 4; (m) carpels, × 2; (n) longitudinal section of carpels, × 2; (o) nectary, face view, × 5; (p) nectary, dorsal view, × 5; (q) leaf, × 1; (r) cross-section of leaf base, × 1; (t) cross-section of widest part of leaf, × 1; (u) mid-peduncle bract, × 1; (v) cross-section of mid-peduncle bract, × 1; (w) pedicellary bract, × 1; (x) cross-section of pedicellary bract, × 1. From the original publication (Cactus and Succulent Journal, volume 13, page 138, figure 80).

Charles Uhl of Cornell, its chromosome number is *n*=about 104. *Echeveria nodulosa* would seem to be closely related, but in the latter species every epidermal cell bulges into a prominent papilla, not merely an occasional one (use hand-lens), and its haploid chromosome number is 16.

As locally cultivated, *E. spectabilis* has proven quite hardy; it is very ornamental with its numerous, large, and bright flowers.

97. **Echeveria goldmani** Rose.

Echeveria goldmani Rose, *in* Britton and Rose, N. Amer. Fl., vol. 22, p. 17, 1905; Poellnitz, *in* Fedde Repert., vol. 39, p. 223, 1936.
Illustration. US no. 91, by Miss Patten, unpublished.

Glabrous subshrub with erect, branching stems to 20 cm. tall or more; leaves laxly rosulate, linear- or oblong-lanceolate, 3 to 5 cm. long, 10 mm. broad or less, deeply concave above, acute, at base narrowed into subtriquetrous petiole 5 mm. wide; inflorescences two to many, equilaterally spicate, to 25 cm. tall; peduncle strict, erect; bracts many, ascending to spreading, oblong-obovate, to 4 cm. long, shortly acuminate; flowers 10 to 15, rather distant; upper bracts 9 mm. long or less, closely resembling sepals; pedicels quite short, even the lowest not over 3 mm. long, thick, bibracteolate, as many as five may be 2-flowered; sepals ascending to appressed, unequal, longest 5 mm. long or less, oblong-ovate, acute, thick, scarcely connate at base; corolla nearly straight, pentagonal, to 10 mm. long, 6 mm. in basal diameter; petals scarcely spreading at tips, with basal hollow short but deep; nectaries reniform, 1 mm. wide. Description from plants locally cultivated, presumably received from Dr. Rose.

Color. Leaves glossy, lettuce- to cosse-green, edges and tip morocco-red, often tinged russet above; lower bracts as leaves; sepals and bractlets lettuce-green, scarlet-red at base; corolla rose-red to scarlet-red; petals inside light salmon-orange; styles viridine-yellow, to morocco-red at tips.

Type. *E. A. Goldman,* 04/802, Comitan, Chiapas, Mexico (US, no. 399990).

Occurrence. Chiapas, Mexico.

Collections. Mexico. Chiapas: Comitan, *Goldman* (US, type; isotypes, BH,F,GH,NY,UC,US, probably all clonotypes from plant grown at Washington, D.C.); mountains near Pasitan, *Matuda,* 34a.

Series 9. SPICATAE (Baker) Berger

Echeveria, ser. Spicatae (Baker) BERGER, *in* Engler Nat. Pflanzenf. ed. 2, vol. 18a,
p. 472, 1930; E. WALTHER, Leafl. West. Bot., vol. 9, pp. 3, 4, 1959.
Courantia LEMAIRE, Jard. Fleur., Misc. 92, 1851; BRITTON AND ROSE, Bull. New
York Bot. Gard., vol. 3, p. 11, 1903; BRITTON AND ROSE, N. Amer. Fl., vol. 22,
p. 32, 1905.
Cotyledon, § Spicatae BAKER, *in* Saunders Refug. Bot. 1, Analytical Table . . . [p. 1],
1869, *pro parte.*
Echeveria, sect. Courantia (Lemaire) BERGER, *in* Engler Nat. Pflanzenf. ed. 2, vol.
18a, p. 481, 1930.

Glabrous subshrubs with small, thinnish, more or less scattered leaves; inflorescence often congested into short, dense spikes or racemes; pedicels rather short or none; bractlets slender; sepals appressed, or somewhat spreading at anthesis; petals rather thin, often yellowish.

TYPICAL SPECIES. *Echeveria rosea* Lindley.

REMARKS. Of the four species placed in his series Spicatae by Baker in 1869, two are pubescent and one is stemless, leaving only *E. rosea.* This last was the basis for Lemaire's *Courantia,* but its characters as conceived by Lemaire, *i.e.,* a filament tube and lack of nectaries, have been found to be illusory. The various species of this series often occur as epiphytes, frequenting tree-trunks, etc., in the moister portions of Mexico and Guatemala.

KEY TO THE SPECIES

A. Flowers rarely or not crowded, if so, then paired on lower pedicels; corolla red.
                 Species of series Nudae
 B. Leaves nearly flat; at least some pedicels 2-flowered; corolla paler. 87. *E. australis*
 B. Leaves concave above, narrower; flowers solitary on each pedicel, the latter very
  short; petals bright red. . . . . 97. *E. goldmani*
A. Flowers crowded, in dense spikes or racemes; corolla pale yellow to pinkish yellow.
                Species of series *Spicatae*
 B. Corolla geranium-pink to jasper-red; sepals broader, linear-oblong, shorter than
  corolla; leaves concave above, elliptic-oblanceolate. Guatemala, Costa Rica.
                 98. *E. pittieri*
 B. Corolla yellowish; sepals and upper bracts narrow, longer than or only slightly
  shorter than corolla; leaves nearly flat, oblanceolate.
  C. Pedicels very short; upper bracts, bractlets, and sepals broader, usually somewhat
   shorter than the corolla; uppermost pedicels all fertile; $n = 51$. Chiapas, Oaxaca,
   Veracruz . . . . 99. *E. chiapensis*
  C. Pedicels sometimes to 5 mm. long; upper bracts, bractlets, and sepals linear-filiform, longer than corolla; uppermost pedicels sterile; $n = 34$. San Luis Potosi
   and Tamaulipas. . . . . 100. *E. rosea*

98. Echeveria pittieri Rose.

(Figure 174).

Echeveria pittieri ROSE, Contrib. U. S. Nat. Herb., vol. 13, p. 296, 1911; ROSE, N.
Amer. Fl., vol. 22, p. 536, 1918; E. WALTHER, Cactus and Succ. Jour. Amer., vol.
7, p. 39, 1935 (as *E. rosea,* in part); POELLNITZ, *in* Fedde Repert., vol. 39, p. 228,
1936; STANDLEY AND STEYERMARK, Flora of Guatemala, Fieldiana, Botany, vol. 24,
pt. 4, 409, 1946.
ILLUSTRATION. U.S. Nat. Herb. photograph no. 715 [see figure 174].

Glabrous subshrub with several ascending branches, to 10 cm. tall or more; leaves laxly rosulate, spreading, elliptic-oblanceolate, acute, 4 to 6 or to 10 cm. long, 20 mm. broad, keeled beneath, above shallowly concave, at base narrowed into petiole 6 mm. wide; inflorescence usually one to each branch, arising from below the foliage, to 20 cm. tall; peduncle erect, to 7 mm. thick at

Figure 174. 98. *Echeveria pittieri* Rose. Plant grown in Washington; apparently collected by C. Werkle on the west coast of Costa Rica (07.250). Photograph from the U.S. National Herbarium, no. 715.

base; bracts numerous, spreading, similar to leaves but smaller, to 4 cm. long; spike dense, equilateral, 3 to 4 cm. long or more, with about 20 flowers; upper bracts linear, shorter than corolla; pedicels not exceeding 1 mm. in length, lowest sometimes 2-flowered, bibracteolate; sepals shorter than corolla, ⅔ of corolla longest to 9 mm. long, somewhat spreading, to ascending, thickish, linear-oblanceolate, acute; corolla campanulate, 12 to 13 mm. long, 6 mm. thick at base, but as much as 11 mm. in diameter at mouth, sharply pentagonal; petals straight, erect or somewhat spreading above, keeled, with distinct basal hollow; carpels tapering into the long, slender styles; nectaries reniform, to 1 mm. wide. Flowers from January on. Description based on living plant received from Dr. Poellnitz.

Color. Leaves courge-green tinged walnut-brown at apex; lower bracts as leaves; upper bracts and bractlets light purplish vinaceous; sepals courge-green to light purplish vinaceous, glaucous in bud; corolla jasper-red to capuzine-buff; petals inside venetian-pink, to etruscan-red above; styles light grape-green; nectaries pinkish cinnamon.

TYPE. *H. Pittier,* 07/1880, collected at lagoon on Volcan Ipala, Guatemala (US, no. 618381).

OCCURRENCE. On rocks or epiphytic, usually in shade but sometimes in the open, 1000 to 2400 m.; Guatemala, Nicaragua, Costa Rica.

COLLECTIONS. Guatemala: lagoon on Volcan Ipala (type, US); Dept. Jutinapa, Volcan Suchitan, northwest of Asuncion Mita, *Steyermark,* 39/43840 (US); Dept Totonicapan, *Standley,* 40/84520 (F); Dept. Quetzaltenango, Volcan Zunil, *Steyermark,* 40/34722 (US); Finca Diamante, *Steyermark,* 42/43840 (F). Nicaragua: Dept. Jinotega, *Standley,* 47/9857 (F). Costa Rica: west coast, *Werkle,* 07/250 (BH). *Cultivated:* Strybing Arboretum, Golden Gate Park, San Francisco by *E. Walther* in 1959 (CAS).

REMARKS. From *E. rosea* and *E. chiapensis,* the present species differs clearly in its shorter spreading sepals, and petals spreading at apex, rose-pink, not yellow. *Echeveria goldmani* has narrower leaves and more distant flowers with appressed sepals. The nearest relation would appear to be an undescribed plant known to occur in Jalisco. In it the leaves are rhomboid-oblanceolate, flat, and shortly acuminate, and the flowers are densely crowded.

Echeveria pittieri was named for Mr. Henry Pittier, well-known collector of Central American and Venezuelan plants.

99. **Echeveria chiapensis** Rose *ex* Poellnitz.
(Figure 175.)

Echeveria chiapensis ROSE *ex* Poellnitz, *in* Fedde Repert., vol. 39, p. 224, 1936.
ILLUSTRATIONS. U.S. Nat. Herb. photograph nos. 278 [see figure 175], 937, unpublished.

Glabrous subshrub to 30 cm. tall, with few spreading branches; leaves laxly rosulate or scattered at end of branches, obovate-oblanceolate, 4 to 7 cm. long, 15 to 25 mm. broad, flat and thin, keeled beneath, mucronate, petiole 8 mm. wide; inflorescences two or three, arising from below the leaves, often decumbent at base, above a dense, equilateral spike to 50 cm. tall; peduncle spreading, to erect above, 5 mm. thick, at base; bracts many, leaflike, spreading, obovate to broadly oblanceolate, acute to mucronate, sharply keeled beneath but otherwise flat, 3 to 4 cm. long; spike 6 cm. long or more, with 15 to 20

Figure 175. 99. *Echeveria chiapensis* Rose. Plant grown in Washington; collected by C. A. Purpus near Esperanza, Puebla, Mexico (Rose greenhouse plant 937). Photograph from the U.S. National Herbarium, no. 278.

flowers; upper bracts to 14 mm. long; pedicels 1 mm. long or less, bearing two linear-deltoid bractlets to 7 mm. long; sepals subequal, longest 10 mm. long, linear, appressed or slightly spreading at anthesis; corolla bluntly pentagonal, to 10 mm. long, 6 to 7 mm. in diameter; petals thinnish with shallow basal hollow; epipetalous stamens borne on petals, episepalous ones free to base; nectaries narrowly reniform, 1.5 mm. wide, oblique. Flowers from August to December. Description based on living plants from Sr. E. Oestlund, collected at Lago Montebello in Chiapas, Mexico.

Color. Leaves lettuce-green, courge-green beneath, somewhat glaucous; lower bracts forest-green to light elm-green, upper bracts tinged testaceous; sepals like upper bracts, but somewhat glaucous and hence pinkish vinaceous, to deep corinthian-red; corolla citron-yellow; carpels deep chrysolite-green; anthers pale lemon-yellow; nectaries margined red.

TYPE. *Rose,* 04/1011, without locality (NY, no. 20952); isotype (NY).

OCCURRENCE. Mexico. Chiapas, Oaxaca, Puebla, Veracruz.

COLLECTIONS. Mexico. *Rose,* 04/1011, probably Chiapas (NY, type).

Chiapas: Pasital, *Matuda,* 36/349 (US). Oaxaca: San Juan del Estado, *L. C. Smith,* 94/475 (GH); Cumbre de los Frailes, Teotitlan, *Conzatti,* 07/2104 (NY,US); San Juan Bautista, near Elto, *Rusby* in 1910 (NY); Dist. Cuicatlan, Coyula, *Conzatti* in 1911 (US). Puebla: on rocks near Esperanza, *Purpus,* 04/R–937 (NY,US); Xuchitl, near Esperanza, *Arsene,* 07/7086 (US), *Arsene and Nicholas,* 10/5148 (US,GH). Veracruz: Jalapa, *P. Maury,* 1884/1088 (NY); Orizaba, *F. Mueller,* 1855/95 (W), *Schlumberger,* 1855/ 176 (NY); mountains towards Tehuacan, *Pringle,* 95/5970 (GH,MEXU).

REMARKS. *Echeveria chiapensis* differs from *E. pittieri* in its longer sepals, longer upper bracts, and clear yellow corolla, as well as in the quite flat leaves. *Echeveria rosea,* too, has yellow petals and very long sepals, but its pedicels may exceed 5 mm. in length, and the upper bracts and sepals are filiform and bright rose in color.

Dr. Uhl of Cornell has determined the number of chromomes as $n = 51$.

While the type is devoid of any data on its source, the annotation by Rose and his choice for a specific name, indicate Chiapas as its home. My material from Lago Montebello agrees completely, as it does also with *Purpus,* 04/R– 937 from the vicinty of Esperanza, as pictured in US photograph number 937. In 1957 I found this species in this general vicinity, atop the first pass leading to Esperanza, just off the Tehuacan-Orizaba highway. There it was in full flower in December, epiphytic on *Crataegus pubescens,* on branches densely laden with ferns, mosses, and *Tillandsia.* This gap in the mountain range permits entrance of the moisture-laden winds from the Gulf of Mexico, which create conditions suitable for success of epiphytes. The plants of *E. chiapensis* had developed stems several feet long, with laxly scattered foliage at their ends, overtopped by the erect, bright red and yellow flower spikes.

100. **Echeveria rosea** Lindley.

(Figure 176. Plate 9, upper; see page 229.)

> *Echeveria rosea* LINDLEY, Bot. Reg., vol. 28, (new ser. vol. 5) pl. 22, 1842; E. WAL-THER, Cactus and Succ. Jour. Amer., vol. 7, p. 39, 1935 (*in part only*); POELLNITZ, *in* Fedde Repert., vol. 39, p. 227, 1936.
> *Courantia echeverioides* LEMAIRE, Jard. Fleur. 1, Misc. 92, 1851.
> *Courantia rosea* (Lindley) LEMAIRE, *op. cit.,* 3, 244, 1853; BRITTON AND ROSE in Bull. New York Bot. Gard., vol. 3, p. 11, 1903; N. Amer. Fl., vol. 22, pp. 32, 33, 1905.
> *Cotyledon roseata* BAKER, *in* Saunders Refug. Bot., vol. 1, no. 3, 1869.
> ILLUSTRATIONS. Lindley, Bot. Reg., vol. 28 (new ser. vol. 5) pl. 22, 1842; Lemaire, *loc. cit.*

Glabrous subshrub to more than 25 cm. tall; branches few, slender, often decumbent, 5 to 8 mm. thick at base; leaves scarcely rosulate, laxly scattered near end of branches, ascending, oblong-oblanceolate, 5 to 9 cm. long, 15 to 20 mm. broad, thinnish, faintly keeled beneath, otherwise flat, somewhat decurved at apex, at base narrowed into subtriquetrous, 7 mm. wide petiole with a basal spur, at apex acute and mucronate; inflorescences arising from below leaves, to 20 cm. long, a dense, equilateral raceme or spike; peduncle ascending, slender, 3 to 5 mm. thick below, glaucous; bracts many, spreading to decurved, oblanceolate, to 35 mm. long, faintly keeled, long-petioled; raceme 8 to 12 cm. long, uppermost sterile; pedicels short, or slender and to 7 mm. long, bearing two bractlets to 15 mm. long; sepals subequal, linear-filiform, free nearly to base, appressed or slightly spreading, to 16 mm. long; corolla 13 mm. long, 6 to 7 mm. in basal diameter; petals thin, scarcely angled on back, not much hollowed within at base, corolla tube to 5 mm. long, bearing the stamens at its upper end (but there is no separate staminal tube); filaments broadened at base; carpels slender; nectaries present, reniform, to 1 mm. wide, secreting an abundance of nectar; follicles widely spreading at maturity. Flowers from January to March. Description of plant sent from Las Canoas, Mexico by Mr. O. Nagel.

Color. Leaves lettuce-green and somewhat glaucous when young, later light brownish olive; peduncle ageratum-violet; lower bracts as leaves but tinged deep vinaceous; upper bracts, bractlets, and sepals daphne-pink to purplish vinaceous; corolla citron-yellow, tips of petals corinthian-red; carpels dull green-yellow, as are the styles and nectaries.

TYPE. Lindley Herbarium, University of Cambridge (?, CGE).

OCCURRENCE. Mexico. Frequently epiphytic; San Luis Potosi (Las Canoas, Tomasopo Cañon); Tamaulipas.

COLLECTIONS. Mexico. San Luis Potosi: 10 miles from Antigua Morelos, *R. Flores,* 51/UCBG–51/642 (UC). Tamaulipas: Victoria, Santa Rita Ranch, *Runyon and Tharp,* 26/75 (NY,US). *Cultivated:* Cambridge, England (type, Lindley Herbarium, CGE); Golden Gate Park, San Francisco, from Tomasopo Cañon, *E. Walther* in 1936 (CAS).

REMARKS. The filiform bracts and sepals, highly colored at anthesis, set this apart from all other species in the genus. Unique as this species is with its striking plume of flowers, it scarcely represents a distinct genus, as conceived by Lemaire and by Rose. There is no true staminal tube, nectaries are clearly present, even if small, and several more or less closely related transitional species are known. The uppermost floral bracts are quite sterile and do not subtend any flowers, another character unknown elsewhere in the genus *Echeveria.* The gametic chromosome number is 34.

In its native home this species occurs most frequently as an epiphyte, as on *Taxodium mucronatum* at Las Canoas, where Mr. O. Nagel, collector for Sr. E. Oestlund of Cuernavaca, found this growing with *Laelia anceps,* and *Tillandsia usneoides.* Mr. C. G. Pringle also collected *E. rosea* here in 1891, taking it from moss-covered branches of *Quercus* species. Mr. F. Schwarz, cactus collector of San Luis Potosi, likewise found this growing on moss-covered oaks, in the high mountains near Ciudad del Maiz, but could find none on the ground.

Echeveria rosea first flowered in England in 1841, the species having been introduced by Lee & Co., of Vineyard near Hammersmith. The genus *Courantia,* proposed by Lemaire, honored J. Courant, an enthusiastic succulent-grower of Ingouville near Le Havre.

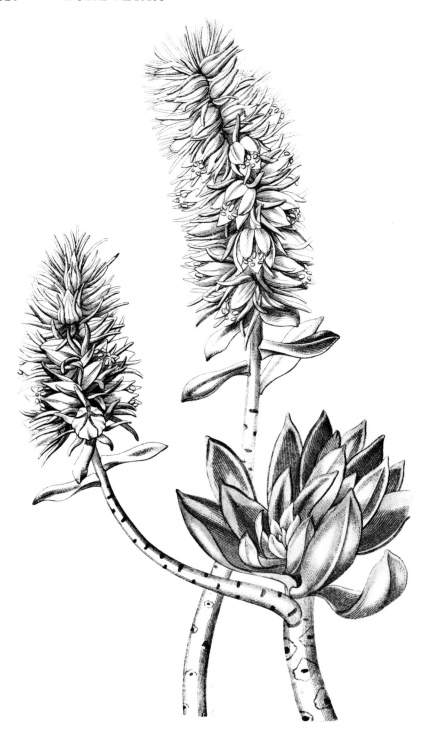

Figure 176.   100. *Echeveria rosea* Lindley. Plant grown at the Royal Horticultural Society, London; imported from Mexico. From the original publication (Edwards's Botanical Register, volume 28, plate 22).

Series 10. ELATAE E. Walther

Echeveria, ser. Elatae E. WALTHER, Leafl. West. Bot., vol. 9, pp. 3, 4, 1959 (Latin).
Cotyledon, § Racemosae BAKER, *in* Saunders Refug. Bot., vol. 1, 1869, *pro parte.*
Echeveria, ser. Racemosae (Baker) BERGER, *in* Engler Nat. Pflanzenf. ed. 2, vol. 18a, p. 472, 1930 *pro parte;* E. WALTHER, Cactus and Succ. Jour. Amer., vol. 7, p. 40, 1935, *pro parte.*
Echeveria, ser. Australes E. WALTHER, Cactus and Succ. Jour. Amer., vol. 7, p. 39, 1935; as to type (English description only). Not *Echeveria,* ser. Australes E. WAL-THER, Leafl. West. Bot., vol. 9, pp. 3, 4, 1959, typified by *E. nuda* LINDLEY. [Cf. Moran, Cactus and Succ. Jour. Amer., vol. 33, p. 138, 1961; MORAN AND MEYRÁN, Cactaceas y Suculentas Mexicanas, vol. 6, p. 82, 1961. Ed.]

Plants glabrous, with evident, sometimes tall, mostly simple stem; leaves medium-sized, densely rosulate or alternately scattered; inflorescence equilateral, racemose, tall and many-flowered; bracts numerous, flat, similar to leaves but smaller; pedicels evident, bracteolate; sepals ascending to spreading or reflexed; corolla cylindroid, broad or narrow.

TYPICAL SPECIES. *Echeveria bicolor* (Humboldt, Bonpland and Kunth) E. Walther.

REMARKS. If we disregard the insufficiently known *E. cuencaensis* and *E. excelsa,* the remaining species form a homogeneous group no doubt closely related. Depauperate forms of *E. bicolor* appear to be common in Venezuela and Colombia, and include *E. bicolor* var. *turumiquirense* and *E. bracteolata,* which may be looked for under *E. quitensis.* Much more field-collected material, preferably of living plants, needs to be studied before a clear concept of the relationships here involved is possible.

I feel certain that *E. bicolor* and *E. venezuelensis* are distinct, despite their close proximity near Caracas; the shape of the corolla and of the petals appears to be decisive.

KEY TO THE SPECIES

A. Pedicels short, less than half the length of the corolla; insufficiently known South American species.
  B. Lowest pedicels mostly 2-flowered; corolla 12 to 14 mm. long. Cuenca, Ecuador.
                                                            106. *E. cuencaensis*
  B. All pedicels single-flowered; corolla 16 to 20 mm. long. Peru. . . 107. *E. excelsa*
A. Pedicels as long as the corolla or longer; plants in cultivation.
  B. Leaves distant, remote, not rosulate; flowers pendant; upper bracts and pedicels abruptly deflexed; sepals strongly ascending. Oaxaca, Mexico.
                                                 103. *E. penduliflora*
  B. Leaves more or less densely rosulate; flowers otherwise.
    C. Sepals reflexed at anthesis; leaves narrow, 10 to 15 cm. long by 5 cm. broad or less, glaucous tinged with purple. Mexico.
      D. Leaves flat or nearly so; corolla 12 to 15 mm. long. . 101. *E. atropurpurea*
      D. Leaves deeply concave above; corolla to 25 mm. long. . 102. *E. canaliculata*
    C. Sepals ascending or somewhat spreading, not reflexed; leaves broader, less than 3 times as long as wide, green or glaucous, not purple-tinged. South American species.
      D. Leaves closely rosulate, usually glaucous; pedicels of even upper flowers elongated; petals broadest near base. . . . . . . 104. *E. venezuelensis*
      D. Leaves subrosulate, green, scarcely glaucous; pedicels of upper flowers short; petals broadest above the middle. . . . . 105. *E. bicolor*

101. Echeveria atropurpurea (Baker) Ed. Morren.
(Figure 177. Plate 10; see page 232.)

> Echeveria atropurpurea (Baker) ED. MORREN, La Belg. Hort., 1874, 156; BRITTON
> AND ROSE, N. Amer. Fl., vol. 22, p. 17, 1905; POELLNITZ, in Fedde Repert., vol.
> 39, p. 229, 1936.
> Cotyledon atropurpurea BAKER, in Saunders, Refug. Bot., vol. 3, pl. 198, 1870.
> Echeveria sanguinea Hort.
> ILLUSTRATIONS. Saunders Refug. Bot., vol. 3, pl. 198, 1870; Walpole no. 73, [see
> plate 10].

Glabrous; stems attaining a height of 10 to 15 cm., to 25 mm. thick; leaves about 20, densely rosulate, oblong-oblanceolate or obovate-spathulate, 10 to 12 cm. long by 50 mm. broad in upper fourth, rather broad at base, moderately thick; peduncle erect, to 30 cm. tall below raceme, bracts crowded, much smaller than leaves; raceme with 20 to 25 flowers, 12 to 15 cm. long, less than 50 mm. across; upper bracts linear, the lowest 12 mm. long; pedicels 9 to 12 mm. long, spreading or the lowest somewhat reflexed; sepals subequal, 4 mm. long (or more), linear-lanceolate, spreading; corolla 12 mm. long, decidedly pentagonal; petals acute; outer stamens inserted at the middle. Description after Baker, loc. cit.

Color. Leaves above dark purple with glaucous bloom; corolla bright red.

TYPE. In Kew Herbarium (?,K).

OCCURRENCE. Mexico, presumably Veracruz.

COLLECTIONS. Mexico. Purpus, 08/4455 (UC), without locality, presumably from Veracruz. Cultivated: Missouri Bot. Gard., C. H. Thompson, 05/304 (MO).

REMARKS. Baker, loc. cit., wrote: "Nearest C. canaliculata, but leaves much broader and spathulately narrowed in lower half, their color characteristic, calyx and corolla much smaller." According to W. W. Saunders, this was first grown by de Smet of Ghent; it appears lost to cultivation at present, but seems to have been grown both at Washington, D. C., and at the Missouri Botanical Garden not too long ago. Aside from E. canaliculata, this should further be compared with my new E. penduliflora, but in the latter the deflexed pedicels and upper bracts are distinctive, the sepals are ascending to appressed, and the corolla is paler pink, with delft-blue tips to the petals.

Figure 177. 101. *Echeveria atropurpurea* (Baker) Ed. Morren. Flowering plant apparently natural size; flower and parts enlarged. Plant grown by W. W. Saunders in Reigate, England; received from Mons. De Smet, of Ghent. From the original publication (Saunders Refugium Botanicum, volume 3, plate 198).

102. **Echeveria canaliculata** Hooker fil.
(Figure 178.)

Echeveria canaliculata HOOKER fil., Bot. Mag., pl. 4986, 1857; BRITTON AND ROSE,
N. Amer. Fl., vol. 22, p. 17, 1905; POELLNITZ, *in* Fedde Repert., vol. 39, p. 230,
1936.
Cotyledon canaliculata (Hooker fil.) BAKER, *in* Saunders Refug. Bot., vol. 1, no. 9,
1869.
ILLUSTRATION. Bot. Mag., pl. 4986, 1857.

Stem short, thick, fleshy to woody, erect, marked with scars of fallen
leaves; when not flowering, the leaves are rosulately crowded, spreading, 10 to
15 cm. long, oblong or somewhat strap-shaped, thick, fleshy, tapering gradually upwards into a slender, almost filiform point, deeply channeled above,
rounded beneath; flowering branch elongated, 35 to 50 cm. tall; lower bracts
similar to rosette-leaves, upper more distant even though numerous, of the
same shape but smaller, at base with blunt spur, but not broadly sessile as
rosette leaves; gradually passing into small, obtuse, upper bracts; raceme equilateral, 15 cm. long or more; pedicels 12 mm. long or more, with minute,
subulate bractlets; sepals equal, linear-lanceolate, spreading-reflexed, much
resembling the bracts; corolla to 25 mm. long, pentagonal; petals erect, shortly
united at base, linear-lanceolate, moderately spreading at tips; ovaries narrowly oblong; nectaries suborbicular, with depression on upper edge; styles
slightly twisted; stigmas globose. Flowers from April on. Description after
Hooker, fil., *loc. cit.*

Color. Leaves glaucous tinged with purple; bracts very glaucous, as are
the sepals; corolla bright brick-red.

TYPE. Perhaps in Kew Herbarium (K).

OCCURRENCE. Mexico. Said to have come from vicinity of Real del Monte,
(?) Hidalgo; recently from Motozintla, Chiapas.

COLLECTIONS. Mexico. Motozintla, *T. MacDougall* in 1958. *Cultivated:*
Dept. of Parks, Bronx, New York (US); Strybing Arboretum, Golden Gate
Park, San Francisco *E. Walther* (CAS).

REMARKS. While this appears to have been in cultivation quite recently at
Dahlem and the Huntington Botanical Gardens, all trace of it is now lost.
Echeveria canaliculata is related to *E. atropurpurea* and *E. penduliflora*. The
latter differs in its flat leaves, strongly nodding flowers with deflexed pedicels
and upper bracts, as well as in a much shorter corolla with appressed sepals.

Echeveria canaliculata finds its closest relation in *E. atropurpurea* which
differs in its flat leaves, shorter corolla, and shorter sepals. South American
species with large leaves resembling this are *E. bicolor* and *E. cuencaensis,*
both of which differ in having shorter corollas and spreading sepals.

Figure 178. 102. *Echeveria canaliculata* Hooker fil. Flowering plant, × 0.7; floral parts enlarged. Plant grown at Kew. From the original publication (Curtis's Botanical Magazine, volume 83, plate 4986).

103. **Echeveria penduliflora** E. Walther.
(Figures 179–180.)

Echeveria penduliflora E. WALTHER, Cactus and Succ. Jour. Amer., vol. 30, p. 151, 1958.

ILLUSTRATIONS. Cactus and Succ. Jour. Amer., vol. 30, p. 151, figs. 86, 87, 1958.

Plant glabrous, caulescent; stem erect, usually simple, to 30 cm. tall or more; leaves scattered alternately or subrosulate at top of stem, thinnish, oblong-oblanceolate, to 14 cm. long and 4 cm. broad, narrowed to 2 cm, at the thick, keeled petiole, faintly keeled beneath, shallowly concave above, at tips upcurved and mucronate; inflorescences one or two, arising from below leaves, to 30 cm. tall; peduncle erect, to 5 mm. thick at base; lower bracts strongly ascending, to 5 cm. long and 15 mm. broad, obovate-oblong, at apex upcurved and acute, shallowly concave above, faintly keeled beneath, spurred at base; racemes many-flowered, unilateral, to 25 cm. long, flexuose, with 60 or more flowers, these strongly pendulous, crowded or remote; upper bracts abruptly deflexed from the spurred base but [the pedicels?—Ed.] becoming erect in fruit, bearing two minute, slender fugacious linear bractlets less than 2 mm. in length; sepals subequal, longest 6 mm. long, linear-deltoid, apiculate, ascending; corolla to 13 mm. long, 9 mm. in basal diameter, 4 mm. at mouth, bluntly pentagonal; petals with shallow basal hollow within; carpels 9 mm. long; nectaries 2 mm. broad, truncate-reniform. Flowers from June on.

Color. Leaves above cerro-green, beneath asphodel-green; peduncle and rachis grape-green; lower bracts as the leaves; upper bracts and sepals pale violet-gray; corolla geranium-pink to peach-red and jasper-pink, tips of petals in buds noticeably delft-blue; carpels white at base, above chartreuse-yellow to kildare-green; styles dull indian-purple; nectaries white.

TYPE. *T. MacDougall,* B–174, in soil between Arroyo de la Y and San Sebastian de los Fustes, Ejutla, elevation about 4,000 feet, Oaxaca, 25 January 1956 (CAS, no. 409846). Clonotype: University of California Bot. Gard., 56.798.

OCCURRENCE. Known only from the type locality.

REMARKS. This species is the most remarkable that has been discovered recently in Oaxaca by Mr. Thomas MacDougall. It shows some similarities to both *E. atropurpurea* and *E. canaliculata,* both of which have the sepals strongly reflexed, and do not show the strongly deflexed pedicels and upper bracts. In *E. penduliflora* the raceme is actually equilateral, but becomes one-sided from one-sided lighting.

Figure 179. 103. *Echeveria penduliflora* E. Walther. From the original publication (Cactus and Succulent Journal, volume 30, page 151, figure 86).

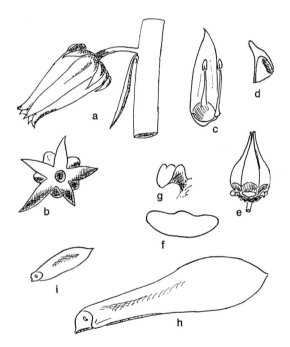

Figure 180. 103. *Echeveria penduliflora* E. Walther. Explanation: (a) flower, × 2; (b) flower from below, × 2; (c) inside of petal, × 2; (d) apex of petal, × 8; (e) carpels, × 2; (f) nectary, front view, × 8; (g) nectary, side view, × 8; (h) leaf, × 0.4; (i) bract, × 0.4. From the original publication (Cactus and Succulent Journal, volume 30, page 151, figure 87).

104. **Echeveria venezuelensis** Rose.
(Figure 181.)

Echeveria venezuelensis Rose, Gentes Herbarum, vol. 2, p. 200, 1930; Poellnitz, *in* Fedde Repert., vol. 39, p. 235, 1936.

Echeveria bicolor E. Walther, Cactus and Succ. Jour. Amer., vol. 7, p. 39, 1935, *in part*.

Illustrations. Gentes Herbarum, *loc. cit.*, p. 202, fig. 104; US Nat. Herb. photographs nos. 1676, 1677, unpublished.

Glabrous; stem evident, to 10 cm. tall or more, usually simple, bearing a dense, terminal rosette of 12 or more leaves; these fleshy, oblanceolate to obovate-cuneate, to 8 cm. long and 45 mm. broad, at apex rounded and mucronate, to acute, margins more or less incurved, especially when young; inflorescences one or two, arising from below the leaves, 30 to 40 cm. tall; peduncle erect; lower bracts as leaves, numerous, spreading, 3 to 5 cm. long; raceme equilateral, with as many as 40 or more flowers; upper bracts narrowly linear-lanceolate, 10 to 15 mm. long, acute, often borne some way up on the pedicel; pedicels 5 to 7 mm. long, ascending, bibracteolate; bractlets linear-oblanceolate, to 6 mm. long; sepals subequal, longest to 8 mm. long or more, widely spreading at anthesis, narrowly deltoid-ovate, acute; corolla pentagonal, 10 mm. long, narrowly urceolate, with only the very base conspicuously gibbose, gradually curved to the shallow constriction just below the slightly spreading tip of the petal, these narrow, acuminate in upper third, bluntly keeled and hollowed within at base; nectaries broad and low. Description after the original description, as amended by the author.

Color. (After Rose), leaves pale green, more or less glaucous, especially beneath; sepals purplish green, glaucous; corolla pinkish; styles purplish.

Type. *Pittier, 13/5932*, collected at Los Chorros, above Dos Caminos, about 12 miles east of Caracas, Venezuela (US, no. 1420623; isotype, GH).

Occurrence. Venezuela: near Caracas and Merida.

Collections. Venezuela: the type; Los Chorros de Tomale, in bushy gorge in savannas, 800 to 1000 m., *Pittier, 17/7043* (US); Los Chorros, *L. H. and E. Z. Bailey, 21/478* (GH,US); Merida, Paramo de Mucuruba, *Gehriger, 30/119* (PH).

Remarks. Further considerations have induced me to retain *E. venezuelensis* as distinct, at least until living material from Venezuela comes to hand. The type of *E. bicolor* Humboldt, Bonpland, and Kunth includes two collections, of which the one from Caracas, number 610, is very fragmentary, while the other, from Pasto in southern Colombia, is possibly another species. However, in this last number 2135, one flower clearly shows the bigibbose shape of the petals, so different from that seen in the present species. In view of the doubt still existing, I am unable to cite any further exsiccatae.

Figure 181. 104. *Echeveria venezuelensis* Rose. Approximately × 0.5. From the original publication (Gentes Herbarum, volume 2, page 202, figure 104).

105. **Echeveria bicolor** (Humbolt, Bonpland and Kunth) E. Walther.
(Figure 182.)

> *Echeveria bicolor* (Humboldt, Bonpland and Kunth) E. WALTHER, Cactus and Succ.
> Jour. Amer., vol. 7, p. 39, 1935; POELLNITZ, *in* Fedde Repert., vol. 39, p. 228,
> 1936.
> *Sedum bicolor* HUMBOLDT, BONPLAND AND KUNTH, Nov. Gen. et Spec., vol. 6, p. 45,
> 1823; DeCANDOLLE, Prodromus, vol. 3, p. 410, 1828.
> *Echeveria bracteolata* LINK, KLOTZSCH AND OTTO, Icones Plant. Rar. Hort. Berol.,
> vol. 2, p. 68, 1844; LINDLEY, Bot. Reg., Misc. matter, vol. 31 (new ser., vol. 8)
> p. 13, 1845. Juvenile stage of *E. bicolor.*
> *Cotyledon bracteolata* (Link, Klotzsch and Otto) BAKER, *in* Saunders Refug. Bot.,
> vol. 1, no. 18, 1869.
> *Cotyledon subspicata* BAKER, *in* Saunders Refug. Bot., vol. 1, no. 30, 1869.
> *Echeveria subspicata* (Baker) BERGER, *in* Engler, Nat. Pflanzenf. ed. 2, vol. 18a, p.
> 473, 1930.

Glabrous; caulescent, stem erect, to 30 cm. tall or more, stout, to 20 mm.
thick, simple above, but with numerous branches arising from base; leaves
subrosulate or crowded, 15 to 20, obovate-cuneate, at apex rounded and strongly mucronate, shallowly hollowed above toward base, keeled beneath, fleshy but
thin, to 9 cm. long and 35 mm. broad, petiole angular; inflorescences two or
more, arising from below the leaves, to 50 cm. tall or more; peduncle stout, to
8 mm. thick, curved below, erect above; lower bracts numerous, spreading to
recurved, broadly-obovate, cuneate, acute and mucronate, flattish, keeled beneath, to 5 cm. long, 35 mm. broad; raceme equilateral, often unilateral due
to one-sided lighting, with as many as 25 or more flowers; upper bracts oblong-

Figure 182.   105. *Echeveria bicolor* (Humboldt, Bonpland, and Kunth) E. Walther. Flow-
ering plant about × 0.75 (about natural size in the original); floral parts enlarged.
From the original publication *Echeveria bracteolata* Link, Klotzsch, and Otto (Icones
Plantarum Rariorum Horti Regii Botanici Berolinensis, volume 2, plate 27).

oblanceolate, acute to shortly acuminate, shallowly concave above, keeled beneath, 12 to 20 mm. long; pedicels 4 to 10 mm. long, 2 mm. thick, bibracteo-late, the bractlets linear-lanceolate, acuminate, 10 to 18 mm. long; sepals sub-equal, longest 12 to 14 mm. long, oblong-lanceolate, acuminate, keeled near apex, ascending to spreading; corolla sharply pentagonal, 14 to 15 mm. long, 12 mm. in basal diameter, 7 mm. at mouth, corolla-tube gibbose at base, constricted at its upper limit where petals become free, the latter again ventri-cose above middle, only to become narrowed again just below the spreading tips; petals broadly obovate-oblong, acuminate, thick, sharply keeled and with deep basal nectar cavity, at apex shortly subulate-apiculate dorsally; carpels 9 to 10 mm. long; nectaries transversely lunate-reniform, truncate, stipitate, to 3.5 mm. broad. Description of living plant growing in the Strybing Arbo-retum, Golden Gate Park, San Francisco, originally received from Dr. Leon Croizat, Caracas, Venezuela.

Color. Leaves cerro-green, to light cress-green beneath, not at all glaucous; peduncle eugenia-red; lower bracts as the leaves, to light bice-green beneath; upper bracts, bractlets, and sepals light cress-green; corolla scarlet-red or peach-red, with edges deep-chrome to apricot-yellow, petals inside light orange-yellow; carpels whitish; styles light green-yellow; stigmas vandyke-red; nectaries white.

TYPE. *Humboldt and Bonpland* no. 610 (P), New Grenada, "crescit in umbrosis, humidis, prope Caracas, alt. 410 hex., Hda. Sr. Blandin; item inter rupes, prope Meneses Pastoensium, alt. 1322 hex. (no. 2135)."

OCCURRENCE. Venezuela: near Caracas (type). Colombia: Sierra de Santa Martha *(Purdie,* type of *C. subspicata);* Dept. Magdalena, about 30 miles inland from Dibulla, near Pasto, southern Colombia; etc.

COLLECTIONS. Venezuela: near Caracas (P, type); Merida, Laguna Negra, Orillas de la Laguna, *Hno. Gines,* 51/1741 (US); Rio Tormero below El Aguila, above Chachapo, *Steyermark,* 44/55674 (F). Colombia: near Pasto, *Humboldt and Bonpland* (P, type); Dept. Boyaca, Nevado del Cocuy, Valle de la Cueva, *J. Cuatrecasas,* 38/1310 (F,US); Cauca, Coconuco, *Kjell von Sneidern,* 39/2337 (F,G,US); Dept Magdalena, Sierra de Santa Martha, *Purdie* (type of *Cotyledon subspicata);* 30 miles inland from Dibulla, *Sei-fritz,* 32/431 (US); College of West Indies Exp., 54/7 (US). *Cultivated:* Strybing Arboretum, Golden Gate Park, San Francisco, from Dr. L. Croizat, Caracas, *E. Walther* (CAS).

106. **Echeveria cuencaensis** Poellnitz.

Echeveria cuencaensis POELLNITZ, *in* Fedde Repert., vol. 38, p. 187, 1935; vol. 39, p. 248, 1936.

Glabrous; stemless (?); leaves oblong or obovate-oblong, mucronate, cer-tainly grayish glaucous (?), red at edges, when mature to 7 cm. long, 25 mm. broad; (scape to 20 cm. tall or more), peduncle elongated; bracts unknown; flowers to over 30 in an equilateral raceme; lowest pedicels somewhat elon-gated, bearing 2 flowers each; pedicels short, about 3 mm. long; upper bracts unknown; calyx tube short, its lobes unequal, acute, to about 7 mm. long, appressed to corolla; corolla about 12 to 14 mm. long (surely red, Poellnitz), its tube short, about 1 to 2 mm. long; segments acute, outcurved above, at edges and towards apex probably yellow or reddish; staminal filaments red, episepalous ones adnate to top of corolla tube, 5 to 6 mm. long, the epipetalous ones borne about 2 mm. higher up on the petals, about 3 mm. long; anthers narrow, about 1 mm. long; carpels erect, somewhat connate at base, red (?), about 5 mm. long; styles erect, red (?), about 2 mm. long. Description after Poellnitz, *loc. cit.*, freely translated by the present author.

TYPE. *Rose, Pachano and Rose,* 18/22941, from near Cuenca, Ecuador (US, no. 1022515).

OCCURRENCE. Ecuador.

COLLECTIONS. The type from near Cuenca; Salle, *W. W. Saunders,* 74/10 (K).

REMARKS. From such a limited amount of material it is difficult to make any accurate comparisons, but *E. cuencaensis* apparently differs from *E. excelsa* from Peru in having longer pedicels, but shorter corolla. The Mexican *E. canaliculata* and *E. atropurpurea* both have much longer pedicels and reflexed sepals.

107. **Echeveria excelsa** (Diels) Berger.

> *Echeveria excelsa* (Diels) BERGER, *in* Engler, Nat. Pflanzenf. ed. 2, vol. 18a, p. 473, 1930; POELLNITZ, *in* Fedde Repert., vol. 39, p. 217, 1936; MACBRIDE, Flora of Peru, Field Mus., Bot. Ser., vol. 13, no. 3, pt. 2, p. 1014, 1938.
> *Cotyledon excelsa* DIELS, *in* Engler, Bot. Jahrb., vol. 37, p. 412, 1906.

Stem (very short) thick at base, 3 to 5 cm. in diameter; leaves subrosulately crowded, oblong-obovate to oblanceolate, markedly narrowed at base, acute, 12 to 15 cm. long, 35 to 40 mm. broad; scape very tall, about 100 to 120 cm. tall, sparingly furnished with bracts that are appressed, remote and gradually becoming smaller; spike narrowly cylindric, with lowest flowers remote (short pedicellate); upper bracts 15 mm. long, 3 mm. broad, oblong-lanceolate, folded upwards; pedicels exceedingly short, only lowest to over 1 mm. long; sepals ovate, 7 mm. long, about 3 mm. broad; petals 16 to 20 mm. long, 5 to 7 mm. broad, lanceolate, implicate, acute, scarlet (with paler, spreading tips). Description after Diels, *loc. cit.*

TYPE. *Weberbauer,* 03/3149, below Estate Cajabamba, between Samanca and Huaraz, Dept. Ancash, Peru, altitude 3300 to 3400 m. (B; destroyed?).

OCCURRENCE. Peru.

COLLECTIONS. The type; Matarragua, *E. Cerrate,* 49/73 (US).

REMARKS. This species is stated to occur in El Valle de Nepena on rocks at 3600 to 3700 m., with *Tillandsia* spp., and *Puya reflexiflora.*

It is to be regretted that this remarkable plant is not in cultivation at present. In its large leaves, tall scape, and large corolla, it stands out in its series, within which it is closely approached only by *E. cuencaensis* from southern Ecuador. The latter appears to differ in having smaller flowers frequently paired, on the lower pedicels at least. In *E. bicolor* the leaves are smaller and broader, in *E. canaliculata* the leaves are deeply hollowed above, in *E. atropurpurea* the flowers are long-pedicelled, and in *E. peruviana* the leaves are shorter and the scape is much lower. *Echeveria chiclensis* is closest geographically.

Series 11. RACEMOSAE (Baker) Berger

Echeveria, ser. Racemosae (Baker) BERGER, *in* Engler Nat. Pflanzenf., ed. 2, vol. 18a, p. 472, 1930; E. WALTHER, Cactus and Succ. Jour. Amer., vol. 7, p. 40, 1935; E. WALTHER, *op. cit.,* vol. 30, p. 44, 1958; E. WALTHER, Leafl. West. Bot., vol. 9, p. 4, 1959.
Cotyledon, § Racemosae BAKER, *in* Saunders Refug. Bot. 1, Analytical Table .... [p. 1], 1869, *pro parte.*

Plants glabrous, but sometimes papillose or lenticular-papillose; stem most often short or none, rarely tall, usually simple, rarely branching below, with lateral roots slender, fibrous, not fleshy; leaves nearly always densely rosulate, small to medium sized; inflorescence equilateral, sometimes unilateral due to one-sided lighting, subspicate to racemose, rarely subpaniculate below; lower bracts sometimes readily detached; pedicels short to elongated, always bracteolate at least in bud, mostly single-flowered; corolla at times narrow, occasionally to 20 mm. long; sepals spreading, to reflexed at anthesis, rarely appressed.

TYPICAL SPECIES. *Echeveria racemosa* Chamisso and Schlechtendal.

REMARKS. After allowance is made for variations due to environmental differences, the species of this series indeed have much in common. The length of pedicels, on which depends whether the inflorescence is spicate or racemose, is a most uncertain character; so that I prefer giving weight to development of the caudex, most species of the series Racemosae being practically stemless. *Echeveria bicolor,* by me placed in the series Elatae may perhaps be better placed here.

KEY TO THE SPECIES

A. Pedicels relatively short and stout.
  B. Sepals more or less appressed, broad, at least as long as the yellow corolla; leaves thinnish, gray-green. Mexico; Oaxaca. . . . . 120. *E. megacalyx*
  B. Sepals widely spreading, shorter than the red and yellow corolla.
    C. Leaves thick, turgid, pale whitish green; bracts broad, ovate-orbicular. Peru.
      119. *E. eurychlamys*
    C. Leaves thinner, green or tinged red; bracts narrower.
      D. Leaves deeply concave above, conspicuously tinged red. Mexico.
        109. *E. lurida*
      D. Leaves at most shallowly concave above, mostly green.
        E. Leaves broad, to 35 mm. wide or more, scarcely 3 times as long as wide, obtuse and mucronate, not glaucous; corolla red. Mexico, Jalapa.
          108. *E. racemosa*
        E. Leaves narrower, scarcely over 25 mm. wide, if so, then over 3 times as long as broad, acute to acuminate, occasionally more or less glaucous; stem distinct in age; corolla red, or red and yellow.
          F. Leaves broader, 5 to 7 cm. long by 25 mm. wide, more or less glaucous; corolla 12 to 15 mm. long, red and yellow. Peru, Bolivia, Argentina. . . . . 121. *E. peruviana*
          F. Leaves narrower, 15 to 20 cm. long by 25 mm. broad, green or brownish; corolla 13 to 20 mm. long, red. Peru. . . . . 122. *E. chiclensis*
A. Pedicels slender, elongated, as long as or longer than corolla.
  B. Leaves and bracts narrow, linear to narrowly lanceolate-oblong.
    C. Bracts few, ovate-deltoid; leaves brownish green. . . . . . 114. *E. whitei*
    C. Bracts numerous, linear, to 45 mm. long or more.
      D. Leaves papillose at least when young, flat above, shortly acuminate; pedicels 1-flowered; corolla reddish. Peru, Matucana. . . . . 113. *E. backebergii*
      D. Leaves not papillose, subterete, obtuse or shortly acute; most lower pedicels 2-flowered; corolla whitish to pale yellow. Bolivia, Chilon, Sucre.
        115. *E. chilonensis*

B. Leaves and bracts broader, ovate to lanceolate.
  C. Sepals more or less appressed, or at most slightly spreading.
    D. Leaves narrow, brownish green, epidermis not at all papillose; lowest pedicels elongated, often 2-flowered; stem evident even if short. Bolivia, Quime.
                            114. *E. whitei*
    D. Leaves broader, with epidermis more or less conspicuously papillose, grey-green, with red edges and keel; pedicels mostly 1-flowered; stem very short or none. Oaxaca.
      E. Leaves conspicuously papillose, the mucronate apex incurved, sepals ascending to very slightly spreading, longest less than half the length of corolla. . . . . 111. *E. moranii*
      E. Leaves minutely papillose, their mucro outcurved; sepals appressed, longest to half the length of the corolla. . . . . 112. *E. proxima*
  C. Sepals usually rather widely spreading.
    D. Leaves, bracts, and sepals conspicuously lenticular-papillose. Mexico, Jalapa, Barranca de Tenampa. . . . . 110. *E. carnicolor*
    D. Leaves, bracts, and sepals not noticeably lenticular-papillose.
      E. Leaves small, rarely or not over 20 mm. broad.
        F. Leaves narrowly oblanceolate. Chiapas. . . . . . . 116. *E. bella*
          G. Leaves not over 4 mm. wide. . . . . 116a *E. bella* var. *bella*
          G. Leaves to 2 cm. wide. . . . . . . 116b. *E. bella* var. *major*
        F. Leaves obovate.
          G. Leaves obovate-oblong, bright green. Colombia. . 117. *E. ballsii*
          G. Leaves obovate-rhomboid, brownish green. Peru, Ollantaytambo.
                            118. *E. westii*
      E. Leaves larger, broader; inflorescence taller.
        F. Leaves broad, 5 to 7 cm. long by 25 mm. broad, more or less glaucous; corolla 12 to 15 mm. long, red and yellow. Peru, Bolivia, Argentina.
                          121. *E. peruviana*
        F. Leaves narrow, 15 to 20 cm. long by 25 mm. wide, brownish green, not glaucous; corolla 13 to 20 mm. long, red. Peru, Chicla.
                        122. *E. chiclensis*

108. **Echeveria racemosa** Schlechtendal and Chamisso.
   (Figure 183. Plate 11; see page 233.)

Echeveria racemosa SCHLECHTENDAL AND CHAMISSO, Linnaea, vol. 5, p. 554, 1830; BRITTON AND ROSE, N. Amer. Fl., vol. 22, p. 18, 1905; POELLNITZ, *in* Fedde Repert., vol. 39, p. 219, 1936.
ILLUSTRATIONS. Maund's Botanist, vol. 1, pl. 11, 1837; Bot. Mag., vol. 64, (new ser. vol. 11) pl. 3570, 1837; Jour. Jard., p. 188, 1836; Cactus and Succ. Jour. Amer., vol. 8, p. 71, figs. 29, 30, 1936; Walpole no. 120 [see plate 11].

Glabrous; stem very short or none, subterranean, roots fibrous; leaves to 15, densely rosulate, spreading, rhomboid-oblanceolate, 5 to 8 cm. long, to 35 mm. broad, shallowly concave above, edges often somewhat lacerate, broadly sessile at base, apex acute and mucronate; inflorescences one or two equilaterally racemose or subspicate, to 50 cm. tall; peduncle strict, erect, stout, to 5 mm. thick at base; bracts ascending, obovate, acute, to 4 cm. long, 20 mm. broad, readily detached; raceme 10 to 20 cm. long, with 25 to 40 flowers; upper bracts to 10 mm. long, linear-lanceolate, upcurved; pedicels slender, to 7 mm. long, bearing two minute bractlets in bud; sepals widely spreading, subequal, longest to 6 mm. long, ovate-deltoid, acute, thick, subterete; corolla conoid-urceolate, to 12 mm. long, 8 mm. in basal diameter, 5 mm. at mouth; petals bluntly keeled, slightly spreading at the acuminate tips, basal hollow short; nectaries reniform, to 2 mm. wide. Flowers from August on. Description from cultivated material collected at Jalapa by the author in 1935.

Color. Leaves light elm-green tinged natal-brown, very lightly glaucous when young; peduncle light grayish vinaceous below; bracts vetiver-green tinged

Figure 183. 108. *Echeveria racemosa* Schlechtendal and Chamisso. Flowering plant about × 0.6 (about natural size in the original); floral parts enlarged. Plant grown at the University of Glasgow. From an article by W. J. Hooker (Curtis's Botanical Magazine, volume 64, plate 3570).

dusky-brown; sepals leaf-green tinged vinaceous-fawn; corolla peach-red to mikado-orange; petals orange-buff inside; carpels pinard-yellow; styles rainette-green to army-brown at tips; nectaries whitish.

TYPE. *Schiede,* 520, Jalapa, on walls. [Editor's note. The type was sought at HAL but not found.]

OCCURRENCE. Mexico, Veracruz, vicinity of Jalapa, on roofs, etc.

342   ECHEVERIA

COLLECTIONS. Mexico. Veracruz: Mirador, *Liebmann,* 1842/12294 (UC); Jalapa, *Rose and Hay,* 01/316 (NY,UC,US), 6124 (US); Xalapa de la Banderilla, *V. Lobato,* 88 (NY). *Cultivated:* F. Weinberg, *Rose,* 11/057 (NY,UC,US); Golden Gate Park, San Francisco, from Jalapa, *E. Walther* 36/CAS.

REMARKS. Jalapa lies at a rather low elevation of about 4700 feet, and consequently does not experience any frosts, but has a heavy rainfall, as is indicated by coffee cultivation and the presence of native tree ferns. Competing with rather lush vegetation, *E. racemosa* has taken refuge on tree branches and on roofs, even growing happily on the quite perpendicular bark of *Araucaria excelsa* in the town square. In view of the extensive collecting done in this vicinity by various botanists, it is surprising to find this species rather poorly represented in herbaria.

Echeveria racemosa is very close to *E. lurida* from the same part of Mexico, but lacks the deeply colored foliage of the latter, and is rather larger in all its parts. *Echeveria carnicolor,* also from near Jalapa, differs in the conspicuous epidermal papillae. Several South American species somewhat resemble *E. racemosa,* most of which differ in having narrower leaves, and otherwise as indicated in our key.

109. **Echeveria lurida** Haworth.
(Figures 184–185.)

Echeveria lurida HAWORTH, *in* Taylor's Phil. Mag. and Ann., vol. 10, p. 418, 1831; BRITTON AND ROSE, N. Amer. Fl., vol. 22, p. 18, 1905.
Cotyledon lurida (Haworth) BAKER, *in* Saunders Refug. Bot., vol. 1, pl. 59, no. 11, 1869.
Echeveria racemosa POELLNITZ, *in* Fedde Repert., vol. 39, p. 219, 1936.
ILLUSTRATIONS. Saunders Refug. Bot., vol. 1, pl. 59, 1869; Bot. Mag., vol. 64 (new ser., vol. 11) pl. 3570, 1837; Bot. Reg., vol. 27, (new ser. vol. 4) pl. 1, 1841.

Glabrous; stem wholly subterranean, with fibrous roots; leaves densely rosulate, narrowly oblong-oblanceolate, acute, 5 to 10 cm. long, 15 to 25 mm. broad, rather deeply concave above, acute; inflorescence equilateral, racemose, to subspicate above, 30 to 50 cm. tall; peduncle erect, 3 to 4 mm. thick at base; lower bracts numerous, spreading, readily detached, obovate-oblong, acute, 2 to 3 cm. long; raceme to 20 cm. long, with 12 to 30 flowers; upper bracts linear-lanceolate, becoming detached at the least touch; pedicels 4 to 6 mm. long, spreading to recurved, bearing the usual two bractlets that are deciduous at anthesis; sepals reflexed, unequal, the longest less than 5 mm. long, ovate-deltoid, acute; corolla 9 to 15 mm. long, conoid-urceolate; petals with usual dorsal keel and basal hollow, slightly spreading at apex; nectaries reniform, about 1 mm. broad. Flowers from October on. Description based on plants grown locally, of unknown source.

Color. Leaves lettuce-green, but tinged dark vinaceous-purple in sun, paler beneath, kildare-green but tourmaline-pink in sun; corolla bright red.

TYPE. None designated. Neotype: Botanical Register, volume 27, plate 1, 1841.

OCCURRENCE. Mexico: Veracruz, vicinity of Orizaba.

COLLECTIONS. Mexico. Veracruz: Corral de Pietra, near Zimapan, *Purpus,* 06/R–235 (UC). *Cultivated:* Flowered in Washington, D. C., *Rose,* 03/531 (US, Walpole drawing). Probably known only in cultivation.

Figure 184. 109. *Echeveria lurida* Haworth. From an article by J. Lindley (Edwards's Botanical Register, volume 27, plate 1). This plate is designated neotype for the species.

344

Figure 185. 109. *Echeveria lurida* Haworth. Leaf, flower, and carpels stated to be and flowering plant evidently also natural size; other parts enlarged. Plant from the Royal Botanic Gardens at Kew. From Baker's monograph (Saunders Refugium Botanicum, volume 1, plate 59).

110. **Echeveria carnicolor** (Baker) Ed. Morren.
　　(Figures 186–187.)

Echeveria carnicolor (Baker) Ed. Morren, La Belg. Hort., vol. 24, p. 158, 1874; Britton and Rose, N. Amer. Fl., vol. 22, p. 18, 1905; Rose, Contrib. U.S. Nat. Herb., vol. 12, p. 393, 1909; Rose, Addisonia, vol. 1, no. 2, p. 25, pl. 13, 1916; Poellnitz, *in* Fedde Repert., vol. 39, p. 220, 1936.
Cotyledon carnicolor Baker, *in* Saunders Refug. Bot., vol. 3, p. 199, 1870.
Illustrations. Saunders Refug. Bot., vol. 3, pl. 199, 1870; Contrib. U.S. Nat. Herb., *loc. cit.*, pl. 46; Addisonia, vol. 1, no. 2, pl. 13, 1916; Moeller's Deutsche Gartenztg., 1930, p. 127.

Glabrous; stem short or none; leaves rosulate, to 20 or more, oblong-oblanceolate, obtusish, thick and turgid, shallowly concave above, rounded beneath, 5 to 7 cm. long or more, 15 mm. broad, epidermis lenticular-papillose; inflorescences two or more, sometimes as many as 12, lateral, spreading to ascending, to over 15 cm. tall, equilaterally racemose, but often branching near base, sometimes unilateral from one-sided lighting; peduncle slender, often decumbent at base; bracts numerous, readily detached and rooting, ascending, oblong-elliptic, acute, curved, to over 2 cm. long; racemes to 7 cm. long, with 6 to 10 or 20 flowers; pedicels slender, to 8 mm. long, bibracteolate; sepals subequal, longest to 6 mm. long, thick, subterete, lanceolate, acute, widely spreading at anthesis, very shortly connate at base, papillose as the leaves; corolla nearly straight, sharply pentagonal, to 10 mm. long, 6 mm. thick at base; petals thick, bluntly keeled, prominently hollowed at base; carpels slender; styles subulate; nectaries reniform, to 1.5 mm. wide. Flowers January and February. Description of living plants originally obtained from the University of California Botanical Garden, traceable to Dr. Rose.

Color. Leaves light cress-green tinged drab; bracts and sepals as the leaves; corolla salmon-orange above, to flesh-color at base, carmine at edges, buff-yellow inside; carpels pinkish vinaceous; styles maize-yellow; nectaries whitish.

Type. None designated. Lectotype: Saunders Refugium Botanicum, volume 3, plate 199, 1870.

Occurrence. Mexico. Veracruz: on rocks and trees in wet rainforest, at foot of easterly slopes of Mt. Orizaba.

Collections. Mexico. Veracruz: Barranca de Tenampa, *C. A. Purpus* in 1906 (NY); Zacuapan, Barranca de Consoquitla, *C. A. Purpus* in 1906 (UC). *Cultivated:* New York Bot. Gard., *Purpus* in 1907 (NY).

Remarks. The epidermal papillae of *E. carnicolor* are a unique feature by which it may be identified without doubt. These lenticular papillae serve to produce an iridescent sheen seen in no other *Echeveria,* except perhaps *E.* 'Mutabilis', a hybrid of *E. linguaefolia,* whose other parent is in doubt, but I feel that this must have been *E. carnicolor.*

Geographically, this species occurs near *E. racemosa* and *E. lurida,* from both of which it differs, aside from its peculiar epidermis, in having much longer pedicels. Other species with papillose epidermis are the shrubby *E. nodulosa* and *E. backebergii* from Peru, with long linear leaves and bracts.

Coming from rather low elevations in a damp region, *E. carnicolor* does best in a warm greenhouse, finding outdoor California a bit too dry.

Chromosome-number is $n = 18$.

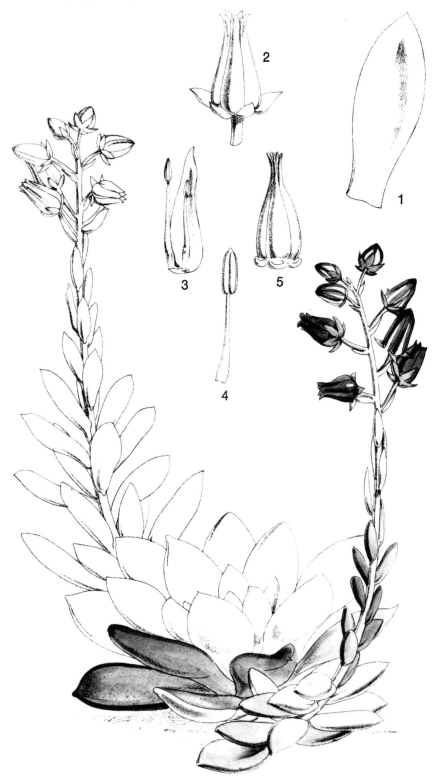

Figure 186. 110. *Echeveria carnicolor* (Baker) Ed Morren. Leaf stated to be and flowering plant evidently also natural size; flower and parts enlarged. Plant grown by W. W. Saunders in Reigate, England. From the original publication (Saunders Refugium Botanicum, volume 3, plate 199). This plate is designated lectotype for the species.

Figure 187. 110. *Echeveria carnicolor* (Baker) Ed. Morren. Plant flowering in Washington, January 1908, about × 0.5; collected by C. A. Purpus in the Barranca de Tenampa, Veracruz, Mexico. From an article by J. N. Rose (Contributions from the U.S. National Herbarium, volume 12, plate 46).

111. **Echeveria moranii** E. Walther, new species.
(Figures 188–189.)

Echeveria moranii E. Walther, sp. nov., pertinens ad ser. Racemosas, glabra; caudice brevissimo; radicibus fibrosis; foliis rosulatis crassis, obovato-cuneatis, carinatis, mucronatis, rubro-marginatis; inflorescentiis racemosis, aequilateralibus vel unilateralibus, usque ad 30 cm. altis, 15-floris; pedunculis flexuosis; bracteis caducis; pedicellis usque ad 10 mm. longis, laxe nutantibus sed erectis post anthesin; sepalis subaequalibus, turgidis, adpressis, corolla brevioribus sub dimidio; corollis conoideis, usque ad 12 mm. longis, corallinis.

Glabrous; stem short, 2 to 3 cm. tall, to 8 mm. thick, simple or ultimately branching below, with fibrous roots; leaves rosulate, to 25 or more, erect to spreading, obovate-cuneate, to 6 cm. long, 3 cm. broad, narrowed to 10 mm. at base, 9 mm. thick near middle, upcurved, shallowly concave above, beneath rounded and keeled, mucronate at the somewhat incurved tips, epidermis of young leaves glistening-crystalline and appearing papillose, the lenticular-hemispheric papillae appear to be solid; inflorescences one or two, racemose, equilateral or unilateral, 20 to 30 cm. (50 cm.) tall; peduncle slender, flexuous, laxly ascending, to 4 mm. thick at base; bracts numerous, strongly ascending, elliptic-oblong, to 3 cm. long, 10 mm. broad, nearly flat above, beneath rounded and faintly keeled, basal spur blunt, hyaline; raceme to 20 cm. long, with about 15 nodding flowers; pedicels slender, 1 mm. thick, to 10 mm. long,

Figure 188. 111. *Echeveria moranii* E. Walther. Flowering plant, × 0.6. Plant photographed in San Diego 12 June 1960; part of the type collection (Moran 6388).

with two minute, linear bractlets, not thickened near apex; sepals appressed, subequal, longest 4 mm. long, ovate-deltoid, acutish, thick, very turgid at base, strongly connate, with one or two basal sutures visible, their thick bases form an umbilicate depression for reception of the slender pedicel; corolla conoid-cylindroid, bluntly pentagonal, to 13 mm. long, 9 mm. in diameter near base, 4 mm. or more in diameter at mouth; petals bluntly keeled, with basal hollow, at apex rather blunt; carpels 8 mm. long; nectaries transversely lunate-reniform, to 3 mm. wide. Flowers from June on. Description from plant cultivated in San Francisco by Victor Reiter, originally received from Cornell.

Color. Leaves above light elm-green to pois-green, beneath tea-green; margins, mucro, and scattered spots on lower surface maroon, with numerous sub-epidermal, anthocyan-containing idioblasts scattered in the parenchyma just below the upper surface; bracts slate-olive; sepals celandine-green to pale bluish-gray; corolla peach-red to coral-red or scarlet; inside of petals orange-buff; carpels pinard-yellow below, towards styles asphodel-green; stigmas maroon; nectaries whitish.

TYPE. Encampamento Agua Blanca, 3 miles north of Totolapan, Oaxaca, Mexico, at 1150 m. altitude, growing on both north and south slopes of a dry cañon, *Reid Moran,* 57/6388 (SD).

CLONOTYPE. Cornell University; University of California.

REMARKS. Well known to all students of succulents by his incisive study of the true relations of *Echeveria* to *Dudleya,* etc., Dr. Reid Moran visited

Mexico in November, 1957, during which excursion he detected at least two new species of *Echeveria*. Plants cultivated locally have now flowered, so that I am able to describe the present item, dedicating it with great pleasure to its discoverer. The new species, while unlike any other previously known, clearly is related to several members of the series Racemosae, as *E. carnicolor,* which has spreading sepals, and *E. whitei* from Bolivia with narrower leaves. Its nearest relation would appear to be another new species, *E. proxima,* collected by Mr. Thomas MacDougall (B–140) near kilo 638, between Oaxaca and Tehuantepec. This last is distinct in the outcurved mucro of the leaves and somewhat longer sepals.

The most striking features of *E. moranii* are the leaf epidermis, the spreading racemes with pendant flowers, borne on exceedingly slender, weak pedicels, and the deep umbilicate base of the calyx.

Dr. Charles Uhl of Cornell has determined the chromosome number of *E. moranii* to be $n=24$.

Figure 189. 111. *Echeveria moranii* E. Walther. Flowers, $\times$ 2. Plant flowering in San Diego 12 June 1960; part of the type collection (Moran 6388).

112. **Echeveria proxima** E. Walther, new species.
(Figures 190–191.)

Echeveria proxima, E. Walther, sp. nov., pertinens ad ser. Racemosas; caudice brevi, simplici; foliis conferte rosulatis, rhomboideo-obovatis, crassis; inflorescentiis aequilateralibus, racemosis, usque ad 20 cm. altis; floribus ad 15, pedicellis usque ad 7 mm. longis, recurvatis, unilateralibus; bracteolis usque ad 2 mm. longis; sepalis adpressis, usque ad ·5 mm. longis, ovato-deltoideis, acutis; corollis usque ad 11 mm. longis et 6 mm. diametro ad basin; petalis excavatis; nectariis 2 mm. latis, reniformibus.

Plants glabrous, with fibrous roots and evident, but short stem, belatedly or not branching; leaves densely rosulate, about 20 or more, to 35 mm. long and 20 mm. broad, spreading to upcurved, thick, subtriquetrous, shallowly concave above, beneath convex and faintly keeled, mucronate, epidermis faintly lenticular; inflorescence equilateral, racemose, to 20 cm. tall or more; lower bracts 10 mm. long, flat, acute; flowers to 15; pedicels slender, to 7 mm. long, strongly curved towards the light, bracteolate, bractlets 2 mm. long; sepals subequal, longest 5 mm. long, appressed, deltoid-ovate, acute, convex on back; corolla to 11 mm. long, about 4 mm. in diameter at mouth, to 6 mm. thick near base; petals bluntly keeled on back, with blunt, subapical mucro and small but distinct basal hollow; carpels 6 mm. long; nectaries to 2 mm. broad, reniform, stipitate. Flowers from June on.

Color. Peduncle ecru-drab; sepals american-green; corolla strawberry-pink to geranium-pink; petals inside mustard-yellow; carpels viridine-yellow above; nectaries whitish.

TYPE. From a plant cultivated in Los Angeles by Don B. Skinner. Mr. Skinner had it from Thomas MacDougall (his B–140) who had collected it in Oaxaca, Mexico in 1957 at kilo 638 (9 miles east of Totolapan) on highway from Oaxaca to Tehuantepec, elevation about 4000 feet (CAS, no. 409845).

REMARKS. This has been mistaken for *E. sessiliflora* but the latter has narrower, longer, thinner, and almost blue leaves. In my key this comes near *E. whitei* from Bolivia, but there the leaves are much longer, narrower, and brownish green.

Figure 190. 112. *Echeveria proxima* E. Walther. Flowering plant, × 0.7.   Plant photographed in San Diego 24 July 1964; collected near the type locality by Thomas MacDougall (B-140, re-collection).

Figure 191.   112. *Echeveria proxima* E. Walther. Flowers, × 2. Plant flowering in San Diego 24 July 1964; collected near the type locality by Thomas MacDougall (B-140, re-collection).

113. **Echeveria backebergii** Poellnitz.

Echeveria backebergii POELLNITZ, *in* Fedde Repert., vol. 38, p. 185, 1935; Fedde Repert., vol. 39, p. 211, 1936.

Plant glabrous, but papillose; stemless, with fusiform-thickened root, becoming cespitose; leaves rosulate, 20 or more, flaccid, minutely papillose at least when young, later only at edges, blade linear-lanceolate, broadest near base, from 6 to 15 cm. or more long, 6 to 15 mm. broad, above shallowly concave, rounded beneath, faintly keeled, apex acute with hooked mucro; inflorescence normally to 30 cm. tall, but often reduced in cultivation, equilaterally racemose, with 10 to 20 flowers; peduncle erect, ascending or spreading, 3 mm. thick below; bracts many, linear-lanceolate, ascending, to 45 mm. long, with sigmoid curvature, uncinate-acute at apex, papillae as the leaves, not readily detached; pedicels 10 to 20 mm. long, their two bractlets minute, filiform; sepals unequal, longest to 10 mm. long, ovate, acute, rounded beneath, thickest near base, scarcely united below, papillose; corolla bluntly pentagonal, 11 to 14 mm. long, about 6 mm. in diameter, nearly straight; petals papillose on keel, connivent at tips, narrowly oblong, with deep basal hollow; carpels slender; nectaries narrowly lunate, stipitate, to 1 mm. wide. Flowers from July on. Description from living plant grown by Mr. V. Reiter, Jr., perhaps from Backeberg seed.

Color. Leaves light hellebore-green to asphodel-green, fading to chamois; sepals and bracts light elm-green; corolla orange to apricot-yellow or empire-yellow; carpels pale green-yellow; styles light bice-green; nectaries yellowish.

TYPE. "Peru: Matucana (an der Lima-Oroya-Bahn) 2600 m. ü. d. M., Curt Backeberg S. 2."

OCCURRENCE. Peru. Matucana, on Lima-Oroya railroad, 2600 m. elevation.

COLLECTIONS. Peru. Matucana, *MacBride and Featherstone,* 22/279, photograph F-1663 (US).

REMARKS. According to Mr. Paul Hutchison, who collected extensively in this part of Peru, no trace of this species was found near Matucana, all the plants seen being *E. chiclensis. Echeveria backebergii* may be merely an aberrant form of that species, but even as such it must be placed on record here. The question of its validity can be settled only after further field collecting.

Mr. Reiter's plant grown from Blossfeld seed, first flowered in 1937.

114. **Echeveria whitei** Rose.
(Figure 192.)

Echeveria whitei ROSE, Addisonia, vol. 10, no. 3, p. 47, pl. 344, 1925; POELLNITZ, *in* Fedde Repert., vol. 39, p. 232, 1936.
Echeveria buchtienii POELLNITZ, *in* Fedde Repert., vol. 36, p. 193, 1934; Fedde Repert., vol. 39, p. 233, 1936.
Echeveria chilonensis E. WALTHER, (not *Sedum chilonense* O. Kuntze), Cactus and Succ. Jour. Amer., vol. 7, p. 40, 1935.
ILLUSTRATIONS. Addisonia, vol. 10, no. 3, pl. 344, 1925; US Nat. Herb. photograph 1842, unpublished.

Plant glabrous, with evident if short stem not or sparingly branching; leaves crowded, subrosulate, narrowly obovate-oblong, acute, thick, 3 to 5 cm. long or more, from 8 to 20 mm. broad, flat above, rounded beneath, upcurved, not papillose; inflorescence equilateral, but often one-sided from one-sided lighting, racemose to subpaniculate; peduncle flexuous, decumbent or laxly spreading, with raceme to 30 cm. long; lower bracts few, early deciduous, deltoid-ovate, acute, appressed, to 10 mm. long; flowers 10 or more; pedicels drooping, to 20 mm. long or more, often 2-flowered below, bearing two minute bractlets near middle; sepals appressed or scarcely spreading, unequal, longest 6 mm. long, linear-lanceolate, acute; corolla 10 to 15 mm. long, 9 to 10 mm. in basal diameter, 6 mm. wide at mouth, urceolate-pentagonal; petals keeled on back, with small basal hollow within; nectaries reniform, to 3 mm. wide. Flowers from February to June. Description from locally cultivated plants.

Figure 192. 114. *Echeveria whitei* Rose. Plant of the type collection, grown at the New York Botanical Garden. From the orginal publication (Addisonia, vol. 10, plate 344).

Color. Leaves light cress-green to mignonette-green, brownish vinaceous in sun, glaucous when young; peduncle orange-cinnamon below, above eosine-pink with bloom; bracts as leaves; sepals grape-green; corolla peach-red below, to coral-red above; petals inside coral-red above to light salmon-orange below; carpels maize-yellow; styles light cinnamon-drab; nectaries whitish.

TYPE. *O. E. White,* 21/220, Quime, Bolivia (US, no. 1111971).

OCCURRENCE. Bolivia: common on dry slope among rocks, Quime; near La Paz.

COLLECTIONS. Bolivia: Quime, *O. E. White,* 21/220 (US, type; NY); Quime, *White,* 22/2292 (US); declivities near La Paz, *Buchtien,* 32/9208 (B, type of *E. buchtienii;* vicinity of La Paz, *M. Bang,* 1890/148 (K,PH,US); Cotana, Illimani, 2450/*Buchtien,* 11/4575 (US).

REMARKS. *Echeveria whitei* was named in honor of Mr. Orlando E. White, curator of plant breeding at the Brooklyn Botanic Garden, where this was first cultivated. In the South American species of the series Racemosae it is distinct by reason of its short but evident stem, the narrow, thick, brownish green leaves, the elongate pedicels, appressed sepals, and bright red corolla. It is quite different from *E. chilonensis,* which has a very short caudex, bright-green linear leaves, more numerous bracts, spreading sepals, and a white corolla, the latter turning yellow in drying. *Echeveria buchtienii* Poellnitz from La Paz appears the same, the difference in length of pedicels stressed by Poellnitz is too inconstant a character. Quime, the type locality of *E. whitei,* is only 80 miles from La Paz, whereas Chilon, the type locality of *E. chilonensis* is 290 miles away, and Sucre is 120 miles distant.

115. **Echeveria chilonensis** (O. Kuntze) E. Walther.

> *Echeveria chilonensis* (O. Kuntze) E. WALTHER, Cactus and Succ. Jour. Amer., vol. 7, p. 40, 1935 (Sept. 15); POELLNITZ, *in* Fedde Repert., vol. 38, p. 191, 1935 (Sept. 30); vol. 39, p. 232, 1936.
> *Sedum chilonense* O. KUNTZE, Rev. Gen. Plant., pt. 3 (2), p. 83, 1898.

Plants glabrous; stem usually short, to 5 cm. long and 10 mm. thick, with offsets near base; leaves not papillose, densely rosulate, to 20, strongly ascending, linear- to oblanceolate-oblong, to 7 cm. long or more, to 15 mm. broad, rather thick, flat above, beneath rounded and faintly keeled, sessile, upcurved, at apex acute or shortly acuminate; inflorescence solitary, equilateral, to 60 cm. tall, racemose above, often subpaniculate below, with 10 to 25 erect or ascending flowers; peduncle stout, to 4 mm. thick at base, erect or strongly ascending; bracts numerous, readily detached, ascending, to 35 mm. long, linear-oblong to narrowly oblanceolate, above flat, rounded beneath, at apex acute; pseudopedicels single-flowered above, to 10 mm. long, bibracteolate, lowest four or five usually with two flowers each and to 30 mm. long, bearing two quite minute, fugacious bractlets; the proper ultimate pedicels 2 to 3 mm. long, bractless; sepals subequal, longest to 8 mm. long, ascending-spreading at anthesis, ovate-oblong to oblanceolate-oblong, subterete, at apex unusually uncinate, that is, with upcurved, hook-like tips; corolla pentagonal, urceolate-cylindroid, to 13 mm. long and 7 mm. thick near base when pressed; petals narrowly ovate-oblong, slightly spreading at tips and there with well-developed, subterminal, dorsal, hooked apiculus; basal nectar cavities shallow; carpels

9 mm. long; nectaries to 2 mm. wide, narrowly transverse-lunate-reniform. Flowers from June on. Description largely from living plant grown by V. Reiter, Jr.

Color. Leaves and bracts cerro-green; peduncle and pedicels cosse-green; sepals spinach-green; corolla often almost white, pale green-yellow to naphthalene-yellow; carpels scheeles-green; nectaries pale green-yellow.

TYPE. *O. Kuntze,* 1892/5, Chilon, Prov. Santa Cruz, Bolivia (NY).

OCCURRENCE. Bolivia: Chilon; Sucre, about 120 miles from Chilon; near LaPaz (UCBG, 56.697).

REMARKS. In leaf shape and the frequently several-flowered lowest pedicels, this resembles *E. whitei,* also from Bolivia. That species differs, however, in having brownish green leaves, fewer bracts, and a coral-red corolla. A plant from the vicinity of La Paz (UCBG, 56.697) has a more evident stem, broader leaves and bracts, and mostly single flowered pedicels, but appears to belong here.

My recognition of *Sedum chilonense* as an *Echeveria* was made possible by loan of the type, through the courtesy of the late Dr. N. L. Britton, of the New York Botanic Garden, which had acquired O. Kuntze's herbarium with funds from the Carnegie endowment. My combination of this in *Echeveria* antedates that of von Poellnitz by about 2 weeks.

Echeveria buchtienii Poellnitz from La Paz is clearly distinct in having obovate-cuneate, reddish-green leaves, few bracts, and a corolla 16 to 18 mm. long, red, not yellow in color. These characters point to its being a form of *E. whitei.* (See "Remarks" under *E. whitei.*)

116. **Echeveria bella** Alexander.
(Figures 193–194.)

> *Echeveria bella* ALEXANDER, Cactus and Succ. Jour. Amer., vol. 13, p. 133, 1941.
> ILLUSTRATIONS. Cactus and Succ. Jour. Amer., vol. 13, pp. 133, 134, figs. 73, 74, 1941.

Glabrous; stem evident, slender, very short, with numerous lateral branches arising from near base causing the plants to appear cespitose; leaves rather crowded, strongly ascending, to 28 mm. long, less than 5 mm. broad, linear-oblanceolate, acute, epidermal cells conspicuous, especially at apex and there semipapillate, somewhat convex on both surfaces, upcurved; inflorescences numerous, equilaterally racemose, to 25 cm. tall; peduncles erect; bracts oblong-oblanceolate, to 23 mm. long and 5 mm. broad, acute, not quite flat above, rounded beneath, thickened toward the basal spur; raceme with 10 to 12 flowers; pseudopedicels slender, to 10 mm. long, each bearing two linear bracts to 7 mm. long, several of the lowest pedicels with two flowers each; sepals widely spreading to somewhat ascending, subequal, to 6 mm. long, linear, subterete, acute; corolla subcylindroid, bluntly pentagonal, about 10 mm. long, 6 mm. in basal diameter, 4 mm. at tips of the slightly spreading petals, these with small basal nectar cavity and subapical mucro; carpels 6 mm. long; nectaries to 1.5 mm. wide, transversely lunate. Flowers from May on. Description from plants cultivated by V. Reiter, Jr., San Francisco, obtained from Dr. J. Meyrán, Mexico City, 1959.

Color. Leaves, bracts, and sepals spinach-green, peduncle pompeian-red;

pedicels carmine; corolla coral-red below, empire-yellow toward apex, carpels pale green-yellow; styles virdine-green; nectaries light yellow-green.

TYPE. *Thomas MacDougall* in 1939, San Cristobal Las Casas, Chiapas, Mexico (NY).

OCCURRENCE. Mexico. Chiapas: vicinity of San Cristobal Las Casas; near San Felipe Ecatepec, on north slopes above valley, forming small, *Sempervivum*-like clusters among rocks (according to MacDougall); Ciudad Las Casas, *Margery C. Carlson,* 49/160-S (F).

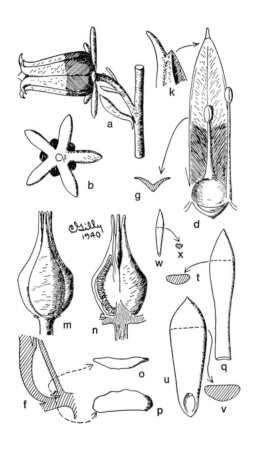

Figure 193. 116. *Echeveria bella* Alexander. Explanation: (a) flower, × 2; (b) flower from below, × 2; (d) inside of petal, × 4; (f) median longitudinal section of petal base, × 8; (g) median cross-section of petal, × 4; (k) apex of petal, the inner face to the right, × 8; (m) carpels, × 4; (n) longitudinal section of carpels, × 4; (o) nectary, face view, × 10; (p) nectary, dorsal view, × 10; (q) leaf, × 2; (t) cross-section of widest part of leaf, × 2; (u) mid-peduncle bract, × 2; (v) cross-section of mid-peduncle bract, × 2; (w) pedicellary bract, × 2; (x) cross-section of pedicellary bract, × 2. From the original publication (Cactus and Succulent Journal, volume 13, page 134, part of figure 74).

Figure 194. 116b. *Echeveria bella* Alexander var. *major* E. Walther. Flowering plant, natural size. Plant photographed in San Diego 29 June 1963; part of the type collection (MacDougall B-180).

116b. **Echeveria bella** var. **major** E. Walther, new.
(Figure 194.)

Echeveria bella var. *major* E. Walther, var. nov. Similis var. *bellae* sed foliis ad 8 cm. longis et 2 cm. latis.

Quite similar to var. *bella,* but differing clearly in having larger leaves, obscurely keeled above, which may be 8 cm. long and 2 cm. broad near apex, to 9 mm. wide at base; only three of the lower pedicels were 2-flowered, the sepals appear somewhat broader and rather more ascending; the corolla is 11 mm. long. Chromosomes $n=15$. Description from material supplied by Dr. C. Uhl of Cornell University. Flowers from March on.

TYPE. Collected on Pan-American Highway near Nabenchauc, before San Cristobal Las Casas, elevation 6000 feet, by Thomas MacDougall, 1958/B–180 (CAS, no. 413925).

Occurrence. Known only from the type locality.

Remarks. All available collections appear to have come from the same vicinity, *i.e.,* near San Cristobal Las Casas; hence I know very little about the range of variation that exists in nature. Even if no intermediate forms should be found, the material here described as var. *major* is scarcely distinct enough for specific rank. I agree with Dr. Alexander in considering this tiny species as having ornamental possibilities, and regret that so far it has continued to be so very scarce. My thanks are due both to Dr. Uhl of Cornell for providing me with material of the var. *major,* and to Dr. J. Meyrán of Mexico City for sparing me a cutting of the typical plant.

Echeveria bella differs from *E. gracilis* in being strictly short-stemmed, more or less cespitose, with smaller, narrower, greener leaves and narrower flowers. Of nearly stemless species with an equilateral inflorescence, few have leaves as small as those of *E. bella;* my new *E. ballsii* comes close, but its sepals are lanceolate, acuminate, and flat, its corolla is different and often nodding. The new *E. westii* differs in having broader, obovate-spathulate leaves. Locally *E. macdougallii* has been confused with *E. bella,* but the former is caulescent, with thick short leaves and a corolla to 16 mm. long.

117. **Echeveria ballsii** E. Walther.
(Figures 195–196.)

Echeveria ballsii E. Walther, Cactus and Succ. Jour. Amer., vol. 30, p. 44, 1958.
Illustrations. Cactus and Succ. Jour. Amer., vol. 30, pp. 45, 46, figs. 26, 27, 1958.

Glabrous; stems evident, but quite short, several arising from base; leaves thick, turgid above, oblong-obovate, acutish, to 35 mm. long, about 10 mm. broad, narrowed to less than 5 mm. at base; inflorescences one or two to each rosette, 25 to 30 cm. tall, equilaterally racemose, but sometimes unilateral due to one-sided lighting; peduncle erect; lower bracts ascending to spreading, narrowly oblong-obovate, to 15 mm. long; flowers about 10, nodding; pedicels to 10 mm. long, their bractlets slender, to 5 mm. long; sepals unequal, longest to 8 mm. long, flat, acuminate, ascending; corolla nearly straight, to 12 mm. long, about 8 mm. in basal diameter; petals spreading at apex, inside with definite basal hollow, nectaries oblique, trapezoid-reniform, to 2 mm. broad. Flowers from August on. Description from living material cultivated in the Strybing Arboretum, Golden Gate Park, San Francisco; plants received from E. K. Balls.

Color. Leaves cosse-green; bracts chrysolite-green; pedicels onionskin-pink; sepals chrysolite- to absinthe-green; corolla peach-red to scarlet; petals pale yellow in shade, pinard-yellow inside; carpels maize-yellow to buff-pink, nectaries whitish.

Type. Cultivated in Strybing Arboretum, Golden Gate Park, San Francisco, *E. Walther,* 4 August 1942, from plant collected in 1939 by E. K. Balls, no. 7587, near Siachoque, Dept. Boyaca, Colombia, elevation 8500 feet (CAS, no. 297644).

Occurrence. Colombia: near Siachoque and west of Bogota.

Collections. Colombia. Dept. Boyaca, Siachoque, 8500 feet *E. K. Balls,* 39/B-7587 (UC,US), as well as the type (CAS) cultivated from this collection; Cundinamarca, Mosquera Hills, 6 miles southwest of Mosquera,

Figure 195. 117. *Echeveria ballsii* E. Walther. From the original publication (Cactus and Succulent Journal, volume 30, page 45, figure 26).

west of Bogota, *H. L. Mason,* 49/13743 (UC). Other collections in U.S. National Herbarium are: *R. M. Schultes,* 46/7222, *Cuatrecasas,* 39/5002, *Barkley, et al.,* 47/17-C-714, *Killip,* 39/33962.

REMARKS. Most of the Colombian material I have seen belongs to the ubiquitous *E. quitensis,* from which *E. ballsii* differs in being nearly stemless, and in having very small thickish leaves. *Echeveria bella* from Chiapas is perhaps the most similar species, but is separated by a distance of 1800 miles and its leaves are not over 18 mm. long nor over 4 mm. broad. Mr. E. K. Balls collected extensively in South America and in Mexico and kindly provided me with living material of this and many other species of *Echeveria*. It was a pleasure to dedicate this species to its discoverer, formerly on the staff of the Rancho Santa Ana Botanic Garden, Claremont, California.

According to Dr. C. Uhl of Cornell, the gametic chromosome number is $n = 40$–42.

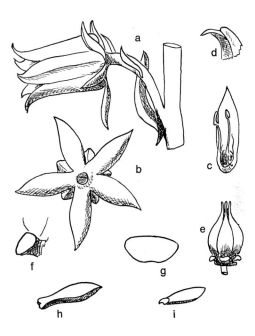

Figure 196. 117. *Echeveria ballsii* E. Walther. Explanation: (a) flower, × 2; (b) flower from below, × 2; (c) inside of petal, × 2; (d) apex of petal, × 8; (e) carpels, × 8; (f) nectary, side view, × 8; (g) nectary, front view, × 8; (h) leaf, × 0.4; (i) bract, × 0.4. From the original publication (Cactus and Succulent Journal, volume 30, page 46, figure 27).

118. **Echeveria westii** E. Walther, new species.

Echeveria westii E. Walther, sp. nov., pertinens ad ser. Racemosas, glabra, caulibus brevibus pauciramosis; rosulis simplicibus vel ramosis; foliis rhomboideo-obovatis, acutis, crassis, usque ad 35 mm. longis et 12–20 mm. latis, fusco-viridibus; inflorescentiis aequilateralibus, racemosis, usque ad 25 cm. altis; pedunculis tenuibus, flexuosis; bracteis obovato-ellipticis, usque ad 14 mm. longis, subteretibus; bracteis superioribus conspicuis; pedicellis usque ad 9 mm. longis; bracteolis 9 mm. longis, acutis, subtriquetris; sepalis subaequalibus, usque ad 10 mm. longis, crassis, acutis; corollis urceolatis, 11–13 mm. longis; petalis apice patentibus; nectariis reniformibus, usque ad 2 mm. latis.

Plants glabrous; stems short, but with evident lateral offshoots; leaves densely rosulate, rhomboid-obovate, cuneate at base, acute, thickish, upcurved, somewhat keeled beneath, above flat or slightly concave, not papillose, 30 to 35 mm. long, 12 to 20 mm. broad, at base 5 mm. wide, with petiole nearly quadrangular in cross-section; inflorescence equilaterally racemose, but often congested and shortened into a few-flowered cyme; peduncle laxly ascending, to 25 cm. tall; lower bracts most readily detached, broadly obovate-elliptic, acute, to 14 mm. long and 8 mm. broad, thick, convex on both sides; upper bracts conspicuous, enveloping buds; pedicels to 9 mm. long, bractlets to 9 mm. long, oblong-lanceolate, acute, subterete or subtriquetrous, readily detached; sepals subequal, longest to 10 mm. long, obovate-oblong, acute, thick; corolla urceolate, 11 to 13 mm. long, 8 mm. in basal diameter; petals with tips incurved, basal hollow distinct; nectaries reniform, to 2 mm. wide. Flowers from July on. Description from plants collected by the late Mr. James West on ruins of Ollantaytambo (UCBG:36. 1850; West nos. 6486, 1850; flowered UCBG, 17 July 1938).

Color. Leaves elm-green tinged chestnut-brown near apex, not glaucous; bracts as the leaves; peduncle oxblood-red; pedicels old-rose; sepals dark cress-green, somewhat glaucous; corolla rose-doree at base, to eosine-pink, at apex empire-yellow; carpels martius-yellow; styles light viridine-yellow; stigmas coral-red; nectaries baryta-yellow.

Type. Herbarium of the University of California no. 1200467, *Paul Hutchison,* 6 July 1959, from plants cultivated in the University of California Botanical Garden, no. 59.430, from specimens collected by Hutchison, no. 1800, on arid rock outcrops among mosses and species of *Peperomia* and *Tillandsia* at Ollantaytambo, elevation 3000 m., Depto. Cuzco, Prov. Urubamba, Peru, 9 November 1957.

Another collection. Peru. Prov. de Urubamba, Dist. de Ollantaytambo, *Herrera,* 25/710 (US).

Remarks. My failure to publish this novel item earlier was due to lack of a type specimen, which only now can be supplied from plants collected by Mr. Paul Hutchison on his 1957 collecting trip to Peru. Within my series Racemosae, where this must be placed, it comes near several small species with rather small leaves, from most of which it differs in the broader rhomboid leaves, dark brownish green in color. Its sepals are spreading, the upper bracts rather broad, somewhat as in *E. eurychlamys;* the leaves are not papillose, glaucous, or whitish.

119. **Echeveria eurychlamys** (Diels) Berger.

Echeveria eurychlamys (Diels) Berger, *in* Engler Nat. Pflanzenf. ed. 2, vol. 18a, p. 473, 1930; Poellnitz, *in* Fedde Repert., vol. 39, p. 221, 1936; F. Macbride, Flora of Peru, Field Mus. Bot. Ser., vol. 13, no. 3, pt. 2, p. 1014, 1938.
Cotyledon eurychlamys Diels, *in* Engler's Bot. Jahrb., vol. 37, p. 411, 1906.

Plant glabrous, stemless; rosettes densely clustered in age; leaves obovate-oblong, to 6 cm. long and to 30 mm. broad, shallowly concave above, beneath rounded and obscurely keeled, at apex rounded and mucronate to acute, margins somewhat hyaline-pellucid; inflorescences two or three, to over 25 cm. tall, erect or ascending, sometimes strongly nodding before anthesis; lower bracts numerous, broadly obovate to orbicular, to 18 mm. long and 12 mm. broad, spreading, recurved, acute and mucronate, rather thick; raceme equilateral, to over 7 cm. long with 12 or more, often rather crowded flowers; upper bracts thick, strongly convex beneath, to 12 mm. long, sessile; pedicels 2 to 3 mm. long or less, stout, bearing two fugacious bractlets; sepals strongly ascending, elliptic, acute, thick, convex above, longest to 8 mm. long, mucronate; corolla erect, 14 to 16 mm. long, 6 to 8 mm. thick, and so rather slender; petals narrow, 4 mm. broad above middle, hollowed at base within; carpels 7 to 8 mm. long, slender; nectaries oblique, lunate-reniform, 2 mm. broad. Flowers from May on. Description of living plant collected by Mr. Harry Johnson.

Color. Leaves asphodel-green to deep greenish glaucous when young, sometimes becoming brownish tinged; lower bracts light cress-green to asphodel-green, upper bracts and sepals the same; corolla bright coral-red; petals inside pinkish buff; carpels primrose-yellow; styles chamois; nectaries straw-yellow.

TYPE. Hda. La Tahona near Hualgayoc, 3100 m., Dept. Cajamarca, Peru, *Weberbauer,* 04/4056 (B, destroyed?). Lectotype: type-photo, Rockefeller Foundation no. 18249 (F).

OCCURRENCE. Peru: Dept. Cajamarca; Prov. Chote.

COLLECTIONS. Peru. Dept. Cajamarca: Hda. La Tahona, near Hualgayoc, *Weberbauer,* 04/4056 (B, type); near Pariocota, above town at 6000 to 8000 feet, with Masdevallia, *H. Johnson,* UCBG, 54.233 (CAS). Prov. Chote: Huambos, *Y. Soukup,* 56/4560 (US). *Cultivated*: V. Reiter's garden, *E. Walther* in 1958 (CAS).

REMARKS. From my observations, limited to a single specimen, I cannot state that the nodding inflorescence is typical. The upper bracts are often borne upon the pedicels, instead of on the peduncle. The unusual leaf color is unique among South American species, and is dupilcated only in the Mexican *E. elegans* and some of its allies. Unfortunately this leaf color is not discernible in dried specimens. The type specimen of *E. eurychlamys* appears to have been burned during the destruction of the Dahlem Herbarium, so that it is indeed fortunate a photo of this was made, thanks to J. F. Macbride and the Rockefeller Fund for photographing type specimens.

In its native habitat, this species occurs in evergreen woods, shrubs, and grass-steppe, associated with such plants as *Bomarea dulcis, Gentiana steubelii, G. arenarioides* and *G. dianthoides, Leontopodium gnaphalioides, Chusquea polyclados, Acaena ovalifolia, Coriaria thymifolia, Befaria weberbaueriana, Rapanea dependens,* and *Syphocampylos weberbaueri.*

The combination of almost white leaves, with an equilateral inflorescence, suffices to distinguish *E. eurychlamys* from all other species of *Echeveria,* and the orbicular upper bracts are a further unique character.

120. **Echeveria megacalyx** E. Walther.

(Figures 197–198.)

Echeveria megacalyx E. WALTHER, Cactus and Succ. Jour. Amer., vol. 31, p. 50, 1959.

ILLUSTRATIONS. Cactus and Succ. Jour. Amer., vol. 31, pp. 50, 51, figs. 25, 26, 1959.

Plant glabrous, not papillose; stem short, in age emitting offshoots at base; roots fibrous, neither fleshy nor fusiform-thickened; leaves numerous, densely rosulate, thin, nearly flat, oblong-spathulate, up- or recurved, to 10 cm. long and 25 mm. broad, shortly aristate-mucronate, epidermis faintly punctate, margins often lacerate when young; inflorescence equilateral, subspicate, at times strongly nodding or scorpioid at apex, to 45 cm. tall; peduncle erect or ascending, to over 8 mm. thick at base; lower bracts obovate, to 3 cm. long, spreading, not readily detached; flowers to 30 or more; upper bracts 10 mm. long, 6 mm. broad; uppermost pedicels very short, lowest 3 to 8 mm. long, their two oblanceolate bractlets to 10 mm. long; sepals often large, leaflike, from two-thirds to as long as corolla, but often smaller, somewhat spreading, obovate-elliptic, acute, subequal, 8 to 10 mm. long, to 6 mm. broad, corolla urceolate, to 8 mm. long, 5 to 8 mm. in diameter at tips of the outcurved petals; petals thin, with shallow basal hollow; carpels approximately 6 mm. long, ridged on face; stamens longer than carpels, nearly as long as petals; styles obliquely capitate; nectaries thin, narrowly lunate, to 1.5 mm. wide. Flowers from July to October. Description of original plant cultivated in Golden Gate Park, San Francisco, 1937.

Color. Leaves grass-green to dark bluish glaucous; peduncle apple-green; bracts and sepals as leaves; corolla dull green-yellow; carpels spinach-green; nectaries yellowish to white.

TYPE. *Thomas MacDougall,* B-187 (UCBG, no. 58.738).

OCCURRENCE. Mexico. Oaxaca: San Juan Mixtepec, Neveria, about 10,000 feet, on rocks in partial shade in pine forest. *T. MacDougall* B-197 is the same, from San Juan Ozolotepec (UCBG, 58.826).

REMARKS. In the series Racemosae this new species stands out by reason of its rather short pedicels, slightly spreading sepals, and greenish yellow corolla. The grayish leaves are reminiscent of those found in *E. eurychlamys* from Peru except that they are turgid; the sepals are spreading, the upper bracts broader and nearly orbicular, and the corolla is red. The clearly fibrous roots prevent placing this in the series Mucronatae, where these structures are always fleshy fusiform.

I first met with this distinct species in Cuernavaca in the garden of C. Halbinger, who had obtained it through Sr. O. Nagel, without any definite locality. When brought to San Francisco, the same plant flowered again, but changed considerably, no doubt in response to the quite different climate in the greenhouse of Golden Gate Park. Loss of that material prevented me from publishing this interesting item at that time, and its recent rediscovery in Oaxaca, by Mr. Thomas MacDougall, was most welcome. Of the locality, Neveria, Mr. MacDougall states: "No habitations here; formerly natural ice was harvested here and packed down to surrounding towns. The 'canoas,' (wooden troughs) in which the ice formed, are still to be seen."

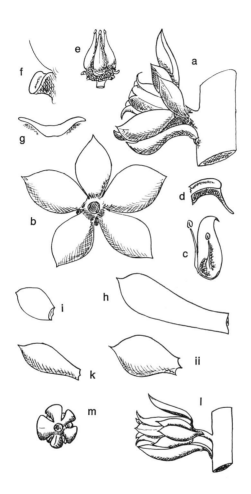

Figure 197.   120. *Echeveria megacalyx* E. Walther. Explanation: (a) flower, × 2; (b) flower from below, × 2; (c) inside of petal, × 2; (d) apex of petal, × 8; (e) carpels, × 2; (f) nectary, side view, × 8; (g) nectary, front view, × 8; (h) leaf, × 0.4; (i) bract, × 0.4; (ii) upper bract, × 2; (k) bractlet, × 2; (l) flower (Cuernavaca), × 2; (m) flower from below (Cuernavaca), × 2. From the original publication (Cactus and Succulent Journal, volume 31, page 50, figure 25).

Figure 198. 120. *Echeveria megacalyx* E. Walther. Explanation: Upper left, flower spike (Golden Gate Park); upper right, flowers (Golden Gate Park); center left, foliage (Cuernavaca); center right, foliage (UCBG, 1958); lower left, scorpioid top of flower spike; lower right, flowers (Cuernavaca, 1937). From the original publication (Cactus and Succulent Journal, volume 31, page 51, figure 26).

121. **Echeveria peruviana** Meyen.

Echeveria peruviana MEYEN, Reise um die Erde, 1, 448, 1834; Walpers Repert. Bot.
  Syst., vol. 5, p. 794, 1845–1846; POELLNITZ, *in* Fedde Repert., vol. 38, p. 192,
  1935; vol. 39, p. 222, 1936; J. F. MACBRIDE, Flora of Peru, Field Mus., Bot. Ser.
  vol. 13, pt. 2, no. 3, p. 1014, 1938.
Cotyledon peruviana (Meyen) BAKER, *in* Saunders Refug. Bot., vol. 1, no. 10, 1869;
  Gard. Chron., 1874, vol. 2, p. 258.

Glabrous; stem evident in age, usually simple, or branching from base;
leaves densely rosulate, to 15 in number, ascending, obovate to oblong-lanceolate, apex straight, acute to cuspidate-acuminate, shallowly concave above,
rounded beneath or obscurely keeled, to 10 cm. long and 25 mm. broad or
more; inflorescences one to three from each crown, erect or ascending, to 35
cm. tall, equilaterally racemose, but sometimes one-sided from uneven lighting;
peduncle stout, to 5 mm. thick at base; bracts few to many, ascending, elliptic-
oblong, acute, slightly convex on both surfaces, scarcely or not keeled, to 35
mm. long; racemes to 12 to 20 flowers, often laxly spreading or erect; pedicels
slender, 5 to 11 mm. long, bibracteolate, bractlets 3 mm. long, fugacious; sepals subequal, longest to 8 mm. long, ascending to somewhat reflexed, deltoid
to oblong-ovate, acute; corolla 11 to 14 mm. long, 8 to 10 mm. in basal diameter, pentagonal, urceolate to cylindroid, petals slightly spreading at the
apiculate tips, with deep basal nectar cavity; carpels 8 to 9 mm. long, sometimes ridged on face; nectaries lunate-reniform, to 3 mm. wide. Flowers from
May to August. Description from living material cultivated locally, originally
from Argentina.

Color. Leaves grass- to cerro- or biscay-green, often tinged reddish at
margins, below and at base, more or less glaucous, especially when young;
peduncle etruscan-red to terra-cotta, dark vinaceous with bloom; bracts spin-
ach- to light lumiere-green, more or less dark greenish glaucous; pedicels vinaceous to congo-pink; sepals sage- to biscay-green, greenish glaucous; corolla
peach-red to light orange-yellow, or empire-yellow; petals inside apricot-yellow; carpels sulphur- to barium-yellow; styles lumiere- to cosse-green; nectaries
sulphur-yellow to citron-yellow.

TYPE. On road from Tacna, near Palca, Peru, *Meyen* (B, perhaps destroyed). Lectotype: type photo, Rockefeller Foundation no. 18248 (F).

OCCURRENCE. Peru: type locality, Dept. Junin and Dept. Lima. Argentina: Dept. Humahuaca and Prov. Jujuy.

COLLECTIONS. Peru. The type; Dept. Junin, Prov. Tarma, between Palca and Carpapata, 2900 m., *Stork,* 39/10967 (F,MO,UC); Tarma, limestone
ledges at 13,000 feet, *Macbride and Featherstone* 22/1061 (F,NY,US);
Depto. Lima, Rio Blanco, *Killip and Smith,* 29/21600 (US). Argentina: cult.
UCBG, 55.795 (CAS,UC); cult. NYBG, *J. West,* 36/6230 (UC), *J. West,*
39 (CAS); Dept. Humahuaca, La Soledad, *Venturi,* 29/8860 (US); Prov. Jujuy, Quebrado de Celato, 3 kilos northeast, Humahuaca (?), 3000 feet, (UC).

REMARKS. In central Peru, *E. peruviana* may appear to overlap the territory of *E. chiclensis,* but the latter is much less xerophytic, its leaves are decidedly narrower, linear-lanceolate, scarcely ever glaucous, often deeply hollowed above, and of a strikingly sigmoid outline at the apex, as are the bracts.

According to Weberbauer (?), *E. peruviana* occurs in the Valle de Tarma,
2700 to 3300 m., on declivities, with *Pellaea nivea, P. ternifolia, Cheilanthes*

lentigera, Notholaena tomentosa, and *Tillandsia* spp., on rocks, *Stenomesson recurvatum, Peperomia nivalis, Ephedra americana, Muehlenbeckia volcanica, Berberis flexuosa, Dodonaea viscosa, Gaya gaudichaudiana, Salvia* spp., *Calceolaria cuneiformis,* and *Mutisia vicifolia.* In the Valle del Rio Rimac this occurs with *Saxifraga magellanica, Peperomia rupicola, Pilea serpyllacea, Villadia dyvrandae,* and *Phacelia peruviana.* In the Valle de Ocros, Rio Pativilea, in grass-steppe, this species grows with *Bomarea ovata, Thalictrum podocarpum, Loasa macrophylla, Colletia spinosa,* and *Lantana scabiosaeflora,* all at 2900 to 3200 m.

Mr. Paul Hutchison of the University of California Botanical Garden reports finding this species growing on rocks and cliffs at Huasahuasi, where it grows in a dry environment, and is not cespitose. Poellnitz, (Fedde Repert., vol. 38, p. 192, 1935) states that according to a letter from Dr. Rose to Dr. White, this species occurs in northern Chile.

Color of corolla varies from red to yellow, according to environment.

122. **Echeveria chiclensis** (Ball) Berger.

> *Echeveria chiclensis* (Ball) BERGER, *in* Engler Nat. Pflanzenf. ed. 2, vol. 18a, p. 473, 1930; POELLNITZ, *in* Fedde Repert., vol. 39, p. 221, 1936; J. F. MACBRIDE, Flora of Peru, Field Mus., Bot. Ser., vol. 13, pt. 2, no. 3, p. 1013, 1938.
> *Cotyledon chiclensis* BALL, Jour. Linn. Soc., vol. 22, p. 38, 1887.
> *Echeveria neglecta* POELLNITZ, *in* Fedde Repert., vol. 38, p. 30, 1935.

Glabrous; stemless or becoming shortly caulescent, cespitose in time, roots thick, fusiform; leaves 12 to 15, ascending, linear to narrowly oblong-oblanceolate, 5 to 15 cm. long or more, 10 to 25 mm. broad, more or less deeply concave above, beneath rounded and obscurely keeled, at apex upcurved to the acute tips, the latter with recurved and cartilaginous apiculus; inflorescences one or several, erect, to over 30 cm. tall, usually simple but sometimes dividing into several erect racemes near base; peduncle stout, to 5 mm. thick below; lower bracts spreading to ascending, oblong-lanceolate, subtriquetrous, somewhat concave above, 25 mm. long or more, out- and upcurved (sigmoid), with the acute apex ending in a cartilaginous-hyaline tip; raceme equilateral, 15 to 20 cm. long, erect, with 15 or more flowers; pedicels relatively stout, 7 mm. long or more, bibracteolate, occasionally the lowest 2-flowered; sepals subequal, longest about 8 mm. long, deltoid-ovate to lanceolate, ascending, not reflexed, acute; corolla 10 mm. long or more (to 20 mm.), pentagonal, cylindroid; petals slightly spreading at tips, with nectar-cavity at base; carpels 8 mm. long; nectaries lunate, to 2 mm. wide. Flowers from June on. Description from plants cultivated at the University of California Botanical Garden, 52.728, Cañon Rio Rimac, above Matucana, east of kilo 85 at 2500 m.

Color. Leaves spinach-green at base, above tinged natal-brown, not glaucous except when quite young; peduncle and rachis lumiere-green; bracts as leaves, but tending to dark vinaceous-drab; sepals celandine-green at base, tips deep purplish vinaceous; corolla lemon-chrome above, grenadine-pink at base (in greenhouse); carpels cosse-green above, paler below; nectaries light chalcedony-yellow.

TYPE. *Ball* in 1882, Chicla, Peru, 12,000 to 13,000 feet (K).

OCCURRENCE. Peru: Chicla, Oroya, Matucana, Rimac Valley, etc.

COLLECTIONS. *Ball* in 1882 (K) Chicla, Peru; *Ruiz and Pavon,* Huanuco (MA); Cante, *Soukup,* 45/2835 (GH); Oroya, *Rose and Rose,* 14/18760 (US), *Kalenborn,* 1918/104, (NY), 1919/105 (GH), *Goodspeed,* 39/11345 (UC). Depto. Lima, Prov. Huarochiri, Quebrada southwest of Matucana, *Goodspeed, Stork and Horton,* 39/11548 (UC); Depto. Lima, Prov. Huarochiri, Infieniello, *P. Hutchison,* 52.1929 (UCBG), Depto. Lima, Prov. Haurochiri, Cañon of Rio Rimac, at Rio Blanca, UCBG, 52.728–3 (cultivated; shows a peduncle branching into several erect racemes near base, or at least some of the lowermost pedicels bear two or more flowers, the result of greenhouse culture).

REMARKS. *Echeveria chiclensis* is quite variable, and when depauperate has been called *E. neglecta* Poellnitz. This last was cultivated at Kew, presumably from plants collected in Peru by Ball. *Echeveria backebergii* Poellnitz, too, may be such a stunted plant, but displays unique papillae on its leaves, bracts, and sepals, so that I am impelled to list it here as a species.

Mr. Paul Hutchison of the University of California Botanical Garden has studied this species in its native habitat. He found it growing on the western Andes in rather damp situations, where there is a foggy season of 6-months' duration. He has kindly provided me with both living and dried material.

Young plants at first produce leaves much narrower and less deeply concave than those of more mature, flowering-size plants. The horny-hyaline tip of the leaves and bracts, as well as the sigmoid curvature, is distinctive, the last being evident even in the ancient type.

Series 12. Mucronatae E. Walther.

Echeveria, ser. Mucronatae E. WALTHER, Cactus and Succ. Jour. Amer., vol. 7, p. 36, 1935; E. WALTHER, Leafl. West. Bot., vol. 9, p. 4, 1959.

Plants glabrous, apparently stemless, but actually caudex very short, almost wholly subterranean, with lateral roots fleshy-fusiform; leaves often few, at times more or less deciduous during dry season, densely rosulate, small to medium-sized; inflorescence equilateral, spicate to racemose or subpaniculate, quite variable, often even on the same plant according to the season; at least uppermost flowers solitary on quite short, bibracteolate pseudopedicels; sepals unequal or subequal, appressed to ascending-spreading; corolla broad or narrow, reddish, red and yellow or clear yellow.

TYPICAL SPECIES. *Echeveria mucronata* Schlechtendal.

REMARKS. Even if this series is well marked by reason of its fusiform roots, etc., its several species are at times difficult to separate, particularly when pressed and dried. In any large range of specimens, from any locality, some will be found to vary in the direction of another species, as for instance, *E. paniculata* may have single-flowered pedicels, while *E. mucronata* may bear several flowers to each branch. Further field work in both northeastern and northwestern Mexico will be required before any final definite species boundaries may be drawn.

Key to the Species

A. Inflorescence normally more or less subpaniculate, usually at least lowest pseudopedicels elongated and each bearing several flowers.
  B. Corolla clear yellow, narrow, to 16 mm. long; sepals ascending-spreading. Hidalgo, San Luis Potosi, etc. . . . . 124. *E. maculata*
  B. Corolla red and yellow, usually broader and shorter; sepals mostly ascending.
    C. Leaves rather thin, nearly flat; lowest pedicels with 3 to 5 flowers. Chihuahua, etc. . . . . 123. *E. paniculata*
    C. Leaves rather thick, deeply concave above; lowest pedicels elongated, even if bearing only one or two flowers each. Hidalgo. . . . . . 125. *E. longipes*
A. Inflorescence normally spicate, or racemose with very short pedicels, very rarely subpaniculate; most pseudopedicels very short and bearing only one, or at most two, flowers each.
  B. Leaves conspicuously bluish-gray. Chiapas. . . . . . . 130. *E. sessiliflora*
  B. Leaves green, scarcely or not glaucous.
    C. Leaves small, rarely over 5 cm. long or over 20 mm. broad; corolla small, mostly not over 10 mm. long. . . . . 129. *E. pinetorum*
    C. Leaves longer and broader; corolla mostly larger, longer.
      D. Leaves rhomboid-obovate, rather thick, more or less concave above, gray-green; inflorescence usually short and dense, elongating in fruit. Valley of Mexico. . . . . 127. *E. platyphylla*
      D. Leaves narrower, oblanceolate to elliptic-oblong, thinnish, nearly flat, at most shallowly concave above, green or slightly glaucous; inflorescence an elongated spike.
        E. Leaves broader, obovate-oblanceolate, dark green; peduncle stout, to 15 mm. thick at base; corolla broad, to 15 mm. long by 10 mm. thick. Serrania de Ajusco. . . . . 128. *E. crassicaulis*
        E. Leaves rather narrower, narrowly oblanceolate; peduncle to 10 mm. thick; corolla relatively narrower.
          F. Corolla clear yellow; flowers rarely borne singly on the pseudopedicels.
                                   124. *E. maculata*
          F. Corolla yellowish tinged red; flowers nearly always solitary on each pedicel. Hidalgo, etc. . . . . 126. *E. mucronata*

123. **Echeveria paniculata** A. Gray.

(Figure 199.)

Echeveria paniculata A. GRAY, Plantae Wrightianae, pt. 1, p. 76, 1850; BRITTON AND
ROSE, N. Amer. Fl., vol. 22, p. 18, 1905; E. WALTHER, Cactus and Succ. Jour.
Amer., vol. 7, p. 36, 1935 (*in part*); POELLNITZ, *in* Fedde Repert., vol. 39, p.
222, 1936.

Cotyledon grayii BAKER, *in* Saunders Refug. Bot., vol. 1, no. 33, 1869.

Echeveria grayii (Baker) ED. MORREN, La Belg. Hort., vol. 24, p. 161, 1874.

ILLUSTRATIONS. Cactus and Succ. Jour. Amer., vol. 7, p. 38, 1935 (photograph of
type).

Glabrous; stemless, with short subterranean caudex and lateral, fleshy-
fusiform roots; rosettes mostly simple, to over 20 cm. in diameter, with as many
as 40 leaves, these spreading horizontally, oblanceolate, acuminate, to 10 cm.
long and 3 cm. broad, rather thin, upcurved at tips; inflorescence mostly solitary, to 50 cm. tall, usually paniculate, but sometimes reduced, with perhaps
only a few of the lowest branches bearing several flowers; peduncle erect; lower
bracts about eight, ascending, ovate-lanceolate, acuminate, thickish, faintly
keeled beneath; branches about six to eight, ascending, each with two to six

Figure 199. 123. *Echeveria paniculata* A.
Gray. Type specimen, approximately × 0.4.
From an article by Eric Walther (Cactus
and Succulent Journal, volume 7, page 38).

flowers; uppermost pedicels short, bibracteolate; sepals unequal, longest to 10 mm. long, deltoid to oblong-lanceolate, thickish, acute, spreading to ascending; corolla conoid-cylindroid, pentagonal, to 12 mm. long, 9 mm. thick at base, 5 mm. wide at mouth; petals keeled, hollowed within at base, apiculate at apex; carpels 9 mm. long; nectaries narrowly transverse-lunate. Flowers from July on. Description from living material received from the University of California Botanical Garden.

Color. Leaves courge-green above, light grape-green beneath, tinged orange-vinaceous at apex in age; peduncle jasper-pink; bracts light bice-green, orange-vinaceous at apex; sepals biscay-green; corolla peach-red at base, above lemon-yellow, as are the inside of the petals; carpels whitish below, above lettuce-green; nectaries whitish.

TYPE. Wislizenus no. 170, Cusihuiriachic, Chihuahua, Mexico (GH).

OCCURRENCE. Northwestern Mexico, Chihuahua, Durango, etc. (See Remarks.)

COLLECTIONS. Mexico. Chihuahua: type collection (GH); hills near Chihuahua City, *Pringle, 85/575* (GH), *Pringle, 86/838* (F,MEXU,NY,US); La Bufa, *Pringle, 87/1237* (ped. 2 to 4 mm. long, 1- to 3-flowered; F,NY, PH, US); dry ledges, Sierra Madre, *Pringle, 88/1600* (BR,G,P,US); 10 to 14 miles west of Hidalgo de Parral, *Gentry, 48/8269* (GH,MO,US). Durango: Tovar, *Palmer, 06/242* (US, ped. 1- to 3-flowered); Otinapa, *Palmer, 06/435* (US, like *E. mucronata); near Durango, *Palmer, 96/916* (GH, all flowers solitary, US). Zacatecas: Mazapil, *F. E. Lloyd* in 1908 (NY). *Cultivated:* University of California Botanical Garden, 53.483, *E. Walther* (CAS).

REMARKS. As delimited here, *E. paniculata* differs from the very similar *E. maculata* in having more ascending sepals and a more reddish corolla which is rather shorter and broader. Its range is northwestern, whereas *E. maculata* is found in Hidalgo, San Luis Potosi, and Queretaro. When depauperate, *E. paniculata* may have a racemose or subspicate inflorescence, in which state it is difficult to separate it from *E. mucronata,* the latter rarely or never having more than a single flower borne on each pedicel. Some of the western material of *E. mucronata* is distinct in having a rather smaller corolla than typical, and in any case cannot be referred to *E. paniculata.*

124. **Echeveria maculata** Rose.

(Figure 200.)

> *Echeveria maculata* ROSE, *in* Britton and Rose, Bull. New York Bot. Gard., vol. 3, p. 7, 1903; BRITTON AND ROSE, N. Amer. Fl., vol. 22, p. 18, 1905; vol. 22, p. 23, 1905 (as *E. schaffneri*); POELLNITZ, *in* Fedde Repert., vol. 39, p. 222, 1936 (as *E. paniculata*); E. WALTHER, Cactus and Succ. Jour. Amer., vol. 7, p. 36, 1935 (as *E. paniculata* in part).
> ILLUSTRATION. Cactus and Succ. Jour. Amer., vol. 7, p. 38, 1935, upper left only.

Glabrous; stem short, mostly subterranean, with lateral, fleshy fusiform-thickened main roots; leaves often deciduous during dry season, 12 to 15 in a dense rosette, narrowly rhomboid-oblanceolate, 7 to 10 cm. long, 15 to 25 mm. broad, acute to acuminate, with distinct, slender, cuspidate mucro, rather thick, shallowly concave above, rounded beneath, upcurved, narrowed to 8 mm. at base; inflorescence usually solitary, equilateral, to 80 cm. tall, either subpaniculate below and spicate-racemose above, or with numerous short mostly 2-flowered branchlets; peduncle to 6 mm. thick at base; lower bracts many, ascending, linear-oblanceolate, subterete, acute, longest to 5 cm. long; lower branchlets bearing two to five sessile flowers each, upper often shorter and single-flowered; ultimate pedicels 1 to 2 mm. long, bibracteolate; sepals unequal, longest to 8 mm. long, subterete, linear, acute, ascending to spreading; corolla narrowly urceolate, to 16 mm. long, 9 mm. thick near base, narrowed to 5 mm. just below apex; petals narrow, thick, sharply keeled on back, deeply hollowed within at base; decidedly spreading at the apiculate tips; nectaries truncate-reniform. Flowers from April on. Description from living plants collected in 1934 at El Salto, Hidalgo, Mexico.

Color. Leaves cerro-green above, light elm-green beneath, sometimes spotted red (as the result of insect-infestation); bracts as the leaves; sepals oil-green to parrot-green; corolla wholly empire-yellow, both inside and out, without any trace of red coloration; carpels straw-yellow; styles light viridine-yellow below, to cosse-green at tips; nectaries straw-yellow.

TYPE. *Rose and Hay,* 1901/217 (6412), near Dublan, Hidalgo, Mexico (US, no. 48364).

OCCURRENCE. Mexico: Hidalgo, San Luis Potosi, Queretaro, Zacatecas, Michoacan.

COLLECTIONS. Mexico. Hidalgo: the type (US); Tula, *Pringle,* 02/11345 (US, all flowers solitary); El Salto, *Rose,* 03/11857 (US), *Pringle,* 03/8778

Figure 200. 124. *Echeveria maculata* Rose. From Cactus and Succulent Journal, volume 7, page 38, the plant from El Salto, Hidalgo, Mexico.

(F,US); Metepec, *Pringle,* 04/11977 (MO,US); Dublan, *Rose,* 01/217 (GH), *Rose,* 03/6412 (NY). Queretaro: Del Cierva de San Juan, *Altamirano,* 05/1742 (US); San Juan del Rio, *Rose, Painter and Rose,* 05/9860 (most flowers single) (MEXU,NY,US), *Rose,* 05/1207 (GH). Michoacan: 5 miles southwest of Quiroga, *Barkley, Westland and Webster,* 47/2713 (F). San Luis Potosi: alkaline plains, Hacienda de Angostura, *Pringle,* 91/3766 (BR,F,G,GH,MEXU,MO,NY,P,PH,UC,US); west slope of Sierra de Alvarez, *R. Moran,* 57/6322 (SD). Zacatecas: Hacienda las Cedras, *F. E. Lloyd,* 08/226 (US). *Cultivated:* La Mortola, *A. Berger* Herb., in 1931 (NY); Golden Gate Park, San Francisco, *E. Walther* in 1934 (CAS, from El Salto).

REMARKS. One plant I collected at El Salto had a large paniculate inflorescence when it bloomed for the first time in the spring of 1935, but when flowering again in the fall of the same year, its branches were nearly all 2-flowered. Such a form can of course receive no taxonomic recognition. From *E. paniculata* the present species would seem to differ in range, color of the corolla, leaf texture, and shape. *Echeveria mucronata* would appear to differ in having a strictly spicate inflorescence, shorter more reddish flowers, and a broader straight corolla.

The specific name *"maculata"* refers to the blotched leaves of the plant cultivated at Washington, D. C., resulting from its having been infested with mealy bugs.

125. **Echeveria longipes** E. Walther.
(Figure 201.)

Echeveria longipes E. WALTHER, Cactus and Succ. Jour. Amer., vol. 7, p. 36, 1935; POELLNITZ, *in* Fedde Repert., vol. 39, p. 248, 1936.
ILLUSTRATIONS. Cactus and Succ. Jour. Amer., vol. 7, p. 38, bottom left, 1935.

Glabrous; stem wholly subterranean, with numerous lateral, fleshy fusiform-thickened roots; leaves rosulate, probably deciduous during dry season, linear-oblong to rhomboid-lanceolate, 8 to 10 cm. long, 15 mm. broad, concave above, rounded beneath, sharply acute; inflorescence solitary, equilateral, paniculate but becoming racemose to spicate above, to 35 cm. tall; peduncle erect, 3 to 6 mm. thick at base; lower bracts numerous, erect, oblong-elliptic, cuspidate, 3 to 4 cm. long; panicle 20 cm. long, elongating in fruit, with 20 or more flowers; branches to 15, lowest to 16 mm. long or more, even if bearing only a single flower, but more often 2-flowered, strongly ascending, bearing three linear, curved, spurred bractlets; upper pseudopedicels shorter and mostly single-flowered; sepals subequal, longest 9 mm. long, narrowly deltoid, subterete-triquetrous, acute, strongly ascending; corolla conoid, to 14 mm. long, 8 to 9 mm. thick at base, 4 mm. in diameter at mouth; petals straight, bluntly keeled, hollowed within at base, slightly spreading at tips; nectaries reniform, 1.3 mm. wide. Flowers from November on. Description as amplified from type material.

Color. Leaves light elm-green, slightly glaucous; peduncle pinkish buff; bracts as the leaves, sepals asphodel-green to dark greenish glaucous; corolla light congo-pink at base, flesh-ocher above, empire-yellow at tips and inside; styles apple-green to chalcedony-yellow toward base.

TYPE. From specimen found by Eric Walther (34/38) on river bank at

Puente Grande, Huehuetoca, Hidalgo, Mexico, and cultivated in Golden Gate Park, San Francisco (CAS, no. 234671).

OCCURRENCE. Mexico. Hidalgo: known only from the type locality.

REMARKS. In the confusing *E. mucronata* complex, *E. longipes* is distinguished by its elongate, yet often single flowered, lower pseudopedicels.

126. **Echeveria mucronata** Schlechtendal.

(Figure 202.)

Echeveria mucronata SCHLECHTENDAL, Linnaea, vol. 13, p. 411, 1839; Hort. Hal., pl. 10, 1841; BRITTON AND ROSE, N. Amer. Fl., vol. 22, p. 15, 1905; POELLNITZ, *in* Fedde Repert., vol. 39, p. 219, 1936.

Cotyledon mucronata (Schlechtendal) BAKER, *in* Saunders Refug. Bot., vol. 1, no. 4, 1869.

ILLUSTRATIONS. Hort. Hal., pl. 10, 1841.

Glabrous; stem quite short, wholly subterranean, with lateral roots fusiform-thickened; leaves semideciduous, rather few, 10 to 15, narrowly rhomboid-oblanceolate, 7 to 9 cm. long, to 25 mm. broad, or more above middle, narrowed to 10 mm. at base, acute, flat above or shallowly concave, rounded beneath; inflorescence an equilateral spike to 50 cm. tall; peduncle erect, to 10 mm. thick at base; lower bracts ascending-spreading, oblong-oblanceolate, to 55 mm. long, shortly acuminate; spike with 15 or more flowers; upper bracts sometimes borne some distance below pedicels, 10 mm. long or less, thick, prominently spurred at base, appressed to corolla; pedicels 1 to 4 mm. long, usually very short, thick, bearing two evanescent bractlets; sepals subequal, longest 9 mm. long, shorter than corolla, somewhat spreading, subterete,

Figure 201. 125. *Echeveria longipes* E. Walther. Type plant, approximately × 0.25. From the original publication (Cactus and Succulent Journal, volume 7, page 38).

acutely mucronate, the hyaline mucro subterminal; corolla urceolate-conoid, 12 to 16 mm. long, 10 mm. in diameter at base, 5 mm. at mouth; petals thick, relatively narrow, prominently keeled and deeply hollowed within at base, slightly spreading at tips, the latter with subterminal, dorsal, often subulate apiculus; nectaries lunate-reniform, to 2.5 mm. wide. Flowers from July on. Description from living plants flowering in Golden Gate Park, San Francisco, collected in El Salto, 1934 by the author.

Color. Leaves courge- to lime-green, slightly or not glaucous, spotted russet; bracts similar to leaves; sepals light cress-green; corolla amber- to straw-yellow, perhaps occasionally tinged red in sun; styles bice-green.

TYPE. *Ehrenberg,* 294, Mineral del Monte, Omitlan, Cuesta Blanca, Hidalgo, Mexico; could not be located at HAL in 1959. Neotype: Hort. Hal., plate 10, 1841.

OCCURRENCE. Mexico: Hidalgo, Chihuahua, Jalisco, Zacatecas, Michoacan, Morelia, Puebla, Durango, etc.

COLLECTIONS. Mexico. Hidalgo: the type (probably lost); El Salto, *Pringle,* 03/8778 (G,GH,MEXU); Buena Vista, *Pringle,* 04/8913 (CAS,G, GH,MEXU,NY,P,PH,US). Chihuahua: Los Organos Mountains, *Harde le Suer* 37/1330 (F). Durango: *Palmer,* 97/4010 (US). Michoacan: Paracho, on road between Uruapan and Guadalajara, *Moore* 48/4055 (BH); Morelia, Cerro de los Nalgas, *Arsene,* 09/2576 (US), Cerro de San Miguel, *Arsene,* 10/ (US); Barranca northwest of Punguato, *Arsene,* 09/10055 (MO,US). Estado de Mexico: Tultenengo, *Rose and Painter,* 03/7866 (US). Puebla: vicinity of Esperanza, *Arsene* 07/10180 (US); Chalcicomula Plaza, *Rose and Hay,* 05/3605 (US); on road to Puebla, "El Corazon," *J. K. Langman,* 40/2655 (PH). Veracruz: Sierra de la Cruz, Orizaba, *H. Schlumberger,* 53/138 (NY, W). Tamaulipas: Cerro Linadero, *Meyer and Rogers,* 2919 (G). Zacatecas: Escobedo, *Rose,* 97/2640 (US). Guanajuato: hills east of San Miguel Allende, *Kenoyer,* 47/2450 (GH).

Some of the material referred here may perhaps belong elsewhere, as for instance *Pringle,* 04/8913 from Buena Vista, which approaches closely E. *crassicaulis. Palmer,* 96/916 from Durango, as well as some other western specimens, may belong to a new species, since here the corolla is much smaller than in the typical material. Living material should be studied from these several localities.

REMARKS. Ehrenberg's material appears to have been lost with the burning of the Berlin-Dahlem Herbarium, but plate 10, in Hortus Halensis, should serve as an adequate neotype. I tried several times to find this near Omitlan, without success, but the living plant described above, from El Salto in Hidalgo, agrees almost perfectly with Schlechtendal's description and with the illustration cited. *Echeveria mucronata* gives the name to the series Mucronatae, of which it was the first species to become known. It differs from its allies in its spicate inflorescence with strictly sessile flowers, scarcely glaucous leaves that are rather narrow and to 9 cm. long, peduncle scarcely over 10 mm. thick, and slender corolla, at least as compared with *E. crassicaulis.* My material from El Salto occurred with *E. maculata,* of which the last differs consistently in its clear yellow corolla and subpaniculate inflorescence.

Figure 202. 126. *Echeveria mucronata* Schlechtendal. Explanation: (1, 2) floral stem and (3) rosette, all × 0.63 (natural size in the original); (4) leaf margin, enlarged; (5) flower, enlarged; (6) floral parts, opened, enlarged. Plant grown at Halle, presumably from one of the original collections of Ehrenberg. From a book by Schlechtendal (Hortus Halensis, plate 10). This plate is designated neotype for the species.

127. **Echeveria platyphylla** Rose.

(Plate 12. See page 236.)

Echeveria platyphylla ROSE, *in* Britton and Rose, Bull. New York Bot. Gard., vol. 3, p. 7, 1903; BRITTON AND ROSE, N. Amer. Fl., vol. 22, p. 19, 1905; POELLNITZ, *in* Fedde Repert., vol. 39, p. 222, 1936.

ILLUSTRATIONS. Walpole no. 46 (US Nat. Herb.) [see plate 12.]; photograph no. 697 (Missouri Bot. Gard., unpublished).

Glabrous; stem short, subterranean, with lateral roots fusiform-thickened; leaves often deciduous during dry season, rosulate, few, horizontally spreading, obovate-rhomboid, at upcurved apex long cuspidate-acuminate, to 55 mm. long, 25 mm. broad; inflorescences one or two, to 40 cm. tall, bearing a dense, equilateral spike with 15 or more crowded flowers; peduncle stout, erect; lower bracts numerous, ascending to appressed, oblong-obovate, cuneate, the acuminate-cuspidate tips hyaline, to 25 mm. long; upper bracts to 16 mm. long, thickish, upcurved, prominently spurred at base; pedicels mostly single-flowered, not over 2 mm. long, but elongating to 5 mm. when in fruit, bearing two large bractlets similar to sepals, the latter erect or slightly spreading, sub-equal, longest to 12 mm. long, deltoid-lanceolate, acute, triquetrous-subterete; (sepals somewhat accrescent in fruit); corolla urceolate-conoid, to 14 mm. long, but often smaller, 9 mm. thick at base, 5 mm. at mouth, sharply pentagonal; petals slightly spreading at tips, deeply hollowed within at base; nectaries reniform, 1 mm. wide. Flowers from June on. Description from living plants collected near Lecheria, Mexico in 1934 by the author.

Color. Leaves light bice- to light elm-green above, kildare-green beneath; peduncle light grape-green; bracts biscay-green; sepals cress-green; corolla amber-yellow above, whitish at base, in age tinged light vinaceous-fawn; carpels and nectaries whitish; styles apple-green.

TYPE. Federal District, Valley of Mexico, *Rose and Hay* 01/202:6393 (US, no. 399920); isotype (MEXU).

OCCURRENCE. Mexico: Estado de Mexico; Hidalgo.

COLLECTIONS. Mexico. Estado de Mexico: Lecheria, *Pringle,* 04/11976 (F,GH,US), *E. Walther* in 1934 (CAS); Llano Grande, *Matuda,* 50/18878 (UC); Pedregal near Tlalpan, *MacDaniels,* /951 (BH). Federal District: type collection. Hidalgo: rocky hills above El Salto, *Pringle,* 03/8778 (CAS, F,G,GH,NY,PH,UC,US).

REMARKS. The broad, rhomboidal, gray-green leaves and the crowded flowers should suffice to distinguish this species from its allies. Its natural habitat appears to be dry, rocky, low hills covered with tall grass, where all vegetation becomes completely dessicated during the dry winters. Here the fleshy roots and deciduous leaves constitute important survival factors.

128. **Echeveria crassicaulis** E. Walther.
   (Figure 203.)

   Echeveria crassicaulis E. WALTHER, Cactus and Succ. Jour. Amer., vol. 7, p. 36, 1935; POELLNITZ, *in* Fedde Repert., vol. 39, p. 218, 1936.
   ILLUSTRATIONS. Cactus and Succ. Jour. Amer., vol. 6, p. 150, figs. 5, 6, 1935; vol. 7, p. 37, 1935.

   Glabrous; caudex very short, subterranean, emitting numerous branching, fusiform-thickened roots; leaves semideciduous during the dry winters, 10 to 15, lying flat on the ground, broadly rhomboid-oblanceolate to elliptic-oblong, 5 to 8 cm. long, 20 to 35 mm. broad, at apex rounded and mucronate, flat above, rounded beneath; inflorescence mostly solitary, equilaterally spicate, often appearing pseudoterminal due to delayed growth of the really terminal vegetative axis, to 60 cm. tall; peduncle erect, stout, to 15 mm. thick at base; lower bracts numerous, lowest similar to leaves, becoming smaller and more obovate-cuneate above, base appressed and spurred, apex outcurved, acutely mucronate, 25 to 40 mm. long; flowers 12 to 30, rather distant; upper bracts closely subtending flowers, very thick, little shorter than the corolla, subterete-triquetrous, acute, the basal spur hyaline; pedicels quite short, to 3 mm. in diameter, bibracteolate; sepals subequal, longest to 10 mm. long, thick, lanceolate, acute, slightly spreading at anthesis; corolla 15 mm. long, 10 mm. in diameter at base, 6 mm. at mouth; petals flattish, thick, broad, bluntly keeled, outcurved at tips, with relatively short, shallow basal hollow; nectaries narrowly lunate-reniform. Flowers from May on. Description from living plants collected at the type locality by the author in 1934.

   Color. Leaves spinach-green, to light elm-green beneath, not at all glaucous; peduncle clear, dull, green-yellow tinged onionskin-pink in sun; sepals spinach-green with reddish mucro; corolla peach- to jasper-red; petals at tips and edges empire-yellow; inside lemon-chrome; carpels baryta-yellow; styles lettuce-green; nectaries pale sulphur-yellow.

   TYPE. Cultivated in Golden Gate Park, San Francisco, from material collected at Cima along old road to Cuernavaca in 1934 by E. Walther, no. 37 (CAS, no. 223002).

   OCCURRENCE. Mexico: Federal District, Estado de Mexico, Puebla, Veracruz.

   COLLECTIONS. Mexico. Federal District: Cima, the type collection (CAS), *Pringle,* 03/11814 (F,GH,US,W), *Rose and Painter,* 03/7175 (GH,US); Serrania de Ajusco, *Pringle,* 96/6490 (F,GH,MEXU,MO,NY,P,PH,US); alpine meadow 20 miles south of Mexico City, *Ortenberger, Paxon and Barkley,* 46/16-M-648 (F). Estado de Mexico: 25 miles southeast of Mexico City, in pine forest at 9000 feet, *Barkley, Rowell and Webster,* 47/2415 (F); 55 kilos southeast of Mexico City, in pine forest, 10,500 feet, *J. N. Weaver,* 42/795 (GH, with *E. alpina*). Puebla: near Esperanza, *Arsene,* 07/10180 (US); Los Chinos, *E. K. Balls,* 38/5304 (US); Mt. Orizaba, at timberline, *Heller and Barber,* 04/23 (F,MO). Veracruz: Sierra de la Cruz, *F. Mueller,* 1853/95 (W).

   REMARKS. As the type locality is of easy access, owing to its location along both the railroad and highway from Mexico City to Cuernavaca, the

present species had been collected there on several occasions previously. Distributed as *E. mucronata,* this material clearly differs from that species in having broader leaves and bracts, longer sepals, and a broader shorter corolla. No trace of any glaucous or pulverulent coating is ever evident.

The plants occur on the edge of an old lava flow, here reaching the unique tussock-grass association found at Cima, on which a tree-stand of *Pinus teocote* provides some shade. Associated plants are *Pinus montezumae, Juniperus mexicana, Symphoricarpos microphylla, Ribes* spp., *Rubus* spp., *Fuchsia* spp. *(Encliandra), Stevia* spp., *Viola* spp., *Gentiana spathacea, Altamiranoa* sp., *Erodium* sp., *Eryngium* sp., *Lamourouxia* sp., and *Festuca tolucensis.*

The plants are hard to find when not in flower, but seeds gathered yielded numerous young plants, all substantially uniform; but in cultivation evidence of hybridization with other garden plants was abundant. Chromosome count is $n = 32$.

129. **Echeveria pinetorum** Rose.
(Figures 204–205.)

Echeveria pinetorum ROSE, *in* Britton and Rose, N. Amer. Fl., vol. 22, p. 20, 1905.
Echeveria sessiliflora var. *pinetorum* (Rose) POELLNITZ, *in* Fedde Repert., vol. 39, p. 218, 1936.
Echeveria huehueteca STANDLEY AND STEYERMARK, Field Mus., Bot. Ser., vol. 23, no. 4, p. 159, 1944; Fieldiana, Bot. Ser., vol. 24, pt. 4, p. 407, 1946.

Glabrous; stem short or none; roots thickly fleshy, fusiform; offsets present; rosettes dense, with as many as 20 leaves; leaves narrowly oblanceolate, acute to acuminate, 2 to 4 cm. long, 10 to 15 mm. broad, rather thick, above flat or shallowly concave, rounded beneath, often denticulate when young; inflorescences one or two, equilateral, sometimes unilateral due to one-sided lighting, spicate, to 30 cm. tall; peduncle erect, to 4 mm. thick below; bracts appressed, obliquely oblong-obovate, acute to shortly acuminate, to 3 cm. long, also denticulate (in type) at U.S. National Herbarium; flowers 8 to 16; upper bracts early deciduous; pedicels usually quite short, only rarely as much as 8 mm. long, bibracteolate at least in bud; sepals unequal, longest 3 mm. long, narrowly ovate, acute; corolla 8 to 10 mm. long, 6 mm. in diameter near base, 4 mm. at mouth, urceolate-cylindroid; petals scarcely spreading at tips, bluntly keeled on back, with distinct, if small, basal nectar cavity; nectaries reniform. Description from living plants cultivated locally, traceable to Dr. Rose.

Color. Leaves olive- to dull green-yellow, at edges tinged carmine; bracts as the leaves; sepals olive-yellow; corolla scarlet at base, grenadine above, apricot-yellow at tip; petals inside lemon-chrome; carpels sulphur-yellow; styles cosse-green, to russet at tips; nectaries white.

◄■

Figure 203. 128. *Echeveria crassicaulis* E. Walther. Explanation: Upper left, flowering plant, approximately × 0.1; upper right, inflorescence a quarter grown, approximately × 0.2; center left, four flowers, approximately × 1.2; center right, flower spike, approximately × 0.2; lower left, first sign of developing flower-stem, approximately × 0.6; lower right, root system of freshly collected plant, approximately × 0.35. From the original publication (Cactus and Succulent Journal, volume 7, page 37).

Figure 204.   129. *Echeveria pinetorum* Rose. Buds and flowers, × 4.
Plant flowering in San Diego, 4 July 1960; from a cited locality, 9 miles
east of Mitla, Oaxaca, Mexico, (Moran and Kimnach 7754).

TYPE. Pine woods 20 miles southeast of Teopisca, Chiapas, Mexico, *Goldman,* 04/R:1013 (US, no. 399735); isotypes (CAS,NY).

OCCURRENCE. Mexico: Chiapas and Oaxaca. Guatemala: Dept. Huehuetenango.

COLLECTIONS. Mexico. Chiapas: the type; near Comitan, Las Margintas, *Matuda,* 5912. Oaxaca: 9 miles east of Mitla, *R. Moran,* 57/6384 (SD,UC).

Guatemala: Dept. Huehuetenango, Cumbre Papal, between Cuilco and Ixmoqui, *Steyermark,* 42/50934 (F, type of *E. huehueteca); Sierra de los Cuchumatanes, above Tunima, *Steyermark,* 42/48373 (F).

REMARKS. While I agree that *E. pinetorum* is rather close to *E. sessiliflora* (which last appears to have come from nearly the same part of Chiapas), I am unable to follow Poellnitz in reducing this to a variety of that species. *Echeveria sessiliflora* seems abundantly distinct in its roots not being fleshy and in its bluish-glaucous leaves (mentioned both by Rose and by Alexander under *E. corallina*). *Echeveria huehueteca* Standley and Steyermark, from Guatemala, does not appear to differ materially. Dr. Steyermark's collection label states: corolla vermilion-red; rachis of inflorescence orange; bracts appressed, dull green, leaves deep green or suffused with dull lavender, *not* glaucous.

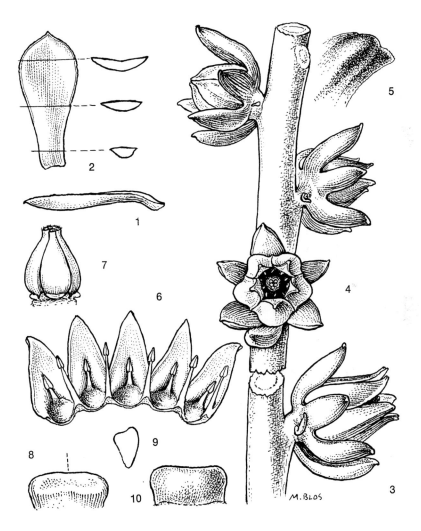

Figure 205. 129. *Echeveria pinetorum* Rose. Explanation: (1, 2) leaf, × 1; (3, 4) flowers, × 3; (5) apex of petal, greatly enlarged; (6) inside of corolla, with stamens, × 3½; (7) carpels, × 3½; (8-10) nectary, × 15. Drawing by Mrs. May Blos, 23 August 1958; plant from east of Mitla, Oaxaca, Mexico (Moran 6384, a cited collection).

130. **Echeveria sessiliflora** Rose.

(Figures 206–207.)

Echeveria sessiliflora ROSE, *in* Britton and Rose, N. Amer. Fl., vol. 22, p. 15, 1905;
POELLNITZ, *in* Fedde Repert., vol. 39, p. 218, 1936, in part.
Echeveria corallina ALEXANDER, Cactus and Succ. Jour. Amer., vol. 13, p. 135, 1941;
MATUDA, Cactaceas y Suculentas Mex., vol. 4, pp. 15, 16, 1959.
ILLUSTRATIONS. Cactus and Succ. Jour. Amer., vol. 13, pp. 134, 135, figs. 74, 76,
1941; Cactaceas y Suculentas Mex., vol. 4, p. 15, fig. 10, 1959.

Acaulescent, leaves numerous in dense flat rosettes, 1 cm. broad, pale blue, somewhat glaucous, lanceolate, acute; flowering stem 15 to 30 cm. high, with numerous ascending lanceolate leaves; inflorescence a very open spike with 12 flowers or more; sepals unequal, acute, much shorter than the corolla; corolla about 8 mm. long, 5-angled. Description by Rose, *loc. cit.*

Plant short-caulescent, the stem 2 to 3 cm. long, eventually branching below; leaves in a loose, terminal rosette, oblanceolate, abruptly acute, 6 to 8 cm. long, 15 to 16 mm. broad, pale green with brownish-purple margins and red apiculus, the whole leaf frequently shaded with brownish pink, very glaucous, the glaucescence producing a soft pinkish tone to the foliage; inflorescence 4 to 5 dm. tall, erect, with bracts similar to the leaves but more green and reduced upwards, the flowering portion roseate-salmon with a glaucous overcast; flowers 20 to 25, multilaterally arranged, sessile or on 1 mm. pedicels which are oblique bulges off the rachis; calyx slate blue-green, the tube 0.5 mm. long, the lobes appressed to the corolla, ovate to ovate-lanceolate, acute, very unequal, the two longest 7 mm. long, the intermediate 6 mm. long, the two shortest 4 mm. long; corolla oblong-conical, 14 mm. long, the petals 3 mm. wide with recurved-spreading tips; stamens opposite the petals 6 mm. long, the filament much flattened, subulate-triangular; stamens opposite the sepals 8 mm. long, the filament terete or nearly so, scarcely enlarged at the base; anthers 1.5 mm. long; honey-sack nearly circular, 2.5 mm. in diameter, 1.25 mm. deep; carpel-cluster 8 mm. long, 5 mm. in diameter, the carpel-bodies 5 mm. long, united 1.75 mm. above the base, white; styles 3 mm. long, apple-green, the stigmas truncate, maroon-purple, the color running 0.75 to 1 mm. down from the apex; nectarine gland flattened-lunate, 2.25 mm. wide. Description by Alexander, of *E. corallina.*

TYPE. Twenty miles southeast of Teopisca, Chiapas, Mexico, *Goldman,* 1904/978 (R:1012) (US); isotype (MEXU).

OCCURRENCE. Mexico: Chiapas.

COLLECTIONS. Mexico. Chiapas: the type; Trinitaria near Zapaluta, cultivated in New York Botanical Garden, *Alexander,* 1940/ (NY, type of *E. corallina* Alexander).

REMARKS. I have been unable to study the type of *E. corallina,* so that my understanding of this species is subject to improvement. I feel certain that *E. corallina* is identical with *E. sessiliflora.* The bluish color mentioned by both Rose and Alexander is distinctive.

According to Alexander, his species is "A rather unattractive plant, but beautiful in flower because of the unusual pastel coloring of the inflorescence. Related to *E. mucronata,* but differing principally in its strongly glaucous character and closely appressed calyx-lobes."

Figure 206. 130. *Echeveria sessiliflora* Rose. Plant grown in Washington, from the Missouri Botanical Garden. Photograph from the U. S. National Herbarium, no. 570.

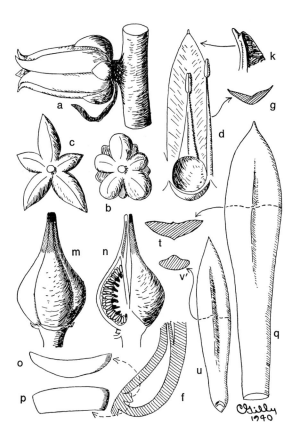

Figure 207. 130. *Echeveria sessiliflora* Rose. Explanation: (a) flower, × 2; (b) flower from below, × 2; (c) flattened calyx, × 2; (d) inside of petal, × 4; (f) median longitudinal section of petal base, × 8; (g) median cross-section of petal, × 4; (k) apex of petal, the inner face to the right, × 8; (m) carpels, × 4; (n) longitudinal section of carpels, × 4; (o) nectary, face view, × 10; (p) nectary, dorsal view, × 10; (q) leaf, × 1; (t) cross-section of widest part of leaf, × 1; (u) mid-peduncle bract, × 1; (v) cross-section of mid-peduncle bract, × 1. From the original publication of *E. corallina* Alexander (Cactus and Succulent Journal, volume 13, page 134, part of figure 74).

Series 13. ECHEVERIA.

Echeveria, sect. and ser. Echeveria E. WALTHER, Cactus and Succ. Jour. Amer., vol. 30, p. 149, 1958.
Oliverella ROSE, *in* Britton and Rose, *pro parte,* Bull. New York Bot. Gard., vol. 3, p. 2, 1903.
Oliveranthus ROSE, *in* Britton and Rose, *pro parte,* N. Amer. Fl., vol. 22, p. 27, 1905.
Echeveria, ser. Vestitae E. WALTHER, Cactus and Succ. Jour. Amer., vol. 7, p. 60, 1935; E. WALTHER, Leafl. West. Bot., vol. 9, pp. 1, 4, 1959.

Plants densely hairy on all exterior portions, including outside of corolla; trichomes elongated, simple or of several uniseriate cells; stemless, or stem evident, often tall, usually branching; leaves rosulate or subrosulate, small to medium-sized; inflorescences various, either of a simple or 2-branched raceme, or spicate, or racemose to subpaniculate or paniculate, in one instance reduced to two or three very large flowers; corolla rather broad, rarely more than twice as long as thick, sharply pentagonal, scarlet; sepals appressed to widely spreading, subequal; petals thick, sharply keeled, their basal nectar-cavity with thick upper rim; stigmas often capitate; nectaries large, usually thick and truncate; styles as long or twice as long as ovaries.

TYPICAL SPECIES. *Echeveria coccinea* (Cavanilles) DeCandolle.

REMARKS. After elimination of *E. nodulosa* with its closely papillose epidermis, *E. spectabilis* with its muriculate surface, and the aberrant *E. semivestita,* in which only the leaves, peduncle, and lower bracts are puberulent, while the corolla is quite glabrous, there remains a group of clearly related species having similar trichomes, chromosome numbers, etc. The hairs are of either of two types, *i.e.,* either multicellular, with the cells in a single row, or with simple, unicellular or solid trichomes.

The Guatemalan *E. macrantha,* which is insufficiently known, is stated to have follicles "sparsely pubescent ventrally with brownish hairs," of which I saw nothing in the closely related *E. amphoralis.*

The last four species in this section, numbers 139 to 142, agree in having simple trichomes, whereas the other hairy species have longer, several-celled, uniseriate hairs.

KEY TO THE SPECIES

A. Leaves merely papillose or muriculate; species in ser. Nudae. . . 95. *E. nodulosa*
                  96. *E. spectabilis*
A. Leaves hairy, pubescent or setose.
  B. Leaves puberulent; corolla glabrous; species in ser. Retusae. . 45. *E. semivestita*
  B. Leaves, bracts, stems, sepals, and corolla hairy.
    C. Rosettes stemless, densely leafy; inflorescence a simple or 2-branched, secund raceme; pedicels bractless.
      D. Leaves uniformly hairy over their entire surface. . . . . 136. *E. setosa*
      D. Leaves with hairs confined to margins and keel. . . . . 137. *E. ciliata*
    C. Plants subshrubs; leaves often scattered or subrosulate; inflorescence mostly equilateral, not secund, sometimes reduced; pedicels bracteolate.
      D. Sepals closely appressed to corolla even at anthesis; leaves thick, turgid.
        E. Lower pedicels evident, with several flowers each; corolla about 16 mm. long, 9 mm. thick; sepals less than half as long as corolla, connate at base; leaves obovate, their hairs sometimes reddish. . . . 133. *E. pulvinata*
        E. Flowers mostly all solitary on rather short pedicels; corolla relatively slender, to 18 mm. long and 8 mm. thick; sepals to more than half the length of corolla, free nearly to base; leaves oblong, white-hairy.
                            134. *E. leucotricha*
      D. Sepals always spreading at anthesis; leaves often thinnish.
        E. Corolla small, less than 2 cm. long.

F. Inflorescence an equilateral spike; pedicels very short or none; upper bracts much exceeding flowers.

    G. Corolla bright scarlet; leaves narrow, oblanceolate, rarely over 18 mm. broad in upper third; sepals spreading or ascending.

                          131. *E. coccinea*

    G. Corolla dull red; leaves broader, obovate-spathulate, scarcely rigid; sepals spreading to recurved. . . . . 132. *E. pubescens*

F. Inflorescence racemose or paniculate; bracts shorter.

    G. Inflorescence paniculate, at least below; corolla small, 12 mm. long or less; leaves thickish; trichomes of several, uniseriate cells.

                          135. *E. pilosa*

    G. Inflorescence usually a simple raceme, most pedicels single-flowered; trichomes simple; corolla to 15 mm. long. . . . 138. *E. pringlei*

E. Corolla large, 2 to 3 cm. long.

    F. Inflorescence many-flowered; corolla 2 to 2.5 cm. long.

        G. Carpels ventrally hairy. . . . . 141. *E. macrantha*

        G. Carpels glabrous.

            H. Corolla scarlet, 22 mm. long; leaves thin, 6 to 9 cm. long, with margins often undulate; stem mostly simple. . 139. *E. carminea*

            H. Corolla red and yellow, to 24 mm. long; leaves flattish, thicker, to 35 mm. long; stem branching. . . . . 140. *E. amphoralis*

    F. Inflorescence few-flowered, usually reduced to one or two, rarely three, large flowers; corolla to 3 cm. long or more, scarlet.

                          142. *E. harmsii*

131. **Echeveria coccinea** (Cavanilles) DeCandolle.

(Figure 208.)

Echeveria coccinea (Cavanilles) DECANDOLLE, Prodromus, vol. 3, p. 401, 1828; BRITTON AND ROSE, N. Amer. Fl., vol. 22, p. 15, 1905; POELLNITZ, *in* Fedde Repert., vol. 39, p. 216, 1936.
Cotyledon coccinea CAVANILLES, Icon. Plant., vol. 2, p. 54, 1793; BAKER, *in* Saunders Refug. Bot., vol. 1, no. 2, 1869.
Echeveria longifolia Hort.
ILLUSTRATIONS. Cavanilles, *loc. cit.,* pl. 170; Herb. Amat. Fl., vol. 2, p. 129, 1817; Loddiges Bot. Cab., pl. 832, 1824; Bot. Mag., pl. 2572, 1825; Herb. Amat. Fl., vol. 1, p. 72, 1828; Cactus and Succ. Jour. Amer., vol. 6, p. 138, fig. 2, 1935.

Plants densely hairy on all exterior portions, trichomes to 2.5 mm. long, of two or three uniseriate cells; stem evident, branching above, to 60 cm. tall; leaves laxly aggregated near end of branches, relatively narrow, oblanceolate, shortly acuminate, 6 to 8 cm. long, rarely to 20 mm. broad, convex beneath, rather deeply concave above, narrowed to a thick, petiole-like base; inflorescences usually one to each branch, to 30 cm. tall or more, a simple, equilateral spike with 25 or more flowers; peduncle stout, erect; lower bracts leaf-like, spreading, to 3 cm. long, early deciduous; upper bracts longer than the flowers; pedicels very short, not over 2 mm. long, stout, bearing two or three bractlets, the latter linear, soon deciduous; sepals ascending to widely spreading, subequal, longest to 13 mm. long, linear-lanceolate, subterete, acute, connate at base, without visible sutures; corolla sharply pentagonal, nearly straight, 10 to 12 mm. long, 8 mm. in basal diameter, 7 mm. at mouth; petals thick, sharply keeled, inside with deep basal cavity having a prominently thickened upper rim; anthers sagittate, even if not as shown in Cavanilles' figure; styles slender; stigmas capitate; nectaries obliquely elliptic, to 1 mm. wide. Flowers from September to December. Description based upon plants collected on Peñas Cosas, Federal District, Mexico, by the author in 1934.

Color. Trichomes colorless; leaves asphodel-green, sometimes tinged red in the sun; bracts and sepals as the leaves; corolla scarlet-red; petals inside

Figure 208. 131. *Echeveria coccinea* (Cavanilles) DeCandolle. Leaf and floral stem about × 0.75 (evidently about natural size in the original). Plant grown in the Royal Botanical Garden in Madrid. From the original publication (Icones et Descriptiones Plantarum. . . ., volume 2, plate 170. This plate is designated lectotype for the species.

mikado-orange, at edges grenadine-pink; carpels whitish to asphodel-green; styles baryta-yellow; stigmas morocco-red; nectaries white.

TYPE. None designated. Lectotype: Cavanilles, Icones Plant., volume 2, plate 170, 1793.

OCCURRENCE. Mexico: Federal District; Hidalgo; Puebla; Oaxaca.

COLLECTIONS. Mexico. Hidalgo: Pachuca, *Neé,* Hisp. ex. Hort. Bot.

Matr. (MA,F, photo); Regla, *P. Maury,* 91/5645 (NY); between Metepec and Zontecomate, *Pringle,* 04/8873 (CAS,G,GH,MEXU,NY,P,PH,UC); Cuesta de Texquedo, kilo 184, Zimapan-Tasquillo, *Moore* 46/1257 (BH, GH). Puebla: Sierra de Guadalupe, *Bourgeau,* 65/739 (GH,P), *E. K. Balls,* 38/5600 (UC,US); Tepeaca-Acatzingo, *Rose and Haugh,* 99/87 (MEXU). Tlaxcala: *Arsene and Nicolas,* 10/5721 (US). Oaxaca: Mixteca Alta, *Galeotti,* 1840/2813 (BR,G,UC). Federal District: Churubusco, *Orcutt,* 10/4267 (F,GH); Peñas Cosas, Cerro de Santa Catarina (flowered in Golden Gate Park), *E. Walther* in 1934 (CAS). *Cultivated:* Bot. Gard. Rome, Herb. de Moise-Etienne Moricand (G).

REMARKS. *Echeveria coccinea* was the first species of the genus to reach Europe, and was cultivated in the Botanic Garden at Madrid prior to 1793, when it was illustrated in Cavanilles' Icones. The excellent figure in question no doubt served to influence DeCandolle when he decided that the American *Cotyledon*-species formed a distinct genus. The early discovery of *E. coccinea* naturally followed from its being native practically in Mexico City. There I found this growing wild on dry walls at the base of the small extinct volcanos known as the Santa Catarina group. Its seedlings were quite abundant there, especially in the root mats of *Notholaena aurea.* Other associated plants noted were *Sedum dendroideum, Senecio praecox, Loeselia mexicana,* and *Dahlia variabilis,* as well as species of *Ageratum, Eupatorium, Anoda, Cardiospermum, Ephedra, Salvia, Mentzelia,* and *Begonia,* with *Sedum oxypetalum, S. moranense,* and *Echeveria glauca* occurring somewhat higher up. A striking feature was the innumerable pepper trees *(Schinus Molle)* dotting the landscape and having the appearance of being native.

The only *Echeveria* species with which *E. coccinea* might possibly be confused is *E. pubescens,* but that differs in having larger, relatively broader leaves and bracts, and a broader more campanulate corolla which is dull red in color, with broader petals and recurved sepals.

Cotyledon spicata Mocino and Sesse, Plantae Novae Hisp., in Naturaleza, 1888, has been referred to *E. coccinea,* but is described as having white flowers, a cymose inflorescence, and terete subulate leaves; it may have been an *Altamiranoa.*

Occasionally found in local gardens is an abberrant form with fasciated stems; this may bear the cultivar name 'Crest.'

132. **Echeveria pubescens** Schlechtendal.

(Figure 209.)

Echeveria pubescens SCHLECHTENDAL, Linnaea, vol. 13, p. 411, 1839; Hort. Hal., vol. 3, p. 17, 1841–1853; BRITTON AND ROSE, N. Amer. Fl., vol. 22, p. 15, 1905; POELL-NITZ, *in* Fedde Repert., vol. 39, p. 215, 1936.
Cotyledon pubescens (Schlechtendal) BAKER, *in* Saunders Refug., Bot., vol. 1, no. 1, 1869; vol. 3, pl. 197, 1870.
ILLUSTRATIONS. Hort. Hal., *loc. cit.,* pl. 9; Saunders Refug. Bot., vol. 3, pl. 197, 1870; von Roeder, Suk., 29.

Plants densely pubescent on all exterior portions, including the corolla; trichomes about 2 mm. long, conical at base, subulate above, of three to four cells in a single row, with the lowest cell the longest; stem to 60 cm. tall, branching above; leaves 8 to 12 in number, obovate-spathulate to obovate-oblanceolate, acute, 6 to 9 cm. long, to 3 cm. broad above middle, concave

Figure 209.   132. *Echeveria pubescens* Schlechtendal. Flowering plant, × 0.6, (natural size in the original); flower and parts enlarged. Plant grown at Halle, presumably from one of the original collections of Ehrenberg. From a book by Schlechtendal (Hortus Halensis, plate 9).

above, with edges upfolded and undulate, beneath faintly keeled near base, somewhat recurved, flaccid yet fragile; inflorescences two or more, arising from below the leaves, to 40 cm. tall, equilaterally spicate, spike with 15 to 25 or more flowers; peduncle stout, erect; lower bracts leaf-like, to 4 cm. long; upper bracts conspicuous, longer than the flowers, narrowly oblong-oblanceolate, to 3 cm. long, recurved, but upcurved near end; pedicels less than 2 mm. long, to 3 mm. thick, with two linear bractlets when young; sepals widely spreading to recurved, subequal, longest to 15 mm. long, linear-oblanceolate, subterete, at base connate but with distinctly visible sutures between the individual sepals; corolla sharply pentagonal, to 10 mm. long or more, rather broad, 9 mm. in diameter near base, to 10 mm. at the open mouth, constricted above base; petals acuminate, thick, sharply keeled, spreading from the middle, incurved at tips, the basal hollow deep, with prominently thickened upper rim; carpels flask-shaped; stigmas capitate; nectaries lunate-reniform, to 1.5 mm. wide. Flowers from January on. Description based upon locally cultivated material.

Color. Leaves cedar-green, their trichomes colorless, but sometimes tinged purplish at first, with stems reddish-brown; bracts and sepals as the leaves; corolla dull saccardo-olive on keel, rose-doree at base and edges, inside buff-yellow; carpels light cress-green above; styles oxblood-red.

TYPE. *C. Ehrenberg,* Mineral del Monte, Regla, Hidalgo, Mexico (HAL?).

OCCURRENCE. Mexico: Hidalgo; Puebla.

COLLECTIONS. Mexico. Hidalgo, the type from Regla. Puebla: Barranca, Hacienda Alamos and Cristo, *Arsene,* 07/1680 (US?). *Cultivated:* Knicker-bocker Nurseries, San Diego (BH); Soldena Gardens, Pasadena, *Floyd* in 1936 (BH).

REMARKS. This species is very close to *E. coccinea,* to which most field collections should be referred. *Echeveria pubescens* would appear to differ amply in its broader leaves and bracts, a broader corolla, and more spreading sepals. My description is based on locally grown plants, actually quite rare in cultivation, and often represented by an abnormal form with twisted and recurved leaves. The latter should be recorded as *E. pubescens* cultivar 'Tortuosa.' I have been unable to relocate this species in its native habitat, and saw nothing but typical *E. coccinea* in that part of Hidalgo.

Schlechtendal's description of the hairs of *E. pubescens* (Hort. Hal., vol. 3, p. 17, 1853), is in full agreement with my observations.

133. Echeveria pulvinata Rose.
(Figure 210. Plate 133; see page 237.)

> *Echeveria pulvinata* ROSE, *in* Britton and Rose, Bull. New York Bot. Gard., vol. 3, p. 5, 1903 (issued Sept. 12); BRITTON AND ROSE, N. Amer. Fl., vol. 22, p. 16, 1905; POELLNITZ, *in* Fedde Repert., vol. 39, p. 214, 1936.
> *Cotyledon pulvinata* HOOKER fil., Bot. Mag., pl. 7918, 1903 (issued Oct. 1).
> ILLUSTRATIONS. Bot. Mag., pl. 7918, 1903; Moell. Deutsche Gartenztg., vol. 26, p. 81, 1911; Walpole, no. 48 (US Nat. Herb.). [see Plate 13].

Subshrub; hairy on all exterior portions; trichomes 3 mm. long or less, of five or more uniseriate cells; stem evident, branching, to 10 cm. tall or more, rusty-pubescent; leaves subrosulate or laxly aggregated near end of branches, obovate, thick, turgid, to 6 cm. long, above nearly flat or very slightly concave, beneath rounded, obtusish and mucronate; inflorescences numerous, arising from below leaves, equilaterally spicate to racemose, or subpaniculate below, to 12 cm. long; peduncle stout, but decumbent at base to ascending above; bracts numerous, ascending, obovate-oblong, to 4 cm. long; flowers 15 or more; pedicels to 15 mm. long, lowest often with two or more flowers, bracteolate, turbinately-thickened below calyx; sepals appressed, less than half as long as corolla, subequal, longest 12 mm. long, deltoid-ovate to oblong-lanceolate, acute, thick, subterete, at base connate but with sutures distinct; corolla urceolate-campanulate, pentagonal, to 16 mm. long and 9 mm. in basal diameter, 7 to 12 mm. wide at mouth; petals thick, sharply keeled, with deep basal hollow, slightly spreading at the acuminate tips, which bear an outcurved dorsal apiculus; carpels stout; stigmas capitate; nectaries truncate, transversely reniform, to 2 mm. wide. Flowers from January to June. Description from living plants grown in local gardens.

Color. Trichomes colorless to rusty-brown in sun; leaves elm-green; bracts and sepals as the leaves, but often pompeian-red at tips; corolla scarlet-red, petals at edges and within empire-yellow; styles peacock-green below, to maroon at tips.

Type. Collected by Pringle, 1894/5641, on dry ledge at 3000 feet, Tomellin Cañon, Oaxaca, Mexico (US, no. 346987). The type sheet holds several different collections, including also material from living plants grown at Wash-

Figure 210. 133. *Echeveria pulvinata* Rose. Plant grown in Washington; collected at North Alban, Oaxaca, Mexico (Rose 4994). Photograph from the U.S. National Herbarium, no. 169.

ington, D. C., and collected at the type locality by Rose and Haugh, (99/4976) and by Rose (01/4994).

OCCURRENCE. Mexico: Oaxaca.

COLLECTIONS. Mexico. Oaxaca: the type collection (US, type; GH); Tomellin Cañon, *Rose,* 01/4994 (US), *Rose and Haugh,* 99/4976 (NY,US); Cerro de San Felipe, *Conzatti,* 96/107 (US); Almoloyas Cañon, *Conzatti,* 06/1686 (GH,MEXU,US). *Cultivated:* Anson Blake garden, Berkeley, Bracelin, 43/2405 (BH,CAS); Orpet Nursery, Santa Barbara, *E. Walther* in 1930 (CAS); flowered in Washington, D. C., *Rose,* 04/4994 (US); Knickerbocker Nursery, San Diego (BH).

REMARKS. *Echeveria pulvinata* is readily distinguished from all other hairy species of *Echeveria* in having an evident caudex, an equilateral inflorescence, bracteolate pedicels, and appressed sepals. In the last character mentioned, it agrees with *E. leucotricha* J. A. Purpus, but the latter differs in having more oblong, narrower leaves with pure white hairs that scarcely ever turn red in the sun, in having mostly solitary flowers on rather shorter stalks, a rather longer, more slender corolla, and sepals that are more than half the length of the corolla, free nearly to base, but without any visible sutures.

A form frequently found in cultivation differs from the type in having its hairs a more intense, more wide-spread rusty color. This has been given the cultivar name, *E. pulvinata* cultivar 'Ruby,' B. K. Boom.

134. **Echeveria leucotricha** J. A. Purpus.
(Figure 211.)

Echeveria leucotricha J. A. PURPUS, Monatsch. Kakteenk., vol. 24, p. 65, 1914; BRITTON AND ROSE, N. Amer. Fl., vol. 22, p. 536, 1918; POELLNITZ, *in* Fedde Repert., vol. 39, p. 215, 1936.
ILLUSTRATIONS. Monatsch. Kakteenk., *loc. cit.,* p. 67; Van Laren, Succ., p. 72, fig. 97, 1934.

Branching subshrub to 15 cm. tall or more; all exterior portions densely covered with conspicuous, colorless, white-appearing hairs quite like those of *E. pulvinata;* leaves laxly subrosulate, oblong-oblanceolate, obtusish and mucronate, 6 to 8 cm. long or more, 20 to 25 mm. broad, upcurved, shallowly concave above, rounded below, thick; inflorescences to 40 cm. long, equilateral, subspicate to subpaniculate; bracts oblong-obovate, to 3 cm. long, ascending; flowers 12 to 15; pedicels short, rarely elongated, mostly single-flowered; bractlets three, linear, to 8 mm. long; sepals free to base, without visible sutures, subequal, longest to 10 mm. long, appressed to corolla, deltoid- or linear-lanceolate, acute; corolla sharply pentagonal, to 18 mm. long, 8 mm. in basal diameter, 10 mm. at thickest part, 7 mm. at mouth; petals somewhat spreading at the shortly acuminate tips, keeled on back, sulcate within, with deep basal hollow; carpels 8 mm. long; styles short; stigmas obliquely capitate; nectaries truncate, transversely reniform, to 2 mm. wide. Flowers from February on. Description based upon plant from the University of California Botanical Garden.

Color. Pubescence of branches becoming indian-red; leaves lettuce-green, often indian-red at tips; bracts, bractlets, and sepals as the leaves; corolla buff-yellow at base where covered by the appressed sepals, spectrum-red on keel, salmon-orange at edges of petals, inside bittersweet-orange above, buff-yellow

Figure 211. 134. *Echeveria leucotricha* J. A. Purpus. Plant grown at Darmstadt. From the original publication (Monatsschrift für Kakteenkunde, volume 24, page 67).

below, carpels martius-yellow; styles to oxblood-red above; stigmas greenish; nectaries apricot-yellow.

TYPE. Collected by J. A. Purpus in 1908, on rocks in mountains near San Luis Tultitlanapa, Sierra de Mixteca, southern Puebla, Mexico (B?).

OCCURRENCE. Mexico. Puebla, vicinity of San Luis Atototitlan, *Purpus,* 07/413, (US); Cerro del Castillo, Caltepec, southern Puebla.

REMARKS. The present species comes quite close to *E. pulvinata,* but would seem to differ amply in having rather longer, narrower leaves with more whitish hairs, a more spicate inflorescence, a corolla to 18 mm. long, and rather more slender, longer sepals, free nearly to base without any evident basal sutures.

135. **Echeveria pilosa** J. A. Purpus.
(Figure 212.)

Echeveria pilosa J. A. PURPUS, Monatsch. Kakteenk. vol. 27, p. 146, 1917; POELL-
NITZ, *in* Fedde Repert., vol. 39, p. 213, 1936.
ILLUSTRATIONS. Monatsch. Kakteenk., vol. 27, p. 147; Cactus and Succ. Jour. Amer.,
vol. 7, p. 86, fig. (upper left), 1935.

Plants closely hairy on all exterior portions, trichomes to 2 mm. long,
spreading, of about four uniseriate cells; stem evident, short, usually simple;
leaves laxly rosulate, to 40, oblanceolate, shortly acuminate, but with thickish
apex, to 7 cm. long, 2 cm. broad, narrowed to 6 mm. at petiole-base, above
concave, rounded beneath; inflorescences two or more, paniculate, becoming
simply racemose or spicate above, to 30 cm. tall; peduncle stout, ascending;
lower bracts many, ascending-spreading, oblong-oblanceolate, acute, to 3 cm.
long; branches five or more, short and few-flowered; pedicels of lower branches
short and bractless, but uppermost to 16 mm. long and bracteolate; sepals
spreading to ascending, subequal, to 15 mm. long, elliptic-oblong, subterete,
acute; corolla sharply pentagonal, rather straight, to 12 mm. long, 10 mm. in
diameter below, narrowed to 6 mm. at mouth; petals broad, with thick keel
and deep basal hollow having a prominently thickened upper rim; carpels
stout; nectaries to 3.5 mm. wide, narrowly trapezoid-reniform. Flowers from
January to December. Description from living plants imported from R. Graessner, Perleberg.

Color. Leaves spinach-green, as are bracts and sepals; corolla with its segments scarlet on keel, salmon-orange at sides, empire-yellow at tips, edges, and
inside; carpels dull green-yellow; styles carmine to spectrum-red.

TYPE. None designated. Lectotype: Kakteenk., *loc. cit.,* figure on page
147.

OCCURRENCE. Mexico. Known only from the type locality, Sierra de
Mixteca, near San Luis Atototitlan, southern Puebla.

COLLECTIONS. Mexico. Puebla: Sierra de Mixteca, near San Luis Atototitlan, *Purpus* in 1909. *Cultivated:* Soldena Gardens, Pasadena, *Floyd* in 1935
(BH).

REMARKS. Dr. Charles Uhl of Cornell reports a chromosome-number of
$n = 24$ for *E. pilosa,* which otherwise is readily distinguished from other hairy
species in its paniculate inflorescence and spreading sepals. Despite the paniculate inflorescence, this species has nothing in common with the series Gibbiflorae, as suggested by A. Berger (Engler's Nat. Pflanzf. ed. 2, vol. 18a, p.
474, 1930).

Figure 212. 135. *Echeveria pilosa* J. A. Purpus. Plant grown at Darmstadt. From the original publication (Monatsschrift für Kakteenkunde, volume 27, page 147). This figure is designated lectotype for the species.

136. **Echeveria setosa** Rose and Purpus.

(Figures 213–215. Plate 14, upper; see page 240.)

Echeveria setosa ROSE AND PURPUS, Contrib. U. S. Nat. Herb., vol. 13, p. 45, 1910; M. L. GREEN, Bot. Mag., pl. 8748, 1918; BRITTON AND ROSE, N. Amer. Fl., vol. 22, p. 538, 1918; POELLNITZ, *in* Fedde Repert., vol. 39, p. 212, 1936.

ILLUSTRATIONS. Contrib. U. S. Nat. Herb., *loc cit.,* pl. 10; Bot. Mag., pl. 8748, 1918; Addisonia, vol. 1, no. 1, pl. 6, 1916; Jacobsen, Handbook of Succ. Plants, vol. 1, p. 385, fig. 419, 1959; Roeder, Sukk., pl. 29; Van Laren, Succ., p. 80, fig. 112, 1934; Desert Plant Life, vol. 20, p. 31, 1948.

Plants densely hairy on all exterior portions; trichomes to 3 mm. long, of six or more uniseriate cells, colorless; rosettes stemless, or very shortly caulescent in age, finally giving out numerous offsets; leaves numerous, as many as 100 or more, turgid, oblanceolate-spathulate, 4 to 5 cm. long, 18 to 20 mm. broad, 5 mm. thick, above nearly flat or somewhat convex, beneath rounded and slightly keeled, at apex acute and shortly mucronate; inflorescences two or more, bearing a simple or 2-branched, secund raceme, to over 30 cm. tall; peduncle ascending, stout; bracts ascending, oblong, acute, thick, biconvex, to 25 mm. long; racemes with 10 or more flowers each; pedicels bractless, to 15 mm. long, somewhat thickened below calyx; sepals subequal, longest to 10 mm. long, ascending, oblong-deltoid, thick, subterete; corolla sharply pentagonal, urceolate, 10 to 12 mm. long, 7 mm. in basal diameter; petals oblong, acute, slightly spreading at tips, thick, sharply keeled, with basal hollow deep but short; carpels flask shaped; stigmas often exserted(?); nectaries oblique, narrowly reniform, to 2 mm. wide; mature follicles widely spreading. Flowers from June on. Description from locally cultivated plants.

Color. Trichomes colorless, leaves spinach-green; bracts and sepals as the leaves; corolla lemon-chrome overlaid with spectrum-red; petals inside empire-yellow; styles cosse-green.

TYPE. Collected by C. A. Purpus, 07/415 (R:07/469), on rocks, Cerro de la Yerba, San Luis Atototitlan, southern Puebla, Mexico (US, no. 592487).

OCCURRENCE. Southern Puebla, Mexico.

COLLECTIONS. Mexico. Puebla, the type. *Cultivated:* Soldena Gardens, Pasadena, *Floyd* in 1935 (BH); Strybing Arboretum, Golden Gate Park, San Francisco, *Dress,* 51/4167 (BH).

Figure 213. 136. *Echeveria setosa* Rose and Purpus. Plant grown by J. A. Purpus in Darmstadt. From the original publication (Contributions from the U.S. National Herbarium, volume 13, plate 10).

Figure 214. 136. *Echeveria setosa* Rose and Purpus. Center of Rosette, × 2.7. Plant grown in San Diego; collected at the type locality (Moran and Kimnach 7721).

Figure 215. 136. *Echeveria setosa* Rose and Purpus. Flowers, × 1.7. Plant flowering in San Diego 4 May 1963; collected at the type locality (Moran and Kimnach 7721).

137. **Echeveria ciliata** Moran.

(Figures 216–217. Plate 14, lower; see page 240.)

Echeveria ciliata Moran, Cactus and Succ. Jour. Amer., vol. 33, p. 131, 1961.
ILLUSTRATIONS. Cactus and Succ. Jour. Amer., vol. 33, figs. 81 (cover), 82, 83, 85 (left), 86 to 91, 1961.

Plant hairy on exterior portions; on leaves trichomes are borne in a narrow line along margins and on keel, a few occur scattered from leaf edge to a distance of 1.5 mm., especially at the broadest portion of the leaf, at apex the three confluent lines of hairs form a conspicuous terminal tuft reminiscent of that seen in *Sempervivium arachnoideum*, trichomes 1 to 2 mm. long, tapering to a thickness of 0.1 or 0.15 at base; stem short, to 7 cm. long in age, and to 2 cm. thick, bearing narrow lines of hairs between leaf bases; rosettes simple (?), hemispherical, densely leafy with 30 to 70 leaves, 5 to 10 cm. in diameter; leaves drying leathery, obovate-cuneate, to 5 cm. long and 35 mm. broad in upper fourth, narrowed to width of 8 mm. at the 8 mm. thick petiole; upper surface nearly flat or somewhat convex, edges subacute, apex mucronate; inflorescence a simple, secund raceme, 4 to 13 cm. tall; peduncle 2 to 3 mm. thick, hirsute, hairs as those on the leaves; racemes to 5 cm. long or more, with four to seven flowers; pedicels ascending, lowest to 12 mm. long; sepals subequal, appressed (?) to spreading, triangular-lanceolate, acute, to 4 mm.

Figure 216. 137. *Echeveria ciliata* Moran. Flowering plant, × 0.7. Type plant (Moran 6395), photographed in San Diego 30 May 1960.

Figure 217. 137. *Echeveria ciliata* Moran. Center of rosette, × 4. Type plant (Moran 6395), grown in San Diego.

long, hirsute; petals about 10 mm. long, hairy on exposed parts, smooth inside and where petal edges overlap in bud; follicles widely spreading at maturity. Description from Reid Moran.

TYPE. From plants growing on "east-facing cliff at about 2100 meters elevation, Cañada [de Tutla] Oaxaca, Mexico (near 17°42′N, 97°38′W), 19 November 1957, Moran 6395; flowering in San Diego 2 June 1960." (SD, no. 51097). [Locality name corrected by Dr. Reid Moran. Ed.]

OCCURRENCE. Known only from the type locality.

REMARKS. I have seen no flowering plants of this new species, but am convinced, from the data provided me by Dr. Reid Moran, that this is indeed very close to *E. setosa,* having been found only 37 miles distant from the type locality of the latter. Its principal difference would appear to be the peculiar arrangement of the leaf-trichomes.

138. **Echeveria pringlei** (S. Watson) Rose.

(Figure 218. Plate 15, upper; see page 241.)

> *Echeveria pringlei* (S. Watson) ROSE, *in* Britton and Rose, Bull. New York Bot. Gard., vol. 3, p. 6, 1903; BRITTON AND ROSE, N. Amer. Fl., vol. 22, p. 16, 1905; POELLNITZ, *in* Fedde Repert., vol. 39, p. 214, 1936.
> *Cotyledon pringlei* S. WATSON, Proc. Amer. Acad. Arts and Sci., vol. 25, p. 148, 1890.

Plant densely pubescent on all exterior portions, trichomes colorless, transparent, to 0.2 mm. long, straight or tapering to base; stem evident, to 10 cm. tall or more, with numerous, decumbent or ascending branches; leaves laxly rosulate or scattered, thinnish, scarcely turgid, to 4 cm. long and 2 cm. broad, oblanceolate to rhomboid-obovate, acute or mucronate, flat or recurved; inflorescences simple, equilaterally-racemose, to 20 cm. long; peduncle spreading, to ascending above; lower bracts rhomboid-obovate, to 3 cm. long, cuspidate-apiculate, recurved; raceme with 12 or more flowers; upper bracts obovate, less than 25 mm. long; pedicels stout, 4 to 8 mm. long, bracteolate; sepals subequal, longest to 14 mm. long, narrowly-lanceolate, acuminate, ascending to spreading; corolla urceolate, sharply pentagonal, to 15 mm. long, 10 mm. thick below middle, 9 mm. wide at mouth; petals sharply keeled, oblong-oblanceolate, acuminate, with subterete apiculus at the slightly spreading tips, at base with deep hollow within; carpels slender, 10 mm. long; nectaries

Figure 218.   138. *Echeveria pringlei* (S. Watson) Rose. Flowering plant, × 0.5. Plant photographed in San Diego 14 November 1964; collected by Señor Zabaleta near Experiencia, Jalisco, Mexico (UCBG 53.1156).

narrowly lunate-reniform, 1.5 mm. wide. Flowers from November on. Description from living plant received from University of California Botanical Garden, 1955.

Color. Leaves and bracts leaf-green, asphodel-green beneath; sepals spinach-green; corolla peach-red to coral-red or scarlet; petals inside apricot-buff; carpels sea-shell pink; styles light hellebore-red; nectaries nearly white.

TYPE. *Pringle,* 1888/1853 (GH; isotypes MEXU,NY,US), collected on dry ledges of barranca, Guadalajara, Jalisco, Mexico.

OCCURRENCE. Region of type locality.

COLLECTIONS. The type collection; barranca at Guadalajara, *Pringle,* 03/ R-870 (flowered, CAS,NY), *Rose and Painter,* 03/870 (GH,MEXU,US).

REMARKS. The living material on which my description is based was collected at Experiencia, near Guadalajara, by Sr. Zabaleta (UCBG 53.1156), not very far from the type locality. According to Dr. Uhl, the chromosome number of *E. pringlei* is $n = 23$, the same as in *E. pulvinata.* The present species differs from related hairy species as follows: from *E. pulvinata* and *E. leucotricha* in its spreading sepals, from *E. coccinea* and *E. pubescens* in its elongated pedicels, from *E. pilosa* and *E. setosa* in its simply racemose, equilateral inflorescence with bracteolate pedicels, and from *E. carminea* and *E. amphoralis* in its smaller corolla. The simple trichomes of the last two species are very similar to those of *E. pringlei.*

139. **Echeveria carminea** Alexander.

(Figure 219.)

Echeveria carminea ALEXANDER, Cactus and Succ. Jour. Amer., vol. 13, p. 138, 1941. ILLUSTRATIONS. Cactus and Succ. Jour. Amer., vol. 13, figs. 75, p. 135. 81, p. 139.

Plants finely pubescent on all exterior parts with simple trichomes 0.1 to 0.2 mm. long; stem evident, to 70 cm. tall, strict, erect, rather slender, sparingly or not branched above; leaves rather few, laxly rosulate or scattered, thinnish, broadly oblanceolate, acutish, 5 to 9 cm. long or more, 25 to 45 mm. broad, narrowed to 7 mm. at base of the subangular petiole, margins usually crispate-undulate, above more or less concave, deeply channeled toward the base when young, later flat, obscurely keeled beneath toward base, rather flaccid; inflorescence an equilateral raceme, usually solitary, arising below the leaves, to 30 cm. tall or more, with eight or more flowers that are often turned toward one side due to one-sided lighting; peduncle rigid, ascending to erect; lower bracts oblong-lanceolate, shortly acuminate, to 6 cm. long and 18 mm. broad, widely spreading to recurved; pseudopedicels 10 to 15 mm. long, bearing two bractlets which are up to 16 mm. long; upper bracts similar to sepals, the latter widely spreading or somewhat recurved, nearly equal, 15 to 20 mm. long, linear-oblanceolate, subterete; corolla broadly urceolate, pentagonal, 20 to 25 mm. long or more, 15 to 18 mm. in greatest diameter narrowed to 13 mm. at mouth; petals thick, dorsally sharply keeled, deeply hollowed within at base, shortly acuminate at the slightly spreading to strongly outcurved, bluntly apiculate tips; carpels to 16 mm. long, quite glabrous; styles slender, but not more than twice as long as ovaries; stigmas obliquely capitate; nectaries lunate-reniform, to over 2 mm. wide, secreting an abundance of nectar. Flowers June and July. Description from plant cultivated locally, received through Sr. C. Halbinger, Mexico City.

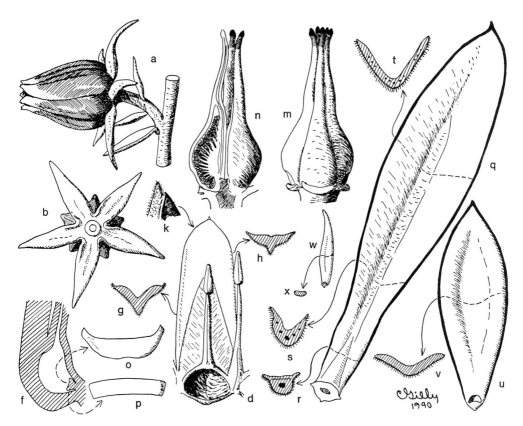

Figure 219. 139. *Echeveria carminea* Alexander. Explanation: (a) flower, × 1; (b) flower from below, × 1; (d) inside of petal, × 2; (f) median longitudinal section of petal, × 4; (g) median cross-section of petal, × 2; (h) cross-section near apex of petal, × 2; (k) apex of petal, the inner face to the right, × 8; (m) carpels, × 2; (n) longitudinal section of carpels, × 2; (o) nectary, face view, × 5; (p) nectary, dorsal view, × 5; (q) leaf, flattened, × 1; (r, s, t) cross-sections of leaf, × 1; (u) mid-peduncle bract, × 1; (v) cross-section of mid-peduncle bract, × 1; (w) pedicellary bract, × 1; (x) cross-section of pedicellary bract, × 1. From the original publication (Cactus and Succulent Journal, volume 13, page 139, figure 81).

Color. Leaves light elm-green above, water-green beneath, at edges army-brown; bracts light cress-green; sepals, upper bracts, and bractlets elm-green; corolla bittersweet-orange; petals inside and at edges baryta-yellow; carpels pale green-yellow; styles lettuce-green; nectaries baryta-yellow.

TYPE. *T. MacDougall,* 38–39/, from mountains west of Tehuantepec, Oaxaca, Mexico (NY).

OCCURRENCE. Mexico. Oaxaca: San Juan del Estado, Santiago Lachi-guiri (according to MacDougall).

COLLECTIONS. *Cultivated:* Golden Gate Park, San Francisco, *E. Walther* in 1940 (CAS).

REMARKS. Among the shrubby, hairy *Echeveria* species, *E. carminea* comes nearest to *E. harmsii* and my new *E. amphoralis.* Of these, the first differs in its inflorescence being reduced to two or three flowers only, with a still longer corolla and much more elongated styles but it agrees with *E. carminea* in having quite similar trichomes.

Echeveria amphoralis has a conspicuously red and yellow corolla and much smaller leaves, at most 35 mm. long, rather flat, and somewhat thicker.

Echeveria spectabilis Alexander differs in its sparingly muriculate leaves, more abundantly branching habit, and somewhat smaller flowers. Its haploid chromosome number is 100–104.

Of the living material supplied by Mr. Thomas MacDougall, quite identical with Dr. Alexander's type, he stated: "It is found in dry, rocky soil, in sun or partial shade, at about 5000 feet, in the mountains west of Tehuantepec, Oaxaca."

140. **Echeveria amphoralis** E. Walther.

(Figures 220–221. Plate 15, lower; see page 241.)

Echeveria amphoralis E. WALTHER, Cactus and Succ. Jour. Amer., vol. 30, p. 149, 1958.

ILLUSTRATIONS. Cactus and Succ. Jour. Amer., vol. 30, pp. 149, 150, figs. 84, 85, 1958. For fig. 85K *read:* trichome, greatly enlarged.

Plant puberulous on all external parts; subshrubby, to 20 cm. tall or more, with numerous ascending branches; leaves numerous, subrosulate or somewhat scattered, obovate-cuneate, mucronate, to 35 mm. long and 20 mm. broad, thickish, subpetiolate; petiole thick; blade shallowly concave above, obscurely keeled beneath; inflorescences several from below the leaves, erect or ascending, to 20 cm. tall; peduncle stout, 4 mm. in diameter at base; lower bracts obovate, mucronate, 30 mm. long, 15 mm. broad, widely spreading; racemes equilateral, each with four to seven flowers; pedicels stout, to 20 mm. long, and 3 mm. thick, bibracteolate, bractlets linear-lanceolate, acute, subterete, to 14 mm. long; sepals subequal, to 14 mm. long, semiterete or somewhat flattened, lanceolate, acute to acuminate, ascending to widely spreading at anthesis; corolla quite large, to 24 mm. long and 14 mm. in basal diameter, 7 to 11 mm. wide at mouth, amphora-shaped, pentagonal; petals sharply keeled on back, apiculate at the somewhat spreading tips, with short basal hollow within; carpels not hairy dorsally, to 18 mm. long with the styles, these last long and slender, to 12 mm. long, somewhat divergent at tips; nectaries transversely lunate-reniform, sharp-edged, to 4 mm. broad; trichomes approximately 0.1 mm. long. Flowers from June on. Description from plant and flowering material furnished by Mr. Don B. Skinner, Los Angeles, 18 June 1958.

Color. Leaves lettuce-green, kildare-green beneath; lower bracts as the leaves; peduncle cosse-green tinged russet-vinaceous; sepals cosse-green; corolla spectrum-red to scarlet at base and middle, with edges and apex of petals conspicuously lemon-yellow; petals inside pale lemon-yellow; carpels white at base, above light yellow-green; styles lettuce-green with faint red lines on inner surface; nectaries white to pale lemon-yellow.

TYPE. *T. MacDougall,* B–82 (UCBG:56.801–1), Tlaxiaco, Rio de Tablas, elevation 7000 feet, Oaxaca, Mexico (CAS, no. 409844).

OCCURRENCE. Mexico. Oaxaca.

REMARKS. This plant is another of Mr. Thomas MacDougall's many discoveries in Oaxaca; its showy red and yellow flowers of good size promise to make it a popular garden ornament. The specific name refers to the shape of the corolla, closely approximating the classic amphora. As a species, this comes near to *E. carminea* Alexander, which differs in having an erect, scarcely

Figure 220. 140. *Echeveria amphoralis* E. Walther. Flowers and rosette, both × 2. Plant of type collection (MacDougall B-82) flowering in San Diego 12 July 1963.

branching stem, with longer, thinner, undulate-margined leaves, and somewhat smaller flowers which are a darker red in color.

Comparisons with *E. macrantha* Standley and Steyermark from Guatemala would also be in order here, except that the latter is not in cultivation at present, and is known to me solely from the very imperfect type material. About the only critical difference of which I can be certain involves the ventrally pubescent follicles.

With *E. carminea* and *E. harmsii,* this new species constitutes a group of related forms within the series *Echeveria,* characterized by their rather large flowers and simple trichomes.

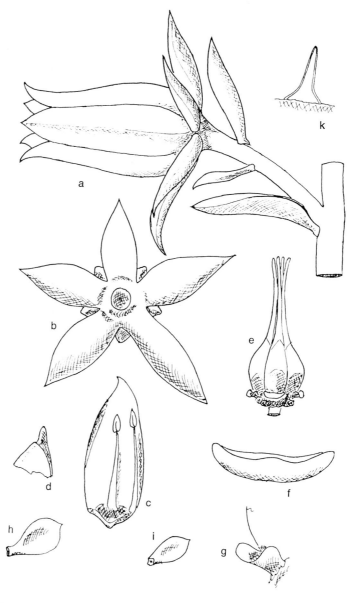

Figure 221.   140. *Echeveria amphoralis* E. Walther. Explanation: (a) flower, × 2; (b) flower from below, × 2; (c) inside of petal, × 2; (d) apex of petal, × 8; (e) carpels, × 2; (f) nectary, inside view, × 8; (g) nectary, side view, × 8; (h) leaf, × 0.4; (i) bract, × 0.4; (k) trichome, greatly enlarged. From the original publication (Cactus and Succulent Journal, volume 30, page 150, figure 85).

141. **Echeveria macrantha** Standley and Steyermark.

Echeveria macrantha STANDLEY AND STEYERMARK, Field Mus., Bot. Ser., vol. 23, no.
4, p. 159, 1944; Flora of Guatemala, Fieldiana, Botany, vol. 24, pt. 4, p. 407, 1946.

Plants erect, suffrutescent, sparingly branched, the branches as much as 1 cm. thick, leafy only at the tips; leaves densely rosulate at the ends of the branches, sessile, rounded-cuneate, 3 cm. long, 20 to 28 mm. wide, broadly rounded or subtruncate at the apex and very shortly spiculate, very broadly cuneate at base, thick-carnose, abundantly but not very densely hirtellous on both surfaces, pale yellowish green, the margins rose-colored; peduncle stout, 45 mm. long, about 3-flowered, the fruiting pedicels 8 mm. long, thick, densely hirtellous; sepals almost free, 8 mm. long, lanceolate-oblong, gradually narrowed to the obtuse apex, densely hirtellous; corolla in age persistent, pubescent outside, 2 cm. long, the petals narrowly lanceolate, gradually attenuate to the apex, acutely carinate dorsally; follicles 15 mm. long, sparsely pubescent (ventrally) with brownish hairs, the body lanceolate-oblong, 8 mm. long, attenuate into a slender beak of about the same length.

TYPE. *Julian A. Steyermark,* 1939/32808, collected on dry rocky slopes, between Montana Miramundo and Buena Vista, between Jalapa and Lago Ayarya, altitude 2000 to 2200 m., Dept. Jalapa, Guatemala (F, type; US, isotype).

OCCURRENCE. Guatemala, known only from the type collection.

REMARKS. *Echeveria macrantha* (type) has three visible follicles; none of these is truly "sparsely pubescent"; the epidermis seems to be wrinkled longitudinally, these striae creating an appearance of appressed hairs.

"The species is noteworthy for its exceptionally large flowers and of course, among Guatemalan species, for its pubescence. Eric Walther considers it synonymous with *E. pringlei,* a Mexican species." (Standley and Steyermark, *loc. cit.*)

142. **Echeveria harmsii** J. F. Macbride.
(Figures 222–223. Plate 16, upper; see page 244.)

Echeveria harmsii J. F. MACBRIDE, Field Mus., Bot. Ser., vol. 11, no. 1, p. 22, 1931;
E. WALTHER, Cactus and Succ. Jour. Amer., vol. 7, p. 60, 1935; POELLNITZ, *in*
Fedde Repert., vol. 39, p. 213, 1936.
Oliverella elegans ROSE, *in* Britton and Rose, Bull. New York Bot. Gard., vol. 3, p. 2,
1903.
Cotyledon elegans (Rose) N. E. BROWN, Bot. Mag., pl. 7993, 1905.
Oliveranthus elegans (Rose) ROSE, *in* Britton and Rose, N. Amer. Fl., vol. 22, p. 27,
1905.
Echeveria elegans (Rose) BERGER, *in* Engler Nat. Pflanzenf. ed. 2, vol. 18a, p. 472,
1930. Not *E. elegans* Rose.
ILLUSTRATIONS. Bot. Mag., pl. 7993; Van Laren, Succ., p. 86, fig. 115, 1934.

Plant minutely pubescent on all exterior parts, trichomes simple, approximately 0.2 mm. long, tapering from a broad base; stem evident, freely branching above, to 30 cm. tall or more; leaves laxly aggregated near end of branches, broadly lanceolate to spathulate, acute, thick, above nearly flat or slightly concave, keeled beneath, 2 to 3 or 5 cm. long, 1 cm. broad or more; inflorescences often numerous, 10 to 20 cm. tall, simple or often 2-branched near base, reduced to one or two, less often three flowers; peduncles slender, curved-

Figure 222. 142. *Echeveria harmsii* J. F. Macbride. Flowering plant about natural size; floral parts enlarged. Plant of the type collection, grown at Kew. From an article by N. E. Brown (Curtis's Botanical Magazine, volume 131, plate 7993).

ascending, 4 mm. thick at base; bracts few, ascending-spreading, oblong-obovate, cuneate, acute, to 2 cm. long, often deciduous at flowering time; pedicels to 3 cm. long, two bracteolate, the bractlets oblong-linear and to 14 mm. long; sepals subequal, to 18 mm. long, spreading upcurved, oblong-lanceolate, acute; corolla narrowly urceolate, pentagonal, to 33 mm. long, 16 mm. in greatest diameter, narrowed to 12 mm. at mouth, ratio of length to diameter 2.1 x 1; petals elliptic-oblong, sharply keeled, acute and apiculate, with small but deep basal cavity, the latter with prominent, thick upper rim; stamens 20 to 35 mm. long; ovaries short, stout, much exceeded by the slender styles that are up to four times the length of ovaries and reach nearly to the mouth of the corolla; nectaries narrowly transverse-lunate, to 3 mm. wide. Flowers from June on. Description from locally cultivated material.

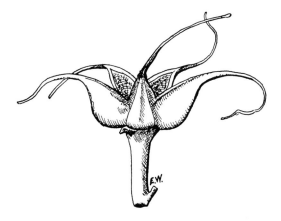

Figure 223. 142. *Echeveria harmsii* J. F. Mac-bride. Ripe follicles, × 2.5. From the Journal of the Cactus and Succulent Society of America, volume 2, page 409.

Color. Leaves lettuce- to lime-green, at tips and edges morocco-red; bracts, bractlets, and sepals as the leaves; corolla scarlet-red, with edges and inner surface of petals pale lemon-yellow; styles maize-yellow to dragonblood-red above; stigmas maroon; nectaries empire-yellow.

TYPE. Found in cultivation at Amecameca, Estado de Mexico, Mexico, *Rose and Hay*, 1901/6073 (US, no. 395878).

OCCURRENCE. Mexico; at present known only from the type locality.

COLLECTIONS. The type, found in cultivation. *Cultivated:* Western Nursery, San Franscico, *Eastwood* in 1920 (CAS); A. Kuester, San Francisco, *Eastwood*, 11/337 (US).

REMARKS. Even today Rose's dictum that this was "the most remarkable of all American *Crassulaceae*" is still valid, even if his creating of a monotypic genus for its reception cannot be followed. *Echeveria harmsii* culminates a line of development, in the series Echeveria, where several species are notable in having a pubescence of short simple hairs and medium-sized to large or very large corollas. In *E. harmsii,* the few-flowered inflorescence clearly represents a reduced state, from such larger inflorescences as we find in *E. carminea* and in *E. amphoralis*. In both of these the inflorescence is racemose, with five or more pedicellate flowers. In *E. harmsii* there are 19 haploid chromosomes.

In its large corolla and greatly elongated styles, *E. harmsii* approaches *E. longissima*, of the series Longistylae. The latter species is distinct in its wholly glabrous leaves possessing palisade-cells, its stemless, dense rosettes, and its very slender corolla, with a length-to-width ratio of nearly 4 to 1, and with correspondingly elongated styles and stamens.

Because of its exceptionally showy flowers, *E. harmsii* is a popular garden and greenhouse subject. While it grows readily from cuttings, the finest plants we have seen were grafted on an understock of *Sedum,* such as *S. dendroideum* or *S. praealtum*. Several showy hybrids have been raised by Mr. Victor Reiter, Jr., with *E. harmsii* for one parent, as *E.* 'Victor' and 'Set Oliver,' etc. (see the section on hybrids).

In July 1957, *E. harmsii* received an Award of Merit from the Royal Horticultural Society, a well deserved distinction.

Series 14. LONGISTYLAE E. Walther.

Echeveria, ser. Longistylae E. WALTHER, Leafl. West. Bot., vol. 9, pp. 1, 4, 1959.

Plants wholly glabrous; stem very short or none, mostly simple; leaves densely rosulate, with palisade cells; inflorescence 1- to 3-branched; racemes few-flowered; pedicels to 14 mm. long, bractless; sepals subequal, to 18 mm. long, ascending to spreading; corolla to 33 mm. long, to 3 times as long as thick; styles to 4 times the length of ovaries; nectaries broadly reniform.

TYPICAL SPECIES. *Echeveria longissima* E. Walther is the only species.

REMARKS. Since this series consists of only a single species, no key is required. The species (and series) is unique in the genus *Echeveria,* for no other species has corolla and styles as long, proportionally, as in *E. longissima.* Only in this one species have my own observations established the presence of true palisade tissue in the leaves. The probable chromosome number of $n=42$, too, is quite rare in the genus.

143. **Echeveria longissima** E. Walther.
(Figures 224–226. Plate 16, lower; see page 244.)

Echeveria longissima E. WALTHER, Cactus and Succ. Jour. Amer., vol. 9, p. 147, 1938.
Echeveria harmsii var. *multiflora* E. WALTHER, Cactus and Succ. Jour. Amer., vol. 7, p. 60, 1935.
ILLUSTRATIONS. Cactus and Succ. Jour. Amer., vol. 9, p. 148, 1938; vol. 27, pp. 108, 109, figs. 73, 75, 1955; photograph of Rose, 09/1717 (US).

Plant wholly glabrous; stem usually quite short, simple, giving out offsets only rarely and belatedly; leaves densely rosulate, to 20, broadly obovate-cuneate, cuspidate-mucronate, thick, beneath rounded, shallowly concave above, to 6 cm. long and 3 cm. broad, with palisade cells; inflorescence to 30 cm. tall, of a simple raceme or 2- or 3-branched; peduncle erect or ascending, to 4 mm. thick near base, in its upper portion bearing 8 to 12 bracts, these slightly spreading, obovate-oblanceolate, shortly cuspidate-acuminate, 2- or 3-spurred at base, to 20 mm. long; racemes secund, with rachis conspicuously zigzag between successive pedicels, illustrating the terminal character of the flowers; flowers 4 to 7 or 12, strongly nodding in bud, spreading at anthesis; upper bracts oblong-obovate, cuspidate, spurred at base, to 12 mm. long; pedicels slender, to 17 mm. long, bractless; sepals subequal, longest to 8 mm. long, ascending to widely spreading, ovate-deltoid to oblong-lanceolate, much connate at base, with subterminal apiculus; corolla very narrowly urceolate-cylindrical, to over 30 mm. long, 10 mm. in diameter near base, with a ratio of length to thickness of nearly 4 to 1, at anthesis the mouth is to 14 mm., but the throat only 6 mm. in diameter; petals narrowly oblong, scarcely keeled, rim of basal hollow tapering above into two ridges that parallel filament, occasionally produced into appendages simulating those found in the genus *Pachyphytum;* stamens to 25 mm. long; anthers to 4 mm. long; carpels 25 mm. long inclusive of ovaries, with the styles proper over 4 times as long as ovaries, the latter only 5 mm. long; nectaries reniform, nearly 3 mm. wide. Flowers from June to August. Emended description from type plant, received through Sr. M. Martínez of Santiago de Mihautlan, Puebla, Mexico.

Color. Leaves cerro-green to light elm-green above, acajou-red beneath, at edges Hays-maroon; bracts light bice-green above, edges and mucro tinged

Figure 224. 143. *Echeveria longissima* E.
Walther. Flower, ca. × 2.3; rosette, ca. ×
0.8. From the original publication (Cactus
and Succulent Journal, volume 9, page 148).

Brazil-red at base, at middle pale greenish yellow, above pois-green; petals inside maize- to buff-yellow below, to grass-green above; carpels pale chalcedony-yellow; styles apple-green; nectaries whitish.

TYPE. Collected by E. Walther from a plant grown in Golden Gate Park, San Francisco, from Puebla, Mexico, from near San Luis Atototitlan (CAS, no. 251052).

OCCURRENCE. Southern Puebla, Mexico.

COLLECTIONS. Mexico. The type; Cerro de Chicamole, 7000 to 9000 feet, Sierra de Mixteca, southern Puebla, *Purpus,* 1909/3953 (NY,UC).

REMARKS. In its long slender corolla, *E. longissima* is unique, being approached therein only by *E. harmsii,* but that species is a densely pubescent subshrub with its inflorescence much reduced, usually consisting of only two flowers, its corolla is relatively broader, and its styles, too, are shorter in relation to the ovaries. No other species of *Echeveria* that I have studied was found to possess true palisade cells, a character that may indicate the most advanced form in the genus. Its gametic chromosome number is probably 42 according to Dr. Uhl.

The thickened rim of the nectar cavities is sometimes produced upwards alongside the epipetalous filaments, simulating the petal-appendages characteristic of *Pachyphytum.* A similar abnormality has been noted in *E. heterosepala* Rose, where it led to the erroneous republication of that as a new species of *Pachyphytum.* However, the latter genus is possessed of enough other distinctive characters to remain valid.

I first had this remarkable species called to my attention by a most fragmentary specimen in the herbarium of the University of California *(Purpus,* 09/3953, UC:136164), which consisted merely of a portion of the inflorescence, without any basal leaves. On visiting Tehuacan in 1934 I asked our guide, Sr. Manuel Martínez, to try and obtain this for me, and 2 months later several plants were received. Sr. Martínez told me that in its native range this is known as "Farolito," or lighthouse. I regret that I have been unable to visit this in its native home and can say nothing of the conditions under which it occurs there.

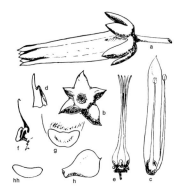

Figure 225. 143. *Echeveria longissima* E. Walther. Explanation: (a) flower, × 1; (b) flower from below, × 1; (c) inside of petal, × 1; (d) apex of petal, × 4; (e) carpels, × 1; (f) nectary, side view, × 4; (g) nectary, front view, × 4; (h) leaf, × 0.2; (hh) cross-section of leaf, × 0.2. From the original publication (Cactus and Succulent Journal, volume 9, page 148).

Figure 226.   143. *Echeveria longissima* E. Walther.   Flowers, × 2. Plant flowering in San Diego 11 June 1966 (Moran 12277), of unknown origin but presumably stemming from the type collection.

Eric Walther's Publications
Pertaining to Echeveria

[Mr. Walther left no bibliography with the manuscript; and since references appear throughout the text, none may be necessary. It seems appropriate, however, to list here all his own contributions to the study of *Echeveria*, some of which are not mentioned elsewhere in the monograph.—Editor.]

1931a. Alwin Berger's "Crassulaceae." Jour. Cact. Succ. Soc. Am., 2: 383–385, 408–411, figs.

1931b. Genus *Pachyphytum*. Cact. Succ. Jour., 3: 9–13, figs. 1–7, 9–16. [Describes *P. chloranthum = Echeveria heterosepala* Rose.]

1932. *Cotyledon, Echeveria*, or *Dudleya?* Leafl. West. Bot., 1: 27–29. [Reprinted in Cact. Succ. Jour. 7: 10–11, 1935.]

1934. *Echeveria* hybrids: A. with *Pachyphytum*. Cact. Succ. Jour., 6: 53–56, figs. 1–6. [Includes key to *Pachyphytum* and *Pachyveria* as grown here.]

1935a. *Echeveria* hybrids: intergeneric crosses. Cact. Succ. Jour., 6: 115–117, figs. [Actually intrageneric. Describes *E.* × *pulvi-carn.*]

1935b. Collecting succulents in Mexico. Cact. Succ. Jour., 6: 137–140, 145, 149–151, 163–165, 185–189, figs.

1935c. Plant hunting in Old Mexico, Part I. Natl. Hort. Mag., 14: 165–174.

1935d. Notes on the genus *Echeveria*: Some new sections, series, species, varieties, and combinations. Cact. Succ. Jour., 7: 35–40, 60–61, 69–72, figs. [Introduction by the editor, p. 34.]

1936a. *Echeveria*: an ideal rock plant for California gardens. Gard. Quart., 4: 26–28.

1936b. Collecting succulents in Mexico, 1935. Cact. Succ. Jour., 7: 137–139, 166–168, 182–184; 8: 18–21, 70–72, figs. 1–31.

1936c. Plant hunting in Old Mexico, Part II. Natl. Hort. Mag., 15: 87–96.

1936d. Phylogeny of *Echeveria*. Cact. Succ. Jour. 8: 82–88, figs.

1937a. Illustrated notes in Crassulaceae: *Thompsonella* Britton & Rose. Cact. Succ. Jour., 8: 100–102, figs.

1937b. Plant hunting in Old Mexico, Part III. Natl. Hort. Mag., 16: 68–76.

1937c. *Echeveria* × *set-oliver* EW, new hybrid. Cact. Succ. Jour., 8: 172–173, figs.

1937d. *Echeveria* hybrids: *Echeveria* × *mutabilis* Deleuil. Cact. Succ. Jour., 8: 191–193, figs. 1–3.

1937e. *Echeveria* hybrids: *Echeveria* × *haageana* Hort. Cact. Succ. Jour., 9: 19–21, figs. [Correction, 9: 82.]

1937f. *Echeveria* hybrids: *Echeveria* × *pulv-oliver* EW, new hybrid. Cact. Succ. Jour., 9: 92–93, figs. 1–3.

1938a. Notes on the genus *Echeveria*, Part 3. Cact. Succ. Jour., 9: 147–148, figs. [Describes *E. longissima.*]

1938b. Notes on the genus *Echeveria*, Part 4. Cact. Succ. Jour., 9: 165–166, figs. [Describes *E. grisea.*]

1938c. Notes on the genus *Echeveria*. Cact. Succ. Jour., 10: 14–15, figs. [Describes *E. pallida.*]

1952. New species of *Echeveria*. Cact. Succ. Jour., 24: 28–29, figs. 11–13. [Describes *E. craigiana.*]

1953. *Sedeveria*, a new bigeneric hybrid. Cact. Succ. Jour., 25: 20–21, figs. 13–14.

1956. *Echeveria "flammea."* Cact. Succ. Jour., 28: 2.

1958a. Further notes on *Echeveria*. Cact. Succ. Jour., 30: 40–48, figs. 21–29. [Describes *E. violescens, E. hyalina, E. ballsii,* and *E. johnsonii.*]

1958b. Further notes on *Echeveria*, Part II. Cact. Succ. Jour., 30: 87–90, figs. 44–47. [Describes *E. macdougallii* and *E. halbingeri.*]

1958c. Further notes on *Echeveria*, Part III. Cact. Succ. Jour., 30: 105–109, figs. 54–57. [Describes *E. affinis* and *E. semivestita* var. *floresiana.*]

1958d. Further notes on *Echeveria*, Part IV. Cact. Succ. Jour., 30: 147–153, figs. 82–89. [Describes *E. albicans, E. amphoralis, E. penduliflora,* and *E. sedoides.*]

1958e. *Echeveria* D.C., localidades conocidas en México, por estados. Cact. Sucul. Mex., 3: 51–54, fig. 30.

1959a. Further notes on *Echeveria*, Part V. Cact. Succ. Jour., 31: 22–25, figs. 11–14. [Describes *E. viridissima* and *E. globuliflora*. A note by Mr. MacDougall (Cact. Succ. Jour., 35: 2, 1963) corrects the locality for *E. globuliflora*.]

1959b. *Echeveria*: conspectus serierum. Leafl. West. Bot., 9: 1–4.

1959c. Los nectarios del género *Echeveria*. Cact. Sucul. Mex., 4: 3–7, figs. 2–6.

1959d. Further notes on *Echeveria*, Part VI. Cact. Succ. Jour., 31: 50–53, figs. 25–28. [Describes *E. megacalyx* and *E. juarezensis.*]

1959e. Dos nuevas especies de *Echeveria*. Cact. Sucul. Mex., 4: 27–31, figs. 15–18. [Describes *E. goldiana* and *E. meyraniana.*]

1959f. Further notes on *Echeveria*, Part VII. Cact. Succ. Jour., 31: 97, 99–102, figs. 31–35. [Describes *E. parrasensis* and *E. longiflora.*]

1959g. *Echeveria* hybrids. Jour. Calif. Hort. Soc., 20: 60–62, fig.

1960. *Echeveria*. Am. Hort. Mag., 39: 73–91, figs. [With an obituary by Elizabeth McClintock.]

Index to Technical Names

New names and principle references in **boldface** type. References to illustrations in *italics*.

Erratum: Page 213. Plate 1, Upper, line 2 of caption: for 0.3 read 3.5.